A RACE OF SINGERS

BRYAN K. GARMAN

A RACE OF SINGERS

WHITMAN'S WORKING-CLASS HERO FROM GUTHRIE TO SPRINGSTEEN

The University of North Carolina Press Chapel Hill & London

AAP- 2554

© 2000
The University of North Carolina Press
All rights reserved
Manufactured in the United States of America
Designed by Richard Hendel
Set in Quadraat and Poplar Types
by Tseng Information Systems
The paper in this book meets the guidelines
for permanence and durability of the
Committee on Production Guidelines for
Book Longevity of the Council on Library
Resources.
Library of Congress
Cataloging-in-Publication Data
Garman, Bryan K.
A race of singers :
Whitman's working-class hero from
Guthrie to Springsteen / Bryan K. Garman.
    p. cm. — (Cultural studies of the United
States)
Includes bibliographical references (p.) and
index.
ISBN 0-8078-2558-1 (cloth: alk. paper) —
ISBN 0-8078-4866-2 (pbk.: alk. paper)
1. Popular music—Social aspects—United
States. 2. Working class—United States—
Songs and music—History and criticism.
3. Whitman, Walt, 1819–1892—Influence.
4. Guthrie, Woody, 1912–1967—Influence.
5. Springsteen, Bruce—Influence. I. Title.
II. Series.
ML3477.G36 2000
781.5′9—dc21   99-058448

04 03 02 01 00   5 4 3 2 1

FOR KAREN

Contents

ILLUSTRATIONS

ACKNOWLEDGMENTS

Writing a book is a self-absorbing and often quite lonely process, one that could not be completed without the assistance and sacrifice of friends, family, and colleagues.

I am grateful to Anthony Seeger, Nick Spitzer, and Pete Daniel for advising my Graduate Student Fellowship at the Smithsonian Institution. Jeff Place, the head archivist at the Smithsonian's Center for Folklife Programs and Cultural Studies, patiently responded to questions and requests and shared his enthusiasm and vast knowledge. Lori Elaine Taylor at the center also offered numerous suggestions. All Guthrie scholars are indebted to her for meticulously indexing and preserving the Woody Guthrie Papers. Stephanie Smith was particularly helpful in obtaining photographs. I am also beholden to the fine reference staff at the Folklife Archive of the Library of Congress, including Joe Hickerson, who was willing to offer both his memories of the folk revival and his knowledge of the library's holdings. I am especially grateful to Nora Guthrie, who on very short notice allowed me to visit the Woody Guthrie Archive in New York. I appreciate the patience and sincerity she demonstrated in responding to my questions about her father. George Arevalo enabled me to navigate the archive's holdings very efficiently.

Seth Cohen of Sure Fire Media, Joy Graeme of Woody Guthrie Publications, Alison Oscar of Jon Landau Management, Evelyn Sasko of the Richmond Organization, Libby Rohman of Special Rider Music, and Pegge Strella of the Chapin Office all provided assistance in securing permissions and photographs. I appreciate the generosity of Seema Weatherwax, Diana Davies, Bruce Springsteen, Bob Dylan, and the Richmond Organization in allowing me to make extensive use of their material.

A number of scholars commented on various parts of this project, including Ralph Bogardus, Paul Buhle, Ed Folsom, Lucy Maddox, Theresa Murphy, Michael Robertson, Jerome Rodnitzky, and Cecelia Tichi. Anonymous reviewers at *Popular Music and Society* and *American Quarterly* were also quite helpful. I thank them for their many insights. Further guidance and support came from Tucker Orbison and Doug Candland at Bucknell University and from Bob and Maureen Ballotta. My students have also provided important emotional sustenance.

I would like to thank several people at Emory University, where I completed my Ph.D. Margot Finn's outstanding seminar on British social history was a landmark in my graduate education, and I am grateful that she supervised a directed reading and an examination field. I am deeply indebted to the members of my dissertation committee, who offered their criticism and advice for six long years. Amy Schrager Lang has been a true advocate. In our hours of conversation, she has offered keen insights that repeatedly forced me to expand and refine my analyses. A true interdisciplinarian, Allen Tullos was particularly helpful in the early stages of this project, graciously supervising a directed reading in folk music and patiently listening to my interpretations of Springsteen. I thank Jonathan Prude for doing far more than is expected of a third chair and for teaching me the discipline of history. His intensity and commitment are remarkable. Tal Stanley made the Institute of Liberal Arts a more meaningful place. I am grateful for his friendship and insights and have the highest regard for his scholarly, political, and cultural labors.

The staff at the University of North Carolina Press was remarkably supportive of this project. David Perry offered a number of important suggestions, and Paula Wald was a meticulous and insightful project editor. I am especially grateful to my editor, Sian Hunter, who immediately understood the scope of the book and whose careful reading of it enabled me to narrow its focus. I also thank her for helping me navigate my way through the process of securing permissions to reprint lyrics and photographs. I appreciate the faith she had in this project and the effort she put forth to make it better.

My family has been a constant source of support. My grandparents, Bill and Gerry Garman and Zelda Brummert, taught me much about the meaning of hard work and have always offered their love. My brother, Brad, never ceases to inspire. His life is a daily reminder of hope and possibility, of happiness and kindness. He is my working-class hero. Part IV is for him. Barbara and Keith Garman were, and still are, my first heroes. This book began on one of the many days I saw my mother sacrifice her own well-being for the good of someone else, or maybe it started when my father popped volume 1 of Dylan's *Greatest Hits* into an eight-track tape player and told me to listen to the words. What I have written in these pages is connected to them in a very real and direct way. For the countless labors of love they performed to build our family, I can give only my thanks, love, and respect. Since they laid the groundwork for my life, Part I, the foundation of the book, is for them.

Finally, I thank Karen Ballotta, who lived this project as much as I did. An outstanding writer, thinker, and critic, she tirelessly listened to me pontificate on the subject, commented on countless drafts, pushed my analysis when it was particularly sluggish, and tried to reign it in when it became overzealous. She offered more suggestions than I can possibly remember, and this book is better because of her selfless efforts. Without her love, boundless faith, constant encouragement, and innumerable sacrifices, this project would have been abandoned long ago. For everything she has done for me, I dedicate *A Race of Singers* to her and pledge my thanks and love.

A
RACE OF
SINGERS

All you can write is what you see.

—Woody Guthrie

INTRODUCTION

Be Radical — Be Not Too Damned Radical

WHICH WHITMAN?

When in 1919 the United States marked the centenary of Walt Whitman's birth, the country was emerging from the shadows of world war only to find itself deeply divided at home. Growing racial tensions prompted a wave of lynchings in the South and a bloody race riot in Chicago that left thirty-three people dead. More than 4 million workers, nearly a quarter of the workforce, participated in unprecedented demonstrations of labor unrest, asserting their rights in the textile, coal, and steel industries.[1] On the heels of the Russian Revolution, the Comintern declared its intention to foment uprisings around the world and recognized the American Communist Party. As corporations, municipalities, and local vigilantes devised methods of intimidation to control such threats, the U.S. government expanded its assault on a variety of radical groups. In 1917, federal agents ransacked the offices of the Industrial Workers of the World; by 1918, Socialist Party leader Eugene Debs had been jailed for sedition; and in late 1919, U.S. Attorney General A. Mitchell Palmer unleashed the first of two raids that led to the arrest of 4,000 leftists, three-quarters of whom were deported.[2]

Many of the approximately 350 newspaper and magazine articles that celebrated Whitman's birth responded to this national crisis. Swept up in the jingoism of victory and the fear of revolution, most writers, Winifred Kirkland among them, relied on Whitman to validate American democracy.[3] Writing for the liberal *Dial*, Kirkland suggested that Whitman was "pre-eminent in expressing what America means to Americans" and opined that his name "brings an instant exhilaration like the sudden sight of the stars and stripes billowing in the breeze."[4] He articulated "ideals for industry that we should like to cherish," and perhaps more important, he would help Americans "recall our clearer motives" of individualism and manifest destiny. The "American, if he is to be the true inheritor of the land that has been given him," argued Kirkland, "needs to tune his soul to wide spaces, unchained cataracts, limitless prairie, and to cities seething with incredible energy. . . . We too need to be spacious like Whitman."[5] Stuart P. Sherman of the *New York Evening Post* also lionized Whitman for his individualism. Worried that communists might claim the democratic bard as their own, Sherman declared that if Whitman had "lived at the right place in these years of Proletarian Millennium, he would have been hanged as a reactionary member of the bourgeoisie."[6] The poet, Sherman argued, "cuts with . . . keenness into the conception of those younger international revolutionary statesmen, who, ignoring individuals, propose to deal with classes . . . and institute a world-wide class war."[7] The *New York Times* echoed Sherman's opinion. Radicals from "the parlor, boudoir, and Greenwich Village" had "started a Whitman cult," but the *Times*, fearing that the poet might be co-opted, unequivocally announced in a headline, "Whitman No Boudoir Bolshevik."[8]

Such conservative interpretations were not unfounded. Whitman certainly sang of individualism and capitalism, maintaining that "riches, and the getting of riches" were an important part of his "programme of culture."[9] But this poet contained multitudes, and as the headline from the *Times* suggests, there was at least one other Whitman, one who lent himself to leftist ideas. Joseph Gollomb of the *New York Evening Post Book Review* alluded to this element when he published an interview with Horace Traubel, Whitman's close friend and literary executor. Playing on the hysteria of the Red Scare, the front-page headline wondered, "Would Whitman Be a Bolshevist?," an inquiry to which Traubel, an ardent socialist, responded negatively. "No 'ism' could pin down Whitman. Might as well try to give shape to the atmosphere," he explained. Whitman's resistance to being labeled did not mean, however, that he accepted the social order as it stood. The poet "may have been against any one trying to raise people to revolution," but he nonetheless "wanted revolution against all that was outgrown and enslaving."[10] Transcripts of conversations between Whitman and Traubel suggest that in the final years of his life, Whitman entertained the possibility of socialist reform. He cursed "the God damned robbers, fools, stupids, who ride their gay horses over the bodies of the crowd" and predicted that their egregious actions would one day "drive us into an inevitable resentment, then revolt, of some sort." "Sometimes, I think, I feel almost sure," said Whitman in particularly uncertain terms, that "Socialism is the next thing coming: I shrink from it in some ways: yet it looks like our only hope."[11]

In the end, Whitman could not relinquish his faith in small-producer capitalism. "Be radical—be radical—be not too damned radical!," he cautioned Traubel.[12] By the 1920s, however, Whitman had become perhaps more radical than he originally had intended. Such left-wing leaders, artists, and intellectuals as Eugene Debs, Michael Gold, and Clifford Odets claimed the Good Gray Poet as the "heroic spiritual grandfather" of their generation and touted him as a posthumous proponent of socialism and communism.[13] His poetry, they insisted, articulated a collective social vision that opposed the exploitative, iniquitous relations that characterized capitalist society. Whitman's cultural politics exerted tremendous influence on the Left's political imagination, but how radical was he? How did he shape left-wing culture in the century that followed his death? How have his cultural politics been transmitted and transformed across generations?

In addressing these questions, A Race of Singers does not purport to assess the diversity of working-class life in the United States. Workers hold myriad opinions about culture and politics, and many alternatives to the tradition I discuss exist. Samuel Gompers and John Lewis, Mother Bloor and Mother Jones, Franklin Roosevelt and Huey Long, George Wallace and Ronald Reagan, Martin Luther King Jr. and Cesar Chavez have often been accepted more enthusiastically by workers than have my cast of characters. A host of related musicians and artists, most of whom I do not discuss, could also boast sizable working-class audiences. Patsy Cline, Kitty Wells, Hank Williams, Johnny Cash, Merle Haggard, and Garth Brooks have been the heroes of workers who listen to country music, and Bessie Smith, James Brown, and Snoop Doggy Dog at various times have appealed to black workers.

A Race of Singers examines the making of an explicit working-class hero, the process by which cultural workers, predominantly nationally recognized white men with leftist leanings, have consciously invoked and evoked specific Whitmanesque ideals to engage class politics. Focusing on artists and intellectuals from Traubel to Gold, Woody Guthrie to Bruce Springsteen, this book demonstrates how the politics of this tradition and of class in general are inextricably enmeshed in constructions of race, gender, and particularly sexuality. I argue that these cultural heroes have promulgated a version of white working-class manhood that has provided the ideological cornerstone of leftist culture and politics for over two centuries. Their rendering of the white male worker not only complicates the construction of class but also compels a consideration of the role sexuality played among those who made up the Left—a term I use to describe a broad spectrum of radicals, including spiritual and Debsian socialists, Trotskyists and Stalinists, members of the Popular Front and New Left, and such cultural radicals as Bob Dylan and Bruce Springsteen.[14] Determined to secure the dignity of the white worker, these heroes largely represented solidarity in terms of male bonding and homoerotic attraction, a strategy that pulled their politics in two directions at once. On the one hand, they envisioned a mutualistic society that emphasized equality, undermined the competitive ethos of capitalism, and imagined a more just social order. On the other, their formulation of solidarity often excluded women and people of color, thereby safeguarding, sometimes inadvertently, the social advantages ascribed to manhood and whiteness.

Although this race of singers descends from a rather insular literary tradition, its members have asked important questions about national identity, questions that reveal much about how Americans have addressed issues of social justice. Because these artists ask what it means to be an American and because they pose that question critically, their work, as my introductory discussion of Whitman indicates, has been scrutinized and endorsed by critics, pundits, and politicians of various ideological stripes. The ambiguity with which their art has been received points to both the pliability and the contradictory nature of the republican rhetoric they endorse. These heroes have dedicated themselves primarily to confronting the most fundamental American quandary: how does one balance individual freedom with social equality? Their desire to be working-class heroes, to rise from the ranks of common men to become quite uncommon, has often done more to exacerbate than to assuage this tension. In many ways, their art and public reactions to it have exposed the limitations of the American reform tradition. These men have at times been remarkably critical of their society, but they have frequently framed their analyses in moral rather than structural terms. Reluctant to rethink economic or political institutions and unable to suspend their faith in the American experiment, they have attributed injustice to the moral failings of individuals (or perhaps corporations), not to the state. Their politics have changed significantly throughout the twentieth century, notably in relation to attitudes about race, gender, and sexuality. And although they have nurtured a particular vision of social justice, they have remained true to Whitman's advice: their songs have been radical but have rarely become too damned radical.

Whitman began to formulate his concept of a working-class hero in October 1846 when he published an unremarkable review of Thomas Carlyle's *On Heroes, Hero-Worship, and the Heroic in History* (1841).[15] "Under his rapt, weird, (grotesque?) style," Whitman asserted, Carlyle had "placed— we may almost say *hidden*—many noble thoughts."[16] When *Leaves of Grass* sprouted from Whitman's imagination nine years later, readers would not have to dig very deeply to unearth Carlyle's influence, a fact Whitman readily admitted. Ralph Waldo Emerson, whose impact on Whitman is well documented, had also authored an essay on heroism, but Carlyle's writings on the subject took root. The poet of democracy chastised this elite Scottish thinker because "he shrank from the people," but when Carlyle died in 1881, Whitman praised him enthusiastically. "It will be difficult for the future to account for the deep hold he has taken on the present age, and the way he has color'd its method and thought," he wrote. "I am certainly at a loss to account for it all as affecting myself."[17]

In his lectures on heroism, Carlyle defined the poet as a hero who expresses the essential character of his nation, serves as that nation's moral arbiter, and conveys this morality in a manner that is musical in both form and content. A product of Enlightenment thought, Carlyle argued that "the progress of mere scientific knowledge" had usurped the heroic function once served by divinities and prophets, and he posited that in this secularized age the poet must become the "heroic figure" who provides humanity with its moral compass.[18] Taking Dante and Shakespeare as prototypes, he identified the poet as "a man sent hither to make [divine mystery] more impressively known to us"; speaking in the "voice of Nature," he manifests "Universal" moral truths.[19] The heroic poet is, in Carlyle's scheme, a necessarily great man, but before he can speak for all humanity, he must transcend his own individuality. In short, he must possess "the justice to put down his own selfishness at every turn"; he must have the ability to "*love*" and "sympathize with" his comrades so that he might become "*virtuously related*" to them.[20]

To develop this relationship, the poet must profess the gospel of "brotherhood" in accord with musical principles, for poetry was quite simply "*musical Thought*":[21]

If your delineation be authentically *musical*, musical not in word only, but in heart and substance, in all the thoughts and utterances of it, in the whole conception of it, then it will be poetical; if not, not.— Musical: how much lies in that! A musical thought is one spoken by an individual that has penetrated to the inmost heart of the thing; detected the inmost mystery of it, namely the melody that lies hidden in it; the inward harmony of coherence which is the soul, whereby it exists, and has a right to be, here in the world.[22]

For Carlyle, "even the commonest speech . . . has something of song in it," and if the poet could capture the essence of a country's vernacular, he could become its spokesperson. It was "a great thing for a Nation that it get an articulate voice; that it produce a man who will speak forth melodiously what the heart of it means." Or as Whitman would later put it, the ideal poet would emerge when his "country absorbs him as affectionately as he has absorbed it."[23]

An engaged observer of antebellum America, Whitman absorbed the cultures and controversies of his moment and represented them in *Leaves of Grass*, a book that echoed many of Carlyle's assertions. "There will soon be no more priests. Their work is done," declares Whitman in the oracular preface of the first edition. To replace the clergy, he would engender a "new breed of poets," a race of "interpreters of men and women and of all events and things."[24] Whitman personified a hero who would turn his attention to the social and political issues of his day and, as he remembered in "A Backward Glance o'er Traveled Roads" (1888), to his era's concomitant "moral revolutions." In his estimation, these revolutions had prompted "the uprisings of national masses," and "with all these new and evolutionary facts, meanings, [and] purposes, new poetic messages, new forms and expressions, [were] inevitable."[25]

Whitman's expressions addressed the historical circumstances of his age and, more specifically, the effects these circumstances had on the common people and what he thought were their common concerns. *Leaves of Grass* engaged the proliferating discourses on sex and sexuality. It responded to demands for gender equality. The poems struggled with the contradictions slavery presented to a nation founded on the ideals of freedom and equality and sought desperately to palliate this conflict in order to preserve the Union. Most important, *Leaves of Grass* confronted the profound moral and economic transformations caused by the industrial revolution. "Without yielding an inch the working-man and working-woman were to be in my pages from first to last," exhorts Whitman in "Backward Glance." "The ranges of heroism with which the Greek and feudal poets endow'd their god-like or lordly born characters—indeed prouder and better based and with fuller ranges than those—I was to endow the democratic averages of America."[26] The industrial revolution had degraded the common American worker, and Whitman was determined to restore his independence and prestige, to celebrate the world not as it was but as he thought it should be. On the surface, Whitman resolves to sing the songs of both the common man and the common woman, both the master and the slave, but this poet viewed "all events and things" through the eyes of white workingmen. As a result, he transformed Carlyle's poet into a working-class hero whose primary responsibility was to protect the interests of his constituency, to extend the rights of freedom and equality to all citizens without abrogating the privileges of manhood and whiteness.

In enumerating his hero's major responsibilities, Whitman follows Carlyle's blueprint and insists that the poet must reveal moral truths to his audience. Whitman took on this task in early childhood when he resolved to compose a "worthy record" of the "foundation of moral America." He intended to play his part in distinguishing a "spiritual and heroic" nation from a nation that, in his lifetime, had replaced traditional principles of fair economic exchange with an unhealthy desire for wealth.[27] The poet hero could reverse this trend by re-moralizing human relationships. The "profoundest service that poems or any other writings can do for their reader," he reasons, "is not merely to satisfy the intellect, or supply something polish'd and interesting, nor even to depict great passions, or persons or events, but to fill him with vigorous and clean manliness, religiousness, and give him a *good heart* as a radical possession and habit."[28] This was a fundamental criterion for the poet hero's cultural work: art should be created not simply for art's sake but to inculcate a sense of moral responsibility in the audience. Poets should subordinate aesthetics to morality, art to politics.

Whitman recognized that "plenty of songs had been sung" about morality but insisted that these songs had been "adjusted to other lands." Alluding to Carlyle's claim that poetry was "musical thought," this hero declares that "no land . . . ever existed so needing a *race of singers*" as the United States and determines that the new poet "would sing . . . solely with reference to America to-day."[29] Whitman might be remembered as the poet of democracy, but as such remarks reveal, he thought of himself and his imagined disciples as singers. In his twilight years, he remembered that his "younger life was so saturated with the emotions, raptures, up-lifts of such musical experiences that it would be surprising indeed if all my future work had not been colored by them." [30] And deeply imbued with music it was. According to biographer David Reynolds, 206 "musical words" appear in *Leaves of Grass*, more than half of which refer to "vocal music." [31] "Solitary, singing in the West," this bard would "strike up for a New World." [32]

When Whitman composed his national opera, he realized that this new race of singers would have to focus on a particular moral issue. The Declaration of Independence, which Whitman identified as the "primary compact of These States," guaranteed American citizens the natural rights of individual freedom and equality, rights that seemed to be in conflict in antebellum America. [33] In Whitman's cultural politics, the poet was responsible for reconciling these two seemingly contradictory impulses, for striking a moral balance. Whitman welcomes "equality's and fraternity's doctrines" and avers that because "Democracy has been so retarded and jeopardized by powerful personalities," "first instincts" often compel the poet to "reduce everything to a dead level." Although "the ambitious thought of [the poet's] song is to help the forming of a great aggregate Nation," this is accomplished "perhaps, altogether through the forming of myriads of fully develop'd and enclosing individuals." [34] Balancing personal liberty with social equality, self-interest with public good, was a fundamental chore for Whitman's poet hero, a chore with which he and his progeny would struggle long and hard.

To obtain this moral balance, Whitman looked not to the courtly traditions that Carlyle's heroes embraced but to the artisan workshop. A workingman's poet from first to last, he transformed the hero from an effete aristocrat to a manly craftsman and based his morality on artisan republicanism, the ideology that governed the workingman's economy. Grounded in the American Revolution's rhetoric of natural rights, artisan republicanism ostensibly granted personal liberty and social equality to those who espoused it—skilled white workingmen. Artisans created a society in which individuals were expected to subordinate their self-interest to the public good. This moral code armed them with a language to resist the economic transformations that would dramatically change the craft system. For example, in the mid-nineteenth century, when enterprising capitalists began to accumulate vast profits at the expense of wage laborers, journeymen invoked the republican ideal to argue that an unequal distribution of wealth threatened principles of equality in particular and the health of the Republic in general. Those who divided labor and refused to pay workers a living wage had, in the artisan's view, acted immorally. To enjoy their natural rights, Americans would have to re-apply moral principles of fairness to all areas of their lives, including the market.

Artisan republicanism was fraught with contradictions, however. Women and African Americans had no citizenship rights in the republic of labor, and when female and black workers began to compete for the artisans' jobs, these skilled white men reached for the familiar crutches of sexism and racism. Whitman imagined a poet hero who based his morality on the republican tradition but who deployed this tradition in a manner that reinscribed racial and gender hierarchies. This ideological blind spot afflicted Whitman throughout his career and often resurfaced in the race of singers who followed in his footsteps.

"From another point of view," writes Whitman, " 'Leaves of Grass' is avowedly the song of Sex and Amativeness, and even Animality." To be sure, Whitman sang the praises of sexual freedom and celebrated the union that sexual relations precipitated. He insists, however, that "meanings that do not usually go along with" sexual conventions "will duly emerge" from his work.[35] What emerged was adhesive love, an idealized emotion between men predicated on homosexual relations. Whitman argued that if Americans were to create a previously unimagined democracy, they would have to forge an unforeseen love and respect for political equals, that is, other white men. Rooted in the homosocial and often homoerotic culture of the artisan workshop, adhesiveness promised that the exchange of sexual pleasure between men would reconcile individual freedom and social equality and promote a radical democracy. Although adhesive love presented the possibility for a gay male identity and had the potential to erode the masculine competitiveness that characterized the marketplace, it also allowed men to strengthen the masculine bonds they formed on the job, prohibited women from engaging in same-sex love, and took for granted both women's participation in the domestic economy and their exclusion from male leisure and work places. As Eve Sedgwick argues in another context, the activities of "men-loving-men" and "men-promoting-the-interests-of-other-men" are closely related, and if Whitman's adhesiveness could restore morality to the market, that market would continue to privilege the constructs of manhood and whiteness.[36]

In short, Whitman created a hero that was radical but not too damned radical. He expressed deep concern for white workingmen and the economic transformations that affected their lives, but rather than rethinking the political economy or the ideologies that undergirded it, he assailed capitalism on moral grounds. He charged the poet with teaching a moral code that opposed the ethos of acquisition and exploitation, a code that, if followed, would eradicate all social distinctions and convey the rights of freedom and equality. Whitman would ceaselessly toil at the task of balancing these rights, but his work remained unfinished. He gestured toward racial and gender equality but ultimately could not conceive of people of color and women as political peers. The poet of democracy sought to protect the natural rights of all Americans but bequeathed to his cultural progeny a legacy that both stimulated and stymied their democratic imaginations.

The Strongest and Sweetest Songs

A Race of Singers begins with an analysis of Whitman's hero and then explores how his legacy has been adopted and adapted from 1892 through the twentieth century. The second chapter examines the process by which the Left identified Whitman as its "heroic spiritual grandfather" and assesses the influence the poet had on anticapitalist cultural workers between 1890 and 1940. No one did more to pull Whitman into left-wing politics than Horace Traubel. Following his comrade's demise, Traubel sought to establish Whitman's reputation as a poet but also introduced him to members of the progressive ethical culture, arts and crafts, and socialist movements. Like his hero, Traubel blindly accepted the republican tradition and espoused a politics of nostalgia that longed to restore an idealized preindustrial order. He relentlessly assailed capitalists and supported the woman suffrage movement, but despite his membership in the Socialist Party, he could not imagine a political economy that differed significantly from Whitman's, nor could he overcome racial prejudices. Traubel did, however, make an important change in the interpretation of his predecessor's cultural politics. In the early twentieth century, when homophobia began to spread among the American middle class, Traubel revised Whitman's adhesiveness in ways that were acceptable to his fellow progressive reformers.

Taking its cue from Traubel, the literary Left of the 1920s and 1930s used Whitman to articulate a radical but androcentric critique of American society. Led by Michael Gold, the Left enthusiastically invoked Whitman's rugged masculinity and collectivist vision to support its revolutionary agenda but struggled to come to terms with his individualism, racism, and sexual politics. Whitman was not, of course, accepted uncritically. Langston Hughes challenged the working-class hero's whiteness, and Tillie Olsen insisted that the construct of masculinity impeded rather than advanced the cause of social justice, in part because it failed to address the realities of gender oppression. If Whitman treated racial and gender politics superficially, artists such as Hughes and Olsen called for a new working-class hero who would confront these issues directly.

Part 2 examines the working-class heroism of Woody Guthrie, analyzing how and why this folksinger constructed himself and was constructed by others as the new Whitman. Guthrie articulated a social vision in which the politics of the body and the body politic, the politics of the bedroom and those of the union hall, were inextricably bound. If Americans intended to alter social relations, Guthrie suggested, they would have to rethink the rules of sexual expression as well as those of economic exchange. Only by discarding their prejudices toward individual bodies — black and white, male and female — could people learn to base relationships on love and cooperation rather than on hate and exploitation. An ardent supporter of the Popular Front, Guthrie readily mixed the metaphors of political and sexual union, embracing the Communist Party and the New Deal with equal fervor and peppering his work with the languages of masculinity and antiracism. Despite his commitment to union politics, however, a significant gap often existed between Guthrie's collectivist theories and their practice. An irrepressible individualist, he was as interested in promoting his own legend as he was in representing the people, and his failure to accept the responsibilities that accompanied his promiscuous sexuality intensified rather than subverted gender inequalities. This itinerant folksinger transformed the working-class hero from a poet to a guitar-slinging traveler of the open road, but his redefinition failed to alleviate the contradictions that were deeply embedded in the concept of heroism.

The focus of A Race of Singers shifts in part 3 to explore how Guthrie succeeded Whitman as the "heroic spiritual grandfather" of a new generation of radicals. I analyze how and why the New Left embraced Guthrie and investigate the ways in which his political reputation has changed through the 1990s. After Guthrie was hospitalized with Huntington's chorea in the mid-1950s, Pete Seeger worked to preserve his legacy by disseminating his music to college students and summer campers. Guthrie's music lost its ideological force in this decade of anticommunism, but young folksingers later rediscovered its radicalism and relocated it in the social movements of the early 1960s. Politically engaged musicians such as Bob Dylan and Phil Ochs invoked Guthrie to promote racial justice but continued to grapple with the familiar problems of individualism and sexism. As Guthrie's popularity increased, however, his image as a left-wing politico was contested. Popular representations refashioned him into a mythical artist who celebrated the American landscape, wrote nationalistic hymns, and represented individual freedom rather than social responsibility. In the 1990s, a variety of socially conscious popular musicians have begun to restore him to his political context, emphasizing his outspoken if tenuous commitment to collectivity, stressing his antiracism and antiwar sentiments, and even recovering the vaguely feminist ideas he expressed.

Perhaps the most influential person to reclaim Guthrie in the 1990s, Bruce Springsteen has consistently drawn on the Dust Bowl Balladeer to place himself in the lineage of the working-class hero. Although Springsteen would absorb Whitman's influence indirectly, he self-consciously adapted Guthrie's music and politics to represent the collective pain, suffering, and injustice working people have historically suffered and to articulate their dreams of a less oppressive future. In part 4, I argue that as the inheritor of a deeply conflicted cultural tradition, Springsteen has produced works that are replete with familiar ambiguities, some of which have been exacerbated by the complexities of commercial culture. During the height of his popularity, Springsteen reified the contradictions of the working-class hero, but his most recent work has challenged the conventions of race, gender, and sexuality and has critically considered how the constructs of heroism and white masculinity have impeded his cultural politics.

What follows, then, is the history of a race of singers who have expressed boundless optimism in the heroic figure that Whitman first imagined in 1855. These singers have both idealized working people and represented the brutality of economic and racial oppression, but they have refused to give into despair, becoming what Guthrie called "hoping machine[s]" who believe that America will one day become the Promised Land.[37] Their faith in American democracy has limited their political vision, a point to which John Lennon, an accomplished cultural worker in his own right, alluded in "Working Class Hero" (1970). Lennon's lone acoustic guitar plods hypnotically along, lulling the listener into the silent resignation and false consciousness that the song addresses. His sardonic voice implies that the construct of heroism encourages passivity by offering the remote prospect of upward mobility. Religion and television and other media promote an ideology that convinces people that they are "classless and free," but Lennon declares that they are "still fucking peasants." For him, "a working class hero is something to be," and when in the final verse he tells his audience that he will lead them on a heroic path, his tone is bitterly ironic. Disillusioned with his own fame, Lennon suggests that the working-class hero is a construct that encourages acquiescence, not revolution.[38] Rather than promoting social change, the hero is a symbol of success, another object to be consumed, an end rather than a means.

Whitman's working-class heroes could not write such pessimistic, defeatist lyrics, nor could they abandon faith in their own abilities to make the republican dream a reality. For the artists I discuss, the working-class hero was not an end in itself, not something to be but, like America, something to become, an unrealized truth toward which to labor. Their work has not been completed. Replete with inconsistencies and inadequacies, these working-class heroes have sustained a particular vision of social justice but have often committed quite unheroic deeds that have arrested rather than advanced democracy. Nearly 150 years after the publication of *Leaves of Grass*, the working-class hero remains something to become; in the words of Whitman, "the strongest and sweetest songs yet remain to be sung."[39]

PROGRAMS OF CULTURE

Imagining a Working-Class Hero

n the five years that preceded the publication of *Leaves of Grass*, Whitman befriended a group of artists and painters who, in 1851, invited him to address the Brooklyn Art Union. Although his speech indicated that the Carlylean connections between art, heroism, and morality weighed heavily on his mind, Whitman expressed a crankiness with the people that did not appear in his poetry. The poet idealized his fellow citizens, but the orator characterized them as money-grubbing philistines. He defined Americans as "a race to whom matter of fact is everything, and the ideal nothing," as people who viewed "most things with an eye to pecuniary profit." The artist, however, had the ability to cure this materialism. He could "go forth into the world and preach the gospel of beauty," could recite a "heroic verse" that would reveal a universal moral code. Like Carlyle, Whitman defined the artist as hero: "I think of few heroic actions which cannot be traced to the artistical impulse. He who does great deeds, does them from his sensitiveness to moral beauty. Such men are not merely artists, they are artistic material. Washington in some great crisis, Lawrence in the bloody deck of the *Chesapeake*, Mary Stewart at the block. . . . All great rebels are innovators . . . . A sublime moral beauty . . . may almost be said to emanate from them. The painter, the sculptor, the poet express poetic beauty in description; for description is their trade, and they have learned it. But the others are heroic beauty, the best beloved of art." [1] Like the leaders Whitman enumerated, a successful artist had the potential to shape the history and character of the nation. In fact, both art and artist could serve a political function that went beyond the holding of public office. The "true Artist" could demonstrate that even the most horrifying despot has "never been able to put down the unquenchable thirst of man for his rights." [2]

Three years after he published *Leaves of Grass*, Whitman continued to find moral and artistic inspiration in song. "A taste for music," he observed, "when widely distributed among a people, is one of the surest indications of their moral purity, amiability, and refinement. It promotes a sociality, represses the grosser manifestations of the passions, and substitutes in their place all that is beautiful and artistic."[3] An ardent fan of opera, the abolitionist Hutchinson Family Singers, and the minstrel show, Whitman was profoundly influenced by antebellum musical forms. By examining his songs under a "moral microscope," an instrument he used to scrutinize the national conscience in Democratic Vistas, we can begin to discern a morality that members of the race of singers he propagated have been eager to tease from his work.[4] The fabric from which Whitman's values were cut was artisan republicanism, an ideology without which his poetic and political tapestries would have certainly unraveled. To be sure, when the poet heard America singing, he listened to the "blithe and strong" voices of mechanics, masons, and carpenters who subscribed to a deeply conflicted but clear and consistent morality that enabled them to resist the acquisitive values of industrial capitalism.[5] Time and again, Whitman reaffirms the ideals he learned as a carpenter's son and printer's apprentice, ideals that simultaneously expanded and contained his democratic vistas.

WHITMAN AND THE ARTISAN IDEAL

Built firmly on the American Revolution's rhetoric of natural rights, artisan republicanism articulated ideas about freedom and equality that were inextricably bound to definitions of gender and race. This ideology belonged to skilled white northern craftsmen who, in the late eighteenth and early nineteenth centuries, served apprenticeships, worked stints as journeymen, and aspired to owning their own shops. These mechanics derived their highly prized economic independence and their sense of manhood from their skills, providing valuable services to the community in exchange for reasonable compensation.

Most artisans did not expect, and in many cases did not desire, to live extravagantly. They sought a "competence" that would enable them to support their families single-handedly but were otherwise wary of wealth. Tight-fisted journeymen were decidedly unpopular with their peers. Men participated in a mutualistic leisure culture characterized by their eagerness to buy drinks for fellow craftsmen at local pubs and formed associations that required them to assist unemployed members of their trades.[6] Wealth, they insisted, concentrated power in too few hands and imperiled the self-evident truths of freedom and equality. Consequently, they viewed greed as an immoral, unrepublican quality that threatened the health of the nation as well as their own freedom and independent manhood. The economic activities of manufacture and commerce were, like all others, subject to the moral laws of religion, and anyone who violated the principles of fair exchange committed a despicable act.[7] Put simply, artisans were determined to prevent the unfettered pursuit of self-interest from making a mockery of the Republic. They held their manly independence sacred but recognized that if they were to maintain what they believed was a state of equality, they must sometimes subordinate their own interests to those of the community.[8]

This idealized equilibrium was disturbed, however, by the economic transformations that beset the workshops between 1810 and 1850. As improved modes of transportation opened regional and foreign markets, a number of enterprising artisans met the rising demand for their goods by implementing new technologies, dividing the labor process into component parts, sending work out to domestic laborers, and ultimately centralizing production under the factory roof. These developments altered the manufacturing process, but more important, they profoundly transformed the values that had characterized preindustrial economic exchange and labor relations. As entrepreneurs commodified labor, they separated it from customary communal and egalitarian values, which resulted in a social organization that was more individualistic and less democratic.[9] Although an employer at the end of the eighteenth century had been obliged to feed and clothe his apprentice in addition to teaching him a trade, by the 1830s, he owed his employees nothing but a wage, and that too was becoming much less of a burden on the employer's bankbook. As trades were deskilled and routinized, employers drew from a vast pool of unskilled immigrant labor and female outworkers, all of whom worked for far less than a journeyman's competence. By 1850, the crafts were "bastardized," and qualified journeymen had difficulty finding positions in which they could properly ply their trades.[10]

The New York City artisans with whom Whitman rubbed elbows did not relinquish their collective ethos easily, and they quickly banded together to protect their economic interests. In 1831, the General Trades Union, an amalgamation of tailors, shoemakers, carpenters, and printers like those to whom Whitman had apprenticed, brandished the labor theory of value to assail greedy employers who had, in the words of one artisan, "disturbed the natural order of things."[11] Raw materials, insisted these journeymen, acquired economic value only after skilled hands transformed them into finished goods, so it was the labor involved in the *production* of manufactures rather than in the *distribution* of them that created wealth. Industrialization turned the artisan's conception of capitalism upside down. As entrepreneurs brokered finished goods, they accumulated tremendous wealth, whereas journeymen saw their standard of living fall dramatically. In an attempt to reassert control over the labor process and stabilize wages, workers organized in opposition to their former masters. But not all craftsmen resisted the temptation of wealth. By 1837, an entrepreneurial class of tradesmen emerged, causing artisan republicanism to bifurcate into two distinct strands: one that upheld skilled white male egalitarianism and collectivity and one that emphasized individual freedom and lent itself to unbridled capitalist development.[12]

Whitman consistently opposed labor unions, not because they pursued a more equitable wage but because he worried that their members "would set on their fellow-workingmen who didn't belong to their 'union' like tigers or other beasts of prey." Such compulsion, he opined, threatened the artisan concept of free and independent manhood.[13] These reservations did not, however, prevent Whitman from railing against entrepreneurs who wrenched republicanism from its egalitarian moorings and used it to promote their own private gain. As early as 1840, he commented on the proliferation of wage labor when he urged the "rich man" to observe the "poor, miserable" workingman who rises "an hour before sunrise, fussing, and mussing, and toiling and wearying, as if there were no safety for his life, except in uninterrupted motion."[14] His disdain for the emerging industrial order reappeared in his editorials in the *Brooklyn Eagle*. Whitman found injustices in the treatment of workers in the city's lead factories, where wages recently had been lowered. Angered by the stingy employers, he sarcastically announced that the "poor manufacturers will save the enormous sum of thirty-seven and one half dollars per week!" Such a paltry figure was "nothing to the rich manufacturers," but to the "poor man," Whitman recognized, it was quite a "serious matter."[15] Disturbed by an economic system that degraded the material and emotional lives of working people and endangered the nation's democratic promise, Whitman condemned the "morbid appetite for money" that his fellow citizens had developed. The "mad passion for getting rich," he explained, "engrosses all the thoughts and the time of men. It is the theme of all their wishes. It enters into their hearts and reigns paramount there. It pushes aside the holy precepts of religion, and violates the purity of justice. The unbridled desire for wealth breaks down the barriers of morality, and leads to a thousand deviations from those rules, the observance of which is necessary to the well-being of our people."[16] Artisans advocated private property and free markets, but when the pursuit of happiness endangered the public good and threatened the concept of justice, many workingmen, as well as Whitman, believed that the moral tenets of republicanism were compromised. If left unchecked, the "morbid appetite" would upset the tenuous balance between personal liberty and social equality.

As artisans formed craft guilds and labor unions to maintain this balance, they reinforced their solidarity by creating a largely homosocial, if not homoerotic, leisure culture. Through their membership in benevolent societies and fire departments, artisans proclaimed their commitment to the community. By sharing rooms in boardinghouses, engaging in wrestling bouts, and, strangely enough, squaring off in bare-knuckled prizefights, they expressed their affection for one another. Because New York City's journeymen spent most of their time with other men and were deeply committed to protecting one another's social and economic interests, it is not surprising that they established intimate relationships.[17] In fact, as historian Elliot Gorn argues, they "focused so much emotional attention on one another" that they frequently described coworkers as "creatures of beauty."[18] This fascination with male bodies presented itself in a wide range of physical activities. Backslapping, hugging, kissing, and bed sharing were routine among same-sex friends in the nineteenth century, and because the concept of a distinct homosexual identity did not emerge until the turn of the century, men and women could participate in homosexual acts without fearing long-term repercussions.[19] This is not to say that such behavior was widely sanctioned or that all, or even most, journeymen indulged in it. Nevertheless, the absence of homophobia and the anonymity of the industrial city allowed for a more fluid sexuality, and it is safe to aver that some workingmen acted on the homoerotic desire that charged their highly physical, masculinized culture. Whitman, who amplifies this impulse in "I Sing the Body Electric," believed that this manly love was particularly prevalent "among the mechanic classes."[20] He celebrated a homoerotic adhesiveness that he found in

The wrestle of wrestlers . . two apprentice-boys, quite grown, lusty, goodnatured, nativeborn, out on the vacant lot at sundown after work,

The coats vests and caps thrown down . . the embrace of love and
resistance.[21]

This culture nurtured a collectivist impulse in which individual freedom was firmly tethered to somewhat limited ideas about equality and
social responsibility. Artisan society was not, however, as egalitarian as
its members imagined. All crafts did not share equal standing in the community, and women, the unskilled, and people of color had little stake
in the society's politics. When black, immigrant, and female workers
began to compete for craftsmen's jobs between 1820 and 1850, racism
and sexism hardened.[22] As women outworkers and factory operatives displaced skilled men, their husbands and fathers viewed them as competitors rather than coworkers and redoubled their efforts to exclude them
from the republic of labor. Even Whitman, who preached gender equality
in his poetry, could not imagine a place for women in the artisan economy. For him, the ideal of the "noble female personality" was the "*wife*
of the mechanic," the "mother of two children, a woman of merely pass-
able English education" who "beams sunshine out of all these duties":
"cooking, washing, child-nursing, house-tending." [23] The wife's "independence" depended on her exclusion from the masculine public, where
her husband had ample opportunities to strengthen his economic position.[24]

As workingmen clung to their masculinity amid the vicissitudes of industrialization, they also held steadfastly to the privileges accrued by their
racial status. David Roediger argues that whiteness was a key component
of the republican man's identity and a physical quality from which he derived considerable social and psychological benefit. Concerned that their
freedom and independence were being taken from them, that industrialization was creating white wage slavery, journeymen responded by defining themselves as *freemen*, a term that clearly distinguished them from
black slaves.[25] Further evidence of white working-class race consciousness appeared in the minstrel show, in which performers and their audiences constructed African Americans as both puerile and savage, and in
the Free-Soil movement, which emerged in 1848 to advocate the abolition of slavery primarily because it threatened the independence of white
laborers.[26]

An ardent Free-Soiler, Whitman toed the party line. For him, slavery
was "a question between the grand body of white workingmen" on one
hand and the "aristocratic owners of slaves" on the other. If slavery was

extended to the territories acquired during the Mexican-American War, if aristocracy replaced democracy, "*that heritage of getting bread by the sweat of the brow*" would perish from the earth, and the "stalwart mass of respectable workingmen" would fade with it. Moreover, Whitman worried that the expansion of slavery would put "an honest poor mechanic in a slave State . . . on par with the negro slave mechanic."[27] Both he and his like-minded audience could not tolerate such leveling, largely because they defined themselves—their freedom, independence, and manhood—in opposition to the degradation that the black slave symbolized.

Whitman revisited such sentiments in an 1858 editorial in the *Brooklyn Daily Times*, entertaining the possibility that blacks might be excluded from the Republic altogether. "Who believes that the Whites and Blacks can ever amalgamate in America? Or who wishes it to happen? Nature has set an impassable seal against it. Besides, is not America for the whites? And is it not better so? As long as the Blacks remain here how can they become anything like an independent race? There is no chance for it." He believed that African Americans could "form a race, a nation," that they might one day become "freemen, capable, self-reliant, mighty." Such success could not, however, "be attained in the United States."[28] Whitman's poetry gestured toward equality, but as he told Traubel in 1890, he "never went full on the nigger question" because the African American "would not do anything for himself—he would only act when prompted to act."[29] Whitman wrote that "man can not hold property in man" and supported the abolition of slavery, but privately he scrawled notes that upbraided blacks for "their passiveness—their character of sudden fits."[30] The poet could never overcome such racist attitudes. For workingmen, and for Whitman, the law of African American inferiority was as natural as the rights of freedom and equality.

Organized around narrowly defined natural rights, artisan republicanism was the complex and contradictory constellation of ideas that provided craftsmen with a moral guide. In theory, this ideology balanced the tension between the individual and the public good, between freedom and equality. In reality, the homosocial and often homoerotic culture that emerged around it undermined its egalitarian designs. By 1850, the constructs of manhood and whiteness had become as important to the artisan's identity as notions of freedom, independence, and equality. Despite such shortcomings, artisan republicanism played an important part in the political and cultural lives of workingmen, arming them with a rhetorical heritage that renounced the morbid appetite for money. When Whitman instilled this ideology in his poet hero, he could not separate its pitfalls from its potential.

THE TRUE PEOPLE

Written in response to the Kansas statehood controversy, *The Eighteenth Presidency!* (1856) demonstrates Whitman's belief that the economic and social crisis posed by slavery could only be reconciled if Americans re-embraced the values of the artisan republic. Although the Compromise of 1850 had eased tensions between North and South somewhat, the Kansas-Nebraska Act (1854) heightened the sectional conflict. The brainchild of Stephen Douglas, an ambitious U.S. senator from Illinois, the act decreed that the residents of the two territories would decide the slavery issue on the basis of popular sovereignty.[31] The Kansas election proved to be a popular travesty. Neighbors from the slave state of Missouri crossed the border to vote early and often, delivering the government to slavery advocates. Despite clear evidence of corruption, President Franklin Pierce failed to intervene. Whitman could not veil his disgust. In his stinging indictment, he reprimands Pierce, declaring that the chief executive "eats dirt and excrement for his daily meals, likes it, and tries to force it on the states."[32] By implicitly supporting the extension of slavery and its aristocratic master class, such "false-hearted men" as Pierce compromised "the main purposes for which the government was established."[33]

Framing his defiant remarks in the terms of the master-apprentice relationship, Whitman insists that only a heroic workingman can recover such purposes. "The young genius of America," he explains, "is not to be emasculated and strangled just as it arrives at a manly age."[34] Like the thousands of journeymen who completed their apprenticeship only to be denied the rewards of manly competence, America was in danger of stalling in adolescence. The artisan's emasculation alone threatened to unsex the country, but this national crisis in gender identity was deepened by politicians who refused to extend the inalienable rights of freedom and equality to the American citizenry. Only when the country's leaders committed themselves to the Declaration of Independence, the document that Whitman calls the "organic" and "primary compact of These States," would America reach manhood.[35]

When he surveys the political landscape, however, Whitman can nowhere find "the spirit of manliness and common sense." He cannot "ob-

serve a single bold, muscular, young, well-informed, well-beloved, reso-
lute American man, bound to do a man's duty." [36] To restore the lapsed
morality of the United States, he calls for a "*heroic*, shrewd, fully-informed,
healthy bodied, middle-aged, beard-faced American blacksmith or boat-
man [to] come down from the West across the Alleghanies [sic], and walk
into the Presidency, dressed in a clean suit of working attire, and with the
tan all over his face, breast, and arms." [37]

Responsible and competent, this idealized hero possesses both physical and moral beauty. Unlike the "sniveling" politicians, he exhibits "a
manly scorn of all [political] parties" and bases his morality on a code
of conduct that seeks to balance individual freedom with the good of the
community, that tempers the pursuit of self-interest with a concern for
mutualism and egalitarianism.[38] The absolute equal of his fellow citizens,
the hero is the craftsman who, by restoring the idealized morality of the
artisan workshop, will lead America to political maturity. He converts
the promises of freedom and equality into realities not only for his own
good but also for the good of what Whitman calls the "*true people*, the millions of *white* citizens, mechanics, farmers, boatmen, manufacturers, and
the like." [39]

FOR THE WORKINGMAN'S SAKE

As *The Eighteenth Presidency!* indicates, Whitman's democratic vistas were
very selective. As he constructed his hero, he remained blind to the
deep contradictions embedded in artisan republicanism and failed to envision a republic in which African Americans and women qualified as
"true people." [40] Indeed, his politics were designed "for the workingman's
sake," were dedicated to securing his place in an uncertain economic
order.[41] To that end, Whitman "get[s] into the stream with" the "roughs
and beards" of America, where he finds "a hospitality which forever indicates heroes." [42] His oracular preface to the first edition of *Leaves of Grass* attacks capitalists who threatened the craft system by devoting themselves
to "years of moneymaking," "to stifling deceits and underhanded dodg-
ings . . . or shameless stuffing while others starve." [43] The morbid appetite
for money had caused master-craftsmen-turned-capitalists to lose sight
of their communal responsibilities, and it was the poet's job to restore
their morality, to become the "equalizer of his age and land." [44] Literature,
Whitman explained, must become "a weapon" that advances "the cause

of the masses," "a means whereby men may be revealed to one another as brothers."[45] To understand the contradictions in Whitman's brotherhood, we must listen carefully to the songs that comprise *Leaves of Grass.*

Whereas his journalism and prose castigated capitalists and politicians for what he believed was immoral behavior, Whitman composed his book of songs to inculcate a sense of "moral beauty" in his audience, to represent the social order not as it was but as he thought it should be.[46] "A Song for Occupations," Whitman's most sustained treatment of the nineteenth-century labor process, is, unlike "Song of Myself" or "Song of the Open Road," a carol that is not *of* workingmen, but one that is written *for* them. The poem identifies a number of economic factors that altered the lives of journeymen, but more important, it attempts to restore the dignity that industrial capitalism stripped from them. Applying the homoeroticism of artisan culture to the fault lines that divided America's cultural and political landscape, Whitman relies on representations of the human body to unite the body politic.

"Song for Occupations" welcomes its audience to the print shop, a workplace in which New York City journeymen of the 1830s and 1840s stubbornly clung to artisan ideals of equality and fellowship. To re-create the homosocial bonds that permeated artisan culture, Whitman opens the poem with an eroticized command that assembles his audience in a spirit of love and collectivity. "Come closer to me," he entreats. "Push close my lovers and take the best I possess / Yield closer and closer and give me the best you possess."[47] He issues this supplication for a sexualized, democratic exchange after the type has been set and the printing presses have run because this transaction is part of the "unfinished business" he must conduct to complete his labors.[48] In the face of economic transformation, Whitman fears that the labor process, its products, and, most important, the worker himself are being redefined in terms of their value to the market.[49] As a result, he strives to restore humanity to the practice of economic exchange. The printer spurns the machines of industrialization, turning from the "cold types and cylinder" that separate him from his male comrades and longing instead for the warm "contact of bodies and souls," the organic essence of human existence.[50] By sexualizing his description of labor, Whitman asserts that in addition to the mechanical elements and processes of the trade, a more valuable organic component exists that is linked directly to the natural law of equality. As he explains in the edition of *Leaves of Grass* that commemorated the centennial of the Revolution, "a fervent, accepted development of comradeship, the beautiful and sane affection of man for man . . . [and] what goes directly and indirectly along with it," would bind the "United States of the future . . . into a living union."[51]

This homosocial solidarity, which Whitman calls "comradeship," "manly love," and "adhesiveness," is central both to his theory of democracy and to the critique he levels in "Song for Occupations." He based his understanding of adhesiveness largely on the "human science" of phrenology, a discipline that claimed Orson Squire Fowler, whose firm distributed the first edition of *Leaves of Grass*, as one of its leading American theoreticians. Dividing the brain into nine "organs" that governed such "faculties" as "observation," "love," and "acquisition," phrenologists carefully measured the cranial dimensions of their subjects and converted the data into something that resembled a present-day personality inventory. Whitman, who had his measurements taken by Fowler's brother Lorenzo in 1849, scored particularly high in "adhesiveness," a quality that, as Fowler defined it, corresponded to Whitman's willingness to "congregate, affiliate, unite with." Fowler suggested that workingmen were particularly adhesive and appropriated the language of the artisan republic in his definition of the term. "HUMAN BROTHERHOOD in all things is its specific aim and mission," he wrote. "All men are brothers, but they have not yet learned this great practical truth." Although he conceived of labor and capital as "mutual friends," Fowler opposed wage labor and proposed that the "co-operative principle, in which each workman SHARES in the profits instead of working for wages, is the true manufacturing policy." He underscored the importance of this mutualism by declaring that "THE COMMON GOOD is also that of the individual," a statement that theoretically, grammatically, and visually subordinates personal gain to public interest.[52]

Although Fowler used the concept of adhesiveness to describe both same-sex and opposite-sex relationships, Whitman applied the term solely to male friendships.[53] His conception of manhood included an implicit heterosexual desire, but he preferred, like his working-class comrades, to associate almost exclusively with men, in part because he found homosocial relations more fulfilling.[54] In a lecture he prepared for a female audience in the 1850s, Whitman argued that "however welcome" the relationship between husband and wife might be, it "does not and cannot satisfy the grandest requirements of a manly soul for love and comradeship." Whereas a woman's love was "invalid" and "transient," the comradely love of men should be experienced with "more wildness, more rudeness."[55] Informed by sentimental novels of the day, the poet thought that heterosexual partners frequently deceived and exploited each other, and he proposed an idealized adhesive love as a politically viable alternative, one that would realize the potential of American democracy.[56]

As the sexualized language of "Song for Occupations" indicates, Whitman was already developing his concept of adhesive love in the first *Leaves of Grass*, but beginning in 1860, he dedicated the "Calamus" poems almost exclusively to exploring the political potential of manly love.[57] "I believe the main purport of these States is to found a superb friendship, exalté, previously unknown," Whitman exhorts in "To the East and to the West," "because I perceive it waits, and has always been waiting, latent in all men."[58] If America was to forge an unforeseen democracy, its citizens, suggested Whitman, would have to create a previously unimagined friendship. "Calamus" begins the search for this idealized relationship by traveling "in paths untrodden," trying to escape "all the standards hitherto publish'd" by a bourgeois society. To "sing" the songs "of manly attachment," individuals would have to discard the "whole past theory of" their lives and "abandon all conformity to the lives around" them; they must renounce the middle-class comforts and conventions located in the "roof'd room of a house" and embrace the roughness of manly love.[59] Whitman fantasizes that "by stealth in some wood" or "back of a rock in the open air" the organic homoerotic love that he believes is "latent" in all men might manifest itself:

Here to put your lips upon mine I permit you,
With the comrade's long-dwelling kiss or the new husband's kiss,
For I am the new husband and I am the comrade.

Or if you will, thrusting me beneath your clothing,
Where I may feel the throbs of your heart or rest upon your hip,
Carry me when you go forth over land or sea;
For thus merely touching you is enough, is best,
And thus touching you would I silently sleep and be carried
    eternally.[60]

Sexual conventions trammeled individual freedom in much the same way as did distinctions based on wealth, so if Americans were to break away from a social structure that had deprived them of their natural rights, they would also have to rethink a social order that controlled the organic impulses of sexuality.[61] In the passage above, Whitman questions constructions of sexuality by refusing to specify the sex of his partner, a strategy that implies that an artificially delineated heterosexuality would be undemocratic because it would restrict the natural expression of love and pleasure solely to male-female relationships and prevent its fair exchange between same-sex partners. Democracy should not make distinctions of any kind, particularly when sexual matters were involved. The natural expression of love, (homo)sexual contact, particularly Whitman's construction of it, had the potential to merge the bodies of political equals —namely white men—in a mutual exchange of pleasure that would bring about unprecedented democratic union of the body politic.[62]

For Whitman, "the special meaning of the Calamus cluster," and of adhesiveness in general, rested not so much in its formulation of an emerging sexual identity as "in [its] political significance," in its ability to cultivate the friendships required to bring about democracy. Only when any "two natural and nonchalant persons," passing leisurely on the street, were willing to kiss each other "on the lips with robust love" would the friendships needed for democracy be forged.[63] This homosocial attraction between men was "the quality that makes the states whole—it is the thin thread—but, oh! the significant thread!—by which the nation is held together, a chain of comrades."[64] For Whitman, sexual and social reform were inextricably linked. Sex, the organic expression of love, would help produce a social order that cultivated the organic rights of equality.[65]

As Whitman constructs the sexual democracy of "Song for Occupations," he tries to eradicate a number of social distinctions that are incongruous with his conception of equality. He discounts "all education practical and ornamental" and expresses his distrust of the "head teacher or charitable proprietor or wise statesman," suggesting that such positions carry with them the "usual terms" of privilege and hierarchy that adhesive love is designed to erode. A democrat must "never" live according these "usual terms" but rather must conduct his or her life according to the principles of the artisan republic:

Neither a servant nor a master am I,
I take no sooner a large price than a small price . . . . I will have my
    own whoever enjoys me
I will be even with you, and you shall be even with me.[66]

Whitman invokes the natural law of equality in a manner that discloses a subtle but important bias. Although it is important that the republican man not be a master, it is paramount that he not be a servant or, even worse, a slave. The poet goes out of his way to identify his constituency as white freemen when, as he questions the "usual terms" of hierarchy, he asks if his readers would be "satisfied" if "the boss" was "employing and paying" them.[67] As master-craftsmen-turned-capitalists uncoupled moral obligations from fiscal ones, journeymen feared that they were being relegated to a state of white slavery and developed the word "boss" to avoid addressing their employers as "masters."[68] Such word games safeguarded the dignity of many workingmen but also revealed the importance of whiteness to their identities and their ideas about freedom and equality. Whitman envisions a world where employer and employee "shall be even with" each other, but understanding slavery primarily as it relates to free white labor, he ultimately fails to put blacks on an equal footing with skilled white men.

This is not to say that *Leaves of Grass* ignores the question of racial equality altogether. As a number of critics note, Whitman based his democratic politics on the assumption that all bodies are equal, and in "I Sing the Body Electric," he was quite willing to put black and white bodies on par with one another. When the narrator encounters a male slave standing on the auction block, he upbraids the "sloven" auctioneer who, blind to the black man's beauty, "does not half know his business." Prospective buyers, the poet tells us, cannot bid "high enough" for this well-formed man. Whitman goes so far as to assert that the slave possesses "the making of the attributes of heroes," that his limbs look the same as "red black or white" limbs, that his veins hold "the same red running blood."[69] The poet sees

> Exquisite senses, lifelit eyes, pluck, volition,
> Flakes of breastmuscle, pliant backbone and neck, flesh not flabby,
>   goodsized arms and legs
> And wonders within there yet.[70]

Such a representation was clearly radical in its day, but Whitman's body politics present significant problems, for he objectifies this black man even as he celebrates him. He opens his description of the auction by calling the slave a "curious creature," a term that, particularly when juxtaposed with his reference to the "Gentlemen" he addresses, brackets his egalitarian intent.[71] He sees in this slave "the start of populous states and rich republics," but is he willing to grant African Americans citizenship in the Republic of the United States?[72] Throughout both his newspaper editorials and *Leaves of Grass*, Whitman consistently capitalizes the words "States" and "Republic" when he refers to the Union.[73] His failure to use capital letters for these words here suggests that although he was willing to include blacks in his poetry, he harbored serious doubts about admitting them to the republic of labor. Indeed, a consideration of black suffrage led him to opine that there was "about as much intellect and calibre (in the mass) [of blacks] as so many baboons" and to conclude that even freed blacks should be disfranchised.[74] The working-class hero might be the poet of masters and the poet of slaves, but the slave could not be a working-class hero.

Even in the radically egalitarian "Song for Occupations," Whitman cannot "go full" on the race question. He doffs his cap to "the slave" and "the negro from Africa" in the same motion that he celebrates "the free Utahan, Kansian or Arkansian," but African Americans' exclusion from productive labor, from the artisan workshop, precludes the possibility that they can become their own masters, that they can mature into *men*. Manliness is a quality Whitman reserves only for the white artisan.[75] He alternately describes African Americans as slaves, "curious creature[s]," "darkey[s]," and "woolypates," referring to them as men only to denote their sex.[76] "This is not only one man," he says of the slave in "I Sing the Body Electric"; "he is the father of those who shall be fathers in their turns."[77] A manuscript written by Whitman in the 1850s prefigures the racial politics of "Song for Occupations":

> And here mechanics work in their shops, in towns—There the
> carpenter shoves his plane—there the blacksmith stands by his
> anvil, leaning on his upright hammer;
>
> . . . .
>
> And here are my slave-gangs, South, at work upon the roads, the
> women indifferently with the men—see, how clumsy, hideous,
> black, pouting, grinning, sly, besotted, sensual, shameless.[78]

Whitman highlights the competence and manliness of white labor by contrasting it to the work done by black slaves. In his view, it matters little whether male or female slaves perform labor, for they are equally inept and incompetent. Defining himself against African Americans, the narrator takes pride in being "neither a servant nor a master" and is especially proud of being free rather than enslaved, white and not black.[79]

Besides failing to break racial barriers, "Song for Occupations" is circumscribed by strict definitions of gender. Given the historical moment under consideration, it is not surprising that the poem contains no analysis of women's subordinate social position, but perhaps it is more important that the only role afforded to women in the productive process is that of the "mother," who "is every bit as much as the father." Whitman further proclaims that the wife is "not one jot less than the husband," but in the unmistakably masculine economy and culture that comprise the poem, gender equality is impossible to achieve.[80] To be sure, few implements used in or products created by traditional women's work appear in Whitman's voluminous account of occupations. He may have longed to lead women "out of these incredible holds and webs of silliness, millinery, and every kind of dyspeptic depletion" that Victorian expectations imposed on them, but he could provide no alternative role for them except that of "perfect Mothers."[81]

Because he believed that the cultivation of manly love alone could achieve democracy, Whitman could not actualize his notions of gender equality.[82] As Eve Sedgwick argues in her study of nineteenth-century British literature, the activities of "men-promoting-the-interests-of-other-men" and "men-loving-men" are located on the same continuum, and in Whitman, these practices converge in a manner previously unfashioned.[83] But the consequences of manly love cut two ways. On one hand, adhesiveness frees men to act on homoerotic desire and has the potential to undermine the exploitative and competitive relations of capitalism and establish equality. On the other hand, Whitman's homosocial economy shores up the political interests of men by assigning women to motherhood and unpaid domestic labor. Moreover, it gives men the leisure and luxury to pursue adhesive relationships, to engage in behavior that strengthens the homosocial bonds of the marketplace, to circumscribe the sexual and social opportunities of women. To a certain extent, Whitman's celebration of sexuality liberated women as well as men, but adhesiveness, the foundation of his democratic vision, says nothing about allowing women to practice same-sex love. Manly love was radical insofar as it presented the possibility for a gay male identity, but because it did so at the expense of gender and arguably racial equality, its implications were profoundly conservative. Only white men, political equals in the artisan republic, could engage in this idealized exchange, and their ability to do so ensured that they would remain more equal than others. At its heart, adhesive love was about preserving, or in the case of workingmen restoring, the privileges of white manhood. Without a dramatic rethinking of gender roles, the manly love of comrades would do more to reinscribe power relations than it would to subvert them.[84]

In the limited context of the white artisan republic, however, Whitman represents a radical democracy in which the individual would have no more or no less than anyone else in the crowd, an assertion that lends itself to the possibilities of socialism. If the opening stanzas of "Song for Occupations" accomplish anything, they assert that the natural law of equality must be recognized. And because equality can only be judged and observed when individuals see themselves in relation to their fellow citizens, Whitman necessarily draws his lovers close to each other. The "equalizer of his age and land," he creates a poetics that locates his lovers in a complex social whole and, as James Dougherty notes, "place[s] him and his reader on a mutual footing":[85]

> If you bestow gifts on your brother or dearest friend, I demand as
>   good as your brother or dearest friend,
> If your lover or husband or wife is welcome by day or night, I must be
>   personally as welcome;
> If you have become degraded or ill, then I will become so for
>   your sake;
> If you remember your foolish and outlawed deeds, do you think that
>   I cannot remember my foolish and outlawed deeds?
> If you carouse at the table I say I will carouse at the opposite side of
>   the table.[86]

In this democratic list, Whitman begins each line with a nearly identical structure that underscores the egalitarian themes the stanza addresses. True to the principles of the artisan republic, the poet assumes a manly pose and proclaims his independence, but he readily subordinates his own interests to the public good by vowing that if working people "become degraded or ill, then [he would] become so for [their] sake."[87] More important, he refuses to make undemocratic distinctions between individuals regardless of prevailing social or sexual mores. He will have whoever enjoys him, making himself equally welcome in the beds of both male and female lovers, for all (white) people are organically equal in his eyes. To express his concern that the new industrial order had degraded America's working people, however, he interrupts his vision of social harmony and camaraderie with a set of questions that suggest that something is amiss. Although he insists that every member of the crowd is "remarkable," he acts as if his lovers respond to his declarations with doubt and disbelief: "Why what have you thought of yourself? / Is it you then that thought yourself less?" As deskilling and an increasingly competitive labor market depressed working people's wages, making their labor worth less in market terms, Whitman feared that people would begin to think of themselves as worth less in human terms as well. "Owning publicly" to deteriorating economic and human conditions, Whitman conducts an "unfinished business" that addresses the privatized nature of economic exchange and seeks to capitalize on human value:

> I bring what you much need, yet always have,
> I bring not money or amours or dress or eating . . . . but I bring
>   as good;
> And send no agent or medium. . . . and offer no representative
>   value — but offer value itself.[88]

By seeking to restore "value itself," Whitman alludes to the labor theory of value that his fellow artisans used to criticize capitalism. His objectified description of occupations suggests that the "natural order of things" — an order in which craftsmen reaped the fruits of their labor — had indeed been disrupted, that somehow people had been reduced to mere objects in the production process.[89] His democratic theory prevents them, however, from seeing themselves as members of a particular class. Rather than providing a model for collective political action, Whitman constructs a poetic program that seeks to reassert the value of the single solitary person, a strategy that at first indicates that he longs to withdraw from the social world. Appealing to Emerson, he speaks of an ethereal "something that comes home to one now and perpetually," something that cannot be "printed or preached or discussed." He tells us that we will not find the source of transcendence in "the President's message," nor in the "state department or treasury departments," nor even "in the census returns or assessors' returns or prices current or any accounts of stock," for all representations, including money, inadequately express the value of human life and labor.[90] Unfortunately, such abstractions abound in industrial America: the people's political will is represented in the president's message, their activities are abstracted into reports made by bureaus, their numbers are converted into census figures.

Whitman reviles representations because they often serve as substitutes for the objects or, even worse, the people they purport to represent. Seeking to recover "value" rather than "representative value," he asserts that humanity is the standard on which all transactions must be based:

> Old institutions . . . . these arts libraries and legends collections —
> and the practice handed along in manufactures. . . . will we rate
> them so high?
> Will we rate our prudence and business so high? . . . . I have no
> objection,
> I rate them high as the highest. . . . but a child born of a woman and
> man I rate beyond all rate.[91]

The natural activity of human labor has been reduced to "the practice handed along in manufactures" and "business." Acknowledging that these representations too are part of human labor, Whitman gives them their due but refuses to value the product, the process, or the profit more than he values the producer. "The sum of all known value and respect," Whitman suggests, is located in the individual who precedes the representation.[92] In this discussion, Whitman appeals to the Emersonian language of idealist individualism by reminding his readers that "all doctrines, all politics and civilization exurge from you," a statement that recalls the "Me myself" of "Song of Myself," where the poet posits an "idle, unitary" individual that somehow stands apart from the social world.[93] Such romantic individualism, argues Alan Trachtenberg, converts the concept of value to something that is "intrinsic, wholly private, free of exchange."[94] For the working-class heroes who would later draw on Whitman for inspiration, however, this revaluing of the individual was crucial. In a world in which workers became extensions of the "cold" machines they operated, their recognition as individuals was an important step in Whitman's poetic rehumanization of the labor process and in his efforts to relocate the source of value in human life.

Just when "Song for Occupations" appears to adopt Emerson's privatized philosophy, however, Whitman poses questions that illuminate the limitations of self-interest:

> Will the whole come back then?
> Can each see the signs of the best by a look in the lookingglass? Is
> there nothing greater or more?
> Does all sit there with you and here with me?[95]

Implying that something greater exists outside the self, Whitman now underscores the individual's connection to a larger social world.[96] He argues that the self is comprised of "your person and every particle that relates to your person," including "what is seen or learned in the street" or "what causes your anger or wonder." [97] In the mid-nineteenth century, however, fewer and fewer people understood the individual's relationship to the social whole and consequently pursued a course of economic self-interest that profoundly altered ideas about value. As many Americans practiced it, self-interest led not, as Emerson had predicted, to social harmony but instead fostered greed, inequality, and unrest. In notebooks he kept in the eight years that preceded the publication of *Leaves of Grass*, Whitman considers this problem, opining that although the "ignorant man is demented with the madness of owning things . . . the wisest soul knows that no object can really be owned by one man or woman any more than another. — The orthodox proprietor says This is mine. I earned or receive or paid for it, — and by positive right of my own, I will put a fence around it, and keep it exclusively to myself . . . dismal and measureless fool not to see the hourly lessons of the one eternal law, that he who would grab blessings to himself, as by right, and deny others their equal chance and will not share with them everything that he has." [98]

As he places the individual within a social context, Whitman comments on the moral failings of acquisitive individualism and identifies some of the effects it has had on the labor process. "What is it that you made money? what is it that you got what you wanted?," Whitman pointedly asks. He answers with a long catalog of his subject, telling us that our reward is "the usual routine . . . . the workshop, factory, yard, office, store, or desk." He intimates that the pursuit of wealth does not bring satisfaction but leads to an increasingly routinized life that values property, processes, products, and profits but not people. Whitman sings of "manufactures . . commerce . . engineering" as well as "the cylinder press [and] the handpress," but his focus remains firmly fixed on tools and products, the mere representations of labor, rather than on the laborers themselves. [99] He sings of

> The anvil and tongs and hammer. . the axe and wedge . . the square
>   and mitre and jointer and smoothingplane;
> The plumbob and trowel and level. . the wall-scaffold, and the work
>   of walls and ceilings . . or any mason-work. [100]

Not once does a smith strike an iron, a printer set his type, a farmer plow his field. Breaking the whole into its parts, dividing the labor process into its components, reducing laborers to their implements, industrial capitalism, Whitman suggests, destroys the culture of the artisan workshop and fragments what he believed to be the wholistic nature of republicanism into atomistic social relations.

This abstracted account of the trades reflects the dehumanizing process of industrialization but simultaneously emphasizes the ways in which the implements of the trades—and by implication the absent laborers who use them—are related to one another. "The pump, the piledriver, the great derrick. . the coalkiln and brickkiln," for example, share mechanical and practical similarities and imply an alliance between workers who must look beyond their individuality to see themselves as an integral rather than a component part of the labor process, their trade, or their society.[101] But again his democratic theory prevents them from seeing themselves as members of a particular class. He locates the possibility for collectivity not in labor unions but in an idealized adhesive love.[102] He allows that the implements of the trade, the "house you live in," "the deposite in the savings bank," the "pay on Saturday night," and even "the purchases" a workingman might make are important parts of his life but suggests that the self is not "in them"; rather, these objects and activities are the mere "themes and hints and provokers" of the self. The true "happiness" of "the whole" exists only within the social relations of the artisan workshop:[103]

Will you seek afar off? You surely come back at last,
In things best known to you finding the best or as good as the best,
In folks nearest to you finding also the sweetest and strongest and
    lovingest,
Happiness not in another place, but this place . . not for another
    hour, but this hour,
Man in the first you see or touch . . . . always in your friend or
    brother or nighest neighbor. . . . Woman in your mother or lover
    or wife
And all else thus far known giving place to men and women.[104]

Whitman again turns away from the "cold" inanimate objects of production and embraces his coworker. By striving to bring individuals in contact with one another, by attempting, in Michael Moon's words, to bring the writer himself "into loving contact with readers," the poet not only eschews the abstractions forged by industrial capitalism but also seeks to transcend the representations he himself creates with "every cross and twirl of the pen."[105] People, not their representatives or their representations, are the source of all value in the economy of "Song for Occupations." In the democratic list that closes the poem, Whitman exhorts that only "When the script preaches instead of the preacher / When the pulpit descends and goes instead of the carver that carved the supporting desk" would he "make as much" of these objects as he makes "of men and women." [106] To ensure that humanity itself was not commodified, Whitman looks to adhesiveness to "counterbalance and offset [the] materialistic and vulgar," to negate distinctions based on wealth and privilege and make "the states whole." [107]

Love, freedom, and equality were the noble ideas on which Whitman based his poetic representations, but like the abstractions he criticizes, his too are mediated, particularly through his republican lens. To be sure, his uncritical acceptance of and nostalgia for the artisan ideal prevented him from imagining an economic program that would address the emerging class structure.[108] When he assayed the unequal distribution of wealth, he saw rapacious individuals, not a capitalist class that exploited a proletariat. Prevailing attitudes about the genre in which he labored also governed his response to injustice. He intended his poetry, as Carlyle suggested, to reveal moral, not economic, truths. His great "language experiment" drew on science, religion, and economics and undoubtedly challenged many poetic conventions. But even his revolutionary free verse and inclusive, proselike line could not convince the arbiters of culture that poetry was an appropriate form for the development of economic theory.[109] Such was never his aim. His ruminations on society were not, as he explains in Democratic Vistas, "the result of studying up in political economy" but instead derived from "the ordinary sense, observing, wandering among men." [110] In his travels, he realized that the seemingly unrestrained development of industrial capitalism posed important problems for the Republic, but he defined these problems as moral, not structural or economic.

Like many members of the artisan republic, Whitman held individual freedom in high esteem, embraced the institution of private property, supported laissez-faire economics, and perpetuated distinctions based on race and gender. These values were widely held by his fellow citizens and were passed on to the artists who followed in his footsteps. But radical components of Whitman's democratic vision also made him a hero of the socialists who invoked his name in the late nineteenth century. First, he articulated a morality that consistently opposed many of the values generated by industrial capitalism. Reducing the vision Whitman creates in

"Song for Occupations," as does one venerable critic, to the mere applica-
tion of a monolithically constructed "antebellum entrepreneurial capitalism" overlooks this crucial achievement.[111] As I have noted, several forms
of capitalism were advanced in the mid-nineteenth century, and Whitman
renounced those that promoted the accumulation of wealth in favor of
one that fostered a sense of equality and community among men. Second,
and perhaps more important, Whitman discerned the relationship between sexual and social oppression, a relationship with which the American Left would struggle to come to terms throughout the twentieth century. He insisted that a radical new democracy could only be forged when
men shared their love, both emotionally and physically, with one another.
Although idealized, these sexual politics posed a clear challenge to many
forms of antebellum capitalism. Whitman was certainly not a socialist,
but as a manuscript he wrote in 1846 attests, he was also not a proponent
of untempered individualism: "Real Democracy, and great riches are in
some sort repugnant to one another. —Riches draw off the attention from
the principles of Democracy which are abstractions, called the rights of
man. —Riches demand the use of the house for themselves. —And men
have frequently to choose whether they will retain one or the other. —My
own opinion is that no amount of riches which numbers can calculate
will ever add up to any live man or any live nation, for the deprivation of
rational liberty and equality." [112]

A "Programme of Culture"

These republican values provided the foundation for Whitman's "programme of culture," which is conveniently summarized in *Democratic Vistas*.[113] A series of three essays completed in 1871, this statement responded
to the "conservative Scotchman" Thomas Carlyle, who in 1867 published
"Shooting Niagara: And After?," a tract that criticized universal (white
male) suffrage on the grounds that it might produce an inferior society. In
his rejoinder, Whitman launched some stinging criticisms at the United
States but ultimately defended the democratic promise to which he dedicated his poetry. *Democratic Vistas* surveyed an industrial landscape that
Whitman could not have envisioned in the 1840s when he wrote about the
indignities and changes that had destroyed the artisan workshops. Ap-
palled by what had transpired since his days as a journeyman, the poet
organizes the essay around a clumsily phrased question: "Is there a great

moral and religious civilization—the only justification of a great material one?"[114] He answers with a resounding "no." Examining the United States under a "moral microscope," Whitman explores a "sort of dry and flat Sahara" where the "depravity of the business classes of our country is not less than has been supposed, but infinitely greater."[115] Although he allows that "riches and the getting of riches" are part of his democratic theory, he observes that most Americans had abandoned faith in the "underlying principles of the States," in part because the government had failed "to inaugurate the respectability of labor."[116]

The "labor question," he asserts, was "beginning to open like a yawning gulf, rapidly widening every year" and forcing America "to sail a dangerous sea of seething currents . . . so dark [and] untried" that he knew not where to turn.[117] These fears continued to plague the poet in "The Tramp and the Strike Question" (1879). Having witnessed the depression of 1873 and the violent railroad strikes of 1877, Whitman thought that the most "press[ing] and perplex[ing]" issue of the day was "social and economic organization, the treatment of working people by employers, and all that goes along with it—not only the wages-payment part, but a certain spirit and principle, to vivify anew these relations."[118] Convinced that the somewhat idealized moral imperatives of artisan republicanism had seeped out of economic relationships, he declares, "If the United States, like the countries of the Old World, are also to grow vast crops of poor, desperate, dissatisfied, nomadic, miserably-waged populations, such as we see looming upon us of late years—steadily, even if slowly, eating into them like a cancer of lungs or stomach—then our *republican* experiment, notwithstanding all its surface-successes, is at heart an unhealthy failure."[119]

To rectify the problems he saw before him, Whitman predictably turns not to politics proper but to culture. As he once told Traubel, "the real work of democracy is done underneath its politics," a point he reiterates in *Democratic Vistas*. Poets, he argues, have the ability to affect "politics far more than popular superficial suffrage."[120] Their work, he suggests, should be "drawn out, not for a single class alone, or for the parlors or lecture-rooms, but with an eye to practical life, the west, the workingmen, the facts of farms and jack-planes and engineers, and of the broad range of the women of the middle and working strata, and with reference to the perfect equality of women, and of a grand and powerful motherhood."[121]

Recalling the preface to the 1855 *Leaves of Grass*, Whitman longs for the development of bards who would create "an aggregate of heroes . . . common to all."[122] Perhaps more important, however, is their responsibility to cultivate a "common ground" between the conflicting impulses that haunted democracy: the tensions between the individual and the whole. These contentious components, he suggests, must be tethered to "the core of democracy," its "religious and moral character," which guarantees personal liberty but prevents individuals from destroying the liberties of others.[123] Singing the praises of the artisan republic, *Democratic Vistas* argues that in order to restore dignity to working people, "these States" needed to enact "the *moral political speculations of ages*, long, long deferr'd, the *democratic republican principle*, and the theory of development and perfection by *voluntary* standards, and self-reliance."[124] To achieve this "spiritualization," Whitman looked to literature to weave the "threads of manly friendship," which he identifies as the "most inevitable twin or counterpart of democracy."[125]

Combining ideas of independence with a concern for the common good, Whitman seeks to restore moral imperatives to economic exchange on an individual basis. "That which really balances and conserves the social and political world is not so much legislation, police, treaties, and dread of punishment," he reasons, "as the latent eternal intuitional sense, in humanity, of fairness, manliness, decorum, &c. Indeed, this perennial regulation, control, and oversight, by self-suppliance, is *sine qua non* to democracy."[126] Whitman reaffirms the notion that all men are individually responsible for practicing morality in the public sphere. The poet hero "furnish[es] the hints, the clue, the start or framework," but "the reader is to do something for himself, must be on the alert."[127] It was the individual's responsibility, not a socialist government's, to enforce the values of the group.[128] Unwilling to renounce the institution of private property, Whitman's democracy requires "men and women with occupations, well-off, owners of houses and acres, and with cash in the bank—and with some cravings for literature, too."[129] Indeed, if he could find no audience, his cultural program would have little influence.

Whitman was radical but not too damned radical.[130] Even as he leveled his criticism against the corporate order, he provided what Sacvan Bercovitch has called a "diagnosis from within," one that reinscribed the contradictions and biases encoded in American notions of freedom and equality.[131] In Whitman's view, the problem was not that these ideas must be radically rethought but simply that America had not yet enabled all of its citizens to realize the self-evident truths. The prejudices submerged in artisan re-publicanism bubbled to the surface of Whitman's poetry, however, and revealed the folly of his faith. His racial politics remained far from egalitarian, and his notion of manly love excluded women from his democratic vision and relegated them to the domestic sphere. The working-class hero may have disdained authority, despised wealth, championed the dispossessed, and served as the "equalizer of his age and land," but he understood equality and freedom within a limited context. His haughtiness, his refusal to recognize anyone as a superior, his love of freedom, and the authority he had to declare "what I assume you shall assume" were predicated on the privileges of manhood and whiteness.[132] Replete with problems and possibilities, contradictions and consistencies, Whitman's concept of the working-class hero has both stimulated and stymied the imaginations of cultural workers from Horace Traubel to Eugene Debs, Woody Guthrie to Bruce Springsteen.

Whitman and the Anticapitalist Imagination, 1890–1940

hen Whitman died in March 1892, his place in American literary history was uncertain at best. His unabashed self-promotion and popular personality won the affection of a small coterie that defended him from all unkind words, but the merits of his poetic achievements were hotly contested in nearly all turn-of-the-century literary journals: for every critic who described him as America's finest poet, another dismissed his verse as doggerel. Such ambivalence may have prevented the poet's country from absorbing him as completely as he absorbed it, but as early as 1860, "Starting from Paumanok" predicted the posthumous fame and influence he would one day enjoy. "See, projected through time," he prophesies, "for me an audience interminable."

> With firm and regular step they wend, they never stop,
> Successions of men, Americanos, a hundred millions,
> One generation playing its part and passing on,
> Another generation playing its part and passing on in its turn,
> With faces turn'd sideways or backward towards me to listen,
> With eyes retrospective towards me.[1]

The "successions of men" and women who have read Whitman would not have assembled if a generation of cultural workers had failed to play their part. Concerned that the poet's legend might be interred with his remains, Horace Traubel and a handful of loyal disciples relentlessly promoted Whitman's literary reputation, publishing a hodgepodge of articles, photographs, and tributes that enabled him to elude obscurity.[2] As Traubel labored to secure Whitman's place in the canon of American literature, he simultaneously refashioned the poet into the prophet of socialism and adjusted his homoeroticism to fit with changing expectations about sexuality. But even as Traubel and his cohorts promoted economic justice, familiar contradictions remained embedded in their politics. Their hero's penchant for individualism as well as the constructs of masculinity and whiteness undermined their egalitarian designs. Nevertheless, their work had important cultural consequences for the American Left, members of which embraced Whitman as their "heroic spiritual grandfather," often challenged the limitations of his vision, and made him more damned radical than either he or Traubel could have imagined.[3]

UNCONSCIOUS INHERITED BIASES

Born in Camden, New Jersey, in 1858, Horace Traubel was the son of Katherine Gunder, a native of Philadelphia, and Maurice Traubel, a German immigrant who worked as a printer and had considerable affection for Leaves of Grass.[4] Horace shared his father's literary tastes, and when Whitman moved to a modest house on Mickle Street in Camden in 1873, the young boy was among the first to befriend him. Over the next twenty years, the two forged an unusually close relationship that David Karsner, Traubel's friend and biographer, described as "one of the most beautiful recorded anywhere in history. . . . It was more sacred, perhaps, than the ties of blood that bind father to son."[5] Traubel visited Whitman daily, organized and preserved his personal papers, and between 1888 and 1892 dutifully recorded their conversations for what would become the nine-volume With Walt Whitman in Camden. In 1894, he founded the Walt Whitman Fellowship, through which he hoped to unite the poet's many admirers. To support his endeavors, Traubel held various jobs, working as a printer's devil, typesetter, editorial writer, factory paymaster, and bank clerk. But he considered his most important work the publication of The Conservator (1890–1919), a monthly that he and his wife, Anne Montgomerie, founded to report on Progressive Era reform organizations and disseminate socialism.[6] When officers at the Farmers and Mechanics Bank of Philadelphia discovered that Traubel's journal espoused leftist ideas, they insisted that he either cease publication or leave his position at the bank. The decision was not difficult. He promptly resigned and devoted himself entirely to singing Whitman's praises.[7]

Traubel's mentor did not approve of his politics. In one of his ideological sparring matches with Traubel, Whitman condemned his understudy for his "radical violence" and warned of the dangers of political revolution. "You must be on your guard," he cautioned. "Don't let your dislike for the conventions lead you to do the old things any injustice."[8] Such advice did not prevent Traubel from becoming the point man in a cultural movement that prescribed Whitman's democratic representations as a cure for the social malaise caused by Gilded Age capitalism. Nor did it dissuade him from using *The Conservator* to connect Whitman to Eugene Debs's Socialist Party. The socialism that Whitman posthumously came to support was as protean as the poet himself, however. Straddling the boundary line that separated a cadre of middle-class intellectuals from an idealized working class, Traubel and his apprentices forged a deeply conflicted program of culture that took shape around changing expectations about sexuality. When an increasingly homophobic society discouraged the Whitmanites from alloying the poet's social and sexual politics, they purged the poet of his homoeroticism, but they used the language of male desire in hopes of resuscitating an imaginary republican past. Whitmanite socialism appealed to women on a number of fronts, but since it was grounded in a nostalgia for the mythic white male worker, it advanced a moral idealism that often failed to assess the complexities of the industrial economy and frequently undermined its claims for gender equality.

The Whitmanites developed their cultural politics during the Progressive Era, a period in which myriad reformers sought to redistribute the wealth, power, and privilege that a new industrial elite had accumulated. Determined to curb the influence of monopolies, many Americans began to contemplate and reembrace the nation's republican heritage. Invoking the Spirit of 1776, reformers did not seek to abandon the current political or economic system but labored instead to oust the tyrannical robber barons and reestablish what Michael Kazin has described as "a moral community of self-governing citizens." [9] To accomplish their goals, to reclaim the birthrights Thomas Jefferson had promised, farmers formed the People's Party, workers joined such organizations as the Knights of Labor and the American Federation of Labor, and middle-class progressives created a variety of organizations designed to address moral and civic issues.

The Society for Ethical Culture (SEC) provided a forum in which Whitmanite socialists could articulate their moral vision. Established in 1877 by Felix Adler, the SEC was an ecumenical organization that emphasized religious "deed not creed." [10] Adler condemned capitalists who recklessly pursued profit and imagined that greed and social injustice could be eliminated if individuals learned to act in a responsible and enlightened manner. To that end, the SEC established schools for working-class children in New York City and organized lecture series and discussion groups to address the most pressing ethical issues.[11] Adler's concern with working-class education was rooted in his belief that unjust labor relations posed the "chief moral question of the day," a question the SEC sought to address through "spiritualism" or ethical socialism.[12] These socialists aimed to create a more caring, egalitarian society without fomenting political revolution. In the republican tradition, they placed great faith in the moral authority of the individual and attempted, as Paul Buhle writes, "to reformulate the basis for order by adjusting existing institutions to self-evident moral laws."[13]

Traubel, who originally launched *The Conservator* to report on the SEC's activities, examined the American landscape under a particularly Whitmanesque "moral microscope."[14] He redefined Andrew Carnegie's Gospel of Wealth as a "perverse gospel," an integral part of a lie that taught individuals that the "wage questions" and the "law of supply and demand" were determined by objective forces that stood apart from ethics. Traubel insisted that all questions, particularly economic ones, were ethical. Pointing to the robber barons' crimes against humanity, he argued that the "founding of our republic would have had little significance if it had done no more" than become "another governmental disciple of the doctrines of devastation or death."[15] America, he acknowledged, had "made her distinct contribution to life and progress," but there did not yet exist a Whitmanesque program of culture that evaluated society on its moral achievements rather than its "material" successes.[16]

In fact, Traubel suggested that the Republic had strayed so far from its original course that it was now time "to organize over again," "to establish men in eternal birthrights."[17] Grounded in the political tradition of natural rights, his socialism did not seek to create a new sense of equality but rather proposed a reorganization that would restore the idealized preindustrial economy Whitman presented in "A Song for Occupations." He aimed simultaneously to "translate man back" to the artisan republic and "advance him to his state as man."[18] "The master workman—when will he come?," asked Traubel in "Craftsmen" (1897), an awkward poem that resurrects Whitman's working-class hero. On his second coming, the "master workman" would revive traditional artisan values, would make sure that the "divine" laws that once governed economic exchange were restored: workers would once again take from "the fund . . . without surplus." Moreover, the master's reappearance would make certain that the factory "bell no longer violates the virgin morning," that the break "is no longer cut short by the whistle that shrieks across the country." "From this day men sung their way through life, into the service of the hand passed the soul, the once-reluctant hours with quick faith enriched the years." [19] As Whitman had sung in "Song for Occupations," Traubel "esteem[ed] the soul above all estrangements—all attempts to confuse it with money-making and greed, with foolish and suicidal accumulations." [20]

Besides providing the foundation for Traubel's labor reforms, "Song for Occupations" enabled socialists to advocate more egalitarian gender relations. In 1907, John Edwin Snyder of the periodical *Socialist Woman* identified "Song for Occupations" as "perhaps the most revolutionary" of Whitman's poems, praising it because it allowed a woman to throw "back the lie . . . of her weakness and independence." [21] Snyder stretched the poem well beyond its ideological boundaries, but Traubel too found inspiration for gender equality in Whitman's republican vision, arguing for a "juster acknowledgment of woman" as "an *individual*" who must be delivered from "domestic thralldom." [22] These opinions, as well as Traubel's willingness to devote considerable space to the "woman question" in *The Conservator*, drew high praise from Mildred Bain, who published a hagiography of Traubel in 1913. According to Bain, Traubel offered a "special message . . . which helps and inspires woman to the fulfillment of herself." [23]

The British expatriate Helena Born, who moved to Boston in 1890 after becoming involved in the English socialist movement, shared Bain's opinion that Whitmanite socialism could lead to the liberation of women.[24] One of the most radical contributors to *The Conservator*, Born approached Traubel in 1898 about reviewing Charlotte Perkins Stetson's (later Gilman) *Women and Economics*. In her letter of inquiry, she suggested that "the importance of the subject would justify a liberal allowance" of space and insisted that her article should not be "condensed" after its submission.[25] Her enthusiastic review questioned the conventions of marriage and observed that although the "old sanctuaries" of politics and the church had recently undergone modest reform, few people had called for change "in the sanctuary of the home" as persuasively as Stetson.[26] Anticipating the radical feminism of Alice Paul, Born renounced all privileges afforded to her sex, even if they were well intentioned. "I find myself as ready to resent special favor and immunities for women as for men, just as I resent the theory that . . . places woman on a pedestal, proffering vain adulation." Such conventions were "rarely sincere," were certainly "not preclusive of demands for menial service," and ultimately violated "the law of equality." [27] Much like the women's rights activists Sherry Ceniza has discussed, Born claimed Whitman as an ally in the struggle for gender equality.[28] In "Whitman's Ideal Democracy," Born argues that the poet "is careful to remind his readers at frequent intervals that his hopes for humanity embrace the female equally with the male, without any sort of reservation." His "ideal woman is fearless and possessed of herself."[29]

Born's analysis is certainly enthusiastic, but turn-of-the-century women could not reach a consensus on the poet's attitudes toward their sex. Helen Clarke and Charlotte Porter were among those who found limitations in Whitman and the socialism his disciples espoused.[30] Prominent members of the Boston branch of the Walt Whitman Fellowship, Clarke and Porter were lovers who coedited the journal *Poet-Lore* from its founding in 1889 until its sale to Richard Badger in 1903. Although *Poet-Lore* was primarily concerned with the study of Shakespeare and Browning, its original location in Philadelphia and Porter's interest in ethical culture organizations ensured that the two women would cross paths with Traubel and contribute to *The Conservator*.[31] Their writings recognized that Whitman allowed the possibility of gender equality but also discerned a tinge of sexism in his work. When the two women coauthored "A Short Reading Course in Whitman" (1894), they contended that the poet defined his concept of comradeship too narrowly: "It is a curious fact, that might possibly strike only the woman reader, that in all his singing of comradeship and friendship he makes no direct reference to comradeship between women."[32] Anxious, perhaps, to appropriate Whitman as a proponent of their lesbianism, they insisted "that the manly love of comrades must include the womanly love of comrades," a love that had "superiority over the love of a husband."[33] Their analysis prefigured a reading that appeared in *Poet-Lore* a year later. Under Clarke and Porter's editorship, Helen Abbot Michael concluded "that after all Whitman has said on woman there remains a feeling of dissatisfaction." In Abbot's view, Whitman could not move beyond a woman's "corporeal attributes," could not capture her "great emotions," could not make her an equal comrade.[34]

Clarke and Porter expressed ambivalence about Traubel as well. They clearly respected the chief Whitmanite but refused to allow his opinions about the poet and his sexism to go unchallenged. In 1890, Traubel condescendingly dismissed the September issue of *Poet-Lore*, which featured articles written exclusively by female critics, as "woman's work from first to last."[35] In a response marked "personal," Porter presaged later feminists who would recognize the power of language to constitute and perpetuate gender inequalities. She angrily retorted, "Making a point of marking distinctions as to female and masculine in literature and art . . . with [such terms as] author*ess*, poet*ess*, editor*ess*, &c, we—Miss Clarke and I—do not believe in, although we did notice, as you did, the occurrence of a table of contents whose leading articles were all by women." [36] If women and men were to be equals, gendered language had to be eradicated and the achievement of female authorship had to go unremarked.

Several years later, Clarke launched an assault of her own. In May 1897, she chastised Traubel for failing to invite women to present papers at the annual meeting of the international Whitman Fellowship. She was further outraged that he expected her and Porter to share one ballot in the election of the fellowship's officers. "Why is it that when women are in charge they always give such a fair representation, but if men are in charge they overlook women if they possibly can?," she asked in a letter to Traubel. Explaining that sexism particularly plagued the Boston branch of the fellowship, she further opined that "co-operation between men and women will be impossible until men show a little more willingness to the parties in cooperation, instead of showing . . . only a desire for personal prominence." [37] By August, her ire had subsided and she issued a lukewarm apology. She assured Traubel that he was "among the few men whose attitude toward women is just and true." His sexism was "not so much intentional as the result of a carelessness men sometimes manifest through an unconscious inherited bias." [38]

Given the historical context, Clarke was right to suggest that Traubel was ahead of his time on issues of gender equality. But she was also quite shrewd to recognize that the bias of sexism suffused Whitmanite socialism. When in "Craftsmen" Traubel asked what social reform might bring the "workman," he constructed the working class in wholly masculine terms and addressed the labor question in a manner that would do as much to restore republican masculinity as it would to eradicate class distinctions.[39] Preoccupied with redeeming the lost privileges of the skilled male worker, he did not consider the future of unskilled immigrant workers, failed to address the issues of working women, and ignored the ways that race functioned in the labor market.

Like their ideas about gender equality, the male Whitmanites' position on race was complicated and contradictory. Lucius Daniel Morse of Atlanta and James Walter Young of Clinton, Tennessee, both of whom sat on the board of directors of the Whitman Fellowship, contributed articles to *The Conservator* that expressed attitudes about African Americans that were widespread in the post-Reconstruction South. Morse praised the slaves of the plantation for being "conscientious, obedient, docile" but argued that since emancipation, the "white man's salutary lessons of honesty, industry, and self-restraint, laboriously but faithfully instilled, have been quickly forgotten." Without the "restraining influence of the dominant race," Morse declared, blacks "would long ere this have resolved themselves back into hordes of howling savages." Young similarly defined African Americans as "a careless, irresponsible, emotional people, with no strictly defined sense of honor or morals; an amiable, good natured race, ignorant, and, of course, devoid of convictions." Suggesting that "a weakening of the moral fibre of the people may in fact result" if African Americans were granted full political rights, he warned that their "lack of mental virility" could possibly "filter into the national life and character." Like Whitman, Morse and Young refused to extend the privileges of manhood to blacks and thereby precluded the possibility that they might become working-class heroes.[40]

This opinion was not, however, universally held by those who wrote for *The Conservator*. In fact, Kelly Miller, the African American dean of the College of Arts and Sciences at Howard University, claimed Whitman as a proponent of racial equality. In an address entitled "What Walt Whitman Means to the Negro" (1895), Miller praised the poet for avoiding the trappings of conventional literature, which, when it addressed African American issues at all, tended to present "ignorant, superstitious, degraded, clownish, cutting jim-crow capers and apish antics for the amusement and delight of white lookers-on." Rather than picturing blacks in "pitiable helplessness," Whitman "endowed [them] with manly qualities and courage." Put simply, *Leaves of Grass* "sound[ed] the key-note of the higher emancipation" of the soul: "No negro, however humble his present station, can read these lines without feeling his humanity stirring within him, breeding wings wherewith to soar." Miller's assessment might have been a bit overenthusiastic, but it indicates that African Americans found such poems as "I Sing the Body Electric," in which Whitman acknowledges the beauty of black bodies, so inspirational that they were willing to overlook his prejudices. "What did he do practically in his lifetime for the negro?," wrote Miller. "Beyond the fact that he imbibed the anti-slavery sentiment of his environments, and that this sentiment distills throughout 'Leaves of Grass,' I do not know. Nor does it matter in the least."[41] It mattered not that, in the poet's own words, he "never went full on the nigger question"; what counted to Miller was that he budged at all.[42]

Traubel inched along too. "If you are a white American you grow grave when you think of the serious negro problem that you have on your hands," he wrote in a review of W. E. B. Du Bois's *Souls of Black Folk* (1903). "But if you happen to be a negro or half negro or colored anyhow you are grave because you have a white problem on your hands." [43] Traubel repeatedly urged his readers to consider "the negro's objection" to whites and was quick to recognize that notions of white "superiority" abridged African Americans' natural rights.[44] "Every time I put up an objection against the negro I am in his way," he reasoned. "I am an enemy of society. I am a foe of the social compact." [45] But like Whitman, Traubel believed that the primary "compact" of the United States was the Declaration of Independence and understood racial politics in terms of the republican past. "If this republic is without class and caste then any negro has as much call as any white man to any fair contest of preferment," he observed.[46] To be sure, the only solution to the race problem could be found through "the way of equal and everlasting opportunity," through efforts that would recover an imaginary past in which men could pursue their livelihoods unencumbered by the burdens of class and race.[47]

Traubel could not, however, conceive of race as a legitimate category of social analysis or oppression. He opined that "the negro makes too much of the negro" and went so far as to suggest that "the negro should stop talking about the negro for a while and commence talking about the white man." [48] Doing so might "plant his feet on competent ground." Rather than "escap[ing] on a racial raft," African Americans, he advised, must "embrace the economic radicalisms that are becoming increasingly prevalent in the north," must cast their lot with and follow the leadership of white working-class heroes.[49] Intellectuals such as Du Bois made much "about the color of . . . skin," but in the end, the black worker was "assailed on the plane of economic exploitation." [50]

Clearly, important inherited biases afflicted the Whitmanites. In 1902, Leonard Abbott declared that their namesake "was thoroughly cleansed of every taint of caste feeling and snobbishness," that his "spirit of equality" was blind to whether an individual was "white or black, high or low, rich or poor, learned or unlearned." Specifically, argued Abbott, Whitman's democracy derived "its logic and strength" from the "concept of organic unity of the world," a concept that owed much to a conflicted republican tradition.[51] M. P. Ball's "Whitman and Socialism" (1898) illustrates an important way that this tradition restricted Whitmanite socialism. Quoting liberally from "Song for Occupations" and *Democratic Vistas*, Ball addressed middle-class concerns that socialism would attack fundamental assumptions of individual achievement and upward mobility. He assured his readers that Whitmanite socialism would not "level everyone up or down," nor would it "do away with *native* inequalities." For many American socialists, the "native inequalities" of women and blacks were as self-evident as the natural truths of liberty and equality that they sought to renew and restore. Indeed, Ball praised Whitman precisely because he sang of the "dignity of labor" rather than the "degraded white slave of industry," because in such works as "Song for Occupations" he sought to reclaim the prestige of white republican manhood.[52] Old habits died hard. Traubel and some of his cohorts began to change their thinking on questions of racial and gender equality, but the idealized master workman remained at the center of their program of culture.

THE CALAMUS SUBJECT

A fervent commitment to the republican tradition impaired the vision of these reformers but enabled them to imagine a social order based on idealized love rather than unbridled competition. If socialists could recover the "sense of unity and comradeship" that Whitman felt for humanity, they could, suggested Abbott, supplant a "plutocracy based upon class rule."[53] The comradeship that the Whitmanites identified was not, however, the manly love on which Whitman had based his program of culture. "I want you some day to write, to talk about me: to tell what I mean by Calamus," Whitman told Traubel during one of their daily conversations. Both the poet and his disciple understood, however, that late-nineteenth-century America was becoming increasingly wary of same-sex relationships. The "respectable" middle class, Whitman suggested, was particularly concerned with "any demonstration between men—any: it is always misjudged: people come to conclusions about it . . . they shake their wise heads—they meet, gossip, generate slander."[54]

Attitudes about same-sex relationships were in part shaped by the pronouncements of turn-of-the-century social scientists. Medical discussions about homosexual acts had begun as early as the 1850s, but by the 1880s, a handful of sexologists, inspired by the scientific impulse to classify behavior, had identified the homosexual as a distinct biological type. Havelock Ellis pioneered the field of sexology in Great Britain and the United States, coauthoring *Sexual Inversion* (1897) with the British Whitmanite John Addington Symonds. The terms "homosexual" and "heterosexual" were not widely used until the 1930s, but as Whitman's remarks suggest, homophobia was already on the rise in the early 1890s. After Ellis and Sigmund Freud, writing in the first decades of the twentieth century, categorized homosexual behavior as "abnormal" and constructed gay men as effeminate, middle-class men in particular began to replace their homosocial leisure pursuits with activities that underscored their attraction to members of the opposite sex.[55] Many of these men made certain that their male friendships did not become emotionally (or sexually) intense and defined themselves in opposition to the "fairy," a style of male homosexuality in which men adopted exaggerated and stereotypical female behaviors.[56] By demonstrating that he desired women only, the middle-class man renounced the effeminacy for which the homosexual stood and, in the process, sought to shore up a masculine authority that the industrial order and feminism had threatened.[57]

To speak frankly about Whitman's homosexuality in this milieu certainly would have damaged his reputation among many of Traubel's middle-class comrades, whose attitudes about same-sex relations followed the shifting contours of American opinion.[58] As a result, the poet's closest followers made a conscious effort to protect their hero from the charge of homosexuality.[59] Traubel and Thomas Harned, his brother-in-law and fellow literary executor, were especially disturbed by a photograph of Whitman and Pete Doyle, a close friend and probable lover of the poet's, staring longingly and lovingly into each other's eyes. They desperately tried (but failed) to prevent the photograph from circulating. Not all of Traubel's efforts to closet Whitman's sexuality were so subtle, however. By 1893, he had left little room for speculation on where he stood on the Calamus question. As he discussed the issue of same-sex love in an 1893 letter to British Whitmanite J. W. Wallace, he fairly ranted: "Homosexuality is a disease—it is muck and rot—it is decay and muck—and Walt uttered the master-cries of health, of salvation, and purity, of growth and beauty."[60]

Motivated by both an emerging homophobia and a surface commitment to feminism, the leading Whitmanites began to redefine the poet's homoerotic concept of adhesiveness as a "co-equal co-operative human collectivity of individuals," male or female.[61] Even when Traubel spoke of Whitman, he referred not to manly love but to "loving humanity."[62] Love, Traubel declared in Whitmanesque terms, was the "thread electric, run from soul to soul," that "mends breaks or heals wounds."[63] He insisted that adhesive love would bind individuals together in the spirit of equality, but when he mentioned adhesiveness in relation to Whitman, he did so in asexual terms.

His decision to downplay Whitman's homoeroticism did not come easily. In September 1905, the British socialist and fellow Whitmanite Edward Carpenter asked Traubel to publish his own views on "Walt's more intimate relations to women & men," a request that Traubel refused only after considerable reflection.[64] In the course of editing *With Walt Whitman in Camden*, Traubel asked Carpenter for advice on whether he should publish Whitman's reply to the infamous John Symonds letter of 1890. When Symonds asked if *Leaves of Grass* advocated homosexuality, Whitman insisted that it did not, underscoring his denial by declaring that he had fathered six children.[65] Although Carpenter accepted Whitman's dubious claim to fatherhood, his correspondence with Traubel suggests that Traubel was reluctant to suppress the homoerotic implications of the poet's work. "It is a difficult question about the letters of Symonds & Whitman on the *Calamus* subject," wrote Carpenter. "Tho' I have not seen Symonds' letter of query, I guess it was a little ill-judged, that it threw upon W. the incubus of defending himself from accusations, & therefore caused W. to write less freely than he might have done. In these ways the publication of these letters will possibly convey false impressions. On the other hand there is further material in W's letter, about his children, which is valuable—& which I suppose is correct."[66] Carpenter worried that Whitman's denial might lead readers to conclude that the poet did not advocate same-sex love, a conclusion that could dramatically alter his politics. But as a gay man, Carpenter understood that the "Calamus subject" must be broached carefully. With this in mind, he advised, "Shall you put in any sort of note just indicating it in a general way—without applying it to particular statements?"[67]

Traubel did not elaborate on Whitman's sexuality, but critics were beginning to take note. As early as 1890, William Norman Guthrie of the *University of the South Magazine* found Whitman "obscene" and castigated him for expressing an "unbearably blasphemous" sympathy and a "brutal or bestial" manliness.[68] Representations of manly love also troubled the critic John Jay Chapman, who in 1897 insisted that the poet's "talk about comrades and Manhattanese car-drivers, and brass-founders displaying their brawny arms round each other's brawny necks, all this gush and sentiment . . . is false to life."[69] Whitman, he contended, had "committed every unpardonable sin against our conventionals, and his whole life was an outrage."[70]

Further speculation occurred in Europe. In *A Problem in Modern Ethics* (1896), Symonds reproduced Whitman's letter of denial and concluded that the poet "entertains feelings at least as hostile to sexual inversion as any law-abiding humdrum Anglo-Saxon could desire."[71] His evidence proved unsatisfying. In 1905, Eduard Bertz, who sought to use Whitman's burgeoning fame to advance the rights of homosexuals in Germany, published an article in which he concluded that the poet "was of a pronounced homosexual type," that 90 percent of Whitman's "impulses . . . were entirely feminine."[72] The discussion resurfaced in the United States the next year when *Current Literature* chastised Bertz and championed a rejoinder authored by Johannes Schlaf.[73] Despite such attempts to sequester Whitman within the confines of respectability, the locks had already been unscrewed from the closet door; the door itself was loosening from the jamb. In *Walt Whitman's Anomaly* (1913), W. C. Rivers declared that Bertz's conclusion was "as sound as an anvil."[74]

Although debates about Whitman's sexuality continued, Traubel did not address the issue directly; instead, following Carpenter's advice, he remarked only "in a general way." Nevertheless, Traubel expressed considerable tolerance for homosexuality in his reviews of Carpenter's works, including *The Intermediate Sex*, in which Carpenter argued that Whitman "could not have spoken . . . with a kind of authority" on same-sex love "if he had not had ample knowledge of its effects and influence in himself and others around him."[75] Traubel did not address this argument but preferred instead to approach the concept of homosexuality in general. "You have heard all the things about the intermediate types," he challenged his audience. "But have you gone further? Have you asked for and been told the rest of the story?" For Traubel, divisions between homosexuality and heterosexuality were more fluid than most people imagined. It was impossible "to cut and dry [sex] into a narrow formula," "to wholly dissever the masculine from the feminine."[76]

Although Traubel did not speak of same-sex love when he discussed Whitman, the Calamus subject remained an integral one in his personal and political lives. Between 1899 and 1905, Traubel forged a remarkably intense adhesive relationship with Gustave Percival Wiksell, a dentist and member of the Boston branch of the Whitman Fellowship. Many mid- and some late-nineteenth-century men addressed one another in idealized and intimate language, but the correspondence between Traubel and Wiksell leaves little doubt that these camerados engaged in sexual relations.[77] "Send me love words to burn into my flesh, sweet brother. Send me your two arms to embrace me. Send me your darling lips run over with kisses," Traubel wrote in 1904. "Soon I will come to you. Then we will be one. The same. One flesh. I and my brother. My brother and me. Does waiting tantalize you?" Anticipation of their trysts clearly titillated Traubel. "Open your arms," he gushed in another steamy letter. "I come to you. You feel me hot and thirsty upon you. I drink for my thirst. And you offer me a full cup. This is what love means when love is love. This is what a brother real is to a brother real." Traubel's marriage apparently did little to temper his passion. When he anticipated an October 1904 visit to Boston, he warned, "I will have the Mrs. with me," but he assured Wiksell that "I will have my hot arms with me too and they will embrace you. My hot lips will kiss you."[78] Wiksell's replies indicate that he welcomed the advances of his "Darling boy lover" with "open arms."[79] To signify their Calamus love, the two men sat for a photograph in which they emulated the loving pose Whitman and Doyle had once struck, a pose that had made Traubel uneasy.[80]

Despite his attempts to silence Whitman's sexuality, Traubel sought to use adhesiveness to effect political change and found an outlet for manly love in Eugene Debs's Socialist Party. Traubel and Debs wrote to each other frequently, and although their letters were not as passionate as the Traubel-Wiksell epistles, the two sets of correspondence exhibit remarkable continuity. "Dear brother, I still feel you near me just as when you took me in your arms when the time came for us to separate the other night," wrote Traubel in 1908. "I am waiting here with radiant memories and strong for the fight."[81] Debs echoed such language. "My dear Horace," he wrote in August of that year. "Just happened to think of you because I had to. Am sending a love thought and already am I enjoying the pleasurable anticipation of seeing you."[82] In November, he jotted a short note that read simply "Love in big letters!"[83] By 1910, the relationship had grown more intense. Debs wrote to Traubel: "It would be impossible for one human being to love another more than I love you. A thousand times I have hoped in my heart that I might sometime be permitted to sit and commune with you and enjoy you to my soul's desire."[84] Middle-class progressives may have spurned manly love, but as a number of historians have demonstrated, workingmen such as Debs seemed to embrace at least its rhetoric.[85]

As Debs assailed capitalism, he drew inspiration from both Traubel and Whitman. In a 1907 letter addressed to the Whitman Fellowship, for example, he identified Whitman's notion of fraternity as "the quin-

Horace Traubel and Eugene V. Debs. Debs Collection, Indiana State University.

tessence of human kinship: Born of freedom, consecrated in brotherhood and expressed in love."[86] The politician and the poet had much
in common. Debs quoted his literary idol in speeches, praised him in
The Conservator, and wept at his grave during the 1904 presidential election.[87] Born the year that *Leaves of Grass* was first published, Debs based his
identity on the artisan ideal, holding notions of self-respect and independence in high esteem and emphasizing communal responsibility.[88] Like
Traubel, he focused his politics primarily on the redemption of the American worker's manhood, but because he supported women's suffrage and,
as his letters to Traubel indicate, because he could adroitly manipulate
the language of sentimentality, he gained considerable popularity among
women. Historian Paul Buhle credits this success to Debs's attempt "to
redeem suffering in a fashion historically associated not with 'manhood'

but with the androgynous Jesus that women churchgoers had substituted for the Calvinist doctrine. Recovery of self-respect, recovery of the republic, meant sacrificing individualism, if necessary, to the needs of fellow humans and to the future society as a whole." [89]

Women certainly found such strategies attractive; Traubel's daughter, Gertrude, even contributed a poem to *The Conservator* in Debs's honor.[90] But Debs's language shared as much, if not more, with a tradition of male bonding and the formulation of Whitmanesque adhesiveness that derived from it than it did with sentimentalism. Steeped in the republican past, his idealized rhetoric had a way of doubling back on itself, of creating a sense of brotherhood that excluded women—and often immigrants and people of color—from the fraternity of labor. Traubel readily discerned the republican origins of Debs's message. As he observed in 1903, "The Debs of fable lighted a fire in the car yards of Chicago. The Debs of fact lighted an idea in the dangerous shadows of the republic." [91] But republican rhetoric could only be so dangerous, could only become so radical, could only push Debs's political imagination so far. As biographer Nick Salvatore argues, his critique of capitalism predictably eschewed serious analysis of race and especially gender. In the end, the former railway worker from Terre Haute viewed women "as subsidiary to his main concerns, in orbit around and tangential to the leading actors in this drama, their fathers, husbands, and brothers." [92]

Adapted by Traubel and Debs, Whitman's adhesiveness simultaneously expanded and constricted democratic vistas. On one hand, brotherly love renounced the competitiveness of industrial capitalism and sought to restore the mutualistic ethos of a bygone era. On the other, that same love, professed in the language of homoerotic desire, was designed to advance the political and economic interests of the white workingman, often at the expense of immigrants, African Americans, and women. The line between men-loving-men and men-safeguarding-one-another's-interests was, as Traubel's and Debs's sexualized language indicates, difficult to detect. In *The Conservator*, however, the demarcations that separated races and genders remained starkly visible. The Whitmanites simply held the "old things" too dear. To achieve social justice, they had to be more damned radical. They had to focus their "moral microscope" on the injustices that plagued the political economy, inequalities deeply imbricated in the republican ideology—and in the poet—they so fervently embraced.

Traubel's association with Debs radicalized his analysis of the political economy. He was quick to celebrate the victory of Pennsylvania's anthracite miners in their 1902 strike and lent implicit but carefully measured support to the Lawrence, Massachusetts, textile strike of 1912, which was led by the Industrial Workers of the World (IWW). Soon after the 23,000 immigrant workers began their struggle for bread and roses that January, members of the Socialist Party began to raise funds and provide shelter for the strikers. Anxious to capitalize on the emergence of class consciousness but wary of the Wobblies' proimmigrant and syndicalist policies, the Socialist Party cautiously reacted to the uprising at its May convention. In preparation for the 1912 presidential election, in which they hoped to tap the middle-class progressive vote, socialists built a prolabor platform that endorsed industrial unionism but condemned the use of sabotage, a technique the Wobblies included in their arsenal.[93]

Traubel readily adopted the party line. Thumbing his nose at the prudential unionism of the American Federation of Labor, he argued that "economic and political organization [should] go hand in hand" and, addressing the IWW, noted that he objected to sabotage not because of "what it does to the proprietor" but because of what it did to the labor movement.[94] Although he viewed sabotage as "suicide," he began to advocate a working-class militancy. IWW tactics may have been reprehensible, "but in so far as the syndicalistic and industrial workers' form of revolt is instrumental in stirring up the crowd and getting the crowd together and inducing the crowd to acknowledge its necessary solidarity," he supported them.[95] Indeed, he recognized that "modern corporations like to reduce people to the status of things" and consequently urged workers to organize, to strike, to "violate" the laws that usurped their natural rights.[96] By the time he published *Chants Communal* (1904), a collection of writings that first had appeared in the socialist weekly, *The Worker*, Traubel was recognized as a leader among members of the American Left. "He is a Communist, and needs not a single qualifying adjective," wrote the leftist scholar John Spargo.[97] He won few accolades among the class of people he sought to reach, however. By 1916, Debs lamented that although Traubel might have been "one of the supreme liberators and humanitarians of his age," it was "a thousand pities that so few of the common people he [had] given his life to actually know him."[98]

The promise of Whitmanite socialism faded when Traubel died in 1919, his spirit carried away, an eyewitness attested, by Whitman's ghost.[99] But thanks to this loyal disciple's relentless efforts, the poet continued to infuse the American Left with important cultural energy. In the 1910s, Traubel had regularly frequented Greenwich Village, spreading Whitman's gospel to a new generation of radicals who labored at such magazines as *The Seven Arts* and *The Masses*. Waldo Frank, Max Eastman, and "Ashcan" artists John Sloan and Robert Henri were among those who read *The Conservator*.[100] By 1915, Floyd Dell, coeditor of *The Masses*, acknowledged Whitman's continuing presence among his comrades.[101] "Walt Whitman seems to have been accepted by Socialists as peculiarly their poet," observed Dell in the *New Review*, a journal to which Traubel occasionally contributed. "In the library of the ordinary 'local' he stands on the shelf not far from Karl Marx." Dell went on to anoint Whitman "the most complete and thorough-going anti-Socialist in all of literature," but a wide range of anticapitalists continued to place the poet in a radical light.[102] A year later, John Dos Passos, the novelist who played a leading role in the defense of Sacco and Vanzetti, insisted that Whitman could provide guidance to an otherwise "rootless" bunch of American writers. Dos Passos invoked and evoked Whitman throughout his literary career and declared that if his fellow novelists intended to produce a culture that was made of more than "steel or oil and grain," they would have to "pick up the glove that Whitman threw at the feet of posterity."[103] Because Whitman insisted that literature could change politics, because he had boundless faith in the future, he provided leftists with a model for their cultural work.

These artists reacted to the crises of American capitalism in a variety of ways, practicing politics marked by personal differences and internecine struggles although they were unified in their opposition to prevailing economic structures. Their interpretations of Whitman were similarly variegated, yet they faced remarkably familiar problems when they transported the artisan poet to the twentieth century. As they sought to unseat the captains of industry, they struggled with Whitman's individualism, his homoerotic vision, his racial politics, and his construction of manhood. By the end of the Great Depression, the limits of Whitman's cultural politics began to manifest themselves to a new generation of artists. As they remade Whitman to suit the exigencies of their own historical moment, many of these intellectuals rationalized his ideological shortcomings and adapted his homoeroticism, whereas others, notably Langston Hughes and Tillie Olsen, refashioned their hero in a manner that renounced the very prejudices he seemed to propagate.

Mike Gold, the editor of *The Liberator* and *New Masses*, assumed a leadership role in Communist Party cultural politics, establishing the ground rules for revolutionary art in his influential essay "Proletarian Realism" (1930). With their hopes buoyed by the stock market crash of 1929, communists held that capitalism and, in Gold's words, "bourgeois culture [were] in the process of decay" and suggested that left-wing writers must do their best to expedite the decomposition.[104] Whitman assumed a prominent role in Gold's cultural theories. "I have read him so many different times and in such varying moods that I believe I could sit down and write a book about him without a moment of research," he explained. "He is part of me for better or worse."[105]

Whitman's influence was particularly discernible in Gold's "Towards Proletarian Art" (1921), a landmark essay that provided the framework for "Proletarian Realism." Citing *Democratic Vistas*, Gold embraced Whitman's sexual language and identified the poet as the "heroic spiritual grandfather" who would "spawn" a new generation of radical writers. Whitman provided a blueprint for the "method of erecting this proletarian culture," and now that he had "aroused" the masses, they could "relieve" their predecessor of his "massive labors." Although Whitman had long been misunderstood as a "prophet of individualism," Gold argued, he "knew the masses too well to believe that any individual could rise in intrinsic value above them." This poet was an "unafraid," "powerful," and "strong" cultural patriarch, the first artist to recognize that "a mighty national art" could only "arise . . . out of the soil of the masses." Gold acknowledged that Whitman might have "fallen short of the entire truth" but insisted that the "lusty great tree" of revolution would sprout from the seeds the poet had sown.[106]

Gold's working class was, like Whitman's, predictably and unmistakably male. In this manifesto for proletarian literature, the poet both fathers the next generation and carries it to term, a rhetorical act that eliminates women altogether from both procreative and creative processes. Indeed, Gold provided little room for women or women's rights in his cultural politics. He anticipated that under his editorship the *New Masses* might produce a "Jack London or a Walt Whitman," "a wild youth of about twenty-two, the son of working-class parents, who himself works in the lumber camps, coal mines, and steel mills, harvest fields and mountain camps of America."[107] Gold built such celebrations of manhood on the cultural heritage of the labor movement that, as Elizabeth Faue argues, "forged a web of symbols which romanticized violence, rooted solidarity in metaphors of struggle, and constructed work and the worker as male."[108] "Send a giant who can shame our writers back to their task of civilizing America. Send a soldier who has studied history," exhorted Gold in his description of the ideal communist critic. "Send a strong poet who loves the masses, and their future. Send someone who doesn't give a damn about money. Send one who is not a pompous liberal, but a man of the street. . . . Send no coward. Send no pedant. Send us a man fit to stand up to skyscrapers. . . . Send no saint. Send an artist. Send a scientist. Send a Bolshevik. Send a man."[109]

Following Gold's lead, the leftist critic Granville Hicks fused the languages of revolution and masculinity in *The Great Tradition* (1935), a history of American literature that reflected the radical politics of the proletarian literature movement. Hicks praised authors who took up the manly task of the revolution but dismissed the work of the most acclaimed women writers. Willa Cather "could do nothing but paint pretty pictures," Ellen Glasgow was bound to a "sentimentality that . . . robbed her of her creative force," and Edith Wharton's work "ended in romantic trivialities."[110]

The critic found Clifford Odets much more inspirational, however. The principal playwright of the radical Group Theater, Odets became the darling of the literary Left when he wrote *Waiting for Lefty* (1935), a one-act agitprop based on the New York City taxi drivers' strike of 1934. Banned in several American cities, this proletarian masterpiece inspired Depression era audiences to rise to their feet chanting its revolutionary message "STRIKE! STRIKE! STRIKE!" in unison with cast members.[111] Odets issued this call to arms in masculine terms. When, in the final scene, the character Agate urges his union brothers to strike, he addresses them as "*Ladies and Gentlemen*" and describes those men who refuse to strike as "ladies . . . wearin' pants."[112] In the context of the incendiary rhetoric that follows, the implications of this opening statement are clear: real men will strike. When Lefty, the representative for whom the union members wait before they cast their ballots, is found murdered, only the most unmanly of men would refuse Agate's plea: "It's war! Working class, unite and fight!"[113] Hicks enthusiastically dubbed the play an "irresistible appeal for action" grounded in a "sure sense of working-class reality."[114] That Odets self-consciously emulated Whitman did not hurt his cause. Determined to become the Whitman of the stage, he named his son after the Good Gray Poet and published an essay entitled "Democratic Vistas in Drama" (1937) in the *New York Times*.[115]

Whitman was widely popular in leftist circles, but his masculine appeal was complicated by the question of his sexuality. The Communist Party of the United States, like the larger society in which it was embedded, had little public tolerance for same-sex relationships. Following the Russian Revolution in 1917, Lenin's government legalized homosexuality to permit the people, suggested a Soviet pamphlet in 1923, to pursue their "needs and natural demands," but by 1934, Stalin had officially outlawed homosexual acts, a policy that the U.S. Communist Party readily adopted.[116] That homophobia would arise in the American Left is not surprising. Seeking to stabilize the crisis in gender roles caused by the Great Depression, Americans in the 1930s redoubled their efforts to control homosexuality. Hollywood studios agreed to exclude representations of same-sex relations from the screen, and the police force in cities such as New York placed well-known gay meeting places under strict surveillance.[117] Eager to sell their ideology as "Twentieth Century Americanism," male members of the Communist Party were unwilling to support an agenda that questioned the patriarchal heterosexual family, largely because it could further tarnish their image.[118]

Moreover, strict adherents of Marxism argued that the class struggle and sexuality were distinct discourses. Many of the bohemians who resided in Greenwich Village during the 1910s and 1920s were attracted to Freud and Marx alike, but with the rare exception of such women as Emma Goldman, they tended to divorce the sexual from the social.[119] As self-proclaimed scientists, communists assigned sexuality to the discipline of biology rather than history or sociology and insisted that whereas class politics were an important part of the public sphere, sexual issues should be confined to the private. This position led the Communist Party to adopt a rather conflicted platform: sexuality had nothing to do with the class struggle, but the disclosure of one's homosexuality meant immediate expulsion from the party.[120] The Communist Party would ignore the sexual preferences of cultural workers who promoted class consciousness, however, and plenty met this criterion. Marc Blitzstein, who wrote such leftist musicals as *The Cradle Will Rock* (1937), actor Will Geer, who traveled in Woody Guthrie's folk music circles, and Harry Hay, who would begin the gay liberation movement in 1951, were among the gay or bisexual men who participated in party activities. In the end, the Communist Party adopted the equivalent of a "don't ask, don't tell" policy.

The homoeroticism that pervaded leftist language also could be overlooked because the heterosexuality of the male worker was taken for granted by both the Communist Party and mainstream American culture. By the 1930s, representations of male homosexuals had become so feminized and those of male workers so masculinized that it was virtually impossible to imagine the two categories overlapping.[121] Such perceptions likely prevented many radicals from discerning the homoerotic content of their rhetoric and certainly has discouraged labor historians from recognizing the significant effort the Left expended in discussing and rethinking sexual politics. Gert Hekma, Harry Oosterhuis, and James Steakley go so far as to argue that the Left "repeatedly ascribed homosexuality to the 'class enemy,' contrasting the manly vigor and putative purity of the working class with the emasculated degeneracy and moral turpitude of the aristocracy and haute bourgeoisie."[122] Hard-liners such as Gold publicly adopted this platform, but beneath the weight of dogma, a number of male leftists recognized that love between men, especially Whitman's formulation of it, had much to offer their cultural politics.

Toeing the party line, Gold authored a review of Thornton Wilder's works in 1930 that renounced homosexuality and conflated it with prevailing constructions of femininity. Wilder, he insisted, was the "poet of the genteel bourgeoisie," the proselytizer of "a pastel, pastiche, dilettante religion . . . a daydream of homosexual figures." Because he viewed his subjects "through the eyes of a typical American art 'pansy,' " Wilder "concocted a synthesis of all chambermaid literature" that emitted a distinct "homosexual bouquet." Such unmanly, unrevolutionary art failed miserably when measured against "the language of . . . the vast Whitman."[123]

Gold contended that the language of same-sex love had no place in proletarian literature, but even this rigid ideologue could not eliminate Whitman's eroticized language from his criticism, a language that often functioned to exclude women from the centers of leftist power. As Michael Trask has noted, the Left typically renounced the conventional institutions of dating and marriage and generally maligned women because they distracted men from committing themselves to revolution. Leftist writers consequently formulated an eroticized male solidarity that stood in stark contrast to romanticized heterosexual relationships, which allegedly promoted consumerism and discouraged social change.[124] Gold predictably imbibed such prejudices. Couched in the rhetoric of male bonding, his descriptions of the radical writer John Reed and IWW organizer John Avila were charged with a homoerotic attraction that rivaled Whitman's most provocative work. Gold described Reed as "a cowboy out of the West, six foot high, steady eyes, boyish face; a brave, gay, open-handed young giant" with a "splendid body." [125] His recollections of Avila were similar. "I can't forget Big John Avila. . . . He is my friend," began Gold's reminiscence. Avila was "a tall, sinuous young Portuguese I.W.W., with a handsome Latin face, blue-black hair and a graceful, eager, naive manner that makes people like him." The union brothers so "loved" Avila that "their eyes followed him as he bustled around the hall." [126] As these erotic descriptions suggest, the attraction that existed among male revolutionaries often seemed to be more than ideological. At the level of language, the activities of men-loving-men and men-protecting-one-another's-political-interests coalesced.

Gold may have constructed Whitman as the manly foil to the feminine, homosexualized Wilder, but Whitman's male adhesiveness was so crucial to the leftist cause that in 1926 two prominent cultural workers chastised Emory Holloway for failing to acknowledge the poet's homosexuality in *Whitman: An Interpretation in Narrative*. Former *Masses* editor Max Eastman noted that Whitman "was strongly homosexual" and accused Holloway of "menshevizing" his subject, of transforming him, in the words of Lenin, from a "fighter" into a "reasoner," from a "worker" into a "blabber." By lamenting that Whitman "did not marry a good wife and settle down," Holloway's "tendency [was] to sterilize him, tame him . . . take the great rebel part . . . out of his poetry." [127] An ambivalent supporter of the Marxist Left, critic Lewis Mumford uneasily echoed such claims. Mumford argued that the "honest biographer need not flinch from admitting" Whitman's proclivities, but he himself could not fathom that the poet had acted on his desires. Homosexuality, concluded Mumford, "existed at a subconscious level in Whitman and was sublimated by him, precisely as in most normal lives"; his "heterosexual experiences were sound, normal, full." In this critic's view, adhesiveness was a mere theory that could be "turned into useful social channels," that could slip easily into the language of collectivity and ultimately promote communism or socialism. [128]

Eastman and Mumford received unsolicited support from conservative critic Ludwig Lewisohn. In *Expression in America* (1932), Lewisohn insisted that Whitman's rhapsodies about same-sex love were "profoundly mingled with much communistic sentiment," that his "theme of universal acceptance is . . . almost Russian in its chaotic leveling impulse." When men loved men—a practice Lewisohn identified as "an abnormal channeling of erotic impulses" — they challenged the individualism and competitiveness that undergirded capitalism.[129]

Lewisohn's claims moved Bernard Smith, who coedited the influential *Proletarian Literature in the United States* (1935), to "loud laughter," but Newton Arvin, a gay socialist critic, quite seriously addressed the connection between homoeroticism and socialism in *Whitman* (1938).[130] Arvin admitted that Whitman was "unmistakably homosexual" but, much like Mumford, modified Whitman's sexual politics to suit the socialist cause. Arvin criticized the poet for basing his social vision on idealized love rather than political activity but maintained that Whitman provided the reformer with a useful program of culture. Whitman's "private origins" may have been somewhat "obscure," but unlike most "inverts," he "chose to translate and sublimate his strange, anomalous emotional experience into a political, a constructive, a democratic program."[131] The poet, Arvin declared, had discovered "living images for the abstraction of Fraternity," and although these images "are not available for *normal* men and women," the Left could use these symbols "to preserve, and adapt" the language of adhesiveness "to [its] own purposes."[132]

The ease with which Arvin carried out that adaptation suggests that the homoerotic spirit that pervaded the language of Whitmanite socialists remained intact in the 1920s and 1930s. Struggling, perhaps, with his own sexual identity, Arvin observed that "the line that can be drawn between the normal and the abnormal, though a real one, is at best an uncertain and somewhat arbitrary line, drawn rather for practical convenience than for the sake of absolute distinctions."[133] Arvin was aware that the lines that separate the political — men-advancing-the-interests-of-men — and the private — men-loving-men — are often as unclear as those that mark the heterosexual-homosexual binarism. As he wrote of *Leaves of Grass*, the homoerotic "strain [was] diffused through" the works of male leftists "so widely and so subtly that it cannot be isolated and separated . . . except by an artificial process of analysis." Same-sex love might not have been available to the "normal" people who comprised the Left, but the language of same-sex desire formed an integral part of their politics and continued to promote the interests of the male worker. Whitman assumed a prominent place in the Left's pantheon of heroes, so prominent that he enabled its members to rationalize their use of an eroticized male solidarity that subordinated women in both the capitalist present and the imagined socialist future.

Just as Whitman's sexuality presented peculiar problems to the Left, his racial politics also presented challenges. Whitman was not a proponent of racial equality, but his commitment to the Free-Soil Party was sufficient reason for many African Americans to claim him as an ally in their struggle for racial justice. Since the 1890s, Whitman was associated with progressive racial politics in Philadelphia, where Kelly Miller addressed the Walt Whitman Fellowship in 1895 and Alain Locke, a leader of the Harlem Renaissance and editor of the influential literary anthology *The New Negro* (1925), attended a school run by the Whitmanite-affiliated Society for Ethical Culture.[134] Other important figures in the black arts movement shared Locke's admiration for Whitman, including James Weldon Johnson, Jean Toomer, and Claude McKay.[135]

No one syncretized Whitman, African American aesthetic traditions, and radical and racial politics as effectively as Langston Hughes (1902–67). Hughes was born to parents with multiracial backgrounds in Joplin, Missouri. His appreciation for Whitman began in high school and persisted in such poems as "I Too" (1926), "Let America Be America Again" (1938), and the paean "Old Walt" (1954).[136] He further acknowledged his artistic debt in the introduction to a 1946 edition of Whitman's poems issued by the left-wing International Publishers.[137]

Hughes's association with the literary Left strengthened his attraction to Whitman. Inspired by McKay's editorial work at *The Liberator*, Hughes broke into leftist circles in New York City in the early 1930s, joining the local branch of the John Reed Club, an organization founded by the *New Masses* to cultivate young revolutionary writers.[138] Throughout his life, Hughes vehemently denied that he had joined the Communist Party, but he was at least a remarkably loyal fellow traveler throughout the Depression. Impressed by the involvement of the Communist Party's International Labor Defense in representing the Scottsboro "boys," nine African Americans unjustly charged with raping two white women in Alabama in 1931, Hughes toured the Soviet Union in 1932, served as president of the party-sponsored League of Struggle for Negro Rights, and became a contributing editor to Gold's *New Masses*.[139]

Closely following Communist Party mandates, Gold allegedly monitored African American writers to make certain they did not emphasize racial consciousness at the expense of class struggle, but he was nonetheless fascinated by black cultural expression. After the Communist Party International declared in 1928 that African Americans in the Black Belt comprised a colonial state that should be granted its own political rights, the party recognized that black culture was replete with complicated forms of cultural and political resistance and consequently identified African American art and race consciousness as inherently revolutionary.[140] Black folk music was understood to be particularly subversive, and Gold insisted that in the traditional spiritual he could hear the African American "religious past become transmuted into a Communism of the present."[141] Still, the Communist Party demanded that African American art address economic issues, although its own racist assumptions prevented it from tightly enforcing such guidelines. Hughes commanded the respect of his comrades, but many communists perceived African American culture as an inferior form of folk art and consequently exempted it from the standards that governed the works produced by white artists. Freed from such dogmatism, African Americans often exploited the opportunity to articulate a clear antiracist politics.[142]

Gold has been criticized for failing to support black artists, but although he subordinated race relations to class struggle, he welcomed African Americans into the Communist Party and vowed to treat them with a respect they had not previously enjoyed.[143] Unlike the "night-club rounder and white literary sophisticate" Carl Van Vechten, who simultaneously promoted and exploited black artists, Gold did not want to associate with "a brood of Negro literary bums" who adopted the exoticized and racialized pleasures of "gin, jazz and sex." He instead anticipated "Negro Tolstoys, Gorkys and Walt Whitmans" who, "plowing into the revolutionary movement," would "be a voice of storm, beauty and pain . . . sombre as night with the vast Negro suffering, but with red stars burning bright for revolt."[144] Racist assumptions backed such overenthusiastic proclamations. Unable to accept African American art on its own terms, Gold suggested that black artists should remain within the political and aesthetic parameters set by white artists, who subsumed racial oppression under the umbrella of economy.[145] The proletarian movement harbored such racist attitudes, but as Gold remarked in 1941, it also provided an opportunity for black writers to portray the "sober self-respect and unquenchable aspiration of the Negro people." Due largely to the Left's efforts, Gold prematurely concluded, the era in which an author "of any quality" could represent "the Negro as a strutting clown" had finally ended.[146]

The masculine rhetoric of revolution, the politics of the Left, and Whitmanesque ideas coalesced in Hughes's *New Song* (1938). With a selling price of just fifteen cents, this pamphlet was published by the International Workers Order (IWO) "in the desire to make literature available which would otherwise be out of the reach of wage earners." Claiming a membership of some 140,000, the IWO published Hughes's poems, General Secretary Max Bedacht explained, because this "fraternal society" sought to "establish cultural ties between people of various races and nationalities. . . . Fraternalism means brotherhood; and the poetry of Langston Hughes is a true expression of our ideals because it is an impassioned cry for humanity and brotherhood." [147] Gold, who quoted this passage in his introduction to the pamphlet, concurred: "The Negroes are enslaved, but so are the white workers, and the two are brothers in suffering and struggle." Assembling racial differences under the banner of class oppression, the IWO would, in Bedacht's words, "help break down the artificial barriers erected between people" and, in Gold's, create "that democratic culture of which Walt Whitman prayed and dreamed." [148]

Gold's comment is followed by Hughes's recognizably Whitmanesque "Let America Be America Again," a poem that reveals the limitations of the republican tradition and presents the possibility of a racially egalitarian society. Hughes longs for the country to realize the "dream" that was envisioned in the Declaration of Independence but recognizes that blacks, poor whites, Native Americans, and striking laborers have all been denied the promises of freedom and equality. Advancing the party's integrationist agenda, he suggests that these inequalities are rooted in unjust labor relations. Working people of all colors have poured their blood and sweat into their country, receiving nothing for their pay but an empty dream. As he recounts this rather inglorious history, Hughes acknowledges that America is a "land that never has been yet," but affirming the faith of both Whitman and Marx, he defiantly declares that "America will be!" Invoking Marxist conceptions of property and production, he urges working people to seize the land from their oppressors.[149]

This revolutionary rhetoric was particularly radical in light of the Communist Party's call for the creation of the Popular Front in 1935. With European fascism on the rise, the party urged its members to put their revolutionary hopes on hold so that they might form alliances with all liberal and democratic governments, including the United States, to eradicate the threats posed by Hitler and Mussolini. The result was the formation of a culture that promoted a prolabor, antifascist, antiracist politics.[150] Hughes accepted these political goals but refused to shelve a revolutionary racial and class consciousness. "For honest work / You proffer me poor pay," he says to an employer whom he prepares to strike in the face.[151] Embracing the prevailing rhetoric of the Left, Hughes contends that the racial and class revolution will be the culmination of a decidedly manly struggle. An elderly African American woman joins the Communist Party ranks in "Sister Johnson Marches" and "Open Letter to the South" acknowledges that "shop girls" are part of the working class, but the usually inseparable languages of violence and manhood predominate throughout the remainder of New Song. Indeed, "Open Letter," which renounces Booker T. Washington's endorsement of segregation, depicts a world in which white and African American workers join forces to "kill" prejudice and "smash" racial barriers. To carry out these tasks, workers must recognize that they are all "brothers" who together have the "strength" to conquer both economic and racial oppression. As a black worker extends his hand to his white counterpart, he asserts his manly equality by declaring, "Today, / We're Man to Man." [152]

Like his comrades, Hughes defines political union in terms of male bonding and evokes a homoeroticism that is particularly interesting when viewed in light of widespread speculation about his sexual orientation. In Harlem Renaissance circles, Hughes was assumed to be gay, but as biographer Arnold Rampersad argues, no one has produced "concrete evidence for his reputation," and even his closest friends insisted that his sexuality was known best for its ambiguity.[153] His fanaticism about concealing his sexual identity may have accounted for his fascination with Whitman. Perhaps Whitman's fluid sexuality permitted Hughes to explore his own identity, perhaps the labor movement's equivocal language of brotherly love enabled him to articulate a revolutionary class politics while veiling a sexual politics. To be sure, Hughes elsewhere professed a tolerance for homosexuality.[154] The short story "Blessed Assurance" (1963) explores the plight of a young gay man, and "Café: 3 A.M." (1951) suggests that the line between "normal" and "abnormal" is sometimes difficult to draw.[155] As a pair of detectives search the streets for homosexuals, they debate whether gays and lesbians are degenerates or simply products of nature. Suddenly they see a woman whose appearance confounds them: is she a "Police lady or Lesbian"?[156] Hughes's own sexuality and the language he uses in New Song are as ambiguous as the woman's sexual orientation. Regardless of his own sexual orientation, notions of same-sex love remain at the periphery of Hughes's poems. In the culture of the Popular Front, the language of adhesiveness no longer applied exclusively to white men, but it was still used to promote the interests of the male worker.

What is more important, perhaps, is that the masculine languages of black nationalism and communism converged in radical African American writers such as Hughes, opening a space where black men, long denied the power and privilege afforded to their white counterparts, could both redeem their masculinity and promote racial politics.[157] The Communist Party insisted that race consciousness not overshadow the class struggle, but as Hughes's work indicates, his adherence to Marxist principles did not prevent him from assailing a society that systematically discriminated against all people of color. Like most Americans in the 1930s, the leaders of the Left still held racist sentiments and were certainly not prepared to celebrate an African American as the manly working-class hero. They were, however, willing to allow men such as Hughes to participate in the proletarian literary movement and Popular Front politics.[158] Perhaps the most influential black cultural worker to embrace Whitman as his literary forebear, Hughes defiantly asserted his racial pride, insisting that African Americans claim the rights of manhood and ensuring that the Left could no longer in good conscience exclude blacks from its politics.

WHERE A HUMAN COULD BE A HUMAN

Whitman's emphasis on manhood shaped the strategies of male literary radicals, but his politics did not go uncontested. Perhaps the most important challenge was made by Tillie Lerner Olsen (1912?–), the daughter of Jews who left Russia during the 1905 uprising against the czar. A life of poverty prompted the Lerners to join the Socialist Party and to introduce their daughter to the era's radical journals and magazines. As a member of the Young Communist League, Olsen ably merged her literary and political interests, publishing a short story entitled "The Iron Throat" in the *Partisan Review* (1934). Acclaimed by critics, the story provided the basis for her novel, *Yonnondio: From the Thirties*. After working on the novel from 1932 to 1937, Olsen was forced by the demands of motherhood and wage labor to abandon the project until 1972. Choosing not to revise or augment the original, Olsen assembled the fragments of her text "in arduous partnership" with that "young writer" from the thirties and published it in 1974.[159] Inspired by Whitman's poem of the same title, *Yonnondio* both embraces and criticizes the masculine formulation of proletarian art, calling particular attention to the ways in which individualism and gender constructions conspire to prevent members of the working class from organizing into a collective revolutionary force.[160]

Based on an Iroquois word meaning "lament for the aborigines," Whitman's "Yonnondio" worries that Native Americans will become "utterly lost" in an increasingly urbanized landscape. "No picture, poem, statement, passing them to the future," he observes. "Yonnondio! Yonnondio!—unlimn'd they disappear."[161] Part of Whitman's poetic project was, of course, to represent the unrepresented, and Olsen, who reproduced much of "Yonnondio" in the epigraph to her novel, found this legacy particularly attractive. Discussing Whitman's poem in the early 1970s, she explained, "Myriad of human beings—those who did the necessary industrial work in the last century—lived and died and little remains from which to reconstruct their perished (vanished) lives. About them as about so much else, literature was largely silent, and the charge can be levied: *Nowhere am I in it.*"[162] Conceived under the influence of the proletarian movement, Olsen's *Yonnondio* is an attempt to validate the experience of the working class, particularly working-class women, and to articulate a long-silenced history. Set in the 1920s, this incomplete novel describes the travails and triumphs of Anna and Jim Holbrook and their five children during an arduous three-year journey from the coalfields of Wyoming, to the farmshares of the Dakotas, to the packinghouses of Nebraska.

In the first few pages of the novel, Olsen describes thirteen-year-old Andy Kvaternick the eve before he begins a lifetime of work as a coal miner. Like his father, who was recently killed by a collapsed mine roof, Olsen suggests, Kvaternick will be "sculptured" by "the artist, Coal": "You are brought now to fit earth's intestines, stoop like a hunchback underneath, crawl like a child, do your man's work lying on your side, stretched and tense as a corpse."[163] Despite the unhealthy and unprosperous life Kvaternick seems destined to live, Olsen introduces the hope and possibility of social change. Someday, she predicts, the mines will "swell and break" with the miners' "old tired dreams," causing men, women, and "starved children" to rebel against their employers.[164] The Holbrooks, however, are unable to act on this possibility, perhaps because they are so poor that they lack the necessary strength for revolution, perhaps because they address class oppression through the language of gender.[165]

Jim in particular invokes this language, repeatedly asserting his masculinity to assuage the pain and humiliation of poverty. In one of this brutal novel's rare tender moments, Jim holds his daughter, Mazie, on his lap as she asks why their family does not live as well as "the boss man." Her perplexed and embarrassed father futilely responds that his employer has a higher standard of living because "he's a coal operator," but both he and Mazie somehow feel better about their plight when Jim explains that despite the operator's wealth and power, he could still "lick" his boss in a fight.[166] Exploited and dehumanized at work, Jim calls on the language and privilege of manhood at home to dominate those around him both physically and psychologically. Beating his children occasionally and Anna frequently, he typically blames his wife for their grim financial status. "A woman's goddamn life," he remarks in a representative assault, "sittin' around huggin' a stove."[167] Indeed, Jim habitually devalues the domestic and reproductive labor in which Anna engages, insults to which she responds by attacking his role as breadwinner:

> "Don't touch ya, huh. You don't always talk like that. No wonder I never got anywhere. No wonder nothing ever comes out right. Lots of help I get from my woman."
> "You get plenty of help. Kitchen help, farm help, milkin' help, wash-woman help. And motherin' too."
> "Who asked for your goddamn brats?"
> "Who? I'll never have another, to starve to death with you."
> "No wonder we're starvin'. Look at the woman I got."[168]

Absolving himself of the often onerous responsibilities of child care, Jim maintains that if he did not have "a woman and kids hangin' around [his] neck," he might have made something more of himself.[169] Olsen suggests, however, that child rearing and housekeeping are as demanding and destructive as the life of an industrial worker. In the final chapter, she juxtaposes descriptions of Anna's domestic labor with descriptions of Jim's work in the packinghouse, demonstrating that the constant demands of child care engender a work environment that is as frenetic and exhausting as that created by the speed-up system under which Jim toils. And like the bodies of miners and slaughterhouse workers who daily risk disfigurement and death, Anna's body deteriorates as a result of her labors as a wife and mother.

Olsen amplifies her criticism of manhood when she describes a packinghouse employee named Jim Tracy who quits his job. Professing faith in clichéd "rugged-individualism," the "chancetorise," and the "pursuitof-happiness," Tracy resents the unsafe and unsanitary conditions in which he works and refuses to meet management's demands for increased production. "I'm a man," he declares, "and I'm not taking crap offn anybody, I'm goin to live like a man." Tracy's rhetoric and course of action may have been reasonable and productive in the nineteenth-century workshop, but Olsen understands that in 1920s America such responses are inadequate. Although he has "nothing to sell but [his] labor," Tracy renounces "God Job" and is forced to endure "the tortures of the damned," wandering along the cold streets in search of work. But even if Tracy decided to "grovel to God Job," his fate would not have improved significantly. Once he started a family, he would "see the old lady nag and worry her life away" and watch his "younguns pulpy with charity starches" repeat the ironic chorus after their teacher, "We-are-the-richest-country-in-the-world." The omniscient Marxist narrator of this passage apologizes for being unable to teach Tracy that "individual revolt was no good" and that only collective political action can alter the trajectory of history: "You had to bide your time and take it till there were enough of you to fight it all together on the job, and bide your time, and take it till the day millions of fists clamped in yours, and you could wipe out the whole thing, the whole goddamn thing, and a human could be a human for the first time on earth." [170]

Although she describes revolution in violent terms, Olsen implies that the masculine rhetoric that framed the literary politics of the 1930s hinders rather than helps the formation of class consciousness. Constance Coiner argues that Olsen subverts the trappings of masculine independence and individualism by employing a narrative strategy that never establishes an individual protagonist. Throughout the novel, the narrative point of view shifts between the voices of Mazie, Jim, Anna, and an omniscient narrator whom we hear in the passages that describe the predicaments of Andy Kvaternick and Jim Tracy. By refusing to permit the reader to identify with any single heroic protagonist, Olsen renounces faith in the American ideology of "rugged-individualism," highlights the social and historical forces that shape individuals, and challenges the individualistic conventions of bourgeois art that Gold so relentlessly attacked. Olsen does not wait for an individual hero to lead the working class but rather envisions the day when workers, both male and female, join together in the struggle for equality and social justice.

Olsen augments her criticism of American individualism by suggesting that prevailing gender relations oppress women in much the same way that employers exploit their employees. The Communist Party and the

Whitmanesque literary tradition it embraced did not easily accommodate such analyses. That is not to say that the Communist Party did not create opportunities for women. As Olsen has explained, the party was "absolutely ahead of anywhere else" she could have turned in the 1930s and she "benefited enormously" from her involvement in it.[171] But the Communist Party was not without its shortcomings. Because Marxist theory held that exploitation occurred at the (predominantly male) point of production, communists consequently devalued reproductive and domestic labor and failed to recognize gender as a viable category of social and economic analysis.[172]

Olsen addresses such oversights by subverting prevailing concepts of the working-class hero and imagining a world not where men could be men but where "a *human* could be a *human*."[173] She envisions this egalitarian world by grounding her critique of gender relations in Whitman's poetry. As a pleasantly drunk Jim Holbrook walks the streets of Omaha listening to "a thousand messages of sound that would blend in to music," the opening line of "I Hear America Singing" parenthetically intrudes into the text: "I hear America singing, the varied carols I hear."[174] Much like "A Song for Occupations," this poem romanticizes a masculinized labor process, briefly celebrating the "delicious singing of the mother, or of the wife at work, or of the girl sewing or washing" alongside the skilled productive labor of artisans.[175] Despite her obvious affinity for Whitman, Olsen illustrates that his idealized representations of labor and gender do not adequately address the brutality that many working people, particularly working-class women, faced in the twentieth century.

In the paragraphs that follow the allusion to Whitman, a drunk Jim returns home determined to have sex with Anna, who is sick from a pregnancy he knows nothing about. Although Anna tells her husband that "it hurts too much" to have intercourse, Jim silences her plea and resorts to violent expressions of possession and domination. "Cant screw my own wife," he retorts. "Expect me to go to a whore? Hold still." Physically acting on his claim that women have no "earthly use" save domestic and reproductive labor, Jim dehumanizes Anna, committing a rape that causes a miscarriage and confines his wife to prolonged bed rest. As Olsen describes "blood on the kitchen floor, the two lifeless braids of hair framing [Anna's] face like a corpse," she makes it patently clear that manhood is often a destructive rather than a productive force.[176]

Jim's actions provide an extreme example of gender oppression, but the masculine economies of *Yonnondio* and "I Hear America Singing" restrict women's lives on a daily basis. Like Jim, who regularly spends precious time and wages at a bar after working hours, "the party of young fellows, robust, friendly," in "I Hear America Singing" engage in recreational activities outside the workplace, carousing together "at night" and singing "with open mouths their strong melodious songs." [177] Deprived of such public spaces for recreation, the female figures of Whitman's poem are confined to the home, where, like Anna, they are denied the opportunity to forge meaningful relationships with their peers, exercise their minds, escape the routine of their labor, or develop the expansive self that permeates Whitman's work. To obtain any sense of self "beyond the kitchen," Olsen suggests, women must not be reduced to their bodies but must be acknowledged as productive members of the political, literary, working-class, and human communities to which they belong.[178] In current socio-economic relationships, however, Anna can only recognize her humanity when she becomes "disembodied," when she retreats into an imaginary world untouched by the gendered responsibilities of wife and mother.[179] Determined to "edjicate" her children, Anna suggests that by cultivating their minds—or even by exercising their imaginations—they might escape the "bounded" bodies that sentence them to lives of labor. She tells her daughters, "Learnin's the only hope a body's got in this world," "books" take you "places your body aint ever been, cant ever get to." [180]

Anna temporarily arrives at this place when she and Mazie and her sons Ben and Jimmie leave the imprisoning confines of the house to search leaves of grass for edible dandelions. In a rare moment of leisure, Anna, much like the narrator of "Song of Myself," loafs in the fields and observes the catalpa trees, bees, and butterflies that surround her. In her "magic" communion with nature, her head becomes "balloony" as she slips into a transcendental moment of "happiness and farness and self-ness" that "had nought to do" with her children. In the midst of Whitman's "bright grasses," Anna sings three songs that enable her to free her own voice—and perhaps the "unlimn'd" female voices of Whitman's "varied carols"—from domestic routine. In the natural world, she transcends her gender identity to acquire an expanded, disembodied sense of self, but when she returns to the social world, her identity is once again circumscribed and her singing silenced. The stench of the packinghouse and the persistent needs of her children bring her back to a reality in which "the mother look on her face, the mother alertness, attunement, in her bounded body," return. Anticipating remarks Olsen would make in her 1962 essay "Silences," this scene demonstrates the exigencies of working-class motherhood.[181] "More than in any other human relationship, overwhelmingly more, motherhood means being instantly interruptible, responsive, responsible," she observed. "Children need one *now* (and remember, in our society, the family must often try to be the center for love and health the outside world is not). . . . It is distraction, not meditation that becomes habitual; interruption, not continuity; spasmodic, not constant toil. Unused capacities atrophy, cease to be." [182]

Sadly, life is Anna's unused capacity. Once again, she withdraws into the pain of "a voiceless dream to be endured." [183] In a world of class exploitation and gender oppression, the sense of self that Whitman envisions in his poetry remains beyond the reach of working-class women. His work locates the politics of union and equality in the body, but by representing the brutality and power relationships that manifest themselves in sexual relations, Olsen reveals the limitations of his idealized sexual democracy. In *Yonnondio*, male and female bodies are unequal. As long as Whitman and the Communist Party essentialized women as mother figures and devalued reproductive labor, no one could claim that the wife was "not one jot less than the husband," that the mother was "every bit as much as the father." [184]

Although members of the 1930s Left read only the portion of *Yonnondio* published in the *Partisan Review*, Olsen assessed the possibilities and limitations of the man they exalted as their working-class hero, criticizing some of the ideological shortcomings of the Communist Party as she did so. *Yonnondio* is a powerful literary and theoretical statement that argues that the manly independence and individualism encoded in the working-class hero threaten to undermine attempts to radicalize and organize the working class. Moreover, it illustrates that the construction of the manly hero silenced at least half of that class, limiting women's participation in cultural and political affairs. In the end, the equality of which both Whitman and the Communist Party spoke could only be obtained when women were not reduced to bodies; when their intellectual, physical, and reproductive labors were esteemed as highly as their counterparts'; when their voices were heard in literary and political debates; when the poetry and politics of the Left did not wait for a working-class hero to redeem the privilege, power, and independence of white manhood but collectively struggled to create an art and a world where "a human could be a human for the first time on earth." [185]

Americans in the 1930s anticipated the arrival of a hero who would deliver capitalism from its current crisis and validate the promises of democracy. Many Americans found that man in Franklin Roosevelt, but members of the Left glanced back to Whitman who, as Gold conceded, had shaped their politics "for better or worse." Throughout the 1920s and 1930s, leftists wrestled with their heroic spiritual grandfather's individualism, racism, sexism, and sexuality, patiently awaiting the arrival of a new Whitman who would let America be America for the first time in its history and reveal a place where a human could be a human for the first time on earth. But the ambiguity of Whitman's own republicanism made it difficult to refashion him into an exclusively leftist icon, particularly in the midst of the jingoism and economic prosperity that accompanied World War II. While Gold, Hughes, and Olsen amplified the poet's revolutionary tendencies, others successfully invoked the Good Gray Poet to discredit their efforts. *Time* magazine, for example, celebrated Henry Seidel Canby's *Walt Whitman, an American* (1943) precisely because it saved the poet "from the vagabonds and literary celebrators of the Common Man, and from the authors of the hard-boiled [radical] school who claim him as their parent." Moreover, Canby addressed "the irrelevant charges of homosexuality or of American fascism . . . with the sharpness of a professor putting students in their place."[186] The grandfather of socialism was easily reclaimed by liberal journalists and literary New Critics, who emphasized his individualism rather than his adhesiveness.

In the midst of their rhetorical and ideological gymnastics, leftists began to recognize that a vast majority of the working class was unmoved by what they had to say, not because workers were uninterested in politics and literature but because, like the characters in *Yonnondio*, they lacked the time, the education, and in many cases the disposable income to access it. As Gold observed in his introduction to Hughes's *New Song*, "The lament of every modern poet is that he has no audience in America."[187] More than sixty years after Whitman wrote *Democratic Vistas*, intellectuals were still imagining an idealized working class that had "some cravings for literature" and were determined to create a culture that extended beyond the middle-class parlors and lecture halls.[188] When they stepped outside Greenwich Village literary circles and discovered a hard-traveling, guitar-picking poet from the Dust Bowl, Whitman's orbic bard seemed to appear miraculously before their eyes.

II LIVING LEAVES OF GRASS

Thomas Carlyle's *On Heroes, Hero-Worship, and the Heroic in History* provided Whitman with a template for his working-class hero, but he did not need this Scotsman to convince him that music could play an important role in the formation of a distinctive American culture. In 1845, nearly a year before he reviewed *Heroes*, Whitman commented on the virtues of music in the *Broadway Journal*. He imagined that a simple, unadorned music would "supplant" the aristocratic traditions of the "stale, second hand foreign method," which, "with its flourishes, its ridiculous sentimentality, its anti-republican spirit, and its sycophantic influence," was not appropriate for the United States. Anticipating arguments he would later make about poetry, Whitman observed that music captured a nation's "subtlest spirit," a spirit so irrepressible that it "acts . . . on the nation's very soul," "enter[s] into religious feeling," "tinge[s] the manners and morals," and is "active even in the choice of legislatures and high magistrates." For Whitman, art and politics were inextricably interrelated, and if Americans were to forge a morally responsible society, they would have to replace the courtly traditions of European "art-singing" with an aesthetic that subordinated style to substance in the form of "heart-singing."[1]

Between 1850 and 1852, some members of the New York City press, Nathaniel Parker Willis among them, suggested that Jenny Lind, the sweet-voiced Swedish soprano who had captivated middle- and upper-class audiences alike, had perhaps mastered the art of heart-singing. Lind's cross-class popularity, argued Willis, demonstrated "the slightness of separation between the upper and middle classes of our country . . . and mark[ed] how essentially, as well as in form and name, this is a land of equality."[2] Whitman, however, was skeptical. Recalling the Lind phenomenon in the final years of his life, he admitted that the vocalist might have "had the most brilliant, captivating, popular musical style and expression of any one known," but he did not think that she had done much to promote equality. The "canary, and several other sweet birds are wondrous fine," the Good Gray Poet admitted, "but there is something in song that goes deeper—isn't there?"[3] No matter how sweet her voice, Whitman suggested, this sentimental European woman must be succeeded by a manly bard who would place his finger on the pulse of the American common man and create a music that flourished on "the throbbings of the great heart of humanity itself," that sang the songs of "love, hope, or mirth."[4]

According to Whitman, this "true method" of singing was perfected by the uncourtly Cheney Family Quartet of New Hampshire, a group he had heard in one of the manliest and most democratic of working-class places—a Brooklyn saloon. "Brown-faced" and "stout-shouldered," the three Cheney brothers conjured images of the independent farmer, and the "awkward," "strangely simple," and masculine appearance of their sister indicated her reluctance to conduct herself according to the genteel codes of middle-class women: she "disdain[ed] the usual clap-trap of smiles, hand-kissing, and dancing school bends." On behalf of all democrats, Whitman proclaimed that "we are absolutely sick to nausea" of such aristocratic affectations as "patent leather [and] curled-hair" and declared the "plain" manners of this family "refreshing." The rough music and unadorned appearance of the Cheneys, who renounced the most refined coiffures and conventions, embodied the organic rights on which Whitman founded his theory of democracy.[5]

If Whitman had lived during the Great Depression, he would have found the folksinger Woody Guthrie (1912–67) particularly refreshing. Renowned for his unkempt appearance, homespun manners, and irregular guitar playing, this nasal-voiced Oklahoman shared Whitman's contempt for wealth and insisted that music could deliver democracy to all citizens. In a letter written to the Columbia Recording Company in the early 1940s, Guthrie echoed Whitman's concerns about performers such as Lind, insisting that popular "cocktail songs and the empty, sissy, and scared ones" should be replaced by "the work songs of the working people."[6] Unlike most Tin Pan Alley songs, which assured listeners that in spite of unprecedented unemployment, the work ethic and capitalism were alive and well, folk songs, Guthrie maintained, provided a musician with the manly courage "to turn his back on the bids of Broadway and Hollywood to buy him and his talents out." Perhaps more important, they enabled the musician to imagine a world where "there ain't no rich men, and there ain't no poor men, and every man on earth is at work."[7] Like Whitman, Guthrie believed that music should articulate the concerns of working people and send a "note of hope" and equality ringing through workshops and farmhouses, union halls and statehouses.[8] As he refashioned himself in Whitman's image, Guthrie represented the lives of working people, preserved their cultural traditions, and worked on their behalf to convert the promises of freedom and equality into democratic reality. In his efforts to take culture out of the lecture hall and put it in the factory, fields, and labor camps, he transformed the poet hero into a guitar-carrying, class-conscious balladeer.

Guthrie's heroism was full of contradictions. In the words of his son Arlo, he was "bent in two directions at once: to escape the world and to change the world."[9] In many ways, the directions Guthrie traveled had already been mapped in Whitman's "Song of the Open Road." Like his predecessor, Guthrie chose "not [to] heap up what is called riches" and advised his listeners to "scatter with open hand all that [they] earn or achieve," to "see no possession" that all cannot enjoy on equal terms.[10] In "paths worn in the irregular hollows," Whitman saw "adhesiveness . . . not previously fashioned" and Guthrie found the brotherhood of the labor union. The folksinger taught neither "preference nor denial" and embraced all who approached him, including "the felon," "the beggar's tramp," "the laughing party of mechanics," "the black with his woolly head," and particularly "the thousand beautiful women." He "nourish[ed] active rebellion," challenging his audience to reject all institutions and conventions that impeded the progress of equality.[11]

But if "the profound lesson of reception" was taught on the open road, so was individualism. "Afoot and light hearted," Guthrie celebrated the freedom of the American highway, where, in Whitman's words, he was "loos'd of limits and imaginary lines" that would otherwise prevent him from becoming his "own master total and absolute."[12] An irrepressible individualist, Guthrie too sought to travel in paths untrodden, but as he constructed himself and was constructed by others as the poet laureate of the common man, he stumbled upon roadblocks and blind alleys that Whitman had already charted. Throughout his career, Guthrie struggled with the benefits and liabilities of following in the poet's footsteps, self-consciously looking back to Whitman one moment and purposefully averting his eyes the next. But no matter where he turned on the open road, Guthrie was compelled to plot his course in relation to the Good Gray Poet's.

Besides espousing comparable philosophies of art and politics, Guthrie and Whitman shared biographical similarities: both men came from agrarian backgrounds and identified deeply with the plight of their hard-luck parents. Born in the frontier town of Okemah, Oklahoma, Woodrow Wilson Guthrie, who was named for one of his parents' favorite democratic heroes, was the third child of Charley Guthrie and Nora Belle Tanner. An ambitious autodidact determined to enter the white-collar middle class, Charley Guthrie had already established his reputation as a skilled fistfighter when he was elected district court clerk in Oklahoma's first elections in 1907. So intertwined were his rugged individualism and his political aspirations that in 1911 he led a mudslinging campaign against the local Socialist Party candidates. A firm believer in capitalism and a darling of the local press, Charley exploited his popularity to establish a real estate firm that by 1918 was profitable enough to provide a comfortable home, a herd of Hereford cattle, and a forty-acre farm. His luck ran out when the oil boom hit Okemah in 1920. Unable to adapt to the fast-paced economy, Charley suffered a decline in popularity and political clout, and by 1923, he found himself flat broke. He struggled and schemed to regain his once secure economic status, but until he died in 1956, he lived in poverty and disappointment.[13]

Personal tragedies darkened the Guthries' bleak financial situation. Their daughter, Clara, burned to death in 1919, and in 1927, Charley was badly injured in a fire when Nora, afflicted with Huntington's chorea, a terminal disease that causes the brain and central nervous system to deteriorate steadily, dropped a kerosene lamp on her sleeping husband. By 1928, Nora, then committed to the state asylum in Norman, no longer recognized her children. A year later, with Charley still incapacitated from his accident, Woody began a lifetime of wandering. After working odd jobs as a sign painter, fortune-teller, and street musician, Guthrie began to perform his folk music professionally on a Los Angeles radio show in 1937. His political consciousness already awakened by the economic plight of farmers who left Oklahoma for California following the dust storms of 1935, Guthrie met several members of the Communist Party in 1938 who encouraged him to join them in the struggle for economic justice.

It is unclear and perhaps unimportant whether or not Guthrie became a card-carrying member of the Communist Party, but it is certain that his art was profoundly shaped by party politics. He insisted that "join[ing] hands" with the Communist Party was one of the "biggest" things he had ever done.[14] The communists "gave me as good a feeling as I ever got from being around anybody in my whole life," he wrote in 1947. "I never did really know that the fight had been going on so long and so bad. I never had been able to look out over and across the slum section nor a sharecropper farm and connect it up with the owner and the landlord and the guards and the police."[15] By 1940, he was a serious fellow traveler, a staunch supporter of organized labor, and a key figure in the folk song movement. From roughly 1940 to the presidential election of 1948, this movement was comprised of a loose affiliation of southern white and black musicians who aligned themselves with radical urban want-to-be folks in New York City to advance the antiracist, antifascist, prolabor agenda of the Popular Front. Pete Seeger, Huddie "Leadbelly" Ledbetter, Josh White, Cisco Houston, Sis Cunningham, and Bess Lomax were among the faithful who joined Guthrie, performing class- and race-conscious folk ballads to support such unions as the United Cannery, Agricultural, Packing, and Allied Workers of America in California, the International Workers Order in New York City, and the Congress of Industrial Organizations.[16]

Guthrie may not have been Whitman's heroic artisan, but his life of poverty, tragedy, and wandering enabled him to identify with and understand the lives of working people, to represent their experiences and their concerns in his art, and to work for far-reaching social change. Although he was based in New York City after 1940, he continued to travel throughout the country, participating in a panoply of political and artistic activities. In 1940, he appeared on several major CBS radio shows, recorded folk songs for the Library of Congress and RCA Records, and wrote political columns for the left-wing *Daily Worker*; in 1941, he performed benefits for migrant workers in California; in 1943, E. P. Dutton published his autobiography and he departed on the first of three tours of duty with the merchant marine, during which two of his ships were torpedoed. He served a brief stint in the U.S. Army in 1945 and campaigned for Progressive Party presidential candidate Henry Wallace in 1948.

Although Guthrie was a traveler of the open road, he also had "some cravings for literature." Before Huntington's chorea destroyed his creative impulses in the early 1950s, he had written manuscripts for several novels in addition to composing some 1,000 songs, immense catalogs of poetry and prose, and hundreds of drawings. Moreover, he was remarkably well read. He pulled books from his father's sizable library when he was a child and later read those given to him by left-wing intellectuals, gaining a familiarity with such authors as Charles Darwin, François Rabelais, Carl Sandburg, Irish poet Robert Burns, Russian poet Aleksandr Sergeyevich Pushkin, Karl Marx, and a variety of Asian philosophers. Somewhere along the line, he studied phrenology and, of course, read Whitman, who had a profound influence on his career.[17]

Why I Like the Others and Hate the Others

It is difficult to determine precisely when Guthrie first read *Leaves of Grass*, but his entrance into left-wing circles in 1937 assured that he would come across Whitman sooner rather than later. After 1929, Guthrie traveled from Okemah to live with family in Houston, unsuccessfully attended high school in Pampa, Texas, and eventually wedded Mary Jennings in 1933. His marriage and the birth of a daughter in November 1935 did not curb his wanderlust. Throughout 1936 and 1937, he traveled across the Southwest, eventually ending up in Los Angeles at radio station KFVD. Operated by the liberal-thinking Frank Burke, KFVD aired the *Oklahoma Woody Show* in July 1937, a program that garnered a sizable audience of Dust Bowl migrants and left-wing intellectuals. By November, Guthrie had signed a one-year contract that enabled him to send for Mary and their two daughters. This attempt at domesticity was short-lived. Growing impatient with the program's commercial format, Guthrie began to criticize KFVD's sponsors on the air, and in the spring of 1938, he jumped a boxcar to investigate migrant worker conditions throughout the state. He returned to Los Angeles via Texas with a newfound concern for the plight of the migrant, and by the time Burke introduced him to Communist Party member Ed Robbin in the fall, he had already written many of the politically astute Dust Bowl ballads. Robbin invited Guthrie to sing at a Communist Party rally and convinced the young artist to become a fellow traveler of the party. Soon thereafter, Guthrie was contributing a column of folksy political commentary to *People's World*, the Communist Party organ on the left coast.[18]

If Guthrie had not read Whitman before he met Robbin, he had certainly done so by the time he made the acquaintance of Will Geer in 1939. The radical actor best known for his role on the 1970s television series *The Waltons*, Geer recalled that he had once discovered the folksinger reading *Leaves of Grass* and that they had discussed the book at length.[19] The poet's ideas quickly took root. In the summer of 1939, Guthrie staked his claim as the people's poet, singing in migrant labor camps outside Bakersfield before following Geer in January 1940 to the mecca of Whitmanesque thought, New York City. Fascinated by this bastion of radicalism, Guthrie aligned himself with cultural workers who sought to keep Whitman's democratic vision alive. As regular contributors to the *Daily Worker*, he and Mike Gold developed a mutual admiration. Gold's *Jews without Money* (1930) was one of Guthrie's favorite books, and when Guthrie's autobiography was published in 1943, Gold responded with an enthusiastic review that constructed the folksinger in the image of his heroic spiritual grandfather.[20] "Woody . . . has become one of the true voices of American folk song," Gold declared in the *Worker Magazine*. "For years he has traveled the roads with his guitar and made up ballads about American life and sung them everywhere. He has been heard in hobo jungles, along the western skid roads, in lumber camps and boxcars and at hundreds of working clubs, union halls, and communist gatherings." Guthrie was a man of the people whose book was "harsh and painful," whose songs "reek of poverty and genuine dirt and suffering." [21]

It was also in New York City that Guthrie fortuitously met Alan Lomax, who welcomed him into the canon of American folk music that men like his father, John, and socialist poet Carl Sandburg had been assembling in a particularly Whitmanesque manner.[22] Sandburg, whose *Chicago Poems* (1916) and *The People, Yes!* (1936) assiduously mimicked Whitman, compiled the songs of the people in *American Songbag* (1926). Meanwhile, the elder Lomax, a student of renowned Harvard folklorist George Kittredge, documented the songs of one of America's most unique and manly occupations in *Cowboy Songs and Other Frontier Ballads* (1910).[23] In his collector's notes, Lomax also invoked the people's poet. "To paraphrase slightly what Sidney Lanier said of Walt Whitman's poetry," he wrote, cowboy songs "are raw collops slashed from the rump of Nature," filled with a "profanity and vulgarity that pleases rather than repulses." "The broad sky under which [the cowboy] slept," he continued, "the limitless plains over which he rode, the big, open, free life he lived near to Nature's breast, taught him simplicity, calm, directness. He spoke out plainly the impulses of his heart. But as yet so-called polite society is not quite willing to hear." [24]

Alan Lomax apprenticed himself in his father's trade and began to interpret the folk through his leftist political sympathies. Both Lomaxes, as well as music scholars B. A. Botkin and Charles Seeger, approached their discipline from a "functionalist" point of view that prompted them to conceive of folklore not as a fixed aesthetic form of the past but as a vibrant part of the present. Practicing what Botkin called "applied folklore," functionalists claimed that they could help scholars reconstruct social history as well as inspire Americans to forge a democratic culture. By the late 1930s, they received federal funding to establish the Archive of Folk Song at the Library of Congress and to coordinate folklore research through the Works Progress Administration and the Federal Writers Project. Alan Lomax and Botkin continued to combine their politics with their profession when in 1946 they served on the board of directors of People's Songs, a song-writing collective that Seeger's son, Pete, organized to promote Popular Front values after the end of World War II.[25]

The preface to the Lomaxes' *Our Singing Country* (1941) declared Whitman's influence on the book, which celebrated the triumph of individualism, the joys of the open road, a disdain for bourgeois custom, and the emergence of a distinct American music commensurate with the country's democratic spirit:

> These people have been wanderers, walking and riding alone into the wilderness, past the mountains and the broad rivers, down the railroad lines, down the highways. Like all wanderers, they have been lonely and unencumbered by respect for the conventions of life behind them. Remembering the old songs in their loneliness, throwing up their voices against prairie and forest track, along new rivers, they followed the instincts of their new experience and the old songs were changed so as to belong to their life in the new country. New songs grew up inconspicuously out of the hums of the old, thrusting out in new directions in small, but permanent, fashion.[26]

"The common man, the individual, is everything in American folk song," Alan Lomax would later write, but like Whitman's poetry, folk song had the potential to join Americans together in social union.[27] An advertising flier produced by the Columbia Lecture Bureau called attention to Lomax's "social" "approach to music" and described his journeys across the country: "He has captured the voices of the American people. . . . He has visited the penitentiaries of the South; he has journeyed over the rough mountain roads of Eastern Kentucky, explored New England farms and Michigan lumber camps, recorded voodoo ceremonies, listened to songs on the sponge docks of Nassau." Columbia professed that Lomax's multicultural music collection could unite "housewives, jazz musicians, Negro convicts, lake sailors, mountain midwives and many other strange and original people" in a democratic community, even if that community, as the words "strange and original" suggest, still accepted white canons of taste as the norm.[28]

When Lomax first saw Guthrie perform at the Grapes of Wrath Evening, a benefit for Dust Bowl migrants that Geer organized in New York City in March 1940, he immediately recognized that the artist's burgeoning radicalism and profound knowledge of the folk tradition uniquely qualified him to be the people's poet.[29] "Woody really fulfilled Whitman's ideal for a poet who would walk the roads of the country and sing the American story in the language of the people," Lomax remarked in 1988. "He felt that songs should wake people up, should help people understand their environment better, and be more willing to do something about it." [30] Even more important was Guthrie's commitment to building community among the various polities of the United States. As he wrote Lomax in 1940, his job as a cultural worker was "to just keep a plowing right down the avenue watching what I can see and listening to what I can hear and trying to learn about everybody I meet everyday and try to make one part of the community feel like they know the other part and one end of it help the other end." [31] Guthrie embodied the political and cultural tradition that Lomax sought to construct and document, and within the course of a year, Lomax recorded him for the Library of Congress and secured lucrative contracts for his protégé to perform on WCBS radio in New York City. He later encouraged Guthrie to write an autobiography and various works of fiction, and in 1940 convinced RCA to record *Dust Bowl Ballads.* The recording session took place in Camden, New Jersey, Whitman's longtime home.

Guthrie's expansive knowledge of folk music indicated that although he had some cravings for literature, he was also steeped in a tradition that had little to do with the radical intellectuals and writers he encountered in New York City. In fact, even as he embraced Whitman and the Left, Guthrie suggested that many, if not most, bourgeois artists did little more than produce patronizing caricatures of working-class people. "My people / Are not quaint," he suggests in a poem from the late 1940s:

It makes me sore to hear or to see or to read
How you big long-haired writers
Whack away at my people

Chew and cut and saw away at my people
Grind and drill and whittle away at them
Trying to make out like you are their Savior
Or their way shower
Or their finder
Or their discoverer.[32]

Far too many radical writers, Guthrie suggested, had explored and exploited the lives of working people in self-serving aesthetic experiments, and consequently, the people he knew had been lost in literature. He was determined to recover the people on their own terms and in their own language, to "pick," as he wrote to Moses Asch of Folkways Records in 1947, "stones about Dust Bowl people that John Steinbeck did not write about." [33] By the late 1940s, he questioned even the long-haired Whitman's ability to speak for the common man: "Does Whitman, Sandburg, and Pushkin, either one, actually talk in the lingo . . . of the kinds and breeds of working people I've met and dealt with?" Guthrie did not believe they did, largely because he saw "more to be lots sadder about than" all of these poets put together.[34]

Guthrie recognized that capitalism and the experiences of working people had changed dramatically since the appearance of *Leaves of Grass*. Whitman had witnessed the rise of industrialization and the economic downturn of 1873, but the Great Depression brought human suffering that even this visionary could not have foreseen. As nearly one-third of the labor force searched for employment during the Depression decade, farmers in the South and Midwest struggled to subsist. Per capita income in Mississippi was halved between 1928 and 1933, and wheat farmers in Cimarron County, Oklahoma, watched the value of their crop plummet from $1.2 million in 1931 to $7,000 in 1933.[35] Conditions were not significantly better in urban areas. In 1931, New York City hospitals attributed nearly a hundred deaths to starvation. With few employment prospects, an army of up to 1 million workers wandered throughout the nation, perhaps 20 percent of whom were teenage boys.[36]

Because he knew poverty and suffering firsthand, Guthrie could not ignore the historical realities he encountered on the open road. He too sang of a democratic future, but rather than idealizing class relations, he represented the pain and injustice that working people faced by discussing "the real stuff" of class struggle and "us[ing] the Truth . . . like a spring of cold water" to bring about social reform.[37] Guthrie considered the "hurt song" the appropriate form for the representation of the travail of working-class life. As a boy in Okemah, he had "picked up" songs on street corners, "learned to jig and dance along the sidewalks to things called portable phonographs," and listened carefully to the traditional tunes his parents sang at home. According to a brief autobiographical narrative Guthrie wrote in 1947, Guthrie's father "sang his Negro and Indian square-dances and Blueses," and his mother taught him "all of the songs and ballads her parents knew, and there were lots that were neither Scotch nor Irish, but Mexican, Spanish, and many made up by Negroes in the South." These ballads were not all hurt songs, but with Clara's death, the family's dire financial situation, and Nora's deteriorating health, the words she sang became much darker. As her mental faculties deteriorated, Nora, remembers Guthrie, "commenced to sing the sadder songs in a loster voice, to gaze out of our window and to follow her songs out and up and over and away from it all, away over yonder in the minor keys." Faced with a deep sense of personal loss, poverty, and uncertainty, Guthrie recalls, "I heard all of the hurt songs over in a wilder way. These were the plainest days that I remember and the songs were made deepest in me along in these seasons. This was the time that our singing got the saddest."[38] Written in working-class language, hurt songs express the collective pain, suffering, and injustice working people have historically experienced and articulate their dreams of a less oppressive future. As he traveled throughout America, Guthrie used hurt songs such as rural blues and traditional ballads to relate his own pain and suffering to the pain and suffering of downtrodden migrant workers and African Americans and to encourage them to join him in the pursuit of social justice.

By using songs to express working-class social and political concerns, Guthrie tapped a musical tradition to which Whitman alluded in "I Hear America Singing." As early as 1800, cobblers bemoaned the automation of the shoemaking trade in "Peg and Awl"; in the 1830s, journeymen composed songs that assailed fledgling capitalists for their greed; and from the 1860s through the 1890s, skilled workers invoked the republican tradition, the rhetoric of manhood, and the morality of Christianity to protest industrial relations in thousands of song-poems, many of which appeared in newspapers alongside the works of Whitman and John Greenleaf Whittier. This largely masculine song tradition presented itself in many major labor movements of the late nineteenth century, including those of the Knights of Labor and the People's Party.[39] Meanwhile, African Americans syncretized their own musical traditions from their African past and enslaved present, using spirituals, ballads, and blues to chronicle and transcend oppressive circumstances.[40]

Perhaps the most familiar part of labor's musical heritage was created by the revolutionary Industrial Workers of the World (IWW). Forged in the collective fires set in 1905 by such labor leaders as Daniel De Leon, Eugene Debs, and Big Bill Haywood, the IWW steadfastly opposed the elite craft unionism of the American Federation of Labor (AFL) and offered one big union in which workingmen and women of all skill levels, colors, and ethnicities could unite. As syndicalists, the Wobblies envisioned a society in which workers rather than capitalists controlled the means of production, a social structure their members sought to build not with the ballot box but with direct action: Wobbly tactics included the threat, if not the reality, of the strike, sabotage, and violence. Although the IWW was unable to attract more than 150,000 workers at any given time, in the first decade of its existence, Wobblies conducted successful organizing campaigns and strikes among migrant laborers, hard-rock miners, timber workers in the West, and textile workers in the Northeast. Often subject to severe repression by local authorities, the union was essentially decimated when federal agents raided its offices in 1917.[41]

To promote its political strategies, the IWW created a culture comprised of newspapers, pamphlets, cartoons, and, perhaps most important, songs that encouraged the manly worker to unite with his comrades against their oppressors. Joe Hill, a Swedish immigrant who worked at various odd jobs across the United States between his arrival in 1901 and his incarceration in 1914, became the undisputed bard of Wobbly culture. Somewhere on his travels, Hill began to write class-conscious songs that eventually popularized *The Little Red Songbook*, an anthology of ballads first published by the Spokane, Washington, local. Often based on well-known tunes, Hill's songs were accessible jingles that promoted political action by satirizing capitalism. "A pamphlet, no matter how good, is never read more than once," he wrote in 1914, "but a song is learned by heart and repeated over and over." Music could reach more workers than could published material, and Hill used it to circulate the Wobblies' revolutionary message. Sung to the tune of "Sweet Bye and Bye," "The Preacher and the Slave" was perhaps Hill's best-known composition; the song criticized Christian leaders for using religion to justify social inequality. Renaming the Salvation Army the "Starvation Army," Hill encouraged workers to address the realities of class oppression in the here and now rather than waiting to reap the benefits of their eternal reward.[42]

Hill's credentials as a martyr, not a musician, however, transformed him into myth. In 1914, the popular Wobbly was convicted of the murder of a Salt Lake City grocer and his son, despite the fact that the authorities presented a weak case. According to legend, he could have proved his innocence by accounting for his whereabouts during the crime, but because his alibi would compromise a woman's honor, Hill chose the manly road and remained silent. Fellow Wobblies charged that their brother was being executed because he belonged to their union, but their protest, as well as those of the Swedish government and President Woodrow Wilson, did not stay his execution. On 19 November 1915, a stony-faced Hill stared down his firing squad, taunting his executioners by ordering them to discharge their weapons. If this defiant act was not manly enough for the revolution, Hill forever fixed his legendary stature by writing a farewell letter to Haywood. "Don't waste any time mourning," he demanded. "Organize!" Hill's immortality was first celebrated by 30,000 admirers who attended a service in Chicago and was fully consummated when his ashes were distributed to iww locals throughout the world on May Day, 1916.[43]

Such fanfare assured Hill a prominent place in the cultural memory of the American Left. In 1933, Gold suggested that the revolutionary movement needed "a Communist Joe Hill" to inspire the people to action, and by 1936, Earl Robinson, a member of the effete but radical Composers' Collective, and poet Alfred Hayes met at the Communist Party's Camp Unity in New York to collaborate on "The Ballad of Joe Hill." Three years later, Paul Robeson, the black all-American football-player-turned-communist-cultural-worker and civil rights leader, popularized the legend among left-wing audiences by making the song part of his repertoire.[44]

Guthrie first became aware of the Hill legend when he acquired an edition of The Little Red Songbook in the late 1930s, and his interest quickened when he joined the Almanac Singers. In the spring of 1941, Guthrie was in Oregon working for the Bonneville Power Administration, which had hired him to write songs in support of a government project that would bring hydroelectricity to the area. Back in New York City, the Almanacs, at the time comprised of Pete Seeger, Lee Hays, and Millard Lampell, recorded a collection of labor songs entitled Talking Union, which boasted that the group followed "in the tradition of Joe Hill."[45] By June, Guthrie was recording and touring with the Almanacs, who in the fall were visited by the fiery iww orator Elizabeth Gurley Flynn, the inspiration for one of Hill's compositions, "Rebel Girl."[46] Impressed by their commitment, Flynn gave the Almanacs a collection of Hill's papers, which, Hays remembered, Guthrie perused quite thoroughly.[47] Not surprisingly, the IWW martyr exerted considerable influence on Guthrie. Like Hill, Guthrie wrote parodies of old standards, particularly religious songs. For example, he reworked the Carter Family's "This World Is Not My Home," a hymn that longs for the rewards of heaven, into a ballad about the hardships of displacement, "I Ain't Got No Home." Some of Guthrie's more dogmatic compositions, such as "You Gotta Go Down and Join the Union," a rewrite of "Lonesome Valley," also tip their hats to Hill, as does the tribute "Joseph Hillstrom."[48]

Hill certainly obtained heroic stature in the labor movement, but he was not cut from the same cloth as Whitman. More damned radical than the Good Gray Poet, Hill enabled Guthrie to engage in collective politics and support unions in a way that Whitman or even Traubel could not. Like his Wobbly idol, Guthrie endorsed a union that emerged out of dissatisfaction with the AFL. At the 1935 convention of labor's aristocrats, United Mine Workers president John Lewis grew increasingly frustrated with the leadership's refusal to support the organization of industrial workers and, after punching a delegate in the mouth, stormed out of the meeting and founded a union of his own. Under his leadership, the Congress of Industrial Organizations (CIO) launched a militant organizing campaign, winning notable gains in the 1937 strikes against the auto industry and inspiring more than 2.4 million workers to strike in 1941. Along with thousands of other communists and fellow travelers, Guthrie enthusiastically embraced the union and used it to advance his prolabor, antiracist politics. When the Almanac Singers embarked on a nationwide tour in 1941, the CIO returned the favor by arranging much of their itinerary.[49]

Joe Hill and the militancy he represented were important elements of Guthrie's cultural heritage, but Guthrie's relationship to Whitman's ideas about sexuality, gender, the individual, and America was a much more pervasive and complicated component of his artistic vision. And because Guthrie's connections to Hill and the folk tradition were refracted through the lens of the Left's literary politics, it is not surprising that throughout the 1940s, Whitman's mantle rather than Hill's weighed heavily on Guthrie's shoulders.

In particular, Guthrie's invocation of Whitman enabled him to overcome the prejudices that many intellectuals and members of the Communist Party harbored about folk musicians. Even when the party began to include folk songs in its cultural politics, its members did not think music was as politically useful as Guthrie thought it was. In their search for an indigenous tradition compatible with their revolutionary politics, the cultural workers of the party initially rejected folk forms as aesthetically inferior, but by 1935, they recognized that folk songs could be used as organizing tools. The use of folk music in textile strikes in Gastonia, North Carolina, in 1929 and coal strikes in Harlan County, Kentucky, in the early 1930s, the resistive songs of African American communists in Birmingham, Alabama, and the folk traditions taught in labor colleges such as the Highlander Folk Center in Tennessee and Commonwealth College in Arkansas awakened the leaders of the Communist Party to the political potential of folk songs.[50] When New York City radicals met the folk, however, they did not always get what they expected. Workers from the South might sing about low wages or wretched working conditions, but they also might affirm their faith in Christianity or espouse racism. Communists soon realized that many disgruntled workers were more interested in having enough to eat than in participating in a revolution. Moreover, they were somewhat taken aback by the folks' less than urbane appearance and nonacademic musical style. When Harlan County resident Aunt Molly Jackson, for example, performed at a benefit for the coal strikes in 1931, urban radicals balked. Informed by dominant representations of Appalachian folk culture, the crowd of 21,000 expected to see a pleasant woman who sang traditional ballads or strummed the dulcimer but instead heard roughly hewn lyrics and a cappella singing that did not conform to their preconceptions.[51] Sensing her audience's disappointment, Jackson, explained Charles Seeger, readily adapted to her situation. Seeger recalled that "it took [her] only a few months to convert herself, when expedient, from a traditional singer, who seemed never to have given any thought to whether anyone liked or disliked her singing, into a shrewd observer of audience reaction, fixing individual listeners one after another with her gaze, smiling ingratiatingly, gesturing, dramatizing her performance."[52]

Guthrie faced similar challenges when he arrived in New York City. Biographer Joe Klein suggests that the musician was perceived as a sort of "Noble Savage," one of the "natural persons" who Mike Gold insisted would plant the "lusty great tree of revolution."[53] Rough-mannered, naive, and unclean, Guthrie emitted a strangely innocent but compelling masculinity that made him quite popular with left-wing women interested in experiencing proletarian romanticism firsthand.[54] A renowned womanizer, Guthrie initially played the stereotype for all it was worth, but he soon discovered that the prejudices New York City radicals held about him and "the people" in general were constricting. Urbanites frequently dismissed the Dust Bowl Balladeer as an undisciplined, unsophisticated rube, another Will Rogers, who might be interested in political issues but was not a hard-nosed communist.[55] Although he often replicated Rogers's cornpone humor, Guthrie wanted to claim his place as a serious artist and cultural worker, so he and his supporters often modeled his image on a much more respectable hero of the Left, Walt Whitman.

Moses Asch, the son of Yiddish novelist Sholem Asch, was among the intellectuals and cultural workers who compared Woody Guthrie to Whitman.[56] Born to a family of socialists, Asch opened his first recording studio in New York City in 1939 before founding the legendary Folkways Records in 1947. Recording such artists as Leadbelly, Big Bill Broonzy, Etta James, Pete Seeger, Cisco Houston, Brownie McGhee, and Sonny Terry, Asch documented everything from croaking bullfrogs to Irish jigs, creating a meeting place for leftist artists and intellectuals in the process. In 1947, Guthrie commented that he could not imagine a "more progressive atmosphere amongst artists, performers, and engineers" than the one Asch provided.[57] The two men first met in March 1944 when, as Asch remembers, "this rough neck . . . with wiry hair" sat "on the floor of the office" and announced, "I'm Woody Guthrie." Unimpressed by his familiarity, Asch told Guthrie that he had "a helluva way of getting acquainted" with someone, but he soon saw that "a personality emerged that had more than the appearance." As he listened to the self-assured musician, Asch "remembered some early pictures of Walt Whitman" and "saw the resemblance to a great extent of an American expression in terms of a man who struggled, who had a hard time, and who was very sparse in words, but had a lot of things on his mind."[58] Asch thought Guthrie "was a person most illustrative of Walt Whitman," and the generally enthusiastic reviews of Guthrie's autobiography *Bound for Glory* (1943) were quick to make the connection between the two artists as well.[59] "For all I know, Woody has never heard of Whitman and Carl Sandburg," wrote James Fullington of the *Columbus Citizen*, "but he is an amazing expression in the flesh of their common man." The *New York Times* reviewed the book under the Whitmanesque headline "America Singing," and the *New York Post*, *Saturday Review of Literature*, and *Louisville Courier-Journal* all echoed Fullington's observations.[60]

Guthrie did much to promote such comparisons. In 1941, he and his friends Jack and Seema Weatherwax organized a benefit for Dust Bowl

Walt Whitman, *frontispiece to the* 1855 Leaves of Grass. *Rare Book and Special Collections Division, Library of Congress.*

Woody Guthrie, 1941. Courtesy of Seema Weatherwax.

migrants in Los Angeles and traveled to nearby Arvin to invite some of
the families from the Farm Security Administration camp located there.[61]
Photographs taken of Guthrie during this trip unmistakably evoke Whitman. In the most provocative photo, Guthrie postures in a manner remarkably reminiscent of the image of the poet that appeared on the frontispiece of the 1855 *Leaves of Grass*.

Dressed in the garb of a journeyman carpenter, Whitman, the "healthy
bodied, middle-aged, beard-faced American," presents himself as the
quintessential republican man: he wears his hat crookedly, nonchalantly

opens his workshirt at the neck, confidently, if not cockily, rests his right hand on his hip, and leisurely reaches into his pocket with his left.[62] The unmistakable sexual authority and brazen masculinity charge Whitman with the "heroic beauty" that in 1851 he suggested made the poet "the best beloved of art." "I look so damned flamboyant, as if I was hurling bolts at somebody," Whitman said of the pose. "[I was] full of mad oaths— saying defiantly, to hell with you!"[63]

Such defiance, he later explained, "falls in line with the purposes I had in view from the start."[64] Whitman squared off against the greedy masters who destroyed the trades and asserted his individuality and equality on behalf of workingmen everywhere. If employers reduced their employees to products and profits, if they refused to pay properly credentialed journeymen a competence, the "heroic person" in the 1855 *Leaves of Grass* would have none of it. Taking orders from no one, this self-assured craftsman cocked his hat as he pleased indoors and out and invited his listeners to take leave of their increasingly structured and hurried lives by loafing with him on the grass.[65]

In Seema Weatherwax's photograph, the pensive, bearded Guthrie cocks his broad-brimmed hat as coyly as the poet, leaning restlessly on his car, the same type of vehicle that transported him and so many of the Okies he visited along Whitman's open road. Striking the pose of an artist, Guthrie does not stare defiantly at the camera as did Whitman but instead squints purposefully.[66] Weatherwax's caption says her subject "relaxes," but his posture indicates a certain uneasiness. Although he often lived the leisurely life of the artist, Guthrie wanted to be perceived as a worker and consequently projects an air of business. He might follow in Whitman's tradition, but this people's poet could not "set here and look at my paper a half a day between each word / Like Walt Whitman could."[67] Because his people suffered so severely, he did not have the patience to contemplate a single blade of grass. Whereas Whitman's songs idealized economic conditions, Guthrie's conveyed the immediacy of struggle and travail and called for urgent action.

A second carefully composed photograph constructs Guthrie as the singer of the American spirit. Framed by the gate leading to the Shafter Farm Workers Community in Arvin, Guthrie converses with Jack Weatherwax while he stands in perfect alignment with an American flag that flies above the grounds. With his guitar slung across his back, Guthrie poses as the people's poet, the self-proclaimed "prophet singer" who has traveled across the country to declare that the United States is the greatest

Jack Weatherwax and Woody Guthrie converse beneath the entrance to the Shafter Farm Workers Community, Arvin, California, 1941. Courtesy of Seema Weatherwax.

of all poems.[68] His exuberance for America is tempered, however, by the contradictions that exist between the democratic promise represented by the flag and the harsh realities that characterize the camp. If America was indeed the land of freedom and equality, if the work ethic truly enabled every citizen to live the American dream, such government camps would be obsolete. Witnessing the vast armies of the unemployed that flooded into California, Guthrie wondered, as Whitman had nearly seventy years earlier, if the great democratic experiment had failed.

Determined to reverse this failure, Guthrie sang for oppressed workers, hoping to inspire them to reclaim a democratic heritage. In a third photograph, he inserts himself into a crowd of camp residents so that he can take his poetry directly to the people. Because, as Seema Weatherwax remembers, women were preoccupied with domestic chores and child care, Guthrie performs before a predominantly and appropriately male crowd that conducts itself with characteristic masculine decorum. The proud, stoic, and silent faces of the men who stand to the left of Guthrie

Woody Guthrie (center, back to camera) entertains the residents of the Shafter Farm Workers Community, 1941. Courtesy of Seema Weatherwax.

convey their displeasure to Weatherwax, who has asked them to move so that she might have a clear shot of Guthrie. Unaware of the distraction, Guthrie stands with his back to these men, absorbing the crowd before him as he is absorbed by it, playing to an audience that remains transfixed on his every move, riveted on his every word. In fact, the faces recorded in the photograph closely correspond to those that Guthrie described in a letter to the Almanac Singers in 1941. As he sang and talked to workers, he said, "every one of them would lean and look toward me and keep so still and such a solemn look on their faces, there in those little old greasy dirty hovels that it would bring the rising sun to tears. . . . On more than one night, on more than one day, I've heard my Oakie friends ask me, Say mister, you don't happen to be Mister Jesus do you? Come back?" [69]

Come back indeed. The smiles on the faces of some of the men in the photograph are a welcome sign to Guthrie, a sign that suggests that he

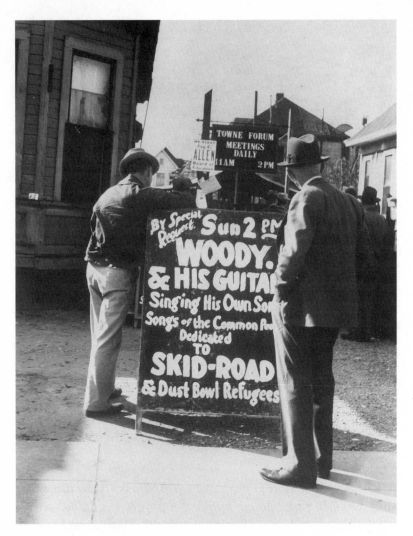

Placard advertising one of Woody Guthrie's benefit performances, 1941.
Courtesy of Seema Weatherwax.

and his people are merging, that the distinctions between artist and audience are blurring. If only in his mind, he becomes the simple man described on a placard advertising the Los Angeles benefit: "WOODY & HIS GUITAR, Singing His Own Songs, Songs of the Common People Dedicated to SKID-ROAD & Dust Bowl Refugees." But the prophet singer's egotism and his self-conscious construction of himself as the common man reveal his desire to become a quite uncommon man. Posing as a 1940s Whitman, he assumes the role of the messiah of his people, of the working-class hero whose heroism threatens the principles for which he stands. By 1946, Guthrie had appropriated Whitman's prophetic language, proposing that a "ballad singer" was better equipped to assume the heroic role that had been reserved for the poet: "He walks across political lines, color lines, conventional and superstitious lines, the lines of jealousy and blind hate, and . . . reaches a place in every person that no other sort of person can reach, and learns things which no other sort of worker nor scientist can reach, not even the family doctor nor the priest nor preacher can reach, no, not even the union organizer." [70]

Guthrie echoes the preface of the 1855 *Leaves of Grass* as well as *Democratic Vistas*, intimating that the people need a great individual artist to speak on their behalf, to teach them a moral and political code that will enable them to realize the promise of democracy. But even as he embraced the cultural legacy Whitman bequeathed him, he felt hamstrung by it. By 1946, he hoped that his audience would not "call [him] another Walt Whitman." [71] As he wrote in a poem entitled "Me and the Others" (1947), he could not "ever be like" his predecessor and in fact did not "want to." [72] But no matter how hard he tried to cultivate plentiful pastures for his own art and politics, Guthrie discovered that Whitman was such a salient part of the Left's cultural memory that he could not escape his influence. [73] The incubus that Whitman and other similar poets placed on him caused him to adopt an unqualified ambivalence toward them, forced him to "like the others and hate the others" at the same time. [74] His cultural ancestor opened the road of possibility for him but also checked his ideas about working-class heroism and shaped the expectations of his audience. To understand how Guthrie confronted these contradictions and to assess how he both reproduced and overcame the limitations Whitman presented to him, we must listen to his songs for occupations.

Both helped and hindered by Whitman's legacy, Guthrie attempted to fuse the poet's sexual politics, the folk tradition, and leftist thought into a democratic vision that responded to world war. European fascism posed serious ideological challenges to the Communist Party of the United States and the folk song movement, particularly after Stalin signed a nonaggression pact with Hitler in August 1939. The Communist Party justified the decision in the name of peace, but the party faithful and their fellow travelers were put in the awkward position of promoting an antifascist platform while their leaders were officially allied with the enemy. In this context, the American Left opposed the war because it would further exploit and endanger working-class lives. "WAR is a game played by maniacs who kill each other," wrote Guthrie in *People's World*. "It is murder, studied and prepared by insane minds, and followed by a bunch of thieves. You can't believe in life and wear the uniform of death."[1] Asserting that the "pore folks" would fight "the rich folks [sic] war," Guthrie criticized proposals for conscription and insisted that "war will end" if the people would simply "strip" the wealthy of their "profits."[2]

The Communist Party and Guthrie promptly changed their tune when the Nazis defied the German-Soviet treaty in June 1941 and the Japanese bombed Pearl Harbor that December. Convinced that songs had the potential to change the world, members of the folk song movement enlisted its music in the battle against the Axis. In Guthrie's view, a song was "a weapon, the same as a gun," and when he was not aiding the war effort by working as a mess boy on merchant marine vessels, he was using his music to defeat fascism abroad and at home. "You dont [sic] have to make a trip to Europe to find a crook," Guthrie contended in an essay written on behalf of the Almanac Singers. Injustices such as racism had not disappeared on the home front, and if workers intended to defeat them, they would have to "stick up for what's right, freedom of speech, press, radio, meetings, collective bargaining, the right to get together for decent pay, hours, rent, prices."[3]

An excerpt of Guthrie's performance on New York City radio station WNYC's *Songs the People Sing* illustrates that his domestic war against fascism challenged American injustices in a manner that relied heavily on Whitman's legacy. A fifteen-minute segment of this half-hour program recorded by Moses Asch constitutes a convenient framework in which to discuss Guthrie's vast and varied art. A male emcee opens the 13 February 1945 broadcast with an introduction that reveals the Whitmanesque character of the folk movement and the reverence with which Americans viewed their democracy, particularly when compared with fascism. "Up and down this broad land of yours and mine, men and women have sung since the very first settlers came," the program's host proclaims. "Pioneers, miners, farmers, field puddlers, millhands, and cotton choppers — they all have their songs." The narrator introduces Guthrie as someone who knows "lots" of these songs of occupations, speaking over a performance of perhaps the folksinger's best-known composition, "This Land Is Your Land."[4]

Written as a response to Irving Berlin's "God Bless America," a song that irked Guthrie because of its unqualified jingoism, "This Land" views Berlin's mountains, prairies, and foaming oceans with a critical eye.[5] Guthrie, who originally gave his song the ironic title "God Blessed America for Me," walked the open road from New York to California, celebrating the national landscape while proclaiming that America was made for all of its citizens. This advertisement for representative democracy is undoubtedly meant to inspire listeners to dedicate themselves to the war effort, but when we consider the emotional core of the original manuscript, it is clear that Guthrie had not forgotten that plenty of "crooks" remained at home who sought to steal the land from the people. Guthrie did not sing the following two verses on the program, but they reveal the disdain he felt for Berlin's idealized representation:

Was a big high wall there that tried to stop me
A sign was painted said: Private Property.
But on the back side it didn't say nothing —
God blessed America for me.

.   .   .   .   .   .

One bright sunny morning in the shadow of the steeple
By the Relief office I saw my people —

As they stood hungry I stood there wondering if
God blessed America for me.[6]

Guthrie's definition of freedom "include[d] 3 square meals a day and a
good job at 'honest' pay," and until all Americans, black or white, were
able to enjoy these freedoms, he was unwilling to remain blind to the injustices he saw in the United States.[7] Profoundly influenced by Whitman's
legacy and sexual politics, Guthrie imagined a promised land that would
guarantee racial and economic equality, but his democratic vistas were
obstructed by familiar barriers of individualism and masculine privilege.

MY BEST SONGS

Guthrie argued that "war songs are work songs," and by opening *Songs
the People Sing* with a cowboy ballad entitled "Ranger's Command," he
immediately tied labor's heritage to the international struggle for freedom and justice.[8] Summoning a national mythology built largely on constructions of masculinity, Guthrie's narrator calls together his fellow cowboys so that he might teach them the manly law of the West: "To hold
a six shooter, and never to run / As long as there's bullets in both of
your guns."[9] To show his listeners how to "fight for their land," Guthrie
presents a brief scenario in which the narrator invites a woman to accompany him and his fellow cowpunchers on a roundup. Not only does the
courageous woman accept the invitation, but she becomes an equal in this
typically masculine world by drinking the cowboys' whiskey and helping
them defend the herd. When a band of thieves attempts to steal some of
the cattle, she defiantly leaps from her bedroll, brandishing pistols in both
hands. The woman is ultimately shot and killed, but by ordering her com-
panions to join in the struggle and engaging in it herself, she becomes an
equal participant in the fight for social justice.[10]

If left-wing artists such as Mike Gold foreclosed opportunities for
women to take part in cultural politics, Guthrie's songs begin to push
them open, albeit very slightly. "Miss Pavlachenko" (1942), for example,
paid tribute to a woman in the Soviet army who killed 257 Nazi soldiers
during the siege of Leningrad, and "Union Maid" (1940) lauded women
for their participation in the labor movement.[11] Written at the request of
Ina Wood, a Communist Party member whom Guthrie and Pete Seeger
visited in Oklahoma City in 1940, "Union Maid" was an uplifting, class-

conscious, and vaguely feminist composition based on an unlikely source —the tune to the Carter Family's "Redwing." The woman in this ballad plays a prominent role in labor politics, attending union meetings and refusing to capitulate to the company "goons" who threaten her. "Oh you can't scare me I'm sticking to the union," she defiantly proclaims. "I'm sticking to the union, till the day I die."[12]

To be sure, Guthrie was more willing to allow women to participate in cultural politics than were many of his comrades. Next to himself, he identified Aunt Molly Jackson and her daughter, Sarah Ogan, two union organizers from Harlan County, Kentucky, as "the most radical, the most militant, and the most topical of" all folksingers.[13] Moreover, a handful of his writings lend themselves to feminist politics. In a manuscript written in 1947, he encouraged women to free themselves from the influence of the "pore sick head poet" who told them "to stay here in these sod walls and laze around sleepy and doze around sheepy while your man is the one to go out and see action." Women, he suggested, should "dance out" to "see fighting," "run factories," and go to "the vote box," and if their men become "jealous" of their accomplishments, women should "dance out to sing equal."[14]

Guthrie's voluminous prose and poetry, which repeatedly draw on Whitman, complicate these gender politics. "Woody loved the sensuality in Whitman," Will Geer remembered. "He had the same wide democratic feeling for his fellow men—liked to move among them, live and touch all their lives."[15] His appreciation for Whitman's sensuality and sexual politics is well presented in "My Best Songs," a long, rambling narrative in which he argues that his best work depicts the naked truths of human existence, particularly those based on the natural laws of freedom, equality, and sex. "In my most naked thoughts I've always laid flat on my back on the beds of *living leaves and grass* counting the tree buds with my hands and the night stars with my toes," he writes in an obvious reference to his cultural forebear.[16] Like Whitman, Guthrie disdains the respectable, well-heeled moral arbiters who "gathered around in robes, coats, suits and dresses, to say what [he should] write, speak, talk, and sing." These men and women, he insists, had devised a "religion" that taught him "to hate and fear, to feel sad and ashamed for [his] own naked flesh skin and body," and to devalue his "own self" in the process.[17] In his view, the unnatural repression of sexuality descended directly from a capitalist class that had "passed a law of our land making [him] a criminal for" enjoying his body. As he explained in an untitled narrative written in the early 1950s, the wealthiest men and women of the country so feared their bodies that they would "pile $50,000.00 worth of pretty colored clothing on top" of them to hide their shame.[18]

Recovering what leftists such as Gold could not, "My Best Songs" underscores the connection between economic and sexual repression by implying that those who govern sexual mores control and destroy the bodies and spirits of the people in much the same way that capitalists exploit the bodies of workers. In a letter to Moses Asch, Guthrie denounced the "bad part of the capitalist system," "this dog eat dog" ethos that characterized the actions of corporations and government agencies. Often followed by federal agents himself, Guthrie argued that economic and political repression were responsible for "killings, murders, rapes . . . and degeneracy" and insisted that capitalists were wedded to this system of control because "they get all of us to fighting against one another, and rob us coming in the fields of production, and going, in the realms of distribution."[19]

Images of thievery, deception, and hatred similarly characterize his criticism of sexual repression. "You are a worser thief than the worst and the bloodiest robber, pirate, bandit, or second-story operator, because you are robbing me of my own human pride and dignity, of my own happiness to dwell here in my own flesh," he declares in "My Best Songs." But sexual mores and the relations of capital did more than inhibit individual freedom; even worse, they conspired to promulgate "hateful, mean, downhearted and downtrodden feelings" that prevented people from uniting against their oppressors. "This shameful feeling of my own self," Guthrie concludes, "would make me so bitter and hateful inside . . . that I would hate and fear every other human body on the face of this earth." As long as individuals feared their own bodies and the bodies of others, they could not successfully unite in the struggle for freedom and economic justice.[20]

As he defines his sexual politics, Guthrie matches Whitman line for line. Whitman declares that "copulation is no more rank . . . than death is," and Guthrie writes that "nothing in this earth life is vulgar to me."[21] Whitman longs to have "soft-tickling genitals rub" against him, and Guthrie speaks of "rubbing bellies of creation . . . stuck together with the glues, foams, [and] juices."[22] In both men's work, political and sexual union are closely related and the democratic ideals on which the United States was founded have the potential to be regenerated through sexual activity.

Whereas Whitman had a predilection for male bodies, Guthrie was renowned for his heterosexual appetites. Alan Lomax recalls that his protégé "worked his way through half the secretaries in the CBS building" soon after his arrival in New York City, and conversations between Lee Hays and Cisco Houston, a close friend who served with Guthrie in the merchant marine and made several cross-country trips with him, corroborate such behavior.[23] In a conversation recorded shortly before Houston's death in 1961, Hays opened the discussion on Guthrie's promiscuity by recalling, "This shriveled, dirty, bearded man that needed a hair cut and a bath . . . really got a gorgeous gal to swoon over him."[24]

In his prosaic representations of sexual relations, Guthrie often constructs himself as a heroic liberator of women but is careful not to dehumanize or degrade his partners. Written in the late 1940s, Seeds of Man, a quasi-autobiographical novel set during his own adolescence, graphically describes intercourse between Guthrie and Helen, his young girlfriend. Clearly the less experienced of the two partners, Helen begs "Sire Guthrie" to make love to her, and although the narrative celebrates male sexuality, both partners play active and equal roles during intercourse. Indeed, they are as concerned with pleasing each other as they are with enjoying themselves, and although Guthrie appears to liberate Helen from her innocence, his careful use of a condom and his nervous performance suggest that the narrative is not merely one of male conquest and braggadocio.[25]

An idealized love and mutual respect characterize all of Guthrie's representations of sexual encounters, including those discussed in "Dear Prostitute," a poem that combines bravado and empathy much like Whitman's "To a Common Prostitute." "Be composed—be at ease with me— I am Walt Whitman, liberal and lusty as Nature," the poet tells his harlot. "Not till the sun excludes you do I exclude you."[26] Rivaling his predecessor's sympathy, Guthrie insists that although he had slept with some thirty prostitutes, he "hated the system of [sex] for profit" and, he tries to transform it into an idealized exchange of love rather than money when he tells his partner that he loved her "even before [he] climbed over on top of [her] body."[27] Guthrie suggests that all sex that expresses love is good and proclaims his goodness by explaining that he truly loved each of his partners. "I never spent an hour nor a night nor a day with any woman I hated. I never slept with a woman I later joked about," he announces in the narrative "My Drunkest Moments." "I gave each woman all I had and she wanted for me to stay and wept to see me go. I wept the same as she wept."²⁸ For Guthrie, sex was ostensibly as much about the sharing of emotions and respect as it was about exchanging physical pleasure.

On the surface, Guthrie's sexuality may have appeared "innocent and playful," and on paper, it seemed to allow women to enjoy sexual relations and the privileges of union in a way that Whitman did not. A fair number of his forays, however, had serious consequences for his partners.²⁹ Married three times, he regularly evaded responsibility for his eight children, leaving them in the care of their mothers while he embarked on his frequent and unannounced wanderings. When Huntington's chorea began to impair his judgment in the late 1940s, the ramifications of his erratic and boorish behavior extended beyond his families, and extramarital affairs were commonplace. Opposed to abortion, he refused to support his longtime friend Jackie Gibson emotionally or financially when she aborted his child in 1947.³⁰ A year later, he launched an erotic letter-writing campaign aimed at several acquaintances, including Mary Ruth Crissman, the sister of his former radio show host, Lefty Lou. Unnerved by his correspondence, Crissman pressed charges that eventually put Guthrie in jail for six months.³¹ Guthrie may have loved all of the women he solicited, but his gender politics were, like the society's in which he lived, far from egalitarian. Like Whitman's, his representations of sex resolved the tension between individual freedom and equality, but in reality, Guthrie's own sexual practices exacerbated this tension because his definition of freedom depended on the subordination of women. Had he not taken the reproductive and domestic labors of his wives, Mary Jennings, Marjorie Mazia Greenblatt, and Anneke Van Kirk, for granted, he would have been unable to walk the open road and perform his cultural work. Such inequalities ultimately tainted his sexual relationships. He may have been concerned with pleasing his partners physically and emotionally, but he also used them to define his masculinity.

Guthrie nevertheless relies on an idealized conception of sex to articulate his politics, particularly in the prose works he authored in the late 1940s and early 1950s. In his point of view, he never sexually exploited any of his partners because he truly loved them, and as "My Best Songs" suggests, when sex is performed in the context of love, it has the potential to emancipate and unite individuals simultaneously. "Use ribbon and your lace to pull me towards you, and I'll use every trick of shadow and shading to pull you closer to me," he writes. "Your legs can't open in a way that I will arrest and give a summons. Your thighs can't move in a way

I'll look up behind my bars. And those rumps, hips, and belly muscles of yours, you could never shimmy nor shake them in a way which I would drag off to my chain gang. . . . I see and taste no sweat any more honest than those drops you have in joy there between your legs. . . . This look and smile, or half-smile, across your face right this very minute, your hair shaking above your eyes, makes Woody Guthrie feel like a lost man getting found." [32]

The resemblance of this description to Whitman's work is so unmistakable that when Will Geer read from the same narrative at the University of Michigan in the early 1970s, a group of students asked him to locate the verse in *Leaves of Grass*.[33] Guthrie mimics the poet in a number of important ways. As Guthrie and his partner draw close together, they echo the opening lines of "A Song for Occupations." In this physical exchange, Guthrie and his lover liberate each other by giving and taking each other's "best." Through the sharing of bodies and fluids, his partner experiences pride and happiness and Guthrie discovers his manhood by liberating her from sexual conventions. In fact, this description of his sexual exploits is in and of itself a celebration of masculinity that confirms his status as manly hero. The flood of sexual detail and the namelessness of Guthrie's lover connote an ebullient universality in which the folksinger will have whoever enjoys him, will reject monogamy so that he might disseminate the "seeds of man" as generously as he can.[34] For Guthrie, sex breaks the bonds of oppression and reunites people on equal terms. "Don't you think we are one? Don't you?," Guthrie asked his second wife, Marjorie, in an explicit 1944 letter that described how he felt during intercourse. "One breath. One warmth. One saliva. One body." [35] Sex allows individuals to merge together without fear, to resolve the conflict between the individual and the other, to blur the distinctions between male and female. Because sex ultimately leads to union, Guthrie implies that its special meaning resides mainly in its political significance.

But does Guthrie's understanding of sexuality allow for Whitman's adhesive love? There is no evidence to suggest that Guthrie was gay or bisexual, but his political vision does call for a radical rethinking of the physical and perhaps sexual relations that take place between men. "I love no woman nor *man* my very tip top," he proclaims in "My Best Songs," "till I see you or help you to get naked." [36] The first chapter of *Bound for Glory*, Guthrie's imaginative autobiography, illuminates his politics of the body, sketching in its opening paragraph a democratic vista that recalls the "embrace of love and resistance" that male wrestlers share in Whitman's "I Sing the Body Electric."[37] "I could see men of all colors bouncing along in the boxcar," he writes in the opening paragraph. "We stood up. We laid down. We piled around on each other. We used each other for pillows. I could smell the sour and bitter sweat soaking through my own khaki shirt and britches, and the work clothes, overhauls and saggy, dirty suits of the other guys."[38]

Although this passage seethes with an energy that eventually erupts into conflict, the sharing of bodies and body fluids introduces the possibility for a democratic social union in which men of all colors—Guthrie later names African Americans, Native Americans, Mexicans, and whites—might embrace each other as equal comrades. The potential for union erodes, however, when bodies are attacked or dishonored: one hobo utters racial epithets, a second accommodates some sickly travelers a bit too reluctantly, and a third hurls a wine bottle across the railcar. Before long, the democratic promise is squandered as Guthrie sees "men fighting against men. Color against color. Kin against kin. Race pushing against race."[39]

But even in this turmoil, Guthrie preserves the possibility for community and cooperation. When a belligerent young hobo attempts to throw Guthrie from a dusty car used to transport cement, an African American whom he befriended earlier in the narrative comes to his aid. Unable to subdue his attacker, Guthrie soon locks his "left arm . . . around the Negro's" to keep from falling from the car.[40] The assailant eventually forces both men out the door, but interracial cooperation between Guthrie and his friend negate the aggressor's efforts, enabling them to reboard the train and resume their travels atop a boxcar. Following this successful collaborative struggle, Guthrie the writer immediately deracializes the two characters to underscore their common humanity. "We laughed at the way our faces looked with the cement all over them, and our eyes watering," he writes. "The black coal dust from the locomotive made us look like white ghosts with black eyes."[41] Guthrie's narrative is not free of racism. He pejoratively refers to his friend as a "colored boy" and privileges the presumed universality of white identity when he deracializes his comrade. Despite these limitations, his egalitarian intentions are clear. The black dust from the coal mixes with the white dust of the cement, creating ghosts—disembodied characters—who unite with each other on equal terms. In the universalist language of the Left, physical differences alone separate the races, so when the difference in skin color disappears, when the white Guthrie locks arms with his black friend, they represent the one big union to which all workers belong.

The sense of physical and comradely unity these men forge immediately strengthens when two boys aged ten and fifteen join them on the car roof. After briefly greeting the two newcomers, Guthrie struggles to protect his guitar from a driving rain and receives immediate and unsolicited assistance from his fellow travelers: the youngest boy offers his sweater to cover the instrument, and the black man promptly strips the shirt from his back. Feeling sorry for his bare-chested friends, particularly the youngest, Guthrie invites the "runt" to sleep by his side, offering his arm as a pillow to break the shock from the unsteady car. When the two later awake, Guthrie is "hugging the little runt around the belly" as the men in the car beneath him sing the African American spiritual "This Train Is Bound for Glory," a song that holds out the promise of spiritual and social redemption.[42] If white men did not fear black bodies, if races loved rather than hated and men embraced rather than attacked one another, they could harness the mutual tenderness, respect, and love Guthrie and his comrades display. If they did so, they might arrive at that glorious promised land where freedom and social equality exist side by side.

As this episode reveals, the open road allowed Guthrie's characters to travel in two directions at once, to pursue their individual freedom and to forge important solidarities. The hoboes who traveled Route 66 and rode the rails during the Great Depression endured tremendous suffering, but many, including Guthrie, recognized that the road afforded them a certain freedom, that it furnished the opportunity to become their own masters, total and absolute. When a man left his home, he flouted the values of a socioeconomic order that threatened to devour him, turning his back on the indignities and monotony of wage labor and reclaiming his manly independence. Without the responsibilities of work or family, he wandered when and where he pleased and reaffirmed his masculinity by demonstrating to himself and his fellow travelers that although he had been humiliated by economic circumstances, he had the strength to navigate the hobo jungle.[43]

But, as Whitman insisted, the road also taught the lesson of reception. Even the most rugged characters in Guthrie's narrative need other men against which to measure their masculinity: they require challengers to fight, audiences for their braggadocio, witnesses to their skills. Perhaps more important, they could not survive without at least the occasional cooperation of their fellow travelers. Hoboes shared scarce food and liquor for nourishment, stories and songs for entertainment, bodies and blankets for survival on cold nights. They shared compassion by nursing comrades who were injured by vigilantes and a variety of accidents peculiar to riding the rails. And it was not unusual for men to have sexual relationships with one another, some of which would last for years. To be sure, homosexuality and pederasty had long been associated with hobo culture, and although *Bound for Glory* does not depict any homosexual encounters, physical contact between men constitutes an important part of Guthrie's idealized politics.[44]

A promotional photograph of Guthrie and Burl Ives taken for the radio program *Back Where I Come From* reinforces Guthrie's formulation of same-sex solidarity. Written by Nicholas Ray (director of *Rebel without a Cause*) and Alan Lomax, the pilot for this program was broadcast on CBS radio's Columbia School of the Air in August 1940. Guthrie, Seeger, Leadbelly, and Josh White were regulars on the short-lived series, which reflected the Popular Front's fascination with "the people" as well as the American desire to create a sense of community amid the social dislocation and isolation bred by the Depression.[45] *Back Where I Come From* drew on this impulse by celebrating small-town America. "The first thing I want to say is that back here, where I come from they call me 'Kip,'" explains New York City literary critic Clifton Fadiman in his polished voice. "The real reason I'm on this program is that I like talking things over and I like American stuff. I like swapping stories, songs, and ideas with the other fellow, I like finding out what things are like back where the other fellow comes from." A discussion of a string of colloquialisms about the weather follows, then Guthrie's "So Long, It's Been Good to Know You," Ives's rendition of "Foggy Dew," and a performance by the African American gospel group, the Golden Gate Quartet.[46]

Staged in Central Park, the photograph of Guthrie and Ives appeals to general knowledge of hobo culture to construct a sense of community in masculine terms. A smiling Guthrie reads a copy of the *HoBo News* as he rests his guitar across his lap and his head on Ives's stomach. Flat on his back, Ives lifts his left arm above his head and welcomes Guthrie to his side. As these two hoboes loaf on the grass, they demonstrate mutual concern for each other's comfort in a manner that recalls the reciprocal relations depicted in *Bound for Glory*: Ives lends Guthrie his body, and Guthrie returns the favor by allowing his friend to use his guitar case as a pillow. Adhering to the iconography of the Popular Front, the photograph uses the metaphor of male bonding to connote ideas about solidarity and brotherhood and predictably excludes women from view. And like the Popular Front solidarity constructed by Langston Hughes, the

Woody Guthrie and Burl Ives pose in Central Park for a publicity photograph for the radio show Back Where I Come From, 1940. *Prints and Photographs Division, Library of Congress.*

brotherhood represented here slips easily into the homoerotic, particularly to an audience that would have been familiar with the sexual practices of hoboes. To be sure, these men demonstrate an intimacy that was not widely accepted by Americans in 1940. In short, they obscure the rigid line that separates the homosocial from the homoerotic, between men protecting one another's interests and men loving one another.

When Guthrie blurs these distinctions in "My Best Songs," *Bound for Glory*, and this photograph, he suggests that if sexual conventions were radically rethought, economic relations could be profoundly transformed. A society that teaches fear of the body forces its members to "hate and fear every other human body on the face of this earth," a hatred that supports capitalist exploitation. For Guthrie, fear of any body—black or white, male or female—inhibits democracy, equality, and, most important, union. "The resolution in my union hall," he declares, "is a command passed on in love for the best welfare of the union members."[47] Issuing a decree for both "the going capitalist" and the "coming communist" orders, he adopts much of Whitman's sexual politics by declaring, "My body shall be my only soul and my only spirit."[48] Any "shape of humanly form," he argues, "is a thing not to be in any way hated, nor in any manner despised [sic] nor even feared, nor shadowed around with insane cold suspicions." Instead, a human body, whether male or female, should "test forever" an individual's "powers to love."[49] In the end, love was the "only medicine" Guthrie believed in. Combining the languages of Whitman and Marxism, he audaciously dispenses orders: "Tell your comrade—Comrade, bend down in dank fear and traps not one second longer—Comrade—your love commands every known (and every unknown) kind of universal energy in existence."[50]

Always a political maverick, Guthrie had difficulty adhering to Communist Party discipline and could not toe the line when it came to issues of sexuality. For him, the politics of the body and the body politic, the politics of the bedroom and those of the union hall, were inextricably bound. Like Whitman, he argued that if Americans intended to alter social relations, they would have to forge a new love that was more intimate and more intense than the love they had imagined under the social relations of capitalism. He did not explicitly advocate Whitman's adhesiveness, but he suggested that men must be willing to express their solidarity and love for one another in a physical manner. And although he often represented collectivity in male terms, he allowed women to "sing equal" in the sexual politics of his poetry. The problem, however, was familiar. Guthrie's understanding of sex and love were so idealized that he was unable to see that his promiscuity widened rather than bridged the chasm that separated self from other, individual from community, men from women. Indiscriminate sexuality may have allowed this lonesome traveler, on the road since age seventeen, temporarily to assuage his own loneliness by connecting with another individual, but in the long run, his philandering and flight from personal responsibility drew the inequalities of gender into sharp relief. His vision of love held out the possibility that society might be redefined along cooperative rather than competitive lines, but when it came to practicing what he preached, particularly in gender relations, something of that promise was squandered.

SINGING THE HISTORY OF RACE AND CLASS

Describing himself as an "educator" rather than an "entertainer," Guthrie articulated a repressed history in which working people fought for social and economic justice.[51] Even more important, he taught his audience how this history related to the struggles the labor movement faced in the 1930s and 1940s. Like many members of the Left, Guthrie saw history not as an exercise in commemoration but as a living process that must be applied to the present. "Our job aint so much to go way back into history," he explained in a letter written to the Almanac Singers in 1941. "Our job is the Here & Now. Today." He insisted, however, that politically active folksingers must "include a Timeless Element in [their] songs. Something that will not tomorrow be gone with the wind. But something that tomorrow will be as true as it is today." [52] In Guthrie's estimation, pain, struggle, and hope marked working-class history, and any art that failed to represent these timeless elements impeded the fight for democracy. Aligning himself with other left-wing cultural workers, he held that art was a "weapon" that "should send fighting people to the field of battle filled with the clear knowledge of what the real enemy is"; if it did otherwise, it was "actually national moral[e] for the fascist enemy." [53] Simply put, if cultural workers did not sing hurt songs that revealed the truth about capitalist relations, they were working for the wrong side.

Situating his cultural analysis within a Marxist framework, Guthrie argued that his audience was not likely to find this history represented in commercial culture. Like Gold, he identified the "workers" as "Real Honest to Goodness People" and reduced the "Rich folks," the clergy, and the police to purveyors of false consciousness. "The Rich folks must have some way of making us poor folks believe their way, so they put out radio programs, sermons, moving pictures, books, magazines, and all sorts of silly advertising," wrote Guthrie in the early stages of his political thinking. "This junk is piled around in the world like a big pile of trash, but most folks believe it, and are sunk in it, and never try to get out of it." [54]

What Guthrie called the "Monopoly on Music" was particularly guilty of churning out capitalist propaganda. "The songs have no guts, no strength, no real spirit, and are opium drams of a few pampered pets who have not evolved upward to the plane of real human being," he vehemently argued, representing capitalist culture in unmasculine terms. Hitler may have "declared war on the world to keep us from being Union," but did the "gals or the bands play or sing a single note about it? Maybe a little fizzle comes out, but it is really a fizzle, a soft, sissified fizzle." Popular musicians may have cheered the Allies to victory, but they did so in such a jingoistic manner that they ignored the democratic principles for which unions struggled and, as a result, produced "sissified" art. Guthrie proclaimed that he would lead the "fight for the right to hear our own real history being sung" to help generate "the real power to go on and on fighting to fix our old world all over new again." Folksinging was indeed a manly and serious activity. If the songs of the people are not preserved, Guthrie argued, their "singing history is killed out," as well as their collective struggle and hope for social justice.[55]

To fulfill the responsibilities of the working-class hero, Guthrie, like many of his contemporaries in radical politics, frequently connected the hurt songs of African American history to the international struggle for freedom. As late as 1937, however, his racial politics were less than egalitarian. In a newspaper article he planned to distribute to his fans at KFVD, he offered a racist representation of blacks who allegedly interrupted a picnic he and friends were having at Santa Monica Beach. Caricaturing the African Americans as "savages," Guthrie complains of an "Ethiopian smell" that pervades the air and grows frightened as he watches their "cannibal" dances.[56] Guthrie changed his tune, however, when a radio listener chastised him for using the word "nigger" on his show. On reading his fan mail, Guthrie immediately apologized for his actions on the air, and as he began to travel in radical political circles, he advocated more egalitarian racial politics. By 1940, he questioned the morality of lynching in the song "Slipknot" and later addressed the racism of the American legal system in "The Furguson Brothers Killing."[57]

Guthrie received perhaps his most important lessons in African American music and history from Huddie Ledbetter. Shortly after Guthrie arrived in New York City, Leadbelly's wife, Martha, invited this disheveled vagabond to live in their apartment, which served as a meeting place for many folk revivalists. The black bluesmen Sonny Terry and Brownie McGhee visited regularly, as did Ives, Lee Hays, Aunt Molly Jackson, and Sarah Ogan. In a narrative entitled "Leadbelly Is a Hard Name," Guthrie expresses a heartfelt respect for his host. He credits the Ledbetters for teaching him "a good bit about making his words plainer, stronger, so as to reach out more and sound louder" and for enabling him "to find [his] listening ear for the history song." Leadbelly, he explains, "wanted to preach history, his own history, his peoples [sic] history, everybody's history," and as he listened to lessons about racism and hunger, Guthrie "could not tell where [his] own personal life stopped and Leadbelly's started."[58]

As Guthrie studied Leadbelly's blues and ballads and learned the stories that inspired them, he recognized that "there was something in [him] as hard and as strong as the thing that [he] knew was in both" Leadbelly and Martha. "I had walked, hitched, begged my rides, played for my chips and tips, sang on field rows, fence rails, side roads, along tough weed beds, and along rattling straws, and had met and seen in my time so many of the people with this same wild hard spot in them, that, well, I had come to hope that we could find some way of learning more of the hard spirit from you folks. . . . I knew that I had never been able to find a name for this feeling that I felt when I heard you folks talk, sing, laugh in the middle of your heart and talk the words that tell your history." [59]

Guthrie may not have been able to give a name to the feeling that characterized the blues and African American experience in general. But he drew on his own hard traveling, his own experience of hunger, loneliness, and economic oppression to understand the emotional core of Leadbelly's history and to empathize with it. For him, the experience of class transcended the boundaries of race and the sharing of hurt songs promoted an interracial understanding of common struggles. African American history and musical traditions such as the blues thus became integral components of Guthrie's hurt songs, in part because they had tremendous political potential. "Negro people were not allowed to talk out openly their hopes, their beliefs and their misery," he explained in *People's World*, but in "their blues and spiritual songs," they "struck a more forceful blow at their oppressor" than they could have struck with "pamphlets, books, or sermons." [60] As W. E. B. Du Bois wrote in *The Souls of Black Folk*, in African American song "there breathes a hope—a faith in the ultimate justice of things. . . . Sometimes it is faith in life, sometimes a faith in death, sometimes assurance of boundless justice in some fair world beyond. But whichever it is, the meaning is always clear: that sometime, somewhere, men will judge men by their souls and not by their skins." [61] Like Whitman, Guthrie tried to create a democracy where bodies and souls were connected, where they were received without prejudice. His knowledge of and respect for African American traditions enabled him "to reach out more and sound louder," to sing the blues as well as the ballad, to fight against racial and economic oppression, and to provide hope that one day justice would indeed abound.

Although Guthrie had difficulty actualizing his theories of sexual democracy, he was much more successful at practicing antiracist politics. He not only sang about overturning Jim Crow laws but openly flouted them. Jim Longhi offers an example in a memoir about his merchant marine service with Guthrie. Longhi recalls that during his final mission, the folksinger entered the ship's Jim Crow bathroom and began to sing with a group of African American soldiers there. The ship's commanding officer ordered Guthrie to leave, but the musician refused and eventually convinced his superior to allow the black soldiers to perform with him in a "white" area of the ship.[62] He continued to defy conventions that discouraged the formation of interracial bands when in 1942 he founded the Headline Singers, which included Leadbelly, Terry, and McGhee. Keeping pace with such leaders as A. Philip Randolph, who in 1941 threatened to organize a march on Washington if President Franklin Roosevelt did not desegregate defense industry jobs, Guthrie identified similarities between supremacist doctrines in Nazi Germany and those in the United States.[63] "This machine kills fascists," read the makeshift sign affixed to his guitar. When it came to matters of racism, that machine would have to produce antidotes to hatred both at home and abroad.

"John Hardy," the ballad that follows "Ranger's Command" on *Songs the People Sing*, demonstrates how Guthrie adapted traditional folk songs to fit the goals of the labor movement and to advocate racial equality. When in March 1940 Guthrie visited Alan Lomax in Washington, D.C., he continually played the Carter Family's "John Hardy Was a Desperate Man" on his host's phonograph, a practice that won the disapprobation of Lomax's wife, Elizabeth. Long referred to as the "first family of country music," the Carter Family, along with Jimmie Rodgers, became the first country music stars when Okeh Records' talent scout Ralph Peer recorded them at the now legendary Bristol, Tennessee, sessions in 1927. A farmer and sometime sawmill employee from Maces Spring, Virginia, A. P. Carter, his wife Sara, and his sister-in-law and her cousin Maybelle were well known for their performance of white gospel tunes such as "Will the Circle Be Unbroken" and traditional Appalachian folk songs such as "John Hardy." A fan of their music, Guthrie corresponded with the Carters on several occasions between 1938 and 1941 and was deeply influenced by their work. As several music scholars have noted, Guthrie carefully imitated Maybelle Carter's guitar playing and borrowed the tunes from a number of their songs for some of his best-known compositions, including the World War II tribute, "The Sinking of the *Reuben James*." Despite his admiration for these pioneers in country music, Guthrie radically reworked the Carters' version of "John Hardy" when he performed it on *Songs the People Sing*.[64]

Scholars do not agree on the details of the John Hardy legend but concur that it is based on an actual person. Newspaper reports and court records establish that in January 1893 an African American man named

John Hardy shot and killed another black man at Eckman, West Virginia. A member of an infamous gang that regularly burglarized coal camps throughout McDowell County, Hardy was a notorious gambler who swaggered into the Shawnee Camp at Eckman and announced that he would kill the first man who won any money from him. Determined to make good on his promise, he murdered a man who took him for fifty cents, fled by train with an accomplice, and was arrested several hours later. According to oral testimony, citizens were so ecstatic that Hardy had finally been incarcerated that hundreds offered to testify against him and a mob unsuccessfully tried to lynch him. Before he was executed at Welch on 19 January 1894, Hardy maintained that he would never die. After a visit from a white Baptist minister, however, the legendary bandit made his peace with God, was baptized, and publicly admitted his wrongdoing on the gallows.[65]

The Carters' "John Hardy" generally follows this narrative but, in typical ballad form, "leaps" over the details of the murder and "lingers" on its moral and emotional consequences.[66] The Carters immediately locate their ballad in a specific place and call attention to the racial and class relationships that characterize it. In their version, Hardy shoots a man on the West Virginia line, flees the murder scene, and heads for the Keystone Bridge, where he mistakenly thinks he "would be free." The Carters suggest that Hardy might find freedom in Keystone because it was the chief economic and cultural center for African Americans in West Virginia. The expanding coal economy dramatically increased the black population of McDowell County between 1880 and 1910, and although company-employed Baldwin-Felts detectives ruthlessly policed the coal camps in which black workers lived, the industry provided them with greater opportunities for financial and social autonomy than did the traditional occupation of farming.[67] Aided by the emergence of a black middle class, a network of vibrant churches and fraternal orders, and the franchise, McDowell's African Americans demonstrated considerable political power, notably when they organized demonstrations to protest lynchings in 1887 and 1896.[68] Such cultural and political advances must have led local whites to view McDowell County as a threat to the status quo, but when the Carters locate Hardy's capture at the Keystone Bridge, they suggest that African Americans could not escape the arm of white justice and its often racist consequences.

Popular among white ballad singers in Appalachia, particularly in Virginia and West Virginia, "John Hardy" allays fears of racial insubordination by subjecting its protagonist to the moral arbiter of the region, white Christianity.[69] Flouting the values of industrialism, Hardy was a gambler, a murderer, and a womanizer who, according to the ballad, received visits from two "little girls" while he was imprisoned. Despite his dubious moral character, Hardy accepts the status quo before his death by standing on the gallows and proclaiming his faith in the afterlife. Emphasized in newspaper reports of the hanging, Hardy's deference to a white Baptist minister and his remorsefulness performed important cultural work. African Americans in McDowell County may have established a place in which they could enjoy a modicum of cultural independence, but the ballad reminded them and the white balladeers who sang it that blacks must remain subordinate to white values and that all people are subordinated to higher powers, including, perhaps, the power of the coal companies. The Carters' "John Hardy" never questions the validity of this moral structure, nor does it examine how the political economy it undergirds may have shaped Hardy's actions. Instead, it reinscribes and justifies the racial and class hierarchies particular to a place and its historical moment.

Guthrie held the Carters in high esteem, but when the politically conscious folksinger recognized that their ballad did little to promote social change, he reworked the song so that he might channel Hardy's anger and rebellion into a collective struggle for racial and economic equality. Although the first five verses of the two ballads are nearly identical, tears of rage rather than remorse flow from the eyes of Guthrie's Hardy, who, like his fellow African American hero John Henry, asserts his manhood and vows to fight his oppressors. Instead of asking for forgiveness, instead of accepting slavery's oppressive legacy, Hardy declares, "I'll rotten in my grave." This bad man goes defiantly to the gallows, where, just before his execution, his two girlfriends affirm that one day African Americans will win their freedom.

To clarify the meaning of his rendition and to connect it to union politics, Guthrie uses the song to provide a "historic understanding, in terms of the past, the present, and future of the whole human race." Placing Hardy's life in a historical context, Guthrie's 1942 essay, "Big Guns," reveals an understanding of economic and regional history when he states that just "as the midwest had its Jesse James, the southwest its Billy the Kid, Oklahoma Pretty Boy Floyd, the deep south its Stack O'Lee, the Virginias had their desperate little man."[70] Like these outlaws, Hardy demonstrates his dissatisfaction with the social order by lashing out against its constraints, and although his is an individual act, it occurs within parameters that are defined by the collective struggles of working-class blacks. Guthrie's interpretation of the racial hurts that inspired this song is somewhat ahistorical, however. He suggests that when Hardy committed his crime, the West Virginia line demarcated the boundary between freedom and slavery, so when the fugitive escapes to "an old vacated coal mine tunnel" known as "Free Stone," he enters a figurative underground railroad. Although Guthrie became a staunch supporter of racial equality, there is a hint of appropriation in his narrative. Like many left-wing cultural workers in the 1930s and 1940, he implies that racial oppression can be explained in strictly economic terms. In "Big Guns," he says the African American struggle for freedom began when "you got loose from your mean boss and made a run for a better place, a free state, and you went in [the tunnel] a slave and you come out in a free state. And that freedom is the same freedom that men and women are fighting to keep alive today." [71] Guthrie wrongly implies that racism would fade with capitalism.

Nevertheless, he tries to forge connections between white and black workers. More than "just another bad man gone wrong," Hardy becomes a proud and defiant voice in the struggle for social justice, but one that must learn to abide by the collective politics of the labor movement. "Every time a man gets disgusted with trying to live decent in the rich man's system, and jumps out with a couple of forty fives on his hips to try to shoot his way through—the outlaw is beat," explains Guthrie. "Reason why is because he's not organized. He's just by his self. Want to holler, cuss, fight, work to change the world around a little bit better . . . but he's by his self. Bound to lose. . . . The Union does it right." [72]

For Guthrie, union was the elixir for all social ills, so he sought to draw on Hardy's energy, assertiveness, and history to channel an individual act of desperation into a collective movement that protested Jim Crow and oppressive industrial relations. To that end, he followed his performance of "John Hardy" on Songs the People Sing with "Which Side Are You On?," a ballad from what he once called "the fascist country of Harlan County, Kentucky." [73] Harlan had earned this reputation in violent coal strikes that occurred there in the early 1930s. In the spring of 1931, nearly 11,000 coal miners, already subjected to below-subsistence wages and inflated prices at company stores, went on strike when local operators cut their pay by 10 percent. Despite the tenacious effort of their fledgling union, extreme poverty, lack of food, and a firm alliance between state and capital conspired to break the strike. Backed by the authority of Sheriff J. H. Blair and the National Guard, the coal companies promptly, violently, and soundly defeated the leadership of both the United Mine Workers and the Communist Party–affiliated National Miners' Union by January 1932.[74]

Guthrie had great respect for the men and women who led the struggle in Harlan County, particularly Aunt Molly Jackson and her daughter, Sarah Ogan. He so admired Jackson's talents as an organizer and a folksinger that he called her a "woman Leadbelly." Ogan received similar praise for having the courage to sing "into the rifle fire of Sheriff Blair's deputies," and her brother, Jim Garland, sang about "the murderous gun thugs" with such conviction that Guthrie "never had the energy to say that one of his lines needed to be rewritten." For him, "the war that Jim Garland was fighting" was much "bigger and better than" the battle of aesthetics.[75]

Written by Florence Reece, another woman who assumed a leadership role in the Harlan strikes, "Which Side" prohibits the individual acts of defiance in which John Hardy engaged. In Reece's view, miners must align with either the workers or "the bosses," either the union or Sheriff Blair. Guthrie's choice to perform this song during the war years is particularly radical. "Of course, the war's been goin' on now for so long, I guess you know that it's a policy and an aim of most of the unions not to have any things such as strikes, so I hate to even mention that word," he remarked as he concluded the number. "That song was sort of a strike song, but it's changed to sort of history now."[76] Guthrie maintained, however, that the history of Harlan County's struggle was still very much alive. By connecting the old folk ballad "John Hardy" with a more recent hurt song from the Appalachian coal-mining region, he identified the historical and social processes that continued to afflict both black and white working people during the war years.

Moreover, he correctly observed that working people would not let history repeat itself without putting up a fight, even if their unions had taken a no-strike pledge to support the war effort. Shortly after the bombing of Pearl Harbor in 1941, national union and business leaders agreed to cooperate to prevent work stoppages by submitting irreconcilable disputes to the federal War Labor Board (WLB) for arbitration. Rank-and-file members readily defied their leaders' decree, however. Because the WLB did not allow wages to rise as fast as consumer prices and corporate profits and employees were often forced to labor under unsafe conditions, millions of workers demonstrated their disapproval and solidarity by participating in thousands of wildcat strikes. Determined to stabilize production, the federal government curtailed workers' rights by passing the War Labor

Disputes Act in 1943, a law that made it illegal to instigate a strike at a federal defense plant. Once again, labor thumbed its nose at the no-strike order, conducting 377 wildcat strikes in 1943 and 1944. The unrest spread in 1945, when a total of 3.5 million laborers participated in some 4,750 work stoppages. "Workers who engaged in unofficial strikes were not necessarily unpatriotic or unwilling to make sacrifices for the war effort," writes labor historian James Green; "they simply refused to allow management to abuse them by taking advantage of the situation."[77]

So did Guthrie. He ardently supported the Allied cause, but when he introduced "Which Side" to his audience, he returned the focus to the home front. As he traveled "all over" the United States, he said, he "heard all kinds of songs, heard all kinds and colors of people singing about every subject": "about work, and about wages, and about having meetings, about having free speech," rights that were abridged not only in Nazi Germany but also in capitalist America. Leading the world war against oppression did not exonerate the nation of its own sins, a point Guthrie boldly underscores when he attaches his definition of "union" to Abraham Lincoln's. After he repeats the chorus of "Which side are you on?" the second time, Guthrie interjects, "I think in regard to the union Abraham Lincoln asked that same question a few times," a remark that suggests that the labor and civil rights struggles were profoundly American rather than foreign or communist. His cause and Lincoln's were one and the same, and to reject the principle of union, to fail to fight for the end of racism, was tantamount to abandoning faith in government of, by, and for the people. Guthrie's communism was twentieth-century Americanism indeed.[78]

When Guthrie orders his audience to choose sides, he does not ask them to decide between the factions engaged in World War II; their support for the Allies is implied and unquestioned. Rather, he asks his listeners to examine the home front, to ask themselves, world war notwithstanding, whether they are on the side of freedom, justice, and equality or on the side of exploitation and Jim Crow, on the side of the worker or on the side of the capitalist. According to Ed Robbin, these polarities defined Guthrie's Manichaean politics. "His radicalism consisted in the fact that he always knew which side he was on," Robbin recalled years after he met Guthrie at KFVD. "In his songs and in his talk you could see that he always knew who the enemy was—the bankers, the big-moneyed people, the men who ran the munitions factories and helped make wars. It was that simple."[79] The same ideology undergirds his performance on *Songs the People Sing.* If men and women failed to apply the principles of anti-fascism at home with the same passion they applied them abroad, they were on the wrong side of the Union, on the side of hate instead of love.

THE BIGGEST THING I'VE SEEN YET

By opening *Songs the People Sing* with three hurt songs, Guthrie articulates a repressed history in the language and traditions of the people he represents, attempting to merge with his audience in a particularly Whitmanesque fashion. He suffers what they suffer, hopes what they hope, assumes what they assume.[80] "I'm just an old awkward Oklahoma boy," this widely read artist wrote in 1940, "use to shine the governor's shoes and shine his spittoons, and ain't too good to do it again." At times, he was so self-effacing that he disavowed his own compositions. "These here songs ain't mine," he explained in his liner notes to *Dust Bowl Ballads*. "The Government says so, and so does Victor Records, but really they ain't, and I hope that when they are played . . . you say, well, you made 'em up yourself." [81] Guthrie credited the subjects of his songs for his inspiration, trying to form a seamless continuity between himself and his constituency. Despite his stature, he was "no more of a poet" than they were: "You are the poet and your everyday talk is our best poem by our best poet. All I am is just sort of a clerk and climate tester, and my workshop is the sidewalk, your street, and your field, highway, and your buildings." [82] With an acute ear for language and a keen eye for observation, he approached his cultural work with great sympathy and purpose, obtaining an intimate knowledge of the traditions and experiences of working-class people, which, he believed, gave him the authority to speak on their behalf.

Besides enabling him to forge bonds with his potential audience, Guthrie's down-home remarks also preserved the communal ethos of the folk song movement. Scholars defined folk songs as anonymous compositions produced not by individual artists but by various members of a community who orally transmitted the songs and traditions embedded in them from one generation to the next. Because this process emphasized collectivity and collaboration over individuality, those committed to promoting social change readily embraced its values. Seeking both to preserve the folk process and to organize collective political action, many members of the folk song movement discouraged the development of great individual artists who might undermine their egalitarian values. Such a collaborative ethos surfaces in Guthrie's "Great Historical Bum," the final song he performs in the fragment of *Songs the People Sing*. Connecting various struggles of the past with those of the present, Guthrie implies that the "job" of defeating Hitler required a collective effort: soldiers, teamsters, and steelworkers would have to cooperate to break "slavery's chains" and win freedom for the world.[83]

But although "Historical Bum" presents the possibility for equality and cooperation, it reveals some of the ways in which Guthrie's irrepressible individuality worked against this possibility, how his heroic persona separated him from rather than united him with his constituency. Collectivity plays an important part in Guthrie's social vision, but he alone takes credit for accomplishing some of history's "biggest things": he built the Rock of Ages, parted the Red Sea for the Israelites, signed the contract to raise the sun each morning, and single-handedly won the battles at Valley Forge and Bull Run.[84] Guthrie may have his tongue planted firmly in his cheek as he makes such claims, but he also unveils his considerable arrogance. "I told the whole history of my own self and the whole rest of the world throwed in and I called it the Biggest Thing That Man Has Ever Done," he wrote in a draft of the introduction to the self-published booklet, "Ten Songs." "And so far, I'm by a long shot the biggest thing I've seen yet. You got to hear it to believe it." This bit of self-promotion did not make it to press, but its excision did not prevent Guthrie from proclaiming that he was "the most truthful ballad singer of the whole lot of them," largely because many of his peers were "paid big money by the big money side." Guthrie's motives were, in his view, far more noble. "I have decided, long ago, that my songs and ballads would not get the hugs and kisses of the capitalistic 'experts,' simply because I believe that the real folk history of this country finds its center and its hub in the fight of the union members against the hired gun thugs of the big owners."[85] Guthrie believed that his own "work in this field will someday be seen as the most radical, the most militant, the most topical of them all."[86]

Much as Whitman had done in "Starting from Paumanok," Guthrie imagined that successive generations of men and women would look back to him for inspiration. His second wife, Marjorie, recalled that her husband "had a tremendous feeling about himself" and would often tell her that they might be "poor" during their lifetime but "one day [their] kids will be rich."[87] Guthrie rarely expressed such concern for money but frequently demonstrated an unmistakable haughtiness. Cisco Houston recalled that he possessed a "drive for immortality" that often conflicted with his political ideals. "There was always a great contradiction," he told Lee Hays, "of . . . never wanting to prostitute anything that was genuinely himself and yet, wanting to be recognized on the biggest scale possible for what he was." [88] Guthrie was always concerned about maintaining his political credibility, but as his fame grew, it became more difficult for him to preserve his integrity. In the fall of 1940, he became widely popular in New York City, where he signed contracts to appear on *Back Where I Come From* and *Pipe Smoking Time*, a variety show sponsored by the Model Tobacco Company. For both programs, Guthrie took home $350 per week, a salary so outlandish at the time that he had no choice but to bring his first wife, Mary, and their children to New York City. Guthrie soon became uneasy, however, about earning "a salary that beats owning six farms in Oklahoma" while singing about the hardships of the Dust Bowl.[89]

The *New York Sun* added insult to ideological injury by running a feature on Guthrie and his family beneath the headline "Wrath's Grapes Turn to Wine; Woody Guthrie and Git-tar Give It a Bouquet." In this article, Guthrie sounded more like an upwardly mobile entertainer than like the Dust Bowl Balladeer. "Most of the fellers that's connected with the show I'm on has got offices above the thirty-second floor," he told the author of this feature. "Heck, I'm already broadcasting on the [thirty]-second floor, I think the next floor up belongs to the vice-president, and so they ain't much for me to look forward to." [90] The extent of his potential sell-out deepened. Red-baited by the popular press, he stopped writing for the left-wing *Daily Worker* because he feared the repercussions among his employers and was forced to refrain from making political commentary or singing political songs on the air. In January 1941, just two months after his ship seemed to have come in, a guilt-ridden Guthrie left his lucrative career behind and did what he always did when he felt hemmed in—he hit the road for California.[91]

Guthrie's individualism both inspired and contained his effectiveness as a cultural worker. On one hand, his iconoclasm enabled him to question authority and to challenge social conventions. On the other, his desire for fame, his dogmatic approach to folk song, and his own self-righteousness circumscribed his political efficacy. As Houston acutely observed, his individualism "sometimes developed into a kind of anarchy" that permitted him to escape rather than challenge political realities. Houston described Guthrie's departure from *Pipe Smoking Time* as one such anarchistic exercise, suggesting that he needed to "take advantage of the

opposition so to speak to get a little more of what [he] want[ed] across."[92]
For someone who had difficulty following the party line, Guthrie held
remarkably dogmatic views when it came to using folk music for political change. Folk music alone could bring about "the Truth like a spring
of cold water" and inspire the people to political action; all other art—
particularly the films of Hollywood and the music of Tin Pan Alley—
was nothing more than propaganda that kept the wheels of capitalism
turning. The problem, however, was that these commercial forms had a
much larger audience than did folk music, and by refusing to accommodate changing tastes, Guthrie limited his audience. He did, of course, use
popular fora such as *Songs the People Sing* to articulate his radical politics,
but generally he would not alter the style or content of his material to fit
the expectations of large record companies. His view of folk music was so
sacred, his political commitment so deep, that he could not, as he said of
Will Rogers, "work for the bosses and against them" at the same time.[93]

Convinced that he was the premier participant in the folk song movement, Guthrie, recalled Houston, wrote "as though he wanted to be
known . . . as a folk poet" and had an "insatiable desire to be at the center" of every performance. The Almanac Singers sought to preserve the
folk ideal of collaboration by forming an anonymous composers' collective, but Guthrie thwarted their efforts by affixing his signature to songs,
presenting himself as the front man, and complicating the group's vocal
arrangements with his irregular guitar playing.[94] His desire to be identified as a renowned "poet in the folking field" led him quite uninten-
tionally to cut himself loose from the people he represented, to forsake
his goals of community and equality. A tension existed between the Okie
image he projected and the cultural hero he wanted to become, between
representation and act. One minute he identified himself as "just plain
Woody," the next as "Mister Jesus." In one breath, he turned his back on
the commercial recording industry, and in the next, he sang for the Model
Tobacco Company. His poems spoke of the need to distinguish himself
from the mythic persona of Walt Whitman, yet time and again he presented himself as a "prophet singer."[95] This uncommon man was full of
the contradictions that permeated the most ordinary lives.

Perhaps Guthrie's individualism is best explained by the tragic circumstances he experienced. After watching his sister burn to death, his
mother lose her mind, and his father become depressed and humiliated
by economic hard luck, Guthrie took to the road for good in 1929 and
soon discovered that the only person he could count on was himself.

Nora Guthrie, Woody and Marjorie's only surviving daughter—their first daughter, Cathy, burned to death in 1947—has recalled that her father was a very lonely man who had an uncanny ability to form close relationships with people in a brief span of time. It seems that he did not have the skills or desire to develop the deep intimacy required to sustain long-term relationships.[96] He simply had lost too many people he loved and had wandered alone for too long. Participation in a strike, a tour of duty on a merchant marine ship, a performance at a hootenanny, or a casual sexual encounter could temporarily bind him to other people, but for Guthrie, the collective experience provided by these acts quickly dissipated. He longed to be part of something larger than himself but repeatedly returned to the open road, where he struggled to become his own master, total and absolute.

Living Leaves and Grass

After Guthrie completed "Historical Bum" on *Songs the People Sing*, the emcee intervened to read a paragraph John Steinbeck wrote about his favorite Okie folksinger. A great source of pride for Guthrie, the statement illustrates the idealized connections to "the people" that left-leaning intellectuals believed Guthrie had. "Woody is just Woody," wrote the Nobel laureate. "Thousands of people do not know he has any other name. He is just a voice and a guitar. He sings the songs of a people and I suspect that he is, in a way, that people. Harsh voiced and nasal, his guitar hanging like a tire iron on a rusty rim, there is nothing sweet about Woody, and there is nothing sweet about the songs he sings. But there is something more important for those who will listen. There is the will of a people to endure and fight against oppression. I think we call this the American Spirit."[97]

Woody was never "just plain old Woody."[98] He may have been a hero to Steinbeck and to some extent a hero *for* the working class, but it is difficult to say whether he was any more a hero *of* it than was Whitman. His radio show at KFVD, his performances at California labor camps, and his column in *People's World* certainly garnered a migrant following, and even if such efforts did not always politicize his audience, they at least raised their spirits. When he arrived in New York City, he continued to perform for such organizations as the International Workers Order, but as he assembled a coterie of admirers comprised of intellectuals and began to live the life of an artist, his connections to working-class experience weakened.[99] Guthrie attempted to create a common culture that would assemble the various polities of American society into one big union, but although the forms he chose to forge this culture may have been familiar to his intended audience, many of the channels through which he broadcast them were not. Most workers did not buy books published by E. P. Dutton, did not read the review of *Bound for Glory* in the *New Yorker*, did not study Marx or Whitman, and did not advocate the radical racial and sexual politics that Guthrie espoused.

Nevertheless, Guthrie passionately embraced the labor movement, searching for a way to become part of what he described as "a chain of others that can't be broken."[100] Beneath his tough exterior, he wrestled with self-doubt, contradictions, and conflicts, but he performed significant cultural work and redefined the working-class hero in important ways. When he represented the experiences of migrant workers and African Americans, he wrote songs of occupations that Whitman could not have composed. Whereas the Good Gray Poet celebrated the artisan and presented the world as it should be, Guthrie chronicled a history of exploitation, injustice, and suffering and openly assailed those responsible for it. This is not to say that he did not glorify the working class. In his world, workers and farmers were inherently good and he celebrated their moral probity by "sing[ing] the songs that would make [them] take pride in" themselves.[101] This pride, he hoped, would inspire people to struggle collectively for a better world, to imagine a time "when we'll all be union and we'll all be free."[102] He too formulated an idealized sexual politics, but because his people endured more suffering than Whitman's, this working-class hero understood that reform would not occur if capitalism was not dramatically altered. Although he was too impetuous to adhere strictly to Communist Party policy, Guthrie asserted that justice—both economic and racial—would be realized only when cultural workers got "this thing called socialism nailed and hammered up."[103]

Perhaps most obvious, Guthrie transformed the working-class hero into a guitar-carrying vagabond and opened a new road of possibility. As Joe Hill observed, songs enable the singer to tell the same story over and over again, and when Guthrie put his democratic message on phonograph records and the radio, he had the potential to disseminate his politics to an enormous audience. This transformation generated such tremendous energy that by the mid-1950s, successive generations of working-class heroes were turning their faces sideways and backward to listen to

Guthrie's southwestern drawl as well as Whitman's barbaric yawp. When a new generation of cultural workers fought for civil rights and democracy, they looked to "Woody's children," including Bob Dylan, to express their politics.

Despite important triumphs, familiar problems resurfaced in Guthrie's career. His sexual politics challenged the conventions governing relations between men, connected the social to the sexual, and in theory erased gender inequalities. In practice, however, these theories reconfirmed the privileges of manhood and ultimately failed to reconcile the tension between self and other. The fundamental dilemma that vexed Whitman's working-class hero plagued Guthrie as well. How could a man who wanted so desperately to be the messiah of the people forge a democratic culture that balanced individual liberty and social equality? No matter where he wandered, this lonesome traveler tramped an open road lined with "living leaves and grass," encountering and sometimes overcoming the conflicts, contradictions, and prejudices articulated by Whitman. In Woody Guthrie, the Leaves were very much alive indeed.

SEVERAL YARNS, TALES, & STORIES

"The world has already built me a legend," declared Woody Guthrie in 1947, and although the "several yarns, tales, and stories" that he and other cultural workers so meticulously cultivated had made him a renowned "poet in the folking field," he could not have foreseen the extent to which his popularity would grow, particularly after Huntington's chorea permanently hospitalized him in the mid-1950s. Guthrie's ever-brightening legend continued to be placed in the same orbit as Walt Whitman's for the next forty years. Critics Robert Shelton and Pauline Kael, journalist Nat Hentoff, and television personality Charles Kuralt were among those who noted the similarities between the two artists.[1] Such comparisons were perhaps more astute than critics realized, for much as Horace Traubel and the Whitmanites promoted the literary and political reputation of their hero, a cabal of well-wishers and admirers assembled around Guthrie to keep his work and political vision alive.

Largely as a result of the tenacious efforts of Pete Seeger, Guthrie's radicalism weathered the harsh ideological climate of the 1950s and once again flowered in the politics and music of the 1960s folk revival. Initially drawn to his bohemian lifestyle, white college students ultimately discovered Guthrie's political commitments and adapted them to their own concerns, notably the ban-the-bomb and civil rights movements. If Whitman was an intellectual touchstone for the Old Left, Guthrie became a heroic spiritual grandfather of the New.[2] The most successful of his cultural offspring, Bob Dylan embodied both the possibilities and the limitations of his hero's vision. Although Dylan and his fellow balladeers relied on Guthrie's legacy to validate their radicalism and to promote collective politics, the Okie's bequest could not prevent his progeny from becoming entangled in the sexism and individualism that were embedded in the larger culture. By the mid-1960s, Dylan's radical individualism repelled him from the New Left's collectivism, and his avant-garde lyricism and self-conscious artistic pose alienated him from the people Guthrie purported to represent. As the New Left began to fragment at the end of the decade, the meaning of Guthrie's politics was again up for grabs.

THE BALLAD OF PETE SEEGER

Anticommunism thrived in post–World War II America, driving party faithful and the folk song movement underground, into prisons, and before the House Un-American Activities Committee (HUAC). Founded in 1938, HUAC was established as a permanent congressional committee in 1945 and began to wield its power quite forcefully two years later when a federal court ruled that uncooperative witnesses could be cited for contempt of Congress. The year 1947 was extremely difficult for the American Left. In a series of general strikes in 1945 and 1946, laborers had asserted their rights in a variety of industries, threatening to reconstruct the employer-employee relationship. Concerned that these efforts would impede economic progress, Congress sought to contain the unpredictability of wildcat strikes in 1947 by passing the Taft-Hartley Act, which limited the rights of labor unions on a number of fronts: it dramatically curtailed the right to strike, held unions liable for damage done to property during a strike, barred unions from contributing funds to candidates running for federal office, prohibited the closed shop, and required that all union officers declare they were not members of the Communist Party.[3]

Taft-Hartley passed over President Harry Truman's veto, but the chief executive responded to the anticommunist hysteria by requiring federal employees to take a loyalty oath similar to that mandated by Taft-Hartley. Such decrees created an anxiety among left-wing cultural workers that heightened when HUAC opened hearings in Hollywood. In the 1948 presidential campaign, Progressive Party candidate Henry Wallace, whom Guthrie, Seeger, and other members of People's Songs staunchly supported, defended the rights of individual communists by appealing to the First Amendment, but his fourth-place finish behind Truman, Republican Thomas Dewey, and States' Rights Party candidate J. Strom Thurmond indicated that his voice was little more than a muffled cry in the ideological darkness. By 1949, Communist Party leaders were tried and convicted for violating the Smith Act, a statute that criminalized the teaching of subversive ideologies. Swept away in this near hysteria, the Congress of Industrial Organizations purged communists from its ranks, expelling 1.5 million members. The Rosenbergs would not be executed for allegedly selling nuclear secrets to the Soviet Union until 1953, but when Truman committed troops to Korea in 1950, the federal government's stand on dissent was clear. Espousing communism, or any ideology that questioned the political motives of the United States, was tantamount to treason.[4]

As anticommunism forced many Americans to suspend their political commitments, the most influential folk music magazine, Sing Out!, played an important role in circulating Guthrie's leftist legend, reprinting his replies to letters children wrote to him in 1955, featuring him on the cover of a 1957 issue, and publishing various articles and songs. As early as March 1951, Guthrie expressed concern about the United States' unprecedented military power, insisting that the folk song movement would "keep right on going and growing just as long as the whole race of us can duck and dodge that atom bomb blast." Guthrie may have ultimately supported the war against Hitler, but he rediscovered his pacifism when it came to Korea. In August, he responded to a "super-reactionary" friend who praised him for having nothing to do with the Sing Out! "bunch," an accusation to which Guthrie took great offense. "I could not agree any more or any plainer nor any stronger with SING OUT if I had wrote every single word of it," he explained in a letter to the editor. Declaring "which side of things I am and am not on," Guthrie explained that he was on the side of peace, on the side against "race hate and kukluckery," and "on double watch" for the side that opposed the Taft-Hartley Act.[5] He understood, however, that in the current ideological climate such protests and "politicle" commitments might prompt the "FBEye" to haul him "violently off to the latchup." But as Huntington's chorea progressively destroyed his creative faculties, his capacity to engage in cultural politics was greatly diminished. By 1955, he was so infirm that a Federal Bureau of Investigation (FBI) agent recommended that his records be removed from the bureau's active security files.[6]

As Guthrie's condition deteriorated, Seeger intervened to carry forward the politics of the folk song movement. According to Alan Lomax, "the renaissance of American folk song" began in March 1940 when Seeger and Guthrie met at the now legendary Grapes of Wrath Evening in New York City. Like Lomax, the twenty-one-year-old Seeger was mesmerized by this hard-traveling Okie, who became, Seeger explained, "a big piece of my own education." "I didn't know much about America then," Seeger recalled in 1964. "I'd been raised in the East; I really had a rather snobbish attitude: I thought there wasn't anything west of the Hudson River worth seeing, and Woody was the one who taught me different."[7]

By his own admission, Seeger's "actual experience in relating to the American people was zero."[8] His paternal grandfather, who traced his lineage to prominent European families, operated a sugar refinery that amassed a fortune large enough to employ four servants on his vast Hudson Valley estate. Pete's father, Charles, was expected to follow his patriarch's example, but this family maverick was more interested in aesthetics than accounting. After attending Harvard, he pursued an academic career in music that in 1911 led him and his wife, Constance de Clyver Edson, to the University of California at Berkeley. After his political consciousness was awakened at a cocktail party in 1914, Charles began to frequent the offices of the Industrial Workers of the World, a habit that cost him his professorship. By September 1918, Charles and Constance, who separated in 1927, repaired to the Seeger estate. After his return to New York, a despondent Charles fought off a nervous breakdown by becoming involved in the radical Composers' Collective and founding the academic discipline of ethnomusicology.[9]

Determined to have their three sons properly trained in the predilections of their class, the Seegers shipped four-year-old Pete off to his first boarding school, an institution with which he would become quite familiar by the time he entered Harvard in 1936. Within two years of enrolling in his father's alma mater, he began to search for work in New York City while continuing to practice his banjo playing, an avocation he picked up in boarding school. In 1939, Seeger went to work for Lomax at the Library of Congress, and when he heard the rusty-voiced Guthrie perform in 1940, his life was forever changed. Seeger, suggested Lomax, realized that he was hearing "his kind of music" and became a faithful soldier in the crusade "to make it everybody's kind of music." Possessed by a "pure, genuine fervor, the kind that saves souls," Seeger attached himself to Guthrie, seeking initiation into a tradition he found both naive and exotic.[10]

His baptism came by fire. Shortly after meeting Guthrie in March, Seeger accompanied his new mentor on a cross-country trek that exposed him to the conditions and traditions of the less-fortunate workingmen and women who lived outside the Hudson Valley. Fascinated by Guthrie's radicalism, his knowledge of folk music, and his ability to interact easily with working people, Seeger aped his working-class attributes, struggling desperately to overcome the wealth and privilege of his Harvard pedigree. There was more than a hint of affectation in Seeger's pose. Although he would sustain a lifelong commitment to labor politics, he was not cut from the same cloth as Guthrie or Whitman and, consequently, was not the type to recast himself as a working-class hero. Shy and soft-spoken, Seeger lacked Guthrie's boundless ego. Rather than boasting of his own musical talents, he downplayed his role in the folk song movement so that he might call attention to lesser-known participants. "I've gotten too much attention already," Seeger told his biographer David King Dunaway in a particularly self-effacing moment. "Too many people listen to me and not enough to the people I learned from." [11]

Seeger never forgot that he did not belong to the class that tutored him in its musical heritage, mainly because Guthrie would not let him. When Seeger would try to blend the American folk tradition with international folk songs so that the Almanac Singers might appeal to a more diverse audience, Guthrie insisted that only he, a self-proclaimed member of the working class, had the authority to speak on behalf of his constituents and dismissed his friend's efforts as being too commercial. Such remarks often escalated into attacks on Seeger's masculinity and puritan rectitude. "That guy Seeger, I can't make him out," Guthrie once quipped. "He doesn't look at girls, he doesn't drink, he doesn't smoke, the fellow's weird." [12] Tall, thin, baby-faced, awkward, and reserved, Seeger traveled with Whitman's roughs, but even his wife, Toshi, recognized that he was simply "pretending" to be a workingman. [13] No matter how "rustic or exotic his song," explains Robert Cantwell, "Seeger delivered it in the honest accents of New England gentility, with its dignified, rotund vowels, every word articulate, the raised voice of a scholar at the podium, lifted out of its element." [14]

Although the man Moe Asch described as a "non-communicative," private person was ill-suited to travel the heroic path Whitman had blazed, he was strangely well equipped to teach a new generation about Guthrie and the political tradition he embodied. [15] More than any other artist, Seeger was responsible for rekindling the fires of the folk song movement, although in the wake of the 1948 election and the failure of People's Songs, it seemed as though its embers were fading fast. Desperate and depressed, Seeger fanned the flames in a new and unfamiliar way. Rather than retreating into the esoteric artistic and political circles in which he had become so comfortable, he pursued a strategy that just a few years before would have made him recoil: he revived the folk tradition by introducing it into popular culture.

In late 1949, Seeger founded the Weavers with former Almanac Singer

Lee Hays, guitarist Fred Hellerman, and vocalist Ronnie Gilbert. In June 1950, the quartet signed with Decca Records, which hired the Gordon Jenkins Band to back the group's powerful vocal arrangements, a formula that resulted in immediate and widespread success. The Weavers' first single, comprised of the Israeli folk song "Tzena, Tzena, Tzena" and Leadbelly's "Goodnight Irene," sold over 1 million copies and initiated a string of hits including "On Top of Old Smoky," "Wimoweh," "Kisses Sweeter Than Wine," and a version of Guthrie's "So Long, It's Been Good to Know You," which was transformed from a sardonic statement about organized religion into a love song. With the assistance of managers Harold Leventhal and Pete Kameron, the Weavers brought folk music, albeit an expurgated version, to audiences that previously had been unfamiliar with it. Their stardom quickly faded, however, when political pressures surfaced. In 1950, the FBI published *Red Channels*, a report on communist influence in the broadcast industry, which named Seeger as a Communist Party member. Within two years, Gilbert and Hellerman were also identified as communist conspirators. Haunted by intense public scrutiny, the original Weavers disbanded until the political climate cleared enough in 1955 that they could hold a reunion concert at Carnegie Hall.[16]

In addition to being subjected to a relentless attack from the Right, the Weavers incurred the wrath of a disgruntled Left, which was convinced that the musicians had forsaken their political integrity for commercial success. To be sure, the Weavers altered their art, politics, and appearance to achieve their popularity: song lyrics were made more palatable to a white middle-class audience, traditional music was accompanied by orchestral arrangements, formal attire replaced proletarian costumes, and television appearances became more important than performances at hootenannies and union halls. What the critics did not realize, however, was that the Weavers' popularity cut two ways. They may have removed some of the ideological sting from the folk tradition, but because that tradition was rife with political significance, they also radicalized popular music. Seeger with his rotund vowels and Gilbert with her resplendent voice "interpreted the Leadbellys and the Guthries," observed Arlo Guthrie, who "were too foreign for mass tastes."[17] No matter how diluted it was, their interpretation subverted many of the values held by their white middle-class audience, introducing working-class and African American songs of freedom that began to unravel the ideological fanaticism and segregationist attitudes that were woven into the nation's social fabric.

Seeger's self-described role as a "cultural guerrilla" became a bit more challenging, however, when HUAC subpoenaed him in 1955. Citing his First Amendment right to freedom of speech, Seeger assailed his interrogators for their un-American conduct, a tactic that earned him ten citations for contempt. Until 1961, he faced the possibility of serving time for the charges and his name remained at the top of the blacklist. Unable to find steady work, he "kept as home base this one sector of society which refused most courageously to knuckle under to the witch hunters: the college students." On campuses such as Oberlin and Swarthmore, Seeger performed before crowds of privileged young men and women who understood his translation of the folk tradition perhaps better than they would have understood Guthrie's. When he encouraged his young fans to pick up their banjos and guitars to spread the gospel of folk music, more than a few listened. At Oberlin, an inspired Joe Hickerson, a young undergraduate who would go on to become the director of the Folklife Archive at the Library of Congress, organized the Folksmiths, a group of eight students who spent their summer vacations performing at children's camps throughout the Northeast.[18]

According to Hickerson, whose family harbored left-wing sympathies, these young men and women had little interest in politics but simply enjoyed performing the songs of other cultures and teaching them to willing listeners. "We have discovered that we like the dances that people different from ourselves like, and we hope you like them too," read the introduction to "The Folksmiths Dance Kit," a mimeographed collection of songs marketed to camp counselors. Following Seeger's example, many of the songs they taught and performed had political implications. Indeed, even as he was pursued by the FBI and HUAC, Seeger continued to sing songs with pointed political content. In 1956, his concert for the New York Society for Ethical Culture, attended by future Folksmith Ricky Sherover, featured "Talking Atom Blues" and the radical manifesto "Which Side Are You On?," and his second show at Oberlin included popular labor songs such as "Winnsboro Cotton Mill Blues," Merle Travis's "Dark as the Dungeon," and Guthrie's "Worried Man Blues."

When the Folksmiths cut their album *We've Got Some Singing to Do* for Folkways Records in 1958, their musical selections followed a similar pattern. Comprised largely of African American songs that expressed a longing for freedom, their album and the songbook they distributed to a host of summer camps ensured that the political content of folk songs, presently being repressed from America's cultural memory, would not be altogether forgotten. Their version of "Kum Buy Yah," which would be learned by children throughout the country, was, except for perhaps its African origins, completely benign, but the inclusion in their sampler of such songs as "Follow the Drinking Gourd," "Study War No More," and Guthrie's "This Land Is Your Land" and "So Long" had the potential to shoot holes in a postwar consensus predicated on militarism, prosperity, and homogeneity.[19]

By performing Guthrie's songs and telling young audiences about his travels, Seeger publicized Guthrie's reputation, but the musical tribute he and other members of the Old Left organized in March 1956 was perhaps the point of departure for Guthrie's ascent to heroic status. Staged at the Pythian in New York City, the show, dutifully attended by Hickerson, was a coming-out party of sorts for the folk song movement. The country had grown weary of Senator Joe McCarthy's anticommunist crusade, and for the first time in a decade, cultural workers could celebrate their artistic and political mentor without facing the threat of being called before HUAC. Lee Hays and Earl Robinson read from Guthrie's writings, a filmstrip chronicled his career, and Seeger and a half dozen other musicians sang songs from *Dust Bowl Ballads*, the *Columbia River Collection*, and a catalog of union and children's songs. "Vigilante Man," "Union Maid," and "Jesus Christ" restored Guthrie to his radical context, and the determined refrain of "I'm goin' down this road feelin' bad / And I ain't gonna be treated this-a way" prepared the crowd for Guthrie's courageous appearance. As the show drew to a close, Guthrie stood in the balcony where he had watched this musical fete, acknowledging his admirers with a clenched fist while a weeping Seeger led the chorus in a triumphant rendition of "This Land." If the celebration itself did not fix Guthrie's defiant image in America's cultural memory, the sympathy generated for a proud man facing imminent death began to do so.[20]

LEFT TURN

When Seeger toured the college circuit in the mid-1950s, he hoped that his audience would absorb his and Guthrie's radicalism through a sort of cultural osmosis, but he would have to suffer through a few disappointing years before his dream was realized. The Kingston Trio, whose David Guard was inspired in 1957 by a Weavers' concert, topped the pop charts in 1958 with the Appalachian folk ballad "Tom Dooley" and, in ensuing

Pete Seeger at a 1965 peace rally. Copyright © by Diana Davies/Smithsonian Folklife.

years, performed Guthrie's "Hard Ain't It Hard," "This Land," "Pastures of Plenty," "Hard Travelin'," and "Deportee (Plane Wreck at Los Gatos)" with the white-shoed passion of Pat Boone. Meanwhile, Joan Baez, who was present at the same concert, revived traditional Elizabethan ballads with considerable success, but her political awakening would not come until the early 1960s.[21] These young men and women may not have been as politically mature as Seeger would have liked, but on college campuses in the Midwest, at folk festivals in the South, and in impromptu performances at New York City's Washington Square, they were beginning to make Seeger's passion for traditional music their own.

Why did white middle-class college students find the cultural traditions of southern farmers, former slaves, and industrial workers so fascinating? Why did Guthrie's representation of the working-class hero appeal to these young men and women, and how did he shape their politics? The attraction had its roots in postwar socioeconomic conditions that imbued these relatively privileged baby boomers with a peculiar angst. The narrative of these middle-class lives is familiar. Following the economic scarcity and uncertainty of the Great Depression and the unprecedented destruction of a long world war, many white middle-class Americans, particularly in the North, were content to ride the postwar economic boom to prosperity and insularity. They had won for their children the freedom from want that only a decade earlier had seemed almost impossible to obtain, and they were quick to remind their offspring that they should be thankful. Settled snugly into their suburban homes, members of the middle class withdrew into a privatized world in which they surrounded themselves with consumer goods, associated with neighbors who shared their racial and class status, and offered their children the promise of an even more comfortable future. Hard work, a willingness to play by the rules of the game, and, perhaps most important, attendance at a four-year college would ensure that affluence would not skip generations.[22]

Prosperity and conformity bred dissatisfaction if not contempt. This world was a bit too antiseptic, a bit too unreal, a bit too comfortable. To imagine a way out of their boredom, these teenagers reconnoitered the margins of American culture, where they discovered what seemed to be a more diverse, more authentic type of existence. Here they found the rebels James Dean and Marlon Brando, reacted hysterically to the raw sexuality of Elvis Presley, gyrated their own bodies to the rhythms created by such African American artists as Chuck Berry, Fats Domino, and Little Richard, and even dug the free-spirited beatniks on Jack Kerouac's road. These artists offered their audience something parents could not: experience, kicks, and excitement. For children who had grown up facing the threat of nuclear holocaust, the possibility of living a more physically, emotionally, and perhaps even spiritually stimulating life was quite attractive.[23]

Given the existential crisis the bomb inspired, it is not surprising that these students identified with the cultures of working people and African Americans. Many baby boomers perceived the world as a frightening, oppressive place. They were taught to fear the Soviet Union and to worry that Reds lurked even in the shadows of Main Street, a suspicion that the Rosenberg execution seemed to validate. The folk tradition that Seeger and other campfire singers presented to them, however, held the memory of a simpler, kinder, prenuclear era in which the possibility of instant annihilation did not exist. Moreover, a folksy and defiant figure such as Guthrie, whose rickety voice and cornpone humor recalled a romantic agrarianism and whose radical politics tinged him with exoticism, provided a model for those who wanted to wage their own personal rebellion against postwar society.[24] As young people began to take an interest in Guthrie's work and the folk tradition, they sought out the source of their inspiration. Along with Seeger, a handful of groupies joined Ramblin' Jack

Elliot, Ralph Rinzler, and the Kossoy Sisters in gathering around the ill-fated folksinger when he ventured into Washington Square. On Sundays, many supporters visited him in East Orange, New Jersey, where Bob and Sidsel Gleason hosted Guthrie each week.[25]

To many of his admirers, Guthrie was not a political figure but a rebel without a cause, a man whose wandering ways symbolized their adolescent desire to flee from the immense social pressures that forced conformity and nurtured predictability. Lee Hays recalled a revealing discussion he had with one of the folksinger's fans. "Woody represents the irresponsibility, traveling, wandering," a young man told Hays. As a teen, he continued, "you want to break away from your family, from teachers, from school, authority, want to see the world. You don't want to be tied down. You're looking for freedom."[26] Hays averred that Guthrie would have been disappointed if he had known that some of his fans were unaware of his political commitments. Nevertheless, in the late 1950s, many of the young people Seeger carefully tutored understood only one part of Guthrie's complicated and conflicted legacy: they knew he wanted to run from the world, but they did not yet realize the extent to which he wanted to change it. They co-opted his proletarian dress to renounce the plenitude and privilege of their middle-class background and romanticized the hard-traveling life of the hobo because it permitted them to challenge the lives their parents had made for them. But as they came to see Guthrie as a symbol of their own personal rebellion, they soon acquired a vague understanding of his politics. Most middle-class kids discovered Guthrie around the campfire, but a contingent of red-diaper babies existed whose parents had made certain that they knew he was a union man. When the civil rights movement began to gain momentum, Guthrie's political legacy bubbled to the surface.

Songs to Woody

Such were the circumstances under which Bob Dylan claimed Guthrie as his idol. Robert Zimmerman, who changed his name to Dylan shortly after he entered the University of Minnesota in 1959, was born in Duluth in 1941, the son of Jewish merchants, Abraham and Beatrice Stone Zimmerman. Dylan's stay at the university was short, but his exposure to the city of Minneapolis was important, largely because he found an intellectual home in Dinkytown, a bohemian section known for its folk music scene. Here, the aspiring young musician was captivated by Guthrie's *Bound for Glory*, a book that convinced him his future was on the road rather than in the classroom. Dylan left Minnesota in 1960 and, after wandering around the country, arrived in New York City in January 1961. He began to circulate through such popular Greenwich Village folk haunts as Gerde's Folk City and the Gaslight, and in 1962, the legendary impresario John Hammond offered the twenty-one-year-old a recording contract at Columbia Records, which released his self-titled album that March.[27]

The folk and folk-styled songs on the album include Dylan's interpretations of Bukka White's "Fixin' to Die," Blind Lemon Jefferson's "See That My Grave Is Kept Clean," and standards such as "House of the Risin' Sun." This sampler of the folk tradition was assembled from a mythic past to which Dylan painstakingly attached himself. Much like Seeger, who tried to obscure the privileges of his life by affecting the pose of a workingman, Dylan reinvented himself as a weary traveler who had hoboed around the country for most of his young life. At one of his first press interviews in 1961, he told his audience that he had lived in Wisconsin, the Dakotas, New Mexico, and Minnesota and had picked up pointers from Jefferson (who was never seen alive after 1929), the Texas songster Mance Lipscomb, and "an old guy named Wigglefoot."[28] Bored with the predictability and sheltered nature of his middle-class life, Dylan fabricated a past that was romantically authentic, one full of hard traveling and hard living. Whereas his life, like those of his contemporaries, was smothered by relative affluence and characterized by a lack of passion, the itinerant one he imagined was full of adventure and possibility. His voice, suggests the perceptive folk-revivalist-turned-historian Robert Cantwell, came "into dormitory rooms with shocking immediacy. And when, in the spoken preface to his shattering 'Baby Let Me Follow You Down,' he waggishly reported he had learned the song from one 'Rick Von Schmidt,' a 'blues guitar player' from Cambridge, whom he had 'met one day in the green pastures of . . . ah . . . Harvard University,' the folk revival knew it had found one of its own."[29]

Dylan's most important (and real) encounter with the past occurred in East Orange when he moved in temporarily with the Gleasons and struck up a friendship with Guthrie. Intoxicated by his hero's approval, Dylan redoubled his efforts to pose as heir apparent, and when he debuted at Gerde's Folk City, he sported one of Guthrie's old suits for the occasion.[30] A self-described "Woody Guthrie juke box," Dylan recalled that he was "completely taken over by [Guthrie's] spirit."[31] In "11 Out-

Bob Dylan, folksinger, 1965. Prints and Photographs Division, Library of Congress.

lined Epitaphs," the liner notes to *The Times They Are A-Changin'* (1964), he wrote that he dreamed of living in the 1930s, of playing for labor unions and singing for tips.[32] In 1964, Dylan alluded to Guthrie's radicalism, but the songs he wrote for his first album eschew his predecessor's ideological commitments. Dylan derived his knowledge of Guthrie primarily from *Bound for Glory*, a book that offers a somewhat romanticized portrait of the road and the folksinger but, because of editorial decisions, does not address his political activities. As a result, Dylan's initial representation of Guthrie, as "Song to Woody" demonstrates, had little to do with union halls.

Written after Dylan's first meeting with Guthrie, "Song to Woody" announces Dylan's intent to follow in his hero's footsteps. Throughout this song, Dylan authenticates his status as a folk musician, proclaiming a wistful loneliness to a tune lifted from Guthrie's "1913 Massacre" and to lyrics borrowed from "Pastures of Plenty." "I'm out here a thousand miles from my home," sings Dylan in a youthful voice, trying his best to sound like a weather-beaten Okie. Dylan imagines that he has embarked on the same road that Guthrie traveled, yet he ignores the political responsibility to which this open road leads. Like Guthrie, he sees a divided nation that suffers from sickness and hunger, but instead of leveling criticism at it or imagining a way to change it, he celebrates an idealized hobo existence and extols Guthrie's individualism. Dylan observes that few men can boast of Guthrie's accomplishments but provides no sense of the commitments he made or hardships he endured. In fact, when Dylan sings, "The very last thing that I'd want to do / Is to say I've been hittin' some hard travelin' too," he suggests that although he wants to wear Guthrie's mantle, he prefers to avoid the struggles in which his subject engaged. The Guthrie that Dylan represents in "Song to Woody" is a spiritual rather than a political guide, a vagabond who has more in common with Kerouac than with communism, a traveler on a path marked not by struggle but by a relentless search for kicks and self-realization.[33]

"Talkin' New York" and "Hard Times in New York Town," two songs that also revise lines from Guthrie, indicate that Dylan had a superficial understanding of his mentor's politics.[34] "Talkin' " chronicles Dylan's hard luck and, alluding to Guthrie's "Pretty Boy Floyd," conveys his distrust for greedy booking agents when he sings that "a very great man once said / That some people rob you with a fountain pen."[35] A similar skepticism permeates "Hard Times," which draws on a scene in *Bound for Glory* in which Guthrie auditions at the Rainbow Room, which sits atop Rockefeller Center. Guthrie was deeply concerned with maintaining his artistic integrity, so when he auditioned at this monument to the founder of Standard Oil, he demonstrated little respect for its luxurious environs. Unwilling to suspend his politics, he began the audition with a performance of "New York City," a song that condemns "John D's spirit" and suggests that the Rainbow Room was located "a long way's" from the people of the United States.[36] Dylan's "Hard Times" refashions this anecdote to describe his own misgivings about the corruption, high cost of living, and dog-eat-dog ethos he finds in New York City, where "Mister Rockefeller sets up as high as a bird." Dylan articulates a disdain for wealth and privilege, applauding the values of down-home rural folks and disparaging those of city slickers. To be sure, the "dust in [Guthrie's] Oklahoma plains" is "much cleaner than the New York kind." But although Dylan shares Guthrie's disdain for urban and commercial culture, his early songs lack ideological commitment. Rather than attacking the system that breeds economic injustice, Dylan wears his poverty as a badge of honor to convince himself and perhaps his audience that he is as authentic as the Okie he emulates. And, like Guthrie, Dylan refuses to capitulate to hard times, even if they are self-imposed. In 1962, Guthrie's defiant individualism gave Dylan a sense of determination, but it had not yet inspired him to try to change the world.[37]

Within a year, however, Dylan became more cognizant of Guthrie's political legacy.[38] "Woody never made me fear," he explained in "11 Outlined Epitaphs."[39] "For he just carried a book of Man / an gave it t' me t' read awhile." He offers a remarkable reading of Guthrie's book in "Last Thoughts on Woody Guthrie" (1963).[40] A long, rambling free-association poem that recalls the itinerant wanderings of both Whitman and Guthrie, "Last Thoughts" evaluates Guthrie's legacy, describes the despair he felt as he lay dying, and reveals the influence he had on Dylan. The poem commences with an astonishing litany of images that depict a physical, psychological, and social malaise that afflicted Guthrie, Dylan, and perhaps an entire generation. Appealing to the language of "This Land," Dylan sees "the sun-decked desert and evergreen valleys" of Guthrie's world "turn to broken down slums and trash-can alleys." The transformation from the hopeful but nostalgic world Guthrie represents to one filled with destruction and deterioration precipitates a spiritual crisis and leaves people searching for an elusive "something" that can summon the transcendental "something that comes home to one now and perpetually" of which Whitman sang in "A Song for Occupations."[41] Like the mute, bedridden Guthrie, Dylan and his contemporaries long for something or somebody to "open up a new door" of hope for a better future, to help them transcend the anxieties presented by their historical moment. Indeed, Dylan's representation of Guthrie's medical condition might well describe his own state before he read *Bound for Glory*:

And there's something on yer mind that you wanna be saying
That somebody someplace oughta be hearin'
But it's trapped on yer tongue and sealed in yer head
And it bothers you badly when you're layin' in bed.

Dylan reads Guthrie's "book of Man" through a lens of ambivalence that magnifies its individualism, but he begins to decipher its political implications. He suggests that a "Greyhound bus that don't bar no race" might assuage the suffering he describes and insists,

> You need something to make it known
> That it's you and no one else who owns
> That spot that yer standing, that space that you're sitting
> That the world ain't got you beat
> That it ain't got you licked
> It can't get you crazy no matter how many
> Times you might get kicked . . .
> You need something special to give you hope.

Drawing on the hope and determination embedded in Guthrie's canon, Dylan describes a temerity buoyed by the hope for a better future, a hope that is wholly absent from the commercial culture that surrounds him. Hope, Dylan explains, is not located "on a dollar bill / And it ain't on Macy's window sill." Nor is hope to be found in some "fat kid's fraternity house," in "cotton candy clothes," or in the voice of "fifty-star generals and flipped-out phonies." If his audience intends to imagine a better world, Dylan instructs,

> You can either go to the church of your choice
> Or you can go to Brooklyn State Hospital
> You'll find God in the church of your choice
> You'll find Woody Guthrie in Brooklyn State Hospital.

For many, including Dylan, Guthrie was a spiritual guide, a great individual whose working-class behavior, disregard for social convention, and love for the freedom of the open road provided an alternative moral code they could use to resist their cultural fate. "You could listen to his songs and actually learn how to live," Dylan explained.[42] When he and his fellow travelers joined the ban-the-bomb and civil rights movements, however, they recognized that Guthrie could teach them how to live politically as well as individually. As Cantwell writes of the folk revival, the fascination with Guthrie began as part of a "culture of personal rebellion," but "under the influence and authority" of a politically charged folk music tradition, it transformed into a culture of collective politics.[43]

By 1960, the political awakening that Seeger had been anticipating for more than a decade was under way. Following the lunch counter sit-ins in Greensboro, North Carolina, in 1960, the Student Nonviolent Coordinating Committee (SNCC) emerged as an arm of the Southern Christian Leadership Conference to organize students in the battle for civil rights. Meanwhile, Students for a Democratic Society (SDS), which evolved into perhaps the most influential white student group of the 1960s, confronted the threat of nuclear disaster, the vapidity of commercial culture, and the problems of racial and economic injustice by advocating participatory democracy. Before Vietnam War protests escalated in 1965, socially conscious youths rallied around the banners of nuclear disarmament and racial equality, organizing political activities that included Freedom Rides, the March on Washington, and Freedom Summer.[44]

The bohemians Dylan left in Dinkytown characterized their friend as politically unsophisticated, but by 1963, he had become the most commercially successful, if not the most important, voice in this movement.[45] "Whether he liked it or not, Dylan *sang for us*," wrote former SDS president Todd Gitlin. "We followed his career as if he were singing our song; we got in the habit of asking where he was taking us next."[46] Shortly after his arrival in New York City, Dylan began to acquire a political education, in part because he explored Guthrie's work more carefully, in part because his girlfriend, Suze Rotolo, inspired him. Born to a well-educated, politically engaged family, Rotolo belonged to the Congress of Racial Equality (CORE) and encouraged Dylan to follow Seeger's example and put his music to political use. In 1962, Dylan performed at a benefit for CORE at New York University and soon befriended Bernice Reagon and other musicians who provided the foundation for SNCC's cultural programs. Perhaps more important, he met Seeger, who, excited by what his friends had told him about this new talent, escorted Dylan to the offices of *Broadside* magazine. Cofounded in 1962 by Seeger, former Almanac Singer Sis Cunningham, and her husband, Gordon Friesen, *Broadside* was a mimeographed monthly that published topical songs. Through these conduits to the Old Left, Dylan and other young songwriters such as Phil Ochs rediscovered the political Guthrie and began to write their own social commentaries. Dylan's "Talkin' John Birch Society Blues," a satire about anticommunists, was published in the first issue in February 1962, initiating a string of contributions that would appear in *Broadside* over the next two years.[47]

A friend of Guthrie's, Friesen thought many of Dylan's songs were "contrived," but when the young musician produced "Masters of War" for the February 1963 issue, Friesen remarked that Dylan was writing "profound statements" that were even more effective than Guthrie's.[48] Included on *The Freewheelin' Bob Dylan* (1963), "Masters" indicated the extent to which Dylan's political consciousness had matured. Written on the heels of the 1962 Cuban missile crisis, the song points an accusatory finger at the men who produce and threaten to deploy weapons of mass destruction, castigating them for spilling "young people's blood" and warning them that "Even Jesus would never / Forgive what you do."[49] Few songs in the folk tradition and perhaps no song released by a commercial recording company criticized the military-industrial complex with such moral certainty. The politics of *Freewheelin'* did not stop here. "Oxford Town" satirized the segregationist policies of the University of Mississippi; "A Hard Rain's A-Gonna Fall" rendered a haunting, imagistic vision of nuclear holocaust; and the anthemic "Blowin' in the Wind" combined protests against militarism and racism.

Following the release of this album in March 1963, Dylan took his politics on the road, assuming center stage at the July Newport Folk Festival, where, in addition to performing a solo set, he played a prominent role in the program's finale. Peter, Paul, and Mary reprised "Blowin' in the Wind" as the ceremonial closing song of the event and, on its completion, summoned Dylan, Seeger, Baez, and SNCC's Freedom Singers to the stage, where they joined hands in interracial solidarity to sing perhaps the most important song of the civil rights movement, "We Shall Overcome." This symbolic gesture connected the political commitments of the Old Left, embodied by Seeger, to these artists of the New, an association that Dylan worked diligently to strengthen. Later that July, he accompanied Seeger to Greenwood, Mississippi, where SNCC was coordinating a voter registration campaign aimed at African Americans. Enacting a scene that recalled Guthrie's visits to migrant encampments, Dylan played his guitar in a cotton field, striking a chord with workers as he performed "Only a Pawn in Their Game," a caustic commentary on the murder of civil rights leader Medgar Evers. He participated in the March on Washington in August and in December attended a meeting of the SDS. Dylan seemed to have finally comprehended the entirety of Guthrie's "book of Man." By the end of 1963, even Seeger was performing Dylan's compositions.[50]

As a new generation of what Cunningham called "Woody's children" recognized that their beloved vagabond may have also shared their politics, they quickly identified him as their heroic spiritual grandfather. In a special tribute to Guthrie published in the left-wing *Mainstream* magazine in 1963, folksinger Phil Ochs chastised those who were unaware of his politics. "I have run across some people who seem to consider [Guthrie] solely as a writer of great camp songs," wrote Ochs. "They cannot fathom the political significance of a great part of his works." Groups such as the Folksmiths defanged Guthrie for their summer camp audiences, but as many of these campers grew up, they anxiously historicized and adapted his work to suit their own purposes. In Guthrie, the New Left found a tradition that legitimated its own cultural work, that gave authority to a burgeoning political movement dismissed by critics for being young, inexperienced, and insubordinate. Ochs explained that Guthrie's "close association with the unions exemplified the traditional connection between folk music and social movements" and that as the civil rights and pacifist movements unfolded, "it was inevitable that folk music would follow its natural tendency of commentary and identify again with the times."[51] Ochs was an important figure in reestablishing this connection. Whereas Dylan's "Song for Woody" downplayed Guthrie's political legacy, Ochs's maudlin "Bound for Glory" (1963) reminded his audience that Guthrie had steadfastly supported unions and courageously defended his beliefs. Perhaps more important, Ochs urged young Americans to embrace and build on Guthrie's ideological commitment. "Oh why sing the songs and forget about the aim," asked Ochs. "He wrote them for a reason, why not sing them for the same?"[52]

Along with Ochs, the editors of Broadside spearheaded the campaign to remind audiences of Guthrie's original aim, announcing in their first issue that readers should "remember that many of our best folk songs were topical songs at their inception. Few would deny the beauty and lasting value of some of Woody Guthrie's songs."[53] Guthrie was clearly the prototype for the cultural workers that Broadside sought to develop, and as politics changed throughout the 1960s and early 1970s, the editors, particularly Friesen, sculpted Guthrie's legend to meet their own political goals. In 1962, an article on Bound for Glory, the book that inspired so many of Guthrie's New Left admirers, called attention to Guthrie's optimism. Unlike "many modern writers" who tended to represent an "unalterable," "horrible and terrifying existence," Guthrie held "a deep and unshakable conviction that man can change things" for the better. Such politics were reiterated as antiwar demonstrations proliferated in 1965.[54] Emphasizing Guthrie's pacifism, Broadside published his anti–Korean War song, "I've Got to Know," which asked, in a manner prefiguring "Blowin' in the Wind," "Why do your war boats ride on my water? / Why do your death bombs fall from my sky?" Friesen, who published the song along-

side a biographical sketch that trumpeted Guthrie's ties to the Communist Party as well as his integrationist politics, suggested that the song
"could be applicable to Vietnam." He emphasized his point by reprinting
a 1951 letter in which Guthrie remarked that it was time to "bring home
your weary wearies from those crazy pastures of war that I don't want to
own or crave one solitary inch of."[55]

Although *Broadside* made much of Guthrie's antiwar sentiments, it tried
to debunk the reputation he earned as an aimless traveler. The editors
understood that Guthrie's open road was a two-way street that sometimes
led him to run from the world rather than fight to change it, and they
began to worry that his politics had been overshadowed by his vagabond
legend. To rectify this problem, Friesen's biographical sketch quoted letters in which Guthrie apologized for his faults, notably for exhibiting
financial and emotional irresponsibility toward his family and for not
doing as much as he might have done to help in the struggle for social justice. Moreover, Friesen included critical remarks Guthrie made concerning the content of *Bound for Glory*. The book, Guthrie suggested, "shows
you a fairsized chunk of me way back in my kidhood days" but failed to
address the "later and more progressive, the more political parts," which,
in his opinion, were "the better and more useful and more sensible phases
and episodes of my life." Guthrie had included these parts in his original
manuscript, but like all "true good capitalist publishers," E. P. Dutton,
or, more precisely, editor Joy Doerflinger, had censored his work.[56]

Camilla Adams, who authored an account of living in the Almanac
Singers' house in 1941 and 1942, elaborated on Guthrie's "romanticized"
image. After detailing his selfishness, laziness, and heavy drinking, she
drove home the point of Friesen's article: "The kids have a tendency to
emulate his worst aspects as a way of basking in the reflected glory of
his very real gifts."[57] *Broadside* insisted that young people could find those
gifts not by seeking the romanticized freedom and irresponsibility of the
road but by aligning themselves with the collective political struggles in
which Guthrie engaged.[58]

LEFT OUT

Broadside sought to harness Guthrie's cultural energy to promote social
change, but his legacy presented reformers with significant limitations,
particularly when it came to gender politics. The folk song movement of

the 1930s and 1940s included a number of women cultural workers, but since it relied on the masculine languages of labor and revolution, its aims served male revolutionaries far better than they did women. As early as 1953, Irwin Silber denied such charges in *Sing Out!*, insisting that the folk tradition contrasted sharply with the "commercial music industry," which sounded the notes of misogyny. "Certainly there are many examples of male supremacist ideology in our folk songs," he wrote, "but these represent only a small portion of our country's folk heritage which is, by and large, a part of the general democratic expression of our proud history of the struggle for equal rights and genuine *brotherhood*." [59] Shrouded in the mythology of the Popular Front, Silber's language betrays historical realities: the Old Left and the New, the Guthries and the Dylans claimed cultural politics as a predominantly male domain. In both the 1930s and the 1960s, female singers often formed a ladies auxiliary for their male counterparts, performing traditional ballads while the men sang topical selections, watching in awe while traditional musicians and bluegrass revivalists flaunted their instrumental virtuosity, and cooking meals and caring for children while the good men of the Communist Party and the SDS brokered the terms of revolutionary strategy. [60]

A brief discussion of Dylan's relationship with Joan Baez illustrates the sexism that pervaded the New Left. Baez had already acquired a sizable audience when she first saw Dylan play at Gerde's in 1961, and although she was initially underwhelmed, her tepid opinion warmed as she became familiar with his songwriting ability. After performing with him at the 1963 Newport Folk Festival, Baez invited Dylan to join her on a West Coast tour. Audiences responded negatively to her protégé, but their hostility diminished in the wake of Baez's scoldings. As the two young folksingers bolstered each other's reputation, they became romantically involved, although Dylan pursued other women without Baez's knowledge. [61] When Dylan embarked on a tour of Britain in 1965, he had apparently lost interest in Baez but nevertheless invited her to accompany him. She assumed that Dylan would introduce her to his audience as she had done for him, but she would be disappointed. [62]

As early as 1964, Dylan had mocked Baez for relying on a repertoire comprised entirely of traditional ballads, ethnic folk songs, and compositions written by other artists, including himself. "It ain't nothin' just to walk around and sing," he confided to Baez's brother-in-law, Richard Fariña. "Take Joanie, man, she's still singin' about Mary Hamilton [the subject of a traditional folk song]. I mean where's that at? She's walked around on picket lines, she's got all kinds of feeling, so why ain't she steppin' out?" [63] To him, Baez was an interpreter of art rather than a creator of it, a second-rate artist who lacked the genius and originality of such poets as Guthrie and himself. When he departed for Britain in 1965, he had little interest in pledging his time to a mere vocalist, whether for romantic or for artistic reasons. His sentiments solidified in England, where an enthusiastic reception by both critics and audiences confirmed his image as a genius and introduced him to the possibilities of being a sex symbol. Stepping out of a folk ethos that espoused community and anonymity, Dylan had become a star, and as he told Robert Shelton, there was "no place" for Baez in his music or, indeed, in his life. She may have introduced him to her audience, but he was not about to return the favor, insisting that he "didn't owe her nothing." [64]

He gave her abuse and embarrassment. Throughout the tour, he pursued other women, refused to allow Baez to appear with him in concerts, and, before finally asking her to leave, openly criticized her for her lack of creativity when he did not ignore her altogether. *Don't Look Back* (1967), D. A. Pennebaker's documentary of the tour, chronicles this developing disdain. In a scene entitled "Turn, Turn, Turn," Dylan types frantically in his hotel room while manager Albert Grossman, friend Bob Neuwirth, and British singer Marianne Faithful lounge aimlessly, listening with varying degrees of attention as Baez plays a guitar and sings Dylan's "Percy's Song." Feeding the ego of an artist caught in his latest creative spasm, Baez is a lady-in-waiting who eagerly anticipates the words this mythic bard will provide her. She picks up another Dylan composition, "Love Is Just a Four Letter Word," and fawns over Dylan as she tells him she would record this "beautiful" song if only he would finish it.[65]

A disinterested but bemused Dylan takes a brief respite from his typing to remind himself and his groupies of his genius and Baez's lack thereof. " 'Long Black Veil.' Sing 'Long Black Veil,' " he whispers, imitating a fan's request. The meaning is clear. Whereas Dylan's audience entreated him to play any number of his latest compositions, Baez's could do little more than ask her to sing such tired and widely recorded standards as "Long Black Veil." [66] Neuwirth, who begs Baez not to sing, emphasizes Dylan's point when, after an exhausted Baez says she is "fagging out," he implies that artistically speaking, she "fagged out a long time ago." He couches these casual insults in terms of gender and sexuality. After she harmonizes with Dylan on several Hank Williams songs, Baez performs a belly dance, which prompts Neuwirth to remark that "she has one of those see-through blouses that you don't even wanna."[67] Dylan smirks, and an offended Baez, who spent much of the trip in tears, leaves the room, recognizing that love is just a four-letter word after all.

Although Baez was a leading figure in the 1960s folk revival and the politics it represented, her voice was interpretive rather than creative, beautifully feminine instead of nasally masculine, and consequently not as authoritative as the voices of the male cultural workers with whom she shared the stage. To Dylan and the New Left men who adored him, Baez, or any other woman for that matter, was not expected to supply the movement with creative inspiration and, as a result, was, like a sexual partner, interchangeable if not disposable. Former SDS member Marge Piercy commented on such expectations in her essay "The Grand Coolie Damn" (1969), the title of which plays on Guthrie's "Grand Coulee Dam," which Dylan recorded in 1968. Although Piercy does not mention Guthrie, her pun provides the context for an essay that condemns the sexism his generation bequeathed to New Left "coolies," who routinely denigrated women's contributions to the movement. As New Left men assumed public leadership roles, they systematically excluded women from intellectual and cultural labor, largely ignored and ridiculed the suggestions they offered at meetings, and viewed them primarily as domestic laborers and sex objects. "A man can bring a woman into an organization by sleeping with her and remove her by ceasing to do so," wrote Piercy. "A man can purge a woman for no other reason than that he has tired of her, knocked her up, or is after someone else: and that purge is accepted without a ripple."[68] In 1965, Dylan purged Baez.

New Left women took risks, dedicated their lives to the struggle for social justice, and gained important political experience that would help launch the feminist movement of the late 1960s.[69] But because men were the leaders of the New Left, women were relegated to its periphery, where they remained bound by conventional gender relations, as Baez's decision to pose for an antiwar poster in 1967 illustrates. Baez, who was married to draft resistance movement leader David Harris, and two other women in the poster sit provocatively beneath a caption proclaiming, "Girls Say Yes to Boys Who Say No." Baez initially had no inhibitions about lending herself to the cause in such a manner, but when she reflected on the incident twenty years later, she recognized that her actions, and the political ideals of the New Left, both produced and were produced by unequal gender relations. "I thought [the poster] was clever," Baez remembered. "The feminists hated it because it said 'girls' and because the women shouldn't have to answer to anyone, especially men, not yes or no. They wanted the poster taken off the market. I honest to God didn't know what they were talking about. But I kept running back and forth to the kitchen, fixing sandwiches and lemonade [for the male leaders of the draft resistance movement], while they nudged each other and looked in exasperation at the ceiling. David raved on about The Resistance and called women 'chicks.' "[70] Although Baez's status as a performer and her reputation for being something of a prima donna certainly gave her more privileges than many women enjoyed in the New Left, it is clear that most men were not interested in promoting gender equality.[71]

In fact, like many male radicals before them, New Left men were primarily concerned with protecting the interests of their brothers in arms, for even as they imagined a radical new America, they envisioned themselves as its future leaders. Activist Paul Potter recalled that those who entered the SDS "were highly motivated, success oriented, competitive men."[72] According to Piercy, these men soon became career radicals concerned with advancing through the ranks. In her view, local chapters "seem[ed] to act as fraternities," and because their members had renounced potentially lucrative careers, they were not about to allow women, whom Piercy identified as the movement's "part-time workers," to challenge their hegemony. Within the movement, relationships between men and women were based on a "master-servant" model that was not seriously questioned until the late 1960s. "Men in this society," she wrote, "reinforce each other's acted-out manhood in so many rituals, from which the man who truly treats women as his equals will be excluded."[73] When men refused to protect the interests of their brothers, when they relinquished the privileges of manhood, they severed the fraternal bond.

Issued in 1962, the SDS's "Port Huron Statement" articulated its politics in male terms, calling for "fraternity," "human brotherhood," and the development of "personal links between man and man." These word choices played themselves out not only in the political structures of the SDS but in sexual relations as well.[74] The promiscuous heterosexuality of the New Left, suggests Todd Gitlin, consummated a collectivist ethos based on an idealized love and to an extent masked "the homoerotic implications of male bonding" that in many ways drove the movement.[75] By sharing the same sexual partners, male revolutionaries in effect shared their sexuality with other men, cementing the bonds that united them in brotherly love.[76] Gitlin intimates that the activities of men-promoting-the-interests-of-other-men and men-loving-men were perhaps linked more closely than his fellow radicals recognized.

The language of homosociality and homoeroticism extended into the folk song movement. Dylan celebrated male friendship in such songs as "Bob Dylan's Dream" (1963), and Tom Paxton, another of "Woody's children," explored the homosocial relations of political organization in more detail on his album *Rambling Boy* (1964). Another of Guthrie's self-conscious descendants, Paxton presents topical songs that merge the political concerns of the New Left with those espoused by Guthrie.[77] The comic "Daily News" ridicules a media that, by blindly supporting U.S. policy on Vietnam, carried its readers "right along to Never Never Land." "What Did You Learn in School Today?" similarly questions an educational system that taught its students that their country was "always right and never wrong." Concerned with working-class issues, "Job of Work" and "Standing on the Edge of Town" describe the effects of automation on employment and reinscribe masculine constructions of labor, while "A Rumbling in the Land" connects the plight of white working-men to those of an African American, a blacklisted coal miner, and an air force pilot, suggesting that in the 1960s "a great flood [of revolution] is a risin' fast."[78]

Paxton accompanies his radical politics with cloying songs that idealize same-sex relations between men. Echoing both Whitman and Guthrie, the narrator of "Rambling Boy" travels with a comrade who "was a man and a friend always," adhering to the strict codes of manliness by sticking by the narrator in the toughest of times and expressing little concern for money. To be sure, the narrator's "rambling boy" refuses to subordinate his loyalty to his own financial well-being. When the two men inquire about work and their prospective employer says he can hire only one of them, the rambling boy replies that he and the narrator would panhandle before they would sever their union. Death, however, finally forces the two comrades to part; in the third verse, we learn that sickness takes from the narrator his only friend. A painfully mawkish final verse reveals the narrator's longing to reunite with the rambling boy in the afterlife, a hope that punctuates the selection's intense homosocial desire. Simply put, "Rambling Boy" is a love song that contains and expresses a homoeroticism that permeated the work of socially engaged artists from Whitman to Traubel, Hughes to Guthrie.[79] The New Left and its folksingers may not have publicly advocated or participated in homosexual behavior, but as both the SDS's language of brotherly love and Paxton's lyrics indicate, the terms in which members of the New Left articulated their collective social vision easily slipped into the rhetoric of homosociality and homoeroticism, a rhetoric that continued to marginalize women.

LEFT ALONE

Dylan's 1965 tour of Great Britain not only provides insight into the sexual politics of the folk revival but also reveals how individualism played itself out in his art. No longer the folksinger of *Freewheelin'* or *The Times They Are A-Changin'*, Dylan shed his workshirt and blue jeans for shades and black leather, retreating from the social world and taking refuge in the myth of the great artist. By 1964, he categorically renounced his commitment to New Left politics, telling Phil Ochs that topical songs were "bullshit, because politics is bullshit. It's all unreal. The only thing that's real is inside you. Your feelings." [80]

Such remarks rejected the collective values to which he and Baez had committed themselves. Rather than engaging in politics, Dylan reacted to the threat of nuclear war, increasing commercialism, and other social maladies by doing what Emerson and Whitman had done before him: he identified the individual as a moral and creative force that could resist the injustices perpetrated by a morally bankrupt society. His politics did not seek to protect the rights of a particular race or class but assailed society for erecting artificial barriers that deprived individuals of their rights. In fact, one of the criticisms he leveled against such liberal organizations as the Emergency Civil Liberties Committee, which in 1963 gave him its Tom Paine Award, was that they tried to convince him to "look at colored people as colored people," something that Dylan, at least rhetorically, refused to do. "I know [the people of SNCC] on another level besides civil-rights campaigns. I know them as friends," he explained, insisting that they were more than "respectable Negroes," more than mere types.[81] Even when Dylan addressed racial or class issues in his music, he demonstrated the ways in which social injustice affected individual lives. "How many roads must a man walk down / Before you call him a man?," he asked, refusing to identify his subject as an African American.[82] The titles of some of his songs reveal his predilection for defending the civil liberties of individuals. "The Lonesome Death of Hattie Carroll," "The Ballad of Hollis Brown," "The Death of Emmett Till," and "Who Killed Davey Moore?" all suggest that their protagonists' misfortunes were brought about by

Bob Dylan plugs in at the Newport Folk Festival, 1965.
Copyright © by Diana Davies/ Smithsonian Folklife.

arbitrary social forces that curtailed their individual freedom. "I hate injustice, that's why I sing about racial discrimination and freedom," remarked Dylan in 1965. "I preach for people to be able to do the things they want."[83]

A sense of equality backed Dylan's politics, but he ultimately subordinated the egalitarian goals of the "Movement" to the ideal value of personal freedom, largely because he could not "have people sit around and make rules for" him to follow.[84] Like Guthrie, he aspired to greatness and recognized that any ideology, no matter how progressive its politics, could become tyrannical. Although Dylan's individualism contained hints of Whitman and Guthrie, it had also been touched by the French existentialist Albert Camus, who insisted that amid the chaos and absurdity that defined modern existence, the categories of truth and morality, once thought to be timeless and objective, were subject to individual interpretation and evaluation.[85] Such values as freedom and equality were not natural or universal but selectively administered and enjoyed. Seeking to break free of the "unreal" social constructions that shackled his life and his thoughts, Dylan attempted to create an authentic or "real" existence and art that somehow stood apart from the fear, disorder, and dread he saw around him.

For Dylan, creation was revolution. His complex and cryptic lyrics may not have advocated collective politics, but they challenged the conventions of popular music and the limitations of language and, as a scene from *Don't Look Back* reveals, rethought the construction of reality itself. Interviewed by an unsuspecting editor from *Time* magazine, a brusque Dylan deconstructs the reality that such publications create and ridicules the social interests they represent. He argues that the journalist has "too much to lose by printing the truth" in his magazine because doing so would alienate the particular "class" of people who read it. When asked to define the truth, Dylan retorts that it is

> a plain picture of, let's say, a tramp vomiting, man, into the sewer. And you know, and next door to the picture, you know, Mr. C. W. Jones, you know, on the subway going to work, you know, any kind of picture. Just make some sort of collage of pictures which [*Time* does not] do. . . . There's no ideas in *Time* magazine, there's just these facts. Well, you know, which too are switched because even the article which you are doing, the way it's gonna come out, don't you see, it can't be a good article. Because, the guy that's writing the article is sitting in a desk in New York, he's not, he is not even going out of his office.[86]

Dylan created his reality within the same mass media he criticized, but he nevertheless declared that the truth was up for grabs; it certainly could not be found in a prepackaged news story. Throughout 1965, an irreverent Dylan resisted attempts to categorize his work and continued to assault journalists and their manufactured reality. To the often-posed question "Do you think of yourself primarily as a singer or a poet?," he variously replied, "I'm not a folk singer," "I'm not a pop singer," "I'm just a guitar player," "I'm just an entertainer," and "I think of myself more as a song and dance man."[87] When a reporter asked, "What is your real message?," he responded, "Keep a good head and always carry a lightbulb."[88] Politically, his brash individualism and absurdist statements were two-faced: they rejected the collective ethos of the New Left but supported the movement's efforts to redefine reality. What better way to delegitimate the social order than to suggest not only that it is unjust but also that it is unreal and therefore subject to reconfiguration?

Through his virtuosic lyrics, Dylan sought to play out the Camusian assertion that "the theme of permanent revolution is . . . carried into individual experience."[89] As songs such as "Mr. Tambourine Man" indicate, he was more interested in exploring the self than the social. "Then take me disappearin' through the smoke rings of my mind," sang Dylan in a line that many listeners read as a reference to marijuana use. The musician preferred to "forget about today until tomorrow,"[90] an attitude that Baez, who proclaimed her political commitments vociferously if not self-righteously, found outrageous. She maintained that Dylan "criticizes society and I criticize it, but he ends up saying there's not a goddamned thing you can do about it, so screw it."[91]

No longer interested in political movements, Dylan infuriated much of the Old Left. Indeed, after he replaced his acoustic guitar with an electric guitar at the 1965 Newport Folk Festival, Jim Rooney observed in *Sing Out!* that "Bob is no longer a Neo–Woody Guthrie. . . . The highway he travels now is unfamiliar to those who bummed around during the Depression. . . . 'The people' so loved by Pete Seeger are 'the mob' so hated by Dylan."[92] Because the New Left also disparaged the racist and conformist behaviors of "the mob," Dylan continued to inspire its collective politics. "It didn't matter that Dylan's lyrics, for example, were celebrations of strictly private experience," observed Gitlin. "By playing the music together we transformed it into a celebration of our own collective intimacy, love, hilarity. . . . The point was to open up a new space, an *inner* space, so that we could *space out*, live for the sheer exultant point of living."[93] In 1965, Dylan's work was still profoundly political, but his were not the politics of Woody Guthrie. Although Dylan initially embraced the idea of the working-class hero, his existential pose and self-consciously artistic lyrics ultimately separated him from the class of people Guthrie claimed to represent.[94] Nevertheless, Dylan was largely responsible for circulating Guthrie's image in various guises, for recovering his politics and popularizing them among a new generation of radicals. The New Left's appropriation of the Dust Bowl Balladeer did not, however, go unchallenged. As a decade of political turmoil drew to a close, another audience tried to transform him into the bard of American patriotism.

The Politics of Cultural Memory

n 1971, Guthrie's fellow traveler and *Broadside* editor Gordon Friesen observed that his hero's political reputation was once again
being defanged by journalists, politicians, filmmakers, and folk-
lorists. Committed to its hard-boiled leftism, *Broadside* unsuccessfully tried to counter such efforts. Modifying an excerpt from
Vladimir Lenin's *State and Revolution* (1918), Friesen wrote that "the
bourgeoisie and the opportunists . . . are cooperating in this work
of adulterating (Guthrieism). They omit, obliterate, and distort the revolutionary side of (his) teaching, (his) revolutionary soul. They push to the
foreground and extol what is, or seems, acceptable to the bourgeoisie."[1]
Such sensational remarks were aimed at a number of developments that
occurred throughout the mid- to late 1960s. Music publisher Howie Richmond, who had obtained the rights to many of Guthrie's songs after the
Weavers' success, recognized that the poetic landscapes of "This Land
Is Your Land" and "Pastures of Plenty" could bring more commercial
success than union songs and encouraged popular performers to record
them. Determined to secure the financial future of Guthrie's biological
children, the Guthrie Children's Trust Fund welcomed such business ven-
tures. Seeking to expand its namesake's audience, it published various
biographical articles as well as a collection of Guthrie's poems and writings entitled *Born to Win* (1965). Within three decades, the Okie's work
was being employed on behalf of companies with much larger advertising
budgets than the Model Tobacco Company. By the 1990s, both the Ford
Motor Company and Anheuser-Busch would use "This Land" in national
campaigns.[2]

As Guthrie became increasingly popular, journalists and scholars alike
began to emphasize his optimism and individualism at the expense of his
radicalism. John Greenway's *American Folksongs of Protest* (1953) initiated
this critical drift during the McCarthy era, depicting Guthrie as a naive
country bumpkin who was unwittingly and unwillingly manipulated by
the Communist Party. Interviewed for *Northwest Magazine*, Marjorie Guth-

rie further downplayed his ties to communism, insisting that her former husband never joined the party because he "was too much of an individualist."[3] Liberal journalist Nat Hentoff and *Readers' Digest* both spoke about "the rebel" who inspired Bob Dylan and Phil Ochs, but they failed to mention Guthrie's left-wing sympathies.[4] By the late 1960s, Guthrie's reputation seemed to revert to what it had been before the New Left rediscovered his politics. He was a symbol of personal rather than political rebellion.

Two eulogies that appeared in 1966 continued to push Guthrie away from the Left. To recognize his work with the Bonneville Power Administration (BPA), the Department of the Interior named an electrical substation after the folksinger and presented him with a Conservation Service Award. Secretary Stewart Udall's citation further lauded him for his artistry: "You sang that 'this land belongs to you and me,' and you sang from the heart of America that feels this about its land. You have articulated, in your songs, the sense of identification that each citizen of our country feels toward this land and the wonders which it holds. You brought to your song a heart as big as all outdoors, and we are fortunate to have music which expresses the love and affection each of us feels, though we are unable to express it so eloquently, toward this land."[5]

According to Udall, Guthrie was a patriot rather than a radical, a conservationist concerned with the aesthetics of nature rather than a voice in the struggle for social justice. An advertisement in a 1966 issue of the trade publication *Music World* echoed Udall's assessment, proclaiming Guthrie "an influence on America as strong as Walt Whitman." The "nation's most influential folk writer" had "an emotional involvement with America that is pervasive, universal, timeless," read the copy. "Sometimes outraged, always optimistic, never despairing Woody's thousand songs tell a story of patriotism and fierce national pride." The leftist movements in which Guthrie participated certainly leaned on the rhetoric of patriotism, but the meaning of nationalism carried a much different connotation in 1960s America than it did during the Popular Front. As Vietnam War protests escalated, those who pledged allegiance to the flag tended to support military action and the politics of the "establishment."

Much as had been the case with Whitman in the early twentieth century, the conflicts that Guthrie experienced in his own life—his desire to both run from the world and change it—have played themselves out in the interpretations of his work that have been advanced from the late 1960s through the 1990s. What function has Guthrie come to serve in

"...an influence on America as strong as Walt Whitman."

Advertisement promoting Woody Guthrie in Music World, July 1966.
Broadcast Music, Inc. (BMI).

America's cultural memory? Why has he been canonized as a poet who is mentioned in the same breath as Whitman? Given Guthrie's political radicalism, the history of the folksinger's reputation is a curious one. As Cary Nelson argues in his study of canon formation, the process by which artists and their works are remembered or forgotten, celebrated or disparaged, is contingent upon the cultural values and political concerns of a particular historical moment. The cultural arbiters of Cold War America disparaged art that engaged politics and validated those that romanticized "individual achievement." [6] In this milieu, class-conscious works that represented the suffering brought about by social injustice were rarely recognized for their artistic merit—especially when America was fighting a war against communism.

If artists addressed social and political issues, they were, for the most part, valued insofar as they embraced what Nelson calls "the ruling ideology of political indecision lived out in uneasy inner anguish and external inaction." [7] If artists' politics extended beyond self-reflection, if they posed political problems in structural rather than moral terms, their work would likely be dismissed as propaganda. An affiliate of the Communist Party and a proponent of collective politics, Guthrie presented a serious challenge to these criteria. In order for Guthrie to be recognized as one of America's finest artists, to be mentioned alongside Whitman, who since the 1930s had become one of the darlings of conservative New Critics, his reputation would have to be made more agreeable to Cold War tastes. Following the press, other branches of the popular culture industry were quick to bend him in this direction. The motion picture *Bound for Glory* and the various musical tributes held in Guthrie's honor since 1968 have emphasized his artistic ability and iconoclasm, making certain that he would be remembered as radical, but not too damned radical.

BOUND FOR HOLLYWOOD

Seeking to introduce his former client to "the largest possible audience," manager Harold Leventhal took Guthrie's legend to Hollywood in the early 1970s and coproduced the motion picture *Bound for Glory* (1976).[8] The road to production was a difficult one, however, principally because Leventhal was very particular about how Guthrie's story was told. A close personal friend of the Guthrie family, Leventhal felt a tremendous sense of responsibility to them and "preferred *no* film" to one that was "inauthentic, glossy, or dishonest." Because he understood that Guthrie's political commitments were an essential part of his life and work, he wanted to emphasize the historical period in which the musician lived rather than focusing on the artist "as a solemn figure." Leventhal vetoed four scripts before he settled on Robert Getchell's, and after landing director Hal Ashby, whose blockbuster *Shampoo* (1975) gave him considerable clout in the industry, he faced the problem of casting someone to play the hero. Robert De Niro, Dustin Hoffman, and Jack Nicholson were considered, and Kris Kristofferson, Johnny Cash, Bob Dylan, and Arlo Guthrie expressed interest in the part. But Ashby chose David Carradine, whose father, John, had played Preacher Jim Casy in John Ford's *Grapes of Wrath* (1940). Although critics correctly noted that Carradine's Guthrie could have been more passionate, they generally commended his performance and the film as a whole. Bankrolled by United Artists for the then princely sum of $7 million, *Bound for Glory* did not attract large audiences but earned six Academy Award nominations, including one for best picture.[9]

Despite Leventhal's intentions, the film does much more to promote Guthrie as a singular, great artist than it does to represent his political commitments, a problem that concerned Guthrie when the autobiography on which it is loosely based was published in 1943. Guthrie originally entitled his manuscript *Boomchasers*, and when editor Joy Doerflinger renamed it *Bound for Glory*, the author wrote in a concerned letter to Marjorie that it "sounds like I personally am bound for glory, but . . . really it is the common people who are." The book was, of course, bombastic if not solipsistic but maintained a delicate balance between promoting collective politics and mythologizing the individual, a balance that, in Guthrie's view, some of the reviewers overlooked. He worried that critics had spent too much time commenting on "the rambling and gambling of a wild hobo" rather than focusing on the "lick at bad politics and racial barriers that [he] really wanted to hit."[10] "You bragged on me and my guitar and my songs, but you didn't mention the fact that all of my songs are work songs," he reiterated in the *New York Herald Tribune*. "I had the notion that my book, in a jerky way, told at least a part of how our country is jerking itself out of its kinks and waking up above a whole mess of little silly arguments that's been keeping us split apart. . . . I ain't the main thing in my book—not me—but the people, all of them in the forty-eight states that I saw."[11]

Ashby and Getchell acknowledge that Guthrie took some licks at social problems such as poverty and injustice, but because they fail to explore how the political and cultural realities of the 1930s shaped these licks, they dehistoricize their subject and caricature his life, politics, and art. The film *Bound for Glory* follows Guthrie's life between the years 1936 and 1940, ending just as he leaves California for New York City, where, according to him, he did his most important cultural work. The subject's own opinion notwithstanding, Getchell explains that by focusing on these four years, the screenplay explores the "formative" period in which the folksinger began to write and perform topical songs. Rather than relying on Guthrie's "specious" autobiography, Getchell wrote an "original" script in which he "made up all the people except Woody and his first wife," Mary. His poetic license and his disregard for Guthrie's text create two major weaknesses in the film. First, Getchell never allows Guthrie to speak in his own words. Not once does Carradine read from Guthrie's voluminous writings, and Getchell rarely adapts these sources to fit the dialogue. Guthrie is thus depicted as a lonesome and silent traveler rather than a voracious reader, prolific writer, and politically engaged artist. In fact, the filmmakers never permit Carradine to sing one of his songs in its entirety and, as a result, interpret his rather complicated life only through his actions and experiences rather than his art and copiously expressed opinions.[12]

Second, the film is ahistorical. Not only does it omit Guthrie's involvement with the New York Left and invent characters when the real ones would do, but it refuses to address his politics in any significant way. Guthrie's antiracism is briefly acknowledged and his connection to working people is examined at some length, but the film does not consider the ideological commitments that so affected its subject. According to Getchell, Guthrie "was never a Communist *per se*" but simply visited migrant camps and asked workers, "What the hell are you doing? Picking fruit at 4 cents a bushel—does that make sense?"[13] Guthrie's writing and manuscripts, to which Getchell, Ashby, and Leventhal had access, tell a different story. Guthrie considered the day he joined hands with the Communist Party one of the most important days in his life. Marxism, he recalled, taught him "to look out over and across the slum section [or] a sharecropper farm and connect it up with the owner and the landlord and the guards and the police and the dicks and the bulls and the vigilante men with their black sedans and sawed off shot guns."[14]

The historical Guthrie wrote for *People's World* and attended Communist Party meetings, but in the film, his connection to communism is essentially dismissed. Getchell insisted that the "main thing [Guthrie] worked on was trying to help other people," and although this assessment has some validity and Guthrie's politics are sometimes ambivalent, the film reinforces a sense of romantic individualism.[15] The most important thing about the filmic Guthrie is not that he fought for social and economic justice but that he celebrated the American landscape and inspired all people to take pride in themselves and their individual accomplishments. Leventhal may have imagined that cinematographer Haskel Wexler's camera would record an entire social history and maintain the balance between Guthrie's political commitments and his brazen individuality, but throughout this two-and-a-half-hour production, the lens remains myopically focused on Guthrie, ensuring that his legend, rather than the causes for which he fought, was glory-bound.

Ashby begins to construct this heroic narrative in the opening scene. Dressed in a white shirt, khaki pants, and a broad-brimmed hat, Carradine resembles Whitman in the frontispiece to *Leaves of Grass*. He appears in the distance, sauntering through the dry, nearly deserted streets toward Wexler's camera, which immediately highlights the character's quirks and mystical abilities. The narration that introduces the film suggests that Guthrie's most important asset was his ability to make people feel good about themselves, to convince them, the film explains in a rare invocation of Guthrie's words, that they must never let anything get them "plumb down." A firm believer in this bit of folk wisdom, the celluloid Guthrie wastes little time lifting the spirits of those around him. His short walk through town brings him to a service station where three men are listening to a radio on which a Jimmie Rodgers imitator croons, "I'm going to California where the water tastes like cherry wine." Guthrie smirks with skepticism, and the gas station owner admits that he has considered joining the migrant train to California himself, a remark that opens discussion on the tough economic times the Depression and the dust storms have brought to town. Taken aback by their attitude, Guthrie tells his friends that they "sure are depressing" and seizes the next opportunity to give them respite from their worries.

This occasion presents itself when a well-fed customer drives into the gas station. The men quickly jump to their feet to admire his pristine new car, and its driver, amused by their interest, offers a dollar to anyone who can tell his fortune. Guthrie obliges and reveals that he is an astute judge of character if not quite a skilled seer. In a matter of seconds, he discerns from some rather obvious clues that the customer works for an oil company, takes his work seriously, and has a new invention but is uncertain how to market it. Riveted to Guthrie's response, the customer insists that his clairvoyant tell him what course of action he should take, but Guthrie, too wise to venture into territory he knows nothing about, insists that he is no "mind reader." The impressed customer pays Guthrie the sum he promised, praising him as the most accomplished fortune-teller he has ever patronized. Entertained by his performance, Guthrie's friends delight vicariously in his success and in the payment he receives for it.

Such praise inspires Guthrie to put out his shingle as a professional fortune-teller, over the protests of his wife, Mary (Melinda Dillon), who insists that his success was no more than "happenstance." Guthrie soon reveals, however, that his abilities enable him to do far more than simply divert the attention of his friends from their worries. In the next scene, he reluctantly accompanies two women to the home of a friend who, since the death of her daughter, has slipped into a nearly catatonic state. Noticing the cross the sickly woman wears around her neck, Guthrie asks his patient if she believes her daughter is in heaven, and when she nods in assent, he adroitly manipulates the language of Christianity, assuming the role of a preacher if not of Christ himself. He lays his hands on the woman's throat, induces her to drink water, and convinces her to recommit herself to life. By the time he leaves the house, his teary-eyed patient is on the mend, and her astounded friends offer Guthrie a payment he selflessly refuses.

Guthrie's mysterious powers and his compassion do not, however, pay the bills, and Mary criticizes him for not making enough money to feed their children. An embarrassed Guthrie retorts that "there ain't no use in harping on" him about their hard luck, but he is eventually shamed into trying to "make regular money" as a sign painter, an occupation for which he demonstrates considerable talent. But as the film illustrates, he has the impudent nature of an artist and fails miserably at this commercial enterprise, largely because he paints the signs according to his own designs rather than following those his customers submit to him. Ashby repeatedly underscores the point that Guthrie is an extraordinary individual who refuses to accept orders, especially those imposed by his family. In a scene that follows the one in which Mary berates him for not accepting his responsibilities, an emasculated Guthrie reasserts his manhood by going to a local bar and seducing a waitress. A second affair that occurs later in the film suggests that Guthrie often flouted the conventions of marriage, and although his actions are accurately represented as an expression of individualism and male privilege, the film does not address the connections he made between sexual and social reform.

Like the historical Guthrie, Carradine's never manages to bring his politics into the bedroom, as the handful of scenes that include Mary indicate. At Marjorie Guthrie's request, Ashby depicts the tremendous emotional suffering and economic hardship that Guthrie inflicted on his families. The effect of these scenes is minimized, however, by the fact that the remainder of the film lionizes Guthrie and excuses his behavior. Following a scene in which he and Mary have sex, a pensive Guthrie sits on his front porch, slowly and melodramatically playing the tune to "So Long, It's Been Good to Know You" on his guitar while he observes the surrounding shotgun shacks, empty of neighbors who had departed for California. With a nod, he conveys his intentions, and an orchestra picks up where his guitar stops, providing a mawkish backdrop to his preparations to leave his family. Seconds later, he runs from the house and hitches a ride as the melancholy score shifts into a glorious celebration of freedom. This triumphant music and the fact that for the next hour and twenty minutes Mary and the children disappear from the film force the audience to identify with Guthrie, not his family. Even in a later scene, in which Mary reprimands her husband for going out to change the world while leaving his family behind, Guthrie violently reacts to her nagging and justifies his work by insisting that he had to "touch the people." *Bound for Glory* accepts this explanation, suggesting that such behavior was a necessary, if unfortunate, part of Guthrie's politics.

During his trek to California, Guthrie hits some hard traveling that awakens his social consciousness, but the more tightly the film focuses on his political activities, the more blurred and ahistorical it becomes, particularly on racial issues. In the sequences that immediately follow his triumphant departure, Guthrie wanders along a hot, dusty road until he meets an African American man named Slim (Ji-Tu Cumbuka) who teaches him how to jump a freight train. Based on the first chapter of Guthrie's autobiography, this scene implies that Guthrie harbored no racist feelings toward blacks: he and Slim shake hands, strike up an easy if brief friendship, and look after each other in a fight that erupts in the boxcar. But whereas Guthrie's *Bound for Glory* sought to eradicate discrimination within a society that exhibited racism at every turn, Ashby's obliterates race as a social construct and obscures its history and the ways in which Guthrie addressed it.

As a result, the film ignores the important part that race played in defining Guthrie's politics. When he began his radio show on KFVD in California, Guthrie often made racist remarks on the air, but his repudiation of this behavior in 1937 marked an important moment in his ideological transformation. So too did his affiliation with the Communist Party, which provided a language and a forum through which he could articulate his egalitarian politics. Ashby's oversight of these developments leads him to represent racial discrimination as an individual rather than a social problem. Guthrie and Slim spend about fifteen minutes together on the train, but after vigilantes separate them, the hero does not interact with another African American for the remainder of the film. We never see Guthrie defy the politics of segregation by performing with black musicians, nor do we see him speaking out against Jim Crow laws. In fact, the only other reference to race comes when Guthrie sings "Deportee (Plane Wreck at Los Gatos)" before a well-heeled audience. Written in 1948, eight years after the period the film covers, "Deportee" addresses the racism that Mexican workers face, but because Carradine sings only one verse and one chorus of the song, its content is not clearly conveyed. The picture of Guthrie's racial politics that emerges in the film is more than a little fuzzy. Rather than depicting a man who underwent a serious ideological transformation to become a cultural worker who supported antiracist politics, Ashby merely implies that Guthrie was an individual with high moral standards who conducted his politics on a personal level. Guthrie did espouse his politics in his personal relations, but because the script does not allow Carradine to speak in Guthrie's words or sing his songs in their entirety, and because it does not situate him in a larger political movement, the film offers a piecemeal understanding of the musician at best.

The remainder of the film concentrates on Guthrie's career as a radio personality and his involvement with migrant workers, and although it considers his political commitments in this area a bit more carefully, it continues to dehistoricize them. After witnessing the murder of another hobo and experiencing a brush with death himself, Guthrie arrives in California, where he befriends the Johnsons, who, along with their newborn child, are searching the fruit orchards for a decent job. In a scene that recalls the Joad family's first entrance into a migrant camp in Ford's *Grapes of Wrath*, Guthrie and the Johnsons drive into a tent city, staring from the jalopy at the diseased and desperate faces of the weary inhabitants. "What the hell's going on here? How come all these people are living like this?," asks a disillusioned Guthrie. Johnson (Randy Quaid) replies that this camp is "the goddamn same as all the rest" and summarizes the employment practices of California fruit growers: the companies advertise more jobs than they can provide, and because a surplus of workers apply, the employers offer below-subsistence wages. Looking at his surroundings in disbelief, Guthrie remarks that "something oughta be done about this." Johnson replies that the migrants have talked about forming unions but that few families can afford to lose several days of work in a strike.

Guthrie's cultural politics begin to take shape when a fictitious guitar-playing union organizer named Ozark Bule (Ronny Cox) visits the migrant camp and uses music both to entertain and to politicize his audience. "I can see just by looking at you you haven't been doin' like I said and organizin'," he shouts before he sings Joe Hill's "Preacher and the Slave." Beneath the vigilant eyes of company police, Bule leads the campers in an evening of singing and dancing, encouraging Guthrie to sing some of his own songs before the police raid the event. A composite of Ed Robbin, Will Geer, Cisco Houston, Pete Seeger, and perhaps Alan Lomax, Bule enables the filmmakers to simplify Guthrie's political and intellectual growth and to develop the tension that drives the second half of the film.

Part musician, part promotion man, and part union organizer, Bule lands a job for Guthrie at a radio station and convinces him to use his music to organize migrant workers. This forked path presents Guthrie with a complex problem, however. Whereas Bule can easily separate his professional and political lives, Guthrie cannot and begins to perform his political songs on his radio show. When sponsors threaten to withdraw their support, the station manager insists that the musician provide him with a list of songs he plans to play for each show, and despite Mary's and Bule's requests that he comply, Guthrie refuses because he feels that doing so would compromise his political efforts. His concerns increase when, in an awkward and ineffectual scene, Johnson visits him at the radio station. Badly beaten by company agents who charged him on a picket line, Johnson asks Woody to continue to sing his topical songs "'cause ever'body's listenin'." Representing a tension that the historical Guthrie himself helped create, the film suggests that Guthrie the individual, not the union, is making the difference. The musician refuses to forsake his constituency, however. In the ensuing scene, the station manager again demands a copy of Guthrie's set list, which Guthrie surrenders but declines to follow. After defying his employer's orders, he leaves his job so that he might "touch the people."

Guthrie's life was defined by the contradictions that his love for individual freedom and his desire to forge the bonds of equality presented, and although the film is cognizant of this tension, it overemphasizes his individualism at the expense of his collective politics. The production offers scant evidence that Guthrie was part of a sustained political movement led by the Communist Party. He and Bule travel across the countryside to sing for children and talk to workers, but no one mentions their political affiliation, and even when the characters begin to articulate their radical politics, their speeches are always curtailed by violence or hostility. In fact, the only reference to communism that surfaces is an ephemeral and derogatory one made by a migrant worker at an organizational meeting. Two organizers try to convince a hall of men to strike against the fruit growers, and when a skeptical worker exclaims that the two speakers are "commies," the embarrassed leaders try to divert the crowd's attention back to their employer's greed in a manner that apologizes for their implied affiliation. Meanwhile, Guthrie, who has been writing furiously in the corner of the room, emerges to diffuse the tension and the discussion of ideology by performing "Union Maid." The crowd soon jumps to its feet to clap with the music, but when a riot breaks out, Carradine is once again prohibited from singing a song in its entirety. Ashby could have used this scene to dramatize the possibilities and liabilities that communism presented to migrant workers and to Guthrie but instead evades serious representation of political history and ideology.

The union hall scene makes a tenuous connection between Guthrie and the larger labor movement, but the sequence that follows his departure from the radio station all but severs that tie. Seconds after Guthrie fumes out of the station manager's office, the film cuts to a railroad yard, where Guthrie boards the boxcar that will send him glory-bound. Once he jumps the freight train, Wexler's camera begins to mythologize the hero. With both sides of the car open, Guthrie stands in the doorway holding a guitar, his body beautifully silhouetted against the orange sunset that shines through the open doorway on the far side of the train while the music to "Pastures of Plenty" comprises the soundtrack. This larger-than-life portrait, which romantically shows Guthrie braving the dangers and enjoying the beauty of the open road, cuts to a shot of Guthrie singing a verse of "Pastures of Plenty" at a migrant camp and soon returns to a long view of the train cutting across picturesque wheat fields and orchards. Guthrie now sits in the car writing "This Land," the camera tightly focused on his determined face as the setting sun forms a sort of halo around his head. More shots of the landscape follow before we arrive at a fruit-packing plant, where Guthrie sings a fragment of the prounion "There's a Better World A-Comin'." But again the emphasis is on Guthrie rather than the lyrics or the working conditions that inspired him. Confused, almost detached employees watch as company police beat Guthrie unconscious and smash his guitar. Rather than calling attention to the workers or their conditions, the scene extols Guthrie for his courage and tenacity, not for his politics.

The ending of the film continues to celebrate Guthrie the individual artist and to separate him from his Dust Bowl constituency and radical politics. In the penultimate sequence, Ashby relocates Guthrie's defiant Rainbow Room performance to Los Angeles, and when the musician walks out of the fictional swank hotel, he leaves Bule behind him and heads for New York City because it has "people" and "unions." As he departs, Odetta, Pete Seeger, Arlo Guthrie, and other performers sail into a triumphant rendition of "This Land," and the film cuts to Guthrie playing his guitar on a train that steams across a Whitmanesque landscape so breathtaking that it erases the image of the unsightly refugee camps from our memories. This, the closing of the film screams to its audience, is what America and Woody Guthrie are all about: determination, beauty, freedom. The scene is so powerful and mythologizing that it made even Ashby uncomfortable. "We don't want to make Woody a saint," he explained, "but sometimes it's hard, because when you hear one of the songs . . . We did the end of the picture, where he sits on top of the boxcar singing 'This Land Is Your Land,' and when I think about it, Jesus, it scares me." [16] Indeed, as the landscape rolls on, the music becomes subordinate to the voice of Will Geer, who reads from Guthrie's writings and constructs his old friend not as a common man but as an American hero whose brilliant artistic vision, as Udall had foretold, inspires listeners to take pride in our national landscape, in our country, and in ourselves: "I hate a song that makes you think that you're not any good! I hate a song that makes you think that you are just born to lose. Bound to lose. . . . I'm out to sing the songs that will prove to you that this is your world. . . . I am out to sing the songs that make you take pride in yourself and in your work." [17]

Although this passage contains vague references to Guthrie's radical politics, the Marxist origins of "This Land," and perhaps even the injustice represented in the film are submerged in musical eulogy. Country Joe McDonald, Judy Collins, the Weavers, Arlo Guthrie, and a host of other artists perform fragments of various Guthrie songs, honoring the author for his artistry, not his politics. Precisely in tune with the jingoistic fervor that swept America during its bicentennial year, this rousing medley affirms a faith in the individualism, freedom, and beauty that the rugged landscape represents. *Bound for Glory* does not honor Guthrie for his commitment to antiracism or the pursuit of social justice. Nor does it acknowledge that he envisioned a revolutionary sexual politics. Instead, the film honors this temperamental folk poet for his courage, patriotism, and ability to make us take pride in our own individuality. Woody Guthrie did represent all of these things, and to some extent, his bombastic rhetoric and relentless self-promotion are responsible for the myth the film presents. There was much more to this working-class hero, however, than met the camera's eye.

SINGING WOODY'S SONGS

Twenty years after the release of Ashby's *Bound for Glory*, the music video network VH-1 aired a report on a tribute concert sponsored by the Woody Guthrie Foundation and the Rock and Roll Hall of Fame. At the conclusion of the broadcast, the young reporter remarked, "Not only did [Guthrie] do protest stuff, but he was a great songwriter." [18] Like Ashby, she suggested that art and politics were separate discourses, that Guthrie's work could be neatly separated into didactic ballads and beautiful lyrics. Which type of Guthrie's songs has become most prominent in the canon of American music? Which songs are most often performed and hence remembered, and what do these songs say about the politics of American cultural memory? An examination of the tributes staged in Guthrie's honor reveals that his most famous songs are those that emphasize individual struggle and express their politics with ambivalence.

Since Pete Seeger led a cadre of musicians onto the stage of the Pythian in 1956, cultural workers have honored Guthrie in venues ranging from the Hollywood Bowl to Harvard University to Carnegie Hall, in cities ranging from Minneapolis to Austin to Okemah. They have recorded albums of Guthrie material on such labels as Vanguard, Folkways, Warner Brothers, and CBS. [19] Thirteen of these events, to which artists such as Bob Dylan, Arlo Guthrie, Bruce Springsteen, Ronnie Gilbert, and Bernice Reagon have contributed, have disseminated a more comprehensive representation of Guthrie's politics to a sizable national audience, but they too often expurgate the historical and ideological content of the original lyrics and struggle to balance collective politics and individualism. Perhaps the cultural productions most influential in shaping Guthrie's legacy, these tributes tend to honor the artist rather than the causes for which he fought, and consequently, they often devolve into eulogies that acknowledge the horrors of his disease. By the time the participants in these affairs join hands to close the show with a sing-along of "This Land," any radicalism they articulate is often swept away in a surge of patriotism, nostalgia, and sorrow. Although most of these tributes identify their hero as a radical, they make certain that audiences understand that he was not too damned radical.[20]

Seeking to disconnect Guthrie from communist affiliation, artists typically perform songs from Dust Bowl Ballads, many of which articulate a disdain for wealth and privilege in republican terms, which, as we have seen, means they "protest social and economic inequalities without calling the entire system into question."[21] "Do-Re-Mi," the most frequently covered of these ballads, expresses the core of Guthrie's populism by describing the disappointment that farmers face when they leave their dust-blown homes to start their lives anew in California, a place the song sardonically describes in Edenic terms. Hoping to find work in the fruit orchards, these families travel westward along Route 66, but when they arrive at the mythic "sugar bowl," they taste only the most bitter fruits. Whereas border patrols welcome families who have the wherewithal to vacation or purchase a house, they sometimes refuse to admit poorer farmers who will likely drain state or federal relief funds. The United States might pride itself on being a free nation, but, Guthrie intimates, freedom comes with a hefty price tag. "If you ain't got the do-re-mi" to purchase freedom in the form of property, then you are not afforded the material and civic privileges granted to the wealthier citizens of the country. As Whitman did before him, Guthrie castigates a society that makes arbitrary social distinctions based on wealth.[22]

"Pretty Boy Floyd," another favorite of Guthrie admirers, offers a similar critique. Written in the same vein as the outlaw ballad "John Hardy," this composition recounts the story of a man who lashes out at the social system by becoming an Okie Robin Hood. As Guthrie tells it, the legend begins one afternoon when Pretty Boy and his wife travel into town, where they are insulted by a deputy. To preserve his wife's honor, Pretty Boy murders the indecorous lawman, thus embarking on a career as a professional criminal. But despite the "life of shame" he pursues, Pretty Boy leads an honorable existence. With his illegally acquired wealth, he pays a poor farmer's mortgage, provides groceries to the unemployed on Christmas Day, and gives $1,000 bills to the kind folks who feed him. Pretty Boy might be a thief, but according to Guthrie, the crimes he commits are not as deceitful as those perpetrated by bankers and landholders, who execute injustices "with a fountain pen" and concentrate wealth in the hands of the few. In the process, these bankers subscribe to moral tenets that are far more shameful than Pretty Boy's. When Guthrie sings that an outlaw would not "drive a family from their home," he suggests that when bankers foreclose, they commit a legalized form of robbery and celebrates Pretty Boy's protest against it. Although the song glorifies its hero, Guthrie was careful to expose his limitations. "Something went haywire and Pretty Boy took to Outlawing," he explained. "He went to packing shooting irons, blowing his way into the banks where the peoples [sic] money was. Grabbed big sacks of it and give it to the poor folks all up and down the country. He had the right idea but the wrong system." [23] Like John Hardy, Pretty Boy was more than just another bad man, but in order to effect far-reaching and lasting social change, he would have to align himself with fellow workers and participate in a collective struggle. Because such explanations do not accompany the performances of this song in any of the tributes, however, "Pretty Boy" serves not as a sounding board for union politics but as a celebration of an individual's bravery and defiance. [24]

To be sure, the Dust Bowl ballads that tell tales of defiant individualism have been the most popular songs with performers who eulogize Guthrie. "Hard Travelin'," which romanticizes Guthrie's hard life of work and wander, has been performed at nearly every tribute, and variations of "Goin' Down That Road Feelin' Bad" and "Blowin' Down That Old Dusty Road," adaptations of a traditional African American song of faith and determination, are also regular selections. Included in just under half of the productions, "Jesus Christ" expounds populist ideas, extolling this "carpenter true and brave" for telling the rich to sell their belongings and give the proceeds to the poor. But for most of the forty years that tributes have honored Guthrie, entertainers have generally avoided the more ideological ballads "I Ain't Got No Home" and "Vigilante Man." [25]

Written in 1939, "I Ain't Got No Home," a reworking of the Carter Family gospel song "This World Is Not My Home," identifies the failed promises of the work ethic and introduces the possibility for collective politics. Like many Baptist hymns, "This World" teaches individuals to focus on their eternal rewards rather than on their lives on earth, insisting that "my treasures and my hopes are all beyond the blue." Anxious to be reunited with their deceased Christian brethren, the Carters proclaim that they "can't feel at home in this world anymore." This was a lesson a materialist such as Guthrie could not easily learn. [26] As he traveled throughout the Dust Bowl, he saw "another side to the picture" and suggested that the reason many people "can't feel at home in this world any more is mostly because [they] aint got no home to feel at." [27] Rather than singing of spiritual matters, the narrator of "I Ain't Got No Home" focuses on mundane hardships. After the bank repossesses his farm and his wife dies, he searches for economic opportunity only to discover that the deck is stacked against him:

Now I just ramble 'round to see what I can see,
This wide, wicked world is a funny place to be.
The gambling man is rich and the working man is poor.
And I ain't got no home in this world anymore.

As "Do-Re-Mi" suggested, those who have no capital to gamble are condemned to live as second-class citizens. But as this narrator describes the sense of displacement, isolation, and oppression he experiences, he begins to develop a consciousness of his class. Invoking the collectivist language of labor unions, Guthrie sings, "My brothers and my sisters are stranded on this road; / It's a hot and dusty road that a million feet have trod / Rich man took my home and drove me from my door." By using such class-conscious language, Guthrie identifies this farmer's plight as a social rather than an individual problem and begins to nurture a political vision that he sketches more clearly in "Vigilante Man." [28]

As the title suggests, "Vigilante Man" concerns the violence that self-appointed law enforcement officials committed against migrant workers who broke local vagrancy ordinances, rode freight trains illegally, or tried to organize labor unions. Much like the police in "I Ain't Got No Home," the vigilantes harass migrants, but Guthrie notes that these injustices occurred to a *class* of people that, if its members acted in concert, had the potential to transform the situation. Although songs such as "Pretty Boy Floyd" focus on the experiences and reactions of a particular individual, "Vigilante Man" represents the collective pain and suffering of migrant workers. When authorities discover the narrator and a group of other homeless men taking shelter in an "engine house," Guthrie describes the incident in collective terms: the police "come along and chased us out in the rain" and "herded us around like a wild herd of cattle." [29] By connecting his narrator to a group of people, Guthrie struggles, as he suggested in a letter to Alan Lomax, "to make one part of the community feel like they know the other part and one end of it help the other end." [30]

To criticize the immoral practices of corporate culture and promote an alternative politics, Guthrie retells the story of Jim Casy, a character in John Steinbeck's *Grapes of Wrath*, who is killed by company police for trying to organize farmworkers:

> Preacher Casey [*sic*] was just a workin' man
> And he said, "Unite all us workin' men!"
> They killed him in the river, some strange man.
> Was that your vigilante man?

It was. Because company agents refused to recognize a kinship with all human beings, Guthrie suggests, vigilantes enforced the code of a corporate order that placed profits ahead of people. As such, a vigilante man was often quite willing to "shoot his brother and his sister down," to suspend his moral obligations if he could improve his financial situation. If Americans were to construct a free and equal society, Guthrie implies, they would have to replace the acquisitive and self-centered ethos of capitalism with one that emphasized mutuality. For Guthrie, the basis of that ethos was firmly grounded in the language of union if not communism.[31]

The versions of "I Ain't Got No Home" and "Vigilante Man" that have been performed at tributes to Guthrie are noteworthy. At the 1968 concert at Carnegie Hall, African American folksinger Richie Havens gave new meaning to "Vigilante Man" by singing it in the wake of the civil rights movement, a performance that hip-hop artist Michael Franti, then with the group Disposable Heroes of Hypocrisy, echoed nearly twenty-five years later. When Franti performed this ballad of police brutality at a 1992 tribute in New York City's Central Park, the images of the Rodney King beating still emblazoned on the minds of his audience made his performance quite compelling. Whereas Havens and Franti refashioned this composition in a manner that was consistent with Guthrie's racial politics and appropriate to their historical moment, Ray Wylie Hubbard restored the song to its historical context. At a Guthrie celebration staged in 1993 by the vibrant musical community of Austin, Texas, Hubbard arranged an imaginative medley of "Vigilante Man" and "Jesus Christ" to emphasize Guthrie's radicalism.

Although the Havens rendition was originally included on the Warner Brothers record *A Tribute to Woody Guthrie*, an all-star production that was well advertised when it was released in 1972, both Franti's and Hubbard's versions have been less accessible. Franti sang only for those who attended the 1992 concert, and Hubbard's rendition was included on *Pastures of Plenty: An Austin Celebration of Woody Guthrie* (1993), an album not circulated as widely as the Warner Brothers release. Nor did it reach as many fans as CBS Records' 1988 *Vision Shared* project, a tribute to Guthrie and Leadbelly on which Bruce Springsteen recorded both "Vigilante Man" and "I Ain't Got No Home."[32]

Springsteen, who became one of the most recognizable popular musicians with the success of *Born in the U.S.A.* (1984), undoubtedly reached much larger audiences than did Havens, Franti, and Hubbard combined. He performed both songs for the *Vision Shared* album and a documentary of the same title, which aired on the cable network Showtime and was subsequently released as a home video. Although Springsteen supported the efforts of labor unions during the Born in the U.S.A. Tour, the songs he recorded for this project deviated from the original texts in significant ways. Perhaps concerned that references to *The Grapes of Wrath* or organized labor would sound obscure or dated to his audience, Springsteen eliminated the verse about Preacher Casy in "Vigilante Man" and edited "I Ain't Got No Home" so that he did not use the collectivist language of "his brother and his sister." He was not, however, the first major pop star to alter these Dust Bowl ballads in such a manner. When Dylan performed "I Ain't Got No Home" at Carnegie Hall in 1968, he excised all references to collective experience and transformed the song from a class-conscious statement to an individualized country music lament.[33]

Whereas artists have revised the ideological verses of the Dust Bowl ballads, they have generally eschewed the more radical songs in Guthrie's repertoire altogether. "Union Maid," which proclaims its loyalty to organized labor, has been sung in less than half of the tributes, and union songs in general have been extremely unpopular.[34] It is striking that even artists who sing about working-class subjects, notably Springsteen and John Mellencamp, who also appeared on both *Vision Shared* projects, have almost wholly ignored the songs on *Struggle* (1976), an album Folkways re-released in 1990 based on "Woody's insistence that there should be a series of records depicting the struggle of working people in bringing to light their fight for a place in the America they envisioned."[35] In addition to "Hangknot," a topical song that protests lynching, the album features "1913 Massacre," a moving narrative about an incident in which company police incite a riot that kills seventy-three children at a union Christmas party, and "Waiting at the Gate," which blames a deadly mine collapse on corporate greed and negligence.[36]

The choice to deradicalize songs on *Dust Bowl Ballads* or not to perform certain compositions has as much to do with historical realities as it does with the predilections of the artist. Communism was an important cultural and political force in the 1930s and 1940s, but, stigmatized by Stalinism and McCarthyism, it was not tolerated in the post–World War II United States. Whether in the age of Joseph McCarthy or that of Ronald Reagan, who in the 1980s referred to the Soviet Union as "the evil empire," most Americans were unwilling to accept communists as their heroes, so it is not surprising that those who followed in Guthrie's footsteps were quick to dissociate him from the Communist Party and the labor movement in general. Unions no longer claim the number of members nor do they possess the political clout they had during the World War II era, in part because big business has exercised its power, in part because American popular culture celebrates rugged individualism and denigrates collective politics, in part because corrupt leaders in some large unions, notably the United Mine Workers and the Teamsters, betrayed the rank and file in the 1970s and 1980s. Even artists who remain committed to Guthrie's political vision would have difficulty convincing a constituency to embrace his ideology. The Left of which Guthrie was a part pursued the singular goal of economic justice, but the contemporary Left has splintered into identity groups that concentrate on issues such as environmental policy, affirmative action, gender equality, and rights for homosexuals. In this context, it is difficult to advance Guthrie's Marxism as a panacea for the nation's social ills.

As the world continues to retool Guthrie's legend in the light of changing political and cultural realities, what has he come to represent in America's cultural imagination? His legacy might be summarized by considering the two songs most often performed at the tributes, "Pastures of Plenty" and "This Land Is Your Land."[37] Composed in 1941, "Pastures of Plenty" was one of the twenty-six songs Guthrie wrote during the thirty-day period he was employed by the BPA. A champion of this federally funded program, Guthrie praised "Uncle Sam" for taking up this challenge to improve the lives of rural Americans. Many of the songs he wrote for the project, including "Pastures of Plenty," reflect an ambivalence toward his government, however. Although he was certainly disappointed by the ways in which politicians responded to the human suffering brought on by the Depression, he supported such government projects as the BPA, particularly when he viewed them in light of the fascist threat that loomed large in Europe. "Pastures of Plenty" was born of this tension. On one hand, it celebrates the dignity of labor and the beauty of a fecund landscape; on the other, it expresses resentment toward the wealthy farm owners who exploit the migrant labor force.[38]

To be sure, the migrants face hardship: their "poor hands" have "hoed" a "mighty hard row," and they have searched for work in the hot deserts and cold mountains. Without their labor, however, the "green pastures of plenty" would not yield such a bountiful harvest. "California, Arizona, I make all your crops," sings a proud narrator who confidently asserts his indispensable role in the production process. Indeed, he and his fellow agrarian workers are, to paraphrase the People's Party hymn "The Farmer Is the Man," the people who feed us all. They pick peaches and prunes, beets and hops, and even "cut the grapes from your vine / To set on your table your light sparkling wine." Guthrie declares that without labor the earth would not be so productive, but he understands that labor's centrality to the production process goes unrewarded if not unrecognized. Migrant workers do not share in the bounty of their harvest, nor do they share ownership of the land they work. In fact, they occupy a peripheral place in these plentiful fields, a point that Guthrie underscores by assigning ownership of property, beauty, and luxury to the employers for whom his subjects toil. His migrants live "on the edge of *your* city," work "all along *your* green valley," and "cut the grapes from *your* vine" to produce *your* wine. This land is yours but not mine, Guthrie's narrator implies.[39]

Despite their hard work and hard traveling, the migrants are locked out of an organic economy and inserted into what Whitman might call an unnatural social order based on exploitative employment practices and the vast accumulation of wealth. In this system of capitalist agriculture, workers are denied ownership of the fruits of their labor as well as the land, a predicament that leaves them doubly damned. They not only are deprived of the opportunity to derive their subsistence from the land but also are stripped of the natural democratic rights of freedom and equality that their homeland purportedly guarantees them. This oppressive situation prompts Guthrie to offer the possibility of collective action as a way to alter their circumstances. "We'll work in this fight," he sings in the penultimate verse, "and we'll fight till we win." But to what fight does he refer? Does he utter a battle cry for the labor movement? Does he mean that he will participate in the effort to build the Grand Coulee Dam? Or does he resolve to lend his energies to the fight against fascism? He probably intends to do each of these things, but perhaps because he was employed by the federal government when he wrote the song, his radicalism is vague and contained. "Pastures of Plenty" criticizes the social relations of capitalism, but the fact that the song was included on a film produced by the BPA in 1941 suggests that the condemnation must not have been perceived as too severe.[40] Indeed, the final verse obfuscates Guthrie's subtle critique:

> Well, it's always we ramble, that river and I,
> All along your green valley I'll work till I die;
> My land I'll defend with my life if it be,
> 'Cause my pastures of plenty must always be free.

Tom Paxton, who performed this song at the Carnegie Hall tribute, attempted to clarify Guthrie's politics by singing, "My land I'll defend from *corporate* greed," and although this line is in tune with Guthrie's sentiments, the conditions under which he wrote the song would not have permitted him to be so explicit.[41] "Pastures of Plenty" oscillates between resentment and celebration, but its final lines ring with a patriotic martyrdom and a description of a resplendent landscape that muddies Guthrie's political intentions. This migrant worker implies that America has always been a land where all men and women are free, and he is willing to work himself to death to keep it that way. In the end, this song sounds more like a celebration of the land and the work ethic than a condemnation of the economy it undergirds. Guthrie is on the side of the workingman, but he is also on the side of hard work.

"This Land Is Your Land," undoubtedly Guthrie's best-known composition, resonates with a more pronounced affirmation of America, and because it is customarily the final song performed at tribute concerts or included on compilations of Guthrie songs, it has played a prominent part in determining the meaning these productions ascribe to their hero. In what has become standard practice in concert celebrations, an artist usually performs one to three of his or her favorite Guthrie songs, perhaps accompanies another musician during his or her appearance, and then relinquishes the stage until all participants reassemble to lead the audience in a rousing, celebratory version of the song that journalist Colman McCarthy described as "singable, handclappingly lively, and populist."[42] Despite its Marxist origins, "This Land" is a jubilant anthem of affirmation that, when sung in a communal context, becomes, as it did in Ashby's film, an unfettered celebration of the artist who wrote it and the land it represents. In a Whitmanesque sweep from coast to coast, Guthrie walks "that ribbon of highway," admiring a beautiful landscape comprised of "diamond deserts" and "golden valley[s]." "Nobody living could ever stop" this determined traveler from "walking that freedom highway," from tramping the joyous open road of America. Even a no-trespassing sign cannot impede his progress because, as the triumphant refrain authoritatively declares, "this land was made for you and me."[43] It is so euphoric that in 1989 Colman McCarthy, resurrecting a similar campaign waged by Californian Jack Franklin in 1976, proposed that the song be adopted as the national anthem of the United States.[44]

Much like a Whitman poem, "This Land," at least as it is sung in a vast majority of the tributes, represents things not as they are but as the author thinks they should be. And also like a Whitman poem, its romantic vision, which tries to realize the promise of freedom and equality, is often mistaken as an assessment of current social realities rather than an interrogation of them. To be sure, few people know that Guthrie intended the song to serve as a Marxist corrective to Irving Berlin's "God Bless America," and although biographer Joe Klein, Harold Leventhal, and Arlo Guthrie have publicized this fact since 1980, the song is so widely known and so widely sung that their efforts have had little impact on public perceptions of it.[45] Because very few artists sing "This Land" in its entirety, it is virtually impossible to distinguish its patriotism from Berlin's or even from more recent jingoistic songs such as Lee Greenwood's "God Bless the U.S.A." Like any other nationalistic anthem, it uncritically proclaims the United States the land of freedom and equality and lends credence to Guthrie's reputation, in the words of Stewart Udall, as a legendary artist who expressed "the sense of identification that each citizen of our country feels toward this land and the wonders which it holds."[46]

In one verse that was far less optimistic, of course, the narrator wonders if America had made good on its democratic promise. Guthrie drew a line through these words in the original manuscript and never sang them in any of the versions of the song he recorded, a choice that suggests he may have intended the song to be a celebration rather than a criticism. But as the song became more popular near the end of his life, he worried that his original intentions might be lost and charged his son, Arlo, with preserving them. "I remember him coming home from the hospital and taking me out to the backyard, just him and me, and teaching me the last three verses to 'This Land Is Your Land' because he thinks that if I don't learn them, no one will remember," Arlo recalled.[47]

When Arlo was old enough to embark on his own artistic career, he was determined to carry his father's politics with him. His modified talking-blues "Alice's Restaurant" (1967), which catapulted him to national prominence, satirized the police and the draft board with a defiance, folksiness, and humor that must have made his father smile when he listened to it just weeks before his death.[48] A supporter of New Left politics, Arlo was especially interested in preserving the integrity of Woody's canon. As he rehearsed for the Hollywood Bowl tribute three years later, he sternly upbraided program director Millard Lampell, a former member of the Almanac Singers, for encouraging other performers to eliminate or modify the original verses of Guthrie's songs, notably "I Ain't Got No Home."[49] Determined not to compromise his father's intentions, in 1984 he recorded all of the original verses of "This Land" for the soundtrack to the documentary film, *Hard Travelin'*.

The suppression of the "lost" verses reveals an important component of Guthrie's politics as well as those of the artists who have celebrated his work. Like Whitman's, Guthrie's radicalism was often created and contained by his faith in American democracy. Indeed, his nationalism was especially pronounced and perhaps exaggerated in the years between 1940 and 1945, when he was submerged in a Popular Front culture that, in its attempt to defeat fascism, embraced Earl Browder and Franklin Roosevelt with equal enthusiasm. But as his performance on *Songs the People Sing* demonstrated, Guthrie did not accept America uncritically and, at times, stepped outside the rhetoric of nationalism and capitalism to imagine a social order that was quite different from the one in which he lived. As I have mentioned, the original manuscript of "This Land," his most celebrated and recognizably patriotic song, is one of the places where he makes this imaginative leap. As he sees hungry people standing in line to receive relief, he finds himself asking if America really was made for all of its citizens.

The scene contrasts sharply with the remainder of the song. Rather than basking in the radiant light in which the narrator had previously strolled, the people stand in a darkness cast not by the natural landscape but by a church steeple. Based on the pejorative opinions about organized religion that Guthrie articulated in "So Long" and "I Ain't Got No Home," this darkness suggests that religion encourages people to accept their earthly fate passively rather than working to change it. These hungry people wait for their relief in much the same way as they await the rewards of the afterlife. Their patience, unfortunately, breeds poverty. Despite their faith in individualism, independence, and the work ethic, these men and women have been unable to earn a decent living, a fact that compels Guthrie to ask a question Whitman could not. Maybe, he intimates, the social and political structures of American democracy cannot deliver freedom and equality. Maybe the great democratic experiment, despite its best intentions, had failed, and its goals, or at least its means of achieving them, needed to be radically rethought. Maybe, as he wrote in 1946, "the job to be done [was] to get this thing called socialism nailed and hammered up just as fast as we can. . . . This is the only job worth working on. . . . Socialism won't skip a single one of us. It'll not make hoboes nor bums nor dirty backdoor tramps out of any of us."[50]

Guthrie may have been able to extend his imagination outside the republican heritage, but those who have followed in his footsteps have not always recognized the totality of his vision. "He was a rebel and a radical," wrote Lampell in his script for the Carnegie Hall and Hollywood Bowl tributes. "He was against poverty and hunger, bigotry and bargain-basement justice, con artists, jackleg preachers, deputy sheriffs and FBI men. Against the comfortable sonsofbitches who pile up profit out of war."[51] But the Guthrie constructed in the tributes never expresses any doubts that the United States is or could be the land of freedom and equality. The artists who have participated in these affairs over the last five decades—Baez, Dylan, Springsteen, Havens, and Judy Collins, among others—have all used their music to address a variety of social and political issues, but under the persistent pressures of anticommunism and the demands of commercial recording careers, they too have sometimes removed Guthrie from his political context and circumscribed their own political and aesthetic imaginations in the process. They have identified important injustices in their music but have maintained an implicit faith, at least in the tributes, that although America may not yet be the land of freedom and equality, the structures to actualize this dream are firmly in place. Radical but not too damned radical, "Woody Guthrie and the ten thousand songs that leap and tumble off the strings of his music box" have become, as critic Clifton Fadiman wrote in 1943, a "national possession, like Yellowstone and Yosemite, and part of the best stuff this country has to show the world."[52]

In September 1996, however, Nora Guthrie, Woody's daughter and president of Woody Guthrie Publications, began a campaign to disseminate a more comprehensive and historical representation of her father by organizing "Hard Travelin': The Life and Legacy of Woody Guthrie," a two-day conference held at the Rock and Roll Hall of Fame in Cleveland, the cosponsor of the event. The conference assembled academics, music critics, and archivists to discuss such topics as Guthrie's racial and class politics and his influence on American music, and two concerts demonstrated some of the ways in which contemporary recording artists were using Guthrie in their work. The second of these concerts, held at Cleveland's Severance Hall, was particularly interesting because it demonstrated that in addition to being a seminal figure for artists who addressed class politics, Guthrie had also become a touchstone for musicians who sang about the politics of gender and sexuality.[53] Hosted by actor/director Tim Robbins, the Severance concert featured Ani DiFranco, British punk politico Billy Bragg, the Indigo Girls, David Pirner of Soul Asylum, Ramblin' Jack Elliot, Arlo Guthrie, Bruce Springsteen, and Pete Seeger. Although an upbeat version of "This Land" closed the performance, it was clear that these cultural workers intended to recover Guthrie's language of collectivity as well as his reputation for defiance.[54]

The Severance concert was not the first tribute in which topical singers adapted Guthrie's material to advocate women's rights. In 1982, former Weaver Ronnie Gilbert, performing "Union Maid" at a concert staged at the Smithsonian Institution's annual Festival of American Folklife, advised her female listeners to "break out of the mold that you've been sold" and "fight for women's rights."[55] Guthrie's concept of gender equality may have done little to lead this fight during his lifetime, but a handful of his writings lend themselves to feminist concerns. As Tim Robbins introduced Ani DiFranco at Severance Hall, he read a passage from one of Guthrie's works that urged women to "dance out to sing equal."[56]

This passage was a particularly appropriate one to welcome the outspoken DiFranco to the stage. Concerned that major recording studios might temper her lyrics about homosexual love and her caustic songs about sexism and class, DiFranco had danced out of the pop mainstream to form her own company, Righteous Babe Records, in 1990. "I want to base my career in a community, not a corporate system based on greed and amassing fame," explained the musician, who was born in 1971. Her dozen albums, including two that adapt the poetry and writings of Industrial Workers of the World music legend Bruce "Utah" Phillips, express an uncompromising feminist politics that defy conventional constructions of sexual identity. "I personally have a great irreverence toward . . . those labels—queer, straight, bi[sexual]," she explained to Ray Rogers of Out magazine. "For myself, it's always been like, label-shmabel—make me an offer!" DiFranco's outspoken sexual politics have made her popular with a variety of audiences, including gays, lesbians, and bisexuals, and have been expressed at such events as a 1997 concert that commemorated the twenty-fifth anniversary of the Roe v. Wade Supreme Court decision.[57]

DiFranco opened the Severance concert with Guthrie's "Do-Re-Mi" and then, in accordance with the guidelines Nora Guthrie presented to all of the participants, performed two selections from her own material that were written "in the spirit of Woody Guthrie."[58] "Not a Pretty Girl" merges Guthrie's disdain for wealth with a critique of gender constructs. She proclaims that most people of her generation "wouldn't be caught dead working for the man" and suggests that instead they might take up cultural work that will alter the patriarchal relations of the political economy. A self-described "patriot" who is "fighting the good fight," she disavows the constructs of beauty and helplessness that confine women's lives, declaring that she is neither a "pretty girl" nor a "damsel in distress." DiFranco does not need to be carried away by the mythical knight in shining armor and defiantly orders the male "punk" who has taken her in his arms to unhand her. Contrary to social conventions, this woman is quite capable of making it "on her own," a phrase that serves as the acronym for the toll-free telephone number of her fan hotline.[59]

Like DiFranco, Amy Ray and Emily Saliers, who formed the Indigo Girls while they were students at Emory University in 1983, recorded under their own label until they signed with Epic Records in 1988. Extremely popular among lesbians ranging in age from their teens to their forties, the Indigo Girls, both of whom have declared their homosexuality, have engaged in cultural politics in a variety of ways: in 1991, they contributed to *Tame Yourself*, a compilation that benefited People for the Ethical Treatment of Animals; in 1993, they recorded "I Don't Want to Talk About It" for the soundtrack to *Philadelphia*, the Jonathan Demme film about a gay man with AIDS; and in 1995, they organized Earth Jam, a concert held in Atlanta that promoted environmental awareness.[60]

In their Severance Hall performance, they covered two songs from Guthrie's catalog: the traditional folk song "Gypsy Davy" and "Ramblin' Round Your City." Perhaps the most interesting song they performed, however, was "This Train Revisited," a reworking of Guthrie's version of "This Train Is Bound for Glory." Like Guthrie's train, the Indigo Girls' traveled in the 1940s, but rather than heading for the California coast, their boxcars filled with "gypsies, queers, and David stars" were bound for the concentration camps and gas chambers of Nazi Germany.

Forced to wear pink triangles, which have come to serve as a symbol of sexual identity in gay communities, homosexuals were rounded up along with Jews, gypsies, and the infirm to be executed by German soldiers and experimented on by doctors. As the narrator of the song describes the mountains of "skin and bone" and the outpouring of blood that filled these sites of human destruction, she echoes "Vigilante Man" when she asks the perpetrators of these acts if they "belong to the human race." Proclaiming that this railroad car carried her "sisters" and "brothers," she invokes the language of collectivity and intimates that although the human "potential" that these railroad travelers represented is forever gone, memories of their hard travels—and Guthrie's—will continue to inspire cultural workers to make certain that their train remains "bound for glory." Much like the first chapter of Guthrie's autobiography, "This Train Revisited" imagines a utopian world in which brothers and sisters of all ethnicities, sexual orientations, and religions—"gypsies, queers, and David stars"—might one day arrive at the promised land of freedom and equality. Other tributes, notably those staged at Carnegie Hall and the Hollywood Bowl, have identified the sexual themes of Guthrie's work, but none has suggested, as did that of the Indigo Girls, that his sexual and social politics were related.

Some of the artists at the Severance Hall concert took Guthrie's politics in new directions, but others reclaimed his labor radicalism. Elliot Adnopoz, who forty years earlier had attached himself to Guthrie and mimicked his every move, appeared under his stage name Ramblin' Jack Elliot and sang the moving labor ballad "1913 Massacre" in a style eerily reminiscent of his idol. This venerable folksinger was preceded by Billy Bragg, who in 1985 founded Red Wedge, an affiliation of pop stars who used their music to campaign for Labor Party politics. A student of American folk and labor music, Bragg adapted Florence Reece's "Which Side Are You On?" to sing in support of the 1984 coal miner's strike in Great Britain.[61]

Bragg's prolabor performance included "Unwelcome Guest," a tribute to union organizers that, along with the unremarkable "Walt Whitman's Niece," was one of fifteen previously unpublished Guthrie lyrics that Bragg and the American band Wilco set to music on the album *Mermaid Avenue* (1998). He augmented his set with "Farmer-Labor Train," an ideological jingle that Guthrie wrote for Henry Wallace's 1948 presidential campaign. Sung to the tune of "Wabash Cannonball," this song recalls the geographic sweep of "This Land," but rather than focusing on the beauty of the landscape, it is more concerned with the workers who populate it. As this train travels "from the high Canadian Rockies to the land of Mexico," it welcomes miners, farmers, sailors, and, perhaps most important, "folks of every color" to ride the rails to the glory of a working-class government. Echoing the preface to the 1855 *Leaves of Grass*, Guthrie and Bragg imagine a day when a train "full of union men" pull into Washington, D.C., and assume their rightful place in the halls of Congress. By selecting this song, Bragg made his hero more damned radical than he had been in quite some time.[62]

The reclamation of Guthrie's collectivist labor politics continued when Springsteen, the performer around whom the show centered, took the stage. If, as I have suggested, the importance of the collectivist impulse was submerged in the interpretations of "Vigilante Man" and "I Ain't Got No Home" that Springsteen recorded in 1988, it was clearly pronounced in the six-song set he performed at this production. Eight years earlier, Guthrie's references to *The Grapes of Wrath* may have seemed too arcane to Springsteen, but with the release of *The Ghost of Tom Joad* (1995), a collection of narratives about the working class and migrant farmworkers, it was clear that this novel was now central not only to his understanding of Guthrie's cultural politics but also to the formulation of his own.

Springsteen opened his performance with Guthrie's "Tom Joad," a ballad based on Steinbeck's protagonist that condenses the novel to a mere seventeen verses. Rather than editing the language of labor unions from the original text as he did on *Vision Shared*, however, Springsteen enthusiastically embraced Preacher Casy's words, singing, "Us working folks has got to stick together." As Springsteen ended the song, he clearly supported the communal impulse that both Steinbeck and Guthrie nurtured in their work. Paraphrasing Joad's words, he speculates that "everybody might be just One Big Soul" and resolves to dedicate his life to waging war "wherever men are fighting for their rights."[63] In case the audience missed the point, Springsteen reiterated it at the end of his performance. Guthrie's songs, he suggested, were carefully poised on a "spiritual center" that "took you out of yourself" and "got you thinking about your neighbor in some sense." Simply put, his work insisted that "salvation isn't individual . . . [that] maybe we don't rise and fall on our own."[64] Nearly a century and a half after Whitman wrote *Leaves of Grass* and more than fifty years after Guthrie sang "Tom Joad," Springsteen sought to resolve the conflict between individual freedom and social equality by relocating the tradition of working-class heroism to the 1980s and 1990s. Although Springsteen was perhaps the most radical of the American musicians at the Severance performance, his efforts to reclaim Guthrie's political vision were, as we shall see, ultimately circumscribed by the tradition he so enthusiastically and successfully embraced.

IV GHOSTS OF HISTORY

Springsteen and the Burden of Tradition

n August 1974, Bruce Springsteen entered 914 Studios in Blauvelt, New York, to take aim, he recalled twenty years later, at making "the greatest rock 'n roll record ever."[1] At the time, the twenty-five-year-old musician was under tremendous pressure to produce a commercially successful album. His first two releases, *Greetings from Asbury Park, N.J.* (1973), and *The Wild, the Innocent, and the E Street Shuffle* (1973), both had received a warm critical reception, but their disappointing performance in the marketplace and the musician's failure to comply with the two-albums-per-year clause in his contract prompted Columbia Records to question his viability as a popular entertainer.[2] The material Springsteen recorded for *Born to Run* (1975), however, convinced executives that the time was right to cash in on their investment, so they reembraced the man they had once touted as the "New Dylan" and bankrolled a media blitz that landed the little-known musician on the cover of *Newsweek* and *Time* in the same week.[3] The press responded to the publicity campaign with generous doses of hyperbole. *Newsweek* proclaimed Springsteen the "new high priest of rock," a "messiah," and Greil Marcus of *Rolling Stone* praised the "extraordinary dramatic authority that [was] at the heart of" the album and insisted that *Born to Run* was "what rock & roll is supposed to sound like."[4] Robert Ward of *New Times* echoed their enthusiasm. For him, this "tough," "democratic" street "punk" was the type of American "hero" that "Walt Whitman and Jack Kerouac and Otis Redding would have joined hands over."[5]

It was not difficult to connect the poet who lived in Camden with the rock musician who was born some fifty miles northeast along the New Jersey Turnpike. Both men wrote about the lives of working people and shared a passion for the open road, and although they traveled these highways at very different historical moments, they articulated a faith that America's thoroughfares would one day lead them to freedom. "Afoot and light hearted I take to the open road," Whitman declared, "the long brown path before me leading me wherever I choose."[6] His declaration echoes in Springsteen's "Born to Run" and "Thunder Road," a path tramped by working-class men who spend most of their time trying to persuade young women that if they would only step into their cars, the possibilities would be unlimited.[7] By day, the characters in "Born to Run" "sweat it out on the streets of a runaway American dream," and by night, they seek to drive their cars as far and as fast as they can away from the rigors and routine of working-class life.[8] On their travels, they embrace the tenets of individualism and imagine that they might attain the elusive dream of upward mobility. "It's a town full of losers," Springsteen proclaims in "Thunder Road," "and I'm pulling out of here to win."[9] In 1975, this musician was ready to run from the world, but he was not yet committed to changing it.

When he performed "Born to Run" during his 1988 Tunnel of Love Express Tour, however, Springsteen suggested that the meaning of the song had changed dramatically since he first wrote it. Whereas the twenty-five-year-old Springsteen had been focused on attaining his own individual success, the thirty-eight-year-old was more interested in accepting social responsibility. Introducing the song to a concert audience, he explained that although the image of "a guy and a girl" running away was a "nice romantic idea," he ultimately had realized that he would have to "figure out someplace for them to go." The more mature Springsteen recognized that when people do not connect "individual freedom . . . to some sort of community or friends," they often feel that life is "meaningless."[10]

Since the release of *Darkness on the Edge of Town* (1978), Springsteen has consistently recorded material that not only examines the tension between individuality and community but also embraces his working-class roots and articulates a concern for social and economic justice. Inspired by the works of Woody Guthrie, as well as readings in American cultural and political history, he has gradually placed himself in the lineage of Whitman's working-class hero. In the process, he has in large part relied on the language and representational strategies of Guthrie's hurt song to claim popular music as a cultural form in which the collective pain, joy, and hopes of working-class experience can be articulated and historicized. Particularly on *Nebraska* (1982), Springsteen connects this tradition to the social and economic conditions that shaped it, reconstructing a history that often contrasts sharply with standard narratives written about the United States. Heir to Whitman's deeply conflicted legacy, he has produced cultural work fraught with familiar ambiguities, many of which have been complicated by the complexities of popular culture. As he relocated the hero to the 1980s and 1990s, Springsteen labored to expand the frontiers of freedom and equality but bumped up against the limits of history and tradition.

Adam Raised a Cain

Springsteen began to develop an interest in American cultural and political history soon after he severed his ties with his first manager, Mike Appel, in 1976 and signed with Brandeis University graduate Jon Landau, a former critic for *Rolling Stone* who coproduced *Born to Run*. Landau encouraged his client to read such authors as John Steinbeck and Flannery O'Connor and to watch the films of John Ford and, according to Springsteen, taught him "to see things—to see *into* things—and somehow" make his epiphanies "come out in the songs." [11] One of the most important books that Springsteen read during the 1978–79 Darkness on the Edge of Town Tour was Henry Steele Commager and Allan Nevins's *Pocket History of the United States of America*, a narrative that, while professing an unwavering faith in the American experiment, enabled Springsteen to examine the social and economic forces that had shaped his life. First published in 1942, *Pocket History* celebrates the mythic land of freedom and opportunity, asserting that the United States is an "interesting" country "because its people have been conscious of a peculiar destiny, because upon it have been fastened the hopes and aspirations of the human race, and because it has not failed to fulfill that destiny or to justify its hopes." [12] When Springsteen explained the importance of this book to a Cleveland concert audience in 1978, however, he implied that the promise of America had not been fulfilled or justified for a large number of people, including his family. "I found a lot of things [in *Pocket History*] that were important to know, because they helped me understand the way that my life was and the way that my life developed," he remarked. "They helped me understand how when I was a kid all I remember was my father worked in a factory, his father worked in a factory. . . . And the main reason was that they didn't know enough . . . about the forces that controlled their lives. . . . The idea was that [in the United States] there'd be a place for everybody, no matter where you came from, no matter what religion you were or what color you were, you could help make a life that had some decency and dignity to it. . . . But like all ideals, that idea got real corrupted." [13]

Romanticizing the ideological origins of the United States, Springsteen suggested, as did Whitman, that although the tenets on which the Republic were founded were unarguably virtuous, a moral crisis had caused things to go terribly awry. Indeed, as Springsteen evaluated the economy in the late 1970s and early 1980s, he sounded much like a member of the artisan republic. "There's too much greed, too much carelessness," he observed. "I don't believe that was ever the idea of capitalism." [14] The "original idea," which "was initially to get some fair transaction between people, went out the window. And what came in was" a variation of Whitman's "morbid appetite for money" or, in Springsteen's terms, an ethos based on "the most you can get and the least you can give." [15] The "runaway American dream" to which the musician alluded in "Born to Run" was not "about two cars in the garage" but "about people living and working together without steppin' on each other." [16] It was a dream that bore a striking resemblance to the vision Whitman articulated in *Democratic Vistas*, one that called for balancing individual freedom with the public good.

The prevailing ethos of capitalism had not been kind to Springsteen's family. Born to Catholic parents in 1949, Springsteen grew up in Freehold, New Jersey, a small town of some 10,000 people located about fifteen miles from Asbury Park on the Jersey shore and about fifty miles from New York City. Throughout his childhood, Springsteen and his family faced austere circumstances. His father, Douglas, had difficulty securing steady employment, holding various jobs as a factory worker, prison guard, and bus driver, while his mother, Adele, worked as a legal secretary. To make ends meet, they lived with Douglas's parents when Bruce was first born, and then, until Adele, Douglas, and younger daughters Pam and Virginia left for California in 1966, they made their home in a working-class section of town where neighbors worked at a rug mill, Nescafe's coffee plant, or 3M's tape factory.

The family's tenuous financial situation, recalled Springsteen, put an "immense amount of stress" on his mother, who frequently borrowed money from a finance company to purchase Christmas gifts and school clothes for her children but still managed to provide "a sense of stability in the family." [17] Meanwhile, Douglas became withdrawn and embittered and often displayed his frustrations in heated confrontations with his son. After his father completed his shift at the prison, Bruce remembered, he would come home "real pissed off," "shut off . . . every light in the house," and sit alone in the dark kitchen with "a six pack and a ciga-

rette."[18] "When I was a kid, I really understood failure," Springsteen remarked. "In my family, I lived deep in its shadow."[19] Such feelings were
never far from Springsteen's mind. By his own admission, his music could
be "traced directly back to [his] mother and father," and in many ways,
it was about "seeking his [father's] revenge."[20]

The young Springsteen was a self-described loner who found intellectual stimulation not in academics but in popular music. He was moved by
Elvis Presley's 1956 appearance on the *Ed Sullivan Show* and, along with his
mother, who listened avidly to the radio, heard something in the voices
of a number of musicians that could assuage his loneliness and perhaps
redeem his family's less than sanguine economic situation. In fact, as
he again commented on the importance of *Pocket History* to a London
audience in 1980, he suggested that artists such as Presley, Roy Orbison,
the Beatles, and several Motown and country musicians had helped him
imagine a more satisfying life. "I started listening to the radio, and I heard
something in those singer's voices that said there was more to life than
what my old man was doing and the life that I was living," he remarked.
"And they held out a promise that every man has a right to live his life
with some decency and some dignity. And it's a promise that gets broken
every day, in the most violent way. But it's a promise that never, ever dies,
and it's always inside of you."[21]

For the teenage loner who lived in a stern working-class household,
"the lift of rock and roll [was] just incredible."[22] Popular music provided
Springsteen with a creative outlet and a vision of the future. In 1963, he
bought a guitar and began to play in local garage bands. After leading
several groups that played along the Jersey shore and in New York City
throughout the late 1960s and then performing acoustic shows in Greenwich Village, Springsteen auditioned for the legendary Columbia Records
talent scout John Hammond in 1972. Hammond, who had "discovered"
such artists as Billie Holiday, later recalled that during the audition he experienced "a force I'd felt maybe three times in my life." He immediately
signed the young musician, hailing him as the successor to another of his
"discoveries," Bob Dylan.[23]

Springsteen's first three albums were grounded firmly in his working-
class experience, but as songs such as "Born to Run" and "Thunder Road"
suggest, they were more concerned with escaping the economic limits
that circumscribed his life than with confronting them. *Darkness on the Edge
of Town* marked a turning point, however, for it was on this album, Springsteen wrote in 1995, that "I figured out what I wanted to write about, the

people who mattered to me, and who I wanted to be."²⁴ As the working-class men and women on *Born to Run* grew older, Springsteen recognized that they were "living the lives of [his] parents in a certain way" and began to see an "everyday kind of heroism" in their efforts "to lead decent, productive lives."²⁵ These men and women once believed in the romantic myths of the open road but were now learning the hard "facts" about a harsh and highly competitive economic system in which, as Springsteen describes it, a "poor man wanna be rich, / rich man wanna be king."²⁶

As they assess where they stand in this social order, the defiant young characters in *Darkness on the Edge of Town* express outrage at what is happening to their lives but are uncertain where to direct their anger. Inspired by John Ford's film *The Grapes of Wrath*, Springsteen was particularly struck by a scene in which a tenant farmer named Muley is forced from his land by corporations, which rationalize their actions, the film explains, by alluding to "economic changes beyond anyone's control."²⁷ As local bankers and bulldozers prepare to level Muley's home, he tries to hold them off with a shotgun, but because the people he confronts explain that they are simply executing the orders of corporations rather than individuals, he does not know where to point it. The forces that shape the lives of the characters in *Darkness on the Edge of Town* are similarly amorphous, largely because Springsteen himself was not certain where to place the blame for economic oppression. "In the Seventies and Eighties, especially compared to the Sixties, it became awfully hard to identify the enemy," he explained.²⁸ Unlike Guthrie, who was part of a movement that was critical of capitalism, Springsteen does not engage questions of political economy. Nonetheless, his characters begin to understand that their lives are being unjustly affected by economic forces and develop both a nascent consciousness of their class and a desire to alter their circumstances. Even those who ceaselessly adhere to the work ethic and maintain faith in rugged individualism find themselves frustrated, as the narrator of "The Promised Land" attests:

> I've done my best to live the right way
> I get up every morning and go to work each day
> But your eyes go blind and your blood runs cold
> Sometimes I feel so weak I just want to explode
> Explode and tear this whole town apart
> Take a knife and cut this pain from my heart
> Find somebody itching for something to start.²⁹

In "Adam Raised a Cain," a loud, guitar-driven song that examines the darkness that Springsteen's father once cast over his household, the musician attempts to give shape to the nebulous forces that affect his characters' lives, suggesting that they are both social and historical:

In the Bible Cain slew Abel
And East of Eden he was cast,
You're born into this life paying,
For the sins of somebody else's past,
Daddy worked his whole life, for nothing but the pain,
Now he walks these empty rooms, looking for something to blame,
You inherit the sins, you inherit the flames,
Adam raised a Cain.[30]

By recognizing that Cain's actions in part resulted from Adam and Eve's original sin, Springsteen acknowledges that each individual life is shaped by its relationship to the past, and he begins to understand that his father is not wholly responsible for his situation. The injuries of class were not retribution for the "sin" of economic failure committed by working people but the product of an original sin committed *against* them. Unfortunately, this original economic sin is not as easily forgiven as the biblical one, which is absolved by the narrator's baptism. But the possibility for redemption still exists. Inspired by this prospect, his characters do their penance by defiantly enduring disappointment and maintaining faith in the future. Even the disillusioned narrator of "The Promised Land" longs for something to "blow away the lies that leave you nothing but lost and brokenhearted."

Springsteen implies that the American economy and dreams based on consumption and success ruin people's lives, but, uncertain precisely where to point the gun, his protagonists can do little more than "pay the cost"—emotionally and materially—for pursuing the myths these dreams offer.[31] In the process, they embrace empty defense mechanisms that temporarily assuage but do not remove the pain in their hearts. "Mister, I ain't a boy, no, I'm a man / And I believe in a promised land," exclaims an angry Springsteen, asserting his masculinity and professing his faith in the future.[32] These narratives do not explicitly identify the enemy, but they represent the deep wounds inflicted by economic exploitation with an intensity and honesty uncommon in American popular culture. In the darkness of his own working-class experience and in the "mansions of fear" and "pain" in which his father dwelled, Springsteen uncovered the enduring muse for his cultural work.[33]

At the conclusion of the Darkness on the Edge of Town Tour in 1979, Springsteen's emerging historical awareness compelled him to expand his inchoate cultural politics. In the wake of the 1979 Three Mile Island nuclear disaster near Middletown, Pennsylvania, he agreed to headline several shows for Musicians United for Safe Energy, an anti–nuclear power consortium comprised of such popular artists as Graham Nash, Bonnie Raitt, and Jackson Browne. Although he performed at several benefits for the cause, his commitment seemed a bit lukewarm and his participation ambiguous. To the dismay of concert organizers, he refused to condemn nuclear energy in public, and although he had written a song entitled "Roulette" about the Three Mile Island emergency, he chose not to perform or release it until the late 1980s. By August 1981, however, he was prepared to be a bit more outspoken about his commitments. After reading Ron Kovic's *Born on the Fourth of July*, a disturbing narrative about the Vietnam War and the social, psychological, and financial problems its largely working-class veterans faced, Springsteen decided to do something to help veterans such as Kovic get back on their feet. To that end, he staged a benefit concert in Los Angeles for the Vietnam Veteran's Association, an organization that provides services for veterans and lobbies for related issues. The event apparently had a formative effect on Springsteen's social awareness. The concert, he recalled, marked the "first time" he felt as though his music had served a "useful" purpose, and throughout the 1980s and 1990s, he would continue to assess the unsettling legacy the war had bequeathed to veterans and their families.[34]

Springsteen's halfhearted political engagement developed coterminously with an expanding interest in classic country and traditional folk music, which seemed to be particularly useful forms for exploring working-class issues. Prompted perhaps by Landau, Springsteen began to listen carefully to the early recordings of Johnny Cash, Hank Williams, and Jimmie Rodgers, as well as the Folkways *Anthology of American Folk Music* (1952), the standard compendium of traditional performers from which Dylan had distilled his knowledge of the folk canon.[35] Williams's influence was particularly discernible on the title track of Springsteen's next album, *The River* (1980), which echoed the country music legend's "My Bucket's Got a Hole in It" (1949) and "Long Gone Lonesome Blues" (1950).[36] But whereas Williams's "Long Gone Lonesome Blues" is a hilarious lament about a heartbroken man whose luck is so bad that the river in which he plans to drown himself has run dry, there is nothing funny about Springsteen's composition. When the working-class narrator of this dark ballad explains that he lives in a town where "they bring you up to do like your daddy done," [37] he echoes the historical observations of "Adam Raised a Cain" and implies that he and his girlfriend, Mary, are bound to inherit the sins of the past. A remarkably candid and unromantic second verse reveals that the dreams these two young lovers once held have disappeared: "Then I got Mary pregnant / And man that was all she wrote." The finality of this harsh reality is underscored by the narrator's job insecurity, a problem that forces him to ask, "Is a dream a lie if it don't come true / Or is it something worse?" [38] In the case of this couple, the dreams of romantic love and upward mobility are more than just broken promises. Because the fulfillment of such dreams is ostensibly based on individual performance, those who are not lucky enough to have their dreams realized are torn apart by feelings of inadequacy and failure and are often forced to live brutally truncated lives. For Springsteen, these idealized dreams become part of a "cruel and cynical game," like "the carrot-in-front-of-the-donkey game," in which people are set up to struggle for something that is impossible, or at least incredibly difficult, to obtain. [39]

Williams would continue to be an important influence on Springsteen, and although the country legend's music captured what he described as "the hopes and prayers and dreams of what some call the common people," it did not engage politics in any significant way. [40] Williams's painful lyrics and mournful voice were certainly grounded in the realities of class relations, but his hard life as an Alabama tenant farmer, his chronic health problems, and his relentless struggle with alcoholism left him perhaps too badly damaged to imagine a future in which people did not have to experience the injuries of class. If Williams could not provide Springsteen with a model for the working-class hero, Woody Guthrie could.

In November 1980, Springsteen acquired a copy of *Woody Guthrie: A Life* (1980), a cultural biography authored by Joe Klein, a former contributor to *Rolling Stone* and friend of Landau's. Intrigued by the folksinger's ability to combine art with political commitment, Springsteen began to cover "This Land Is Your Land" in his concerts, a practice he continued throughout the River Tour (1980–81) and the Born in the U.S.A. Tour (1984–85). When he introduced the song to his audience at a 1981 performance, he mentioned Klein's book and conveyed the little-known fact that Guthrie had written "This Land" not as an unmitigated celebration of the nation's wonders but as an "angry" response to Irving Berlin's "God Bless America." Reluctant to embrace Guthrie's communist-influenced collectivism, however, Springsteen, like Guthrie himself, performed the song with characteristic ambiguity, omitting the radical "lost" verses and emphasizing aesthetics rather than politics by describing it as "the most beautiful song ever written."[41] His remarkably somber performance nevertheless recovered the doubts that Guthrie expressed in the original manuscript. Springsteen pitched the anthem "way over yonder in the minor keys" and punctuated it with a lugubrious harmonica solo that suggested that if this land had in fact been made for all of its citizens, the original intentions had been compromised. In the face of what he called "large-scale corruption," Springsteen explained, he sang "This Land" "to let people know that America belongs to everybody who lives there: the blacks, Chicanos, Indians, Chinese and the whites. . . . It's time that somebody took on the realities of the eighties."[42] When he confronted the realities of Ronald Reagan's America on Nebraska (1982), it was clear that this land did not belong to all of its citizens.

A Meanness in This World

Nebraska, explained Springsteen, examines the problem of "American isolation: what happens to people when they're alienated from their friends and their community and their government and their job," what happens when they are forced "to exist in some void where the basic constraints of society are a joke," what happens when they look at their own lives as a "kind of joke" as well.[43] An acoustic album Springsteen recorded in his home, Nebraska documents the desperate acts people commit under such circumstances: petty crimes, barroom brawls, suicides, and even mass murders. Throughout the album, Springsteen's haunting vocals, backed with minimal guitar arrangements and sharp harmonica blasts, narrate class-conscious tales of desperation and defiance with an emotional tautness that threatens to unravel at any moment. These grim narratives flow directly from "The River," in part because they explore similar themes, in part because they demonstrate a profound awareness of American musical history and the social conditions that shaped it. Tipping his hat to his heroes, this macabre storyteller twice reiterates Chuck Berry's desperate plea for rock and roll to deliver him from nowhere and at nearly every turn seems to be in dialogue with such Dylan songs as

"The Ballad of Hollis Brown."[44] To be sure, Dylan had a profound influence on Springsteen, but his inspiration for *Nebraska* extended far beyond the 1960s.

"Johnny 99," a song about an unemployed autoworker who kills a man in a moment of drunken desperation, demonstrates that Springsteen refashioned the themes and lyrical conventions of traditional musicians to connect working-class struggles of the present to those of the past.[45] While writing songs for *Nebraska*, Springsteen had been listening to Guthrie's recordings as well as the Folkways *Anthology*, an album on which he heard Julius Daniels's "Ninety Nine Year Blues" (1927) and the Carter Family's "John Hardy Was a Desperate Little Man" (1930). Taken together, these two songs provide, along with the 1980 closing of the Ford Motor Company plant in Mahwah, New Jersey, the narrative structure of "Johnny 99."[46] Springsteen's interpretation of these standards was refracted through the cultural lens of Woody Guthrie, whose music was influenced by Piedmont bluesmen such as Daniels and in particular by the Carters. In fact, as Klein notes in his biography, Guthrie disliked the Carters' social conservatism and rewrote several of their songs, including "John Hardy," to articulate his own political concerns.[47] Following in his hero's footsteps, Springsteen adapts Daniels's blues and the Carters' ballad to create a hurt song for the 1980s, a ballad that expresses the collective pain, suffering, and injustice that working people have historically suffered and articulates their hopes and dreams for a less oppressive future.

"Johnny 99" does not confront the politics of race, but the hurt song tradition on which it draws has its roots firmly planted in the African American musical and narrative traditions that were familiar to Julius Daniels. Born near Charlotte, North Carolina, in 1902, Daniels traveled to Atlanta in February 1927 to record four tracks for Victor Records, including "Ninety Nine Year Blues."[48] The narrator of this song, like Springsteen's protagonist, follows a rather standard plot in American folk song: he is arrested, found guilty, and sentenced to ninety-nine years in prison. Although this rather typical blues song does not, as did the Carters' ballad, refer to a particular historical event, it assembles an array of images, experiences, and geographies through which the musician represents and comments on the racism that followed him on his various travels. Indeed, as the bluesman Robert Johnson implied, racism was a constant "hellhound" on the trail of African Americans, and although Daniels's narrator tries to keep one step ahead of this threat, he is ultimately overrun.[49] A complete stranger in town, the protagonist is immediately identified as a criminal who has violated the "poor boy law," an ordinance that punishes those who commit the crimes of blackness and poverty.[50]

As Houston Baker notes, many blues musicians, Daniels among them, relied on geographic markers to map the locations where blacks most frequently and perhaps universally encountered discrimination and violence.[51] Constantly on the move, this protagonist arrives in yet another nameless town on Monday, and by Tuesday, is transported to the blues geography of the courtroom, a site that is supposed to represent equality and social justice but, in the context of the song and the blues in general, marks the authority of a social order that discriminates against the narrator for both his racial and his economic status. Daniels underscores this point when the judge sentences this offender to ninety-nine years in "Joe Brown's coal mine."[52] This excessive sentence and the downward movement to a subterranean blues geography not only suggest that working-class blacks have been deprived of the opportunity for upward mobility but, by referring to the convict-labor system, acknowledge that the state has historically aligned itself with business interests to use racism to control the labor process.[53] Daniels's character sobs as he accepts the terms of this unjust sentence, but his tears are formed in rage rather than defeat. Like a panoply of "bad man" folk heroes in African American culture, he vows to lash out against this system by "kill[ing] everybody" that has committed an act of racism against him.[54] This character's life has been so devalued that he cannot imagine addressing his oppressive circumstances in a collective manner but can only envision a resistance based on an existential and self-destructive act of defiance.[55]

Whereas Daniels protested the conditions of racism, the Carter Family, as I previously argued, preserve a traditional ballad based on a historical event that confirmed prevailing racial hierarchies. In January 1893, an African American bandit named John Hardy shot a man near the West Virginia state line and, after apologizing for his crimes and embracing the moral authority of white Christianity, was executed. Hardy's deference to a white Baptist minister, his remorsefulness, and his faith in the afterlife reminded the Carters' audience that blacks must remain subordinate to white values. When Guthrie rewrote the Carters' "John Hardy," however, he presented an outlaw who had much more in common with Daniels's character. Rather than deferring to the social order, Guthrie's Hardy remains defiant, insisting that he would die before he would be a slave to white justice and declaring that one day all African Americans would win their freedom.

Springsteen adapts the traditions of Daniels, the Carters, and Guthrie to place the socioeconomic conditions of the 1980s in a historical context. Focusing on the life of a young unemployed autoworker, "Johnny 99" is based on the 1980 closing of Ford's Mahwah facility, which had opened in 1955. Two years after the shutdown, more than half of the 3,359 workers who lost their jobs remained unemployed, and many of those who found other positions had accepted drastic cuts in pay or left their homes to find work in other regions of the country. Douglas Fraser, the president of the United Auto Workers Union, who saw nearly 250,000 of his members lose their jobs in the early 1980s, explained that the "kind of permanent layoff at Mahwah [was] much more shattering than anything that happened in the Depression. At least in the 1930's workers had hopes of being called back to work. In Mahwah they don't." [56] For many working people, the 1980s seemed hauntingly reminiscent of Guthrie's 1930s. In the shadow of Reagan's antilabor policies, the unemployment rate reached a post-Depression high of 11 percent in 1982, union membership fell by 29 percent, industrial cities rapidly decayed, and homelessness became a visible national problem. [57]

To represent these economic transformations, Springsteen, like a traditional balladeer, uses geographic markers to situate his characters in a sort of darkness on the edge of town, a place where nearly all communal relations have been eclipsed. In "Johnny 99," this shadow is cast when Ralph, a victim of the Mahwah shutdown, mounts an unsuccessful job search and repairs to a bar in an unseemly "part of town where when you hit a red light you don't stop." Like migrant workers during the Great Depression, Ralph and many other working people were located on a rather uncertain periphery of the social order in the 1980s, but in this age of deindustrialization, they had little hope that their fate would improve. They watched factories relocate outside the United States, saw their union halls empty, and moved away from traditional working-class communities to search for employment elsewhere, often leaving their families and friends behind. In fact, before the drunken Ralph kills the night clerk, he too faces the possibility of displacement. When the bank prepares to foreclose on his home, it not only threatens to repossess his place of residence but also imperils his connection to his neighbors, friends, and community. Even the bonds that hold together the most basic relationships, including those between parents and children, are broken in this desperate situation. Ralph is the person who is alienated from society, but as his mother and girlfriend weep uncontrollably in the courtroom, it is clear that his actions extend beyond his own life to affect both his and his victim's families. The concept of community may have dissolved, but individual lives were still interconnected.

Ralph's pathetic narrative represents the despair that many working people experienced in the 1980s, but his ambiguous actions are difficult to interpret. He understands that social and economic conditions have undoubtedly shaped his life, but as he addresses the court, he admits that it was more than his debts that led him to a life of crime. In doing so, he refuses to be reduced to a product of historical circumstances.[58] On one hand, his acceptance of personal responsibility and his failure to show remorse echo the actions of Guthrie's John Hardy and seem to adopt the credo of the mass-murdering narrator of "Nebraska," who rationalizes his killing spree by explaining "there's just a meanness in this world." This meanness is not confined to murderers alone but permeates an economic system that defines value exclusively in terms of the market and convinces many of its citizens, as it did Ralph, that the inequalities of class are part of an organic and immutable social order. In a sense, Ralph's greatest tragedy is that he has so deeply internalized these values that he is unable to imagine a rewarding life without economic success. In this atomistic society, his connection to the social order and to other human beings—his family, his union, his employer—has completely eroded.

On the other hand, Ralph subtly criticizes the morality of capitalism by telling the court that he had "debts no honest man could pay" and, despite the circumstances that shape his life, tries to assert what little control he can over his fate. Although nihilistic, his actions provide him with a feeling of significance that the social order cannot offer and foreshadow the attitude of the death row murderer Springsteen represents in "Dead Man Walkin' " (1995). Cut from the same cloth as Guthrie's John Hardy, this criminal remains defiant even when his execution is imminent, coldly remarking, "Sister, I won't ask for forgiveness / My sins are all I have." [59] In the closing verse of "Johnny 99," Ralph similarly refuses to petition the court for forgiveness or mercy. Rather than accepting his ninety-nine-year sentence, he asks the judge to "let 'em shave off my hair and put me on that execution line."

Like "John Hardy," "Johnny 99" could be read as the story of what Guthrie suggested was "just another bad man gone wrong," a ballad of individual failure and moral weakness in which the antihero gets what he deserves. In fact, one critic suggests that Ralph's actions could easily be endorsed by the party of Reagan: "He is no whiner, and by conveniently offering to remove himself from the picture, here is one man who doesn't want to live off the public trough."⁶⁰ Springsteen's treatment of his protagonist is a bit more complicated, however. Grounded in the tradition of Guthrie, the Carters, and Daniels, his ballad is a history of class relations that illustrates the cost of these relations in human rather than economic terms. The economic decisions of the Ford Motor Company and the competitive ethos of capitalism provide a social context for Ralph's actions and have an adverse impact not only on his life but also on the social relations of Mahwah. Like Muley in *The Grapes of Wrath*, Ralph is not certain where to point the gun, but he is so frustrated and outraged that he must aim it somewhere, haphazardly turning it on innocent bystanders and, in effect, on himself. For Springsteen, the "meanness" in *Nebraska* was rooted in an "economic injustice" that "falls on everybody's head and steals everyone's freedom." Because people live with "a greater sense of apprehension, anxiety and fear than they would in a more just and open society," an act such as Ralph's cannot, he suggested in an interview, be explained as a mere "accident," nor can it be rationalized by simply saying "that there are 'bad' people out there." Ralph's behavior was instead "a product of what we have accepted, what we have acceded to. And whether we mean it or not, our silence has spoken for us in some fashion."⁶¹ Ralph's random gunshots may break that silence in a somewhat ambiguous manner, but Springsteen underscores the social origins and ramifications of his actions and insists that he was *more* than just another bad man gone wrong.

This murder ballad considers a violent manifestation of class consciousness, but much of *Nebraska* explores the subtle and ordinary ways that working-class lives are devalued. In "Mansion on the Hill," Springsteen again returns to Hank Williams, reworking his 1947 hit of a similar title, a song that describes a romantic relationship thwarted by class distinctions. Using geography to represent class hierarchies, Williams sings of a woman who, "alone with [her] pride," remains sequestered in her "loveless mansion on the hill" because she refuses to pursue a relationship with the workingman who lives in a cabin "down in the valley."⁶² Springsteen's ballad, which he based on his father's obsession with a mansion outside Freehold, explores how children acquire consciousness of class.⁶³ He too uses geography to delineate social relationships, but this time the mansion, not the workers, is located on the outskirts of town. Since the narrator's early childhood, this imposing structure has served as a constant reminder of the town's economic structure and his place in it. It towers "above the factories and the fields" and is encircled by steel gates, the product of the men who labor in factories located in the town below.[64] This cold, hard steel recalls the lovelessness of Williams's mansion, but more important, it emphasizes the workers' place in the community. The fruits of their labor do not enable them to achieve the dream that the mansion represents but, cruelly and ironically, isolate them from it.

This social geography again relegates the characters to a darkness where they pay the cost for desiring what the mansion symbolizes. Under the darkness of night, the narrator and his sister remain hidden in nearby cornfields while they gaze at the big house's lights and listen to the music and laughter inside. Caught on the outside looking in, the narrator and his family remain firmly within the boundaries of their assigned social space, feeling the silent shame associated with their social status and coming to realize the virtual impossibility of moving from the dark, still, silent streets of their town to the light and laughter they see and hear in the mansion. The laughter in the house is expressed at the expense of the brother and sister's silence, a fact that illuminates the end results of an economy in which the people who live comfortably do so at the expense of those who do not.

The teenage narrator of "Used Cars," however, begins to question the relationships that shape his life and expresses a deep resentment toward the humiliation he faces daily. Brought up to do like his father had done, he has grown tired of passively accepting a situation in which his father works the same dead-end job day in and day out.[65] Having witnessed the failure of the work ethic to deliver the promise of upward mobility, he believes that he can only escape his fate by winning the lottery. As he waits for his number to come in, he expresses a deep sense of shame and bitterness about his family's financial status that manifests itself when they drive through their neighborhood in a "brand new used car." Meddlesome neighbors gather around to comment on the second-rate vehicle, and the boy is so wounded and embarrassed by their patronizing reactions that he longs for his despondent father to tell them to "kiss our asses goodbye." This bitterness and the determined refrain—"I ain't ever gonna ride in no used car again"—capture the pain and humiliation of working-class life, but perhaps more important, they articulate the type of resentment and resistance that Guthrie tried to channel into the collective spirit that drove the labor movement.

But in 1982, Springsteen differed from Guthrie in significant ways.

Nebraska is a mean place, but Springsteen provides no ideas about how it might be made kinder. Critics have noted that his characters were still uncertain where to direct their outrage, where to point the gun, and as a result, they seem to accept that "there's just a meanness in this world."[66] *Nebraska* is filled with narratives of defeat and resignation, but the problem for its denizens is not that they are passive but that they are disconnected. Ralph is certainly willing to take action, and the narrator of "Used Cars" is angry enough to do something, perhaps anything, to change his fate. As Guthrie might suggest, these characters have the right idea but the wrong system, and their real dilemma is not apathy but rather the fact that the coping mechanisms with which they were familiar and perhaps the tradition Springsteen invoked no longer provided them with the tools they needed to imagine a way out of their predicaments. In this hour of deindustrialization, their unions were crippled, their working-class communities disintegrated, their government provided little relief, and the employment opportunities offered by other industries were meager if they existed at all.

By representing the dissolution of communal relations, Springsteen implies that collective bonds must be reestablished before any sense of social justice can be obtained, but he does not articulate an explicit vision for the future. Lacking the broad-based left-wing culture into which Guthrie plugged his hurt songs, Springsteen does not issue a manifesto for change as much as he delivers a state of the union address. His songs nonetheless perform important cultural work, introducing disturbing working-class voices into a popular culture that largely ignores them and challenging the Reagan administration's vision of social harmony and economic recovery. Indeed, Springsteen narrates a revisionist history that proclaims that if this land was made for everyone, a vast number of people did not feel they had a stake in its future. To recover this history, Springsteen carefully delved into working-class music and connected the social struggles of Daniels, the Carters, Williams, and Guthrie to the realities of the 1980s. The struggle to lead a decent, productive life had been going on for a long time, and by aligning himself with musicians such as Guthrie, he identified an alternative American tradition that represented this struggle, one that was not based on the most you can get and the least you can give but sought to balance individual freedom with communal responsibility. When Springsteen relocated this tradition to 1984, however, he learned that the job of being a working-class hero was a tricky business.

Originally written for *Nebraska*, "Born in the U.S.A." is the story of a working-class man who fights in Vietnam, loses his brother in the war, and returns home to discover that his old employer will not rehire him and that his advocate at the Veterans Administration can offer little assistance. By the time we reach the final verse, he stands in a dark "shadow" located between the penitentiary and the refinery, between a life of crime and unemployment, a condition that, when described in the loud and defiant manner in which Springsteen screams the chorus, suggests the betrayal of a birthright both he and his dead brother supposedly fought to defend. Like the characters in *Darkness on the Edge of Town*, he has done his best to live the right way, but he is left with "nowhere to run . . . nowhere to go." [67] The most cursory analysis of these lyrics reveals that the song questions the morality of the war as well as the country's treatment of its working-class veterans, yet many of the 18 million Americans who purchased the album and the more than 5 million who paid to see the 1984–85 tour misconstrued Springsteen's intentions.[68] His defiance was interpreted as patriotic jingoism, and the resonant chorus of "Born in the U.S.A.," sung to "triumphant anthem-like melodies bolstered by ringing guitars and a walloping rhythm section," was understood to be a celebration of a resurgent American militarism.[69] Shot through with discrepancies and inconsistencies, Springsteen's cultural work had, as George Lipsitz writes about popular art in general, "no fixed meanings." Because popular culture is embedded in a conflicted and dynamic network of symbols and ideologies that discourage social change and promote consumerism, "it is impossible to say whether any one combination of sounds or set of images or grouping of words innately expresses one political position." [70] Springsteen's art was already part of a tradition fraught with ideological tensions, and when it was circulated in postmodern America, its meanings were up for grabs.

As had been the case with Whitman and Guthrie, Springsteen lent himself to conservative interpretations. In September 1984, syndicated columnist George Will attended one of Springsteen's concerts and enthusiastically dubbed the musician "a wholesome cultural portent" who punctuated songs about "closed factories and other problems" with "a grand, cheerful affirmation: 'Born in the U.S.A.!' " Will, and no doubt many other Americans, including perhaps Springsteen, conflated this refrain with the xenophobic phrase "Made in the U.S.A.," which unions invoked throughout the 1980s to discourage Americans from purchasing imported goods, particularly automobiles. "If Americans made their products with as much energy and confidence as Springsteen and his merry band make music," opined Will, if laborers reembraced the work ethic, consumers would be more willing to buy American, and "there would be no need for Congress to be thinking" about levying protective tariffs.[71] Seeking to assign blame for workers' tenuous economic position, unions pointed not to the advent of global capitalism but to foreign competitors who would work for far less than Americans. Will suggested that rugged individualism and standards of craftsmanship were on the wane and implied that workers should look in the mirror if they wanted to find the source of their doldrums.

Less than a week after Will published his article, President Reagan, whom Will often advised, pledged his allegiance to Springsteen during a campaign stop in New Jersey. "America's future rests in the message of hope in songs of a man so many young Americans admire: New Jersey's own Bruce Springsteen," remarked the president. "And helping you make those dreams come true is what this job of mine is all about."[72] If Springsteen's goal was to encourage the United States to examine issues of social and economic justice, his intentions had been misunderstood.[73]

The musician was not an innocent bystander in this process. As he would admit after the *Born in the U.S.A.* phenomenon subsided, "the rock and roll idea," and perhaps the concept of the working-class hero, tended to "exalt the cult of personality. . . . And I've been as guilty of it as anybody in my own life."[74] With the Summer Olympic Games being held in Los Angeles and a presidential election slated for November, 1984 was a year of patriotic rhetoric and the flag, a "powerful image" that Springsteen certainly used to his advantage.[75] Although he would try to clarify his cultural politics during the tour, he personally benefited from and helped create the patriotic fervor that swept the nation. The flag appeared on his album cover and hung behind his concert stage, and when he sang the chorus of "Born in the U.S.A." in his performances, he and his audience rhythmically and triumphantly pumped their fists in the air.

Moreover, with the exception of the title song and "My Hometown," most of the other selections on the album were about love, friendship, and, in short, trying to have fun. Such raucous, up-tempo songs as "Darlington County" and "Working on the Highway," replete with references to labor unions, are an integral component of Springsteen's music because their blue-collar characters escape the tediousness of their workday and maintain faith that they will one day "lead a better life."[76] Neither of these tales ends happily; in fact, characters in both songs are arrested in the final verses. But the foot-tapping melodies, Springsteen's joyful "sha la las," and the patriotic context in which he sang them all conspired to work against the serious social criticism that could be found in the album's title track. To many listeners, his material seemed to validate the idea that hard work and persistence would enable them to climb the social ladder. In 1984, Springsteen climbed that ladder to heights unimagined.[77]

It was more than flag waving and the promise of good times, however, that attracted Will to Springsteen. For the horn-rimmed, bow-tied journalist, perhaps the musician's most endearing quality was his unabashed masculinity. Drawing on ideas that had persisted for nearly a century and a half, Will defined work and the working-class hero by fusing the language of American capitalism with notions of masculine skill and performance. Springsteen's four-hour concerts, which provided "vivid proof that the work ethic was alive and well," were the products of a dedicated, determined, and upwardly mobile "blue-collar" "athlete draining himself for every audience." This "national asset," who performed with tremendous "energy and confidence," possessed a "manner" that "affirms the right values."[78]

In an era in which "'values' [were] all the rage," Springsteen apparently not only articulated a love of country and a faith in its economy but embodied the values of manhood as well. Whereas Guthrie had articulated his masculinity and patriotism against the backdrop of the Popular Front, by the 1980s, nationalism and manhood were part of the Republican Party's ideological arsenal, and the image Springsteen projected easily coalesced with its conservatism. "Let's not quibble," writes Will. "Cars and girls" — the subject of many of Springsteen's songs — "are American values." Mobility and manhood, consumption and patriarchy were important components of Reagan's America, and in Springsteen, Will located the furnace in which this national alloy was forged. "There is not a smidgen of androgyny in Springsteen, who, rocketing around the stage in a T-shirt and a headband, resembles Robert De Niro in the combat scenes of *The Deerhunter*," he exclaims. "This is rock for the United Steelworkers, accompanied by the opening barrage of the battle of the Somme."[79]

Will's description provides insight into the complex network of symbols and ideas in which Springsteen's work was consumed and reveals some of the ways in which nationalism, constructions of manhood, and revisions of the Vietnam War intersected in both 1980s popular culture and the Reagan presidency. For conservatives such as Reagan, the 1960s, and Vietnam in particular, fractured concepts of national unity, power, and prestige. The Great Society's social programs, with their socialist overtones, were insidious to the members of the emerging New Right, but the insubordinate young adults who marched in the streets were far more inflammatory. Reagan, who as governor of California deployed the National Guard against unruly Berkeley students in 1969, had little tolerance for the counterculture, defining a hippie as a man who "dresses like Tarzan, has hair like Jane, and smells like Cheetah." [80] This characterization of the New Left castigated male draft resisters not simply for refusing to accept their manly duty to fight for their nation but also for blurring gender roles both in their actions and in their appearance. In the eyes of conservatives, however, these long-haired protesters were not the only contingent that was experiencing a crisis in masculinity. Military strategists and politicians who coordinated the war effort had also acted in a decidedly unmanly fashion, forcing the soldiers in Vietnam to fight the battle against communism, Reagan insisted, "with one hand tied behind them." [81] Cowardly protesters and weak and indecisive bureaucrats, not soldiers, were responsible for America's ignominious defeat.

The Vietnam conflict was only the first in a series of incidents that indicated that America's international status was spiraling downward. Richard Nixon desecrated the presidency with the Watergate debacle, and despite hopes that a change in party leadership would prompt a reversal of national fortunes, Jimmy Carter's administration did little to stem the tide of disappointment. With an economy hamstrung by a global energy crisis and skyrocketing inflation, the soft-spoken Carter urged expansion-minded consumers to downsize their expectations, to live simply rather than extravagantly. In his first television address to the public as president, he encouraged his constituents to lower their thermostats to conserve fuel. To illustrate that he practiced what he preached, the chief executive donned a sweater, apparently to declare his intentions to run the country from a chilly Oval Office. [82]

Uninterested in sacrifice or compromise, many Americans greeted such posturing with a cold shoulder that became even more frigid as they watched the president react to a pair of international crises that surfaced in 1979. In November, Islamic fundamentalists overtook the U.S. embassy in Tehran, Iran, where they held fifty-two hostages for nearly a year and a half. Haunted by media coverage that daily announced the duration of the siege, Carter responded by freezing Iranian assets and attempting several negotiations. His efforts yielded little progress. Under increasing public pressure to resolve the crisis, he exercised his military options in March 1980, approving a mission to rescue the captives. The attempt failed miserably. Eight American soldiers died, the hostages remained imprisoned, and an already uncertain electorate became even more dubious about the strength of both the United States military and its commander in chief.

Carter's response to the Soviet invasion of Afghanistan did little to quell public discontent. Rather than meeting the communist threat against U.S. oil interests with military action, Carter again pursued diplomatic efforts that culminated in a U.S. boycott of the 1980 Summer Olympic Games in Moscow. A staunch supporter of human and civil rights, Carter exhibited a patience and predilection for diplomacy that undoubtedly saved thousands of lives but made him poorly suited to sustaining the support of an electorate that based its national identity largely on notions of prosperity, expansion, and world domination.[83]

Reagan revived a patriotic pride by reaffirming these values within a decidedly masculine framework. If on Carter's watch America had grown weak and effeminate, Reagan pledged that on his it would once again become strong, decisive, self-reliant, and manly. A firm believer in rugged individualism, Reagan sought to dismantle the Democrats' social programs, insisting that the profits generated by a deregulated economy would ultimately "trickle down" to benefit the less fortunate. Moreover, he demonstrated zero tolerance for any groups that threatened national economic or security interests. In 1981, he broke the air traffic controllers' strike by announcing that he would hire replacement workers and bombed Libya for conducting terrorist activities. A 1983 invasion of Grenada again allowed the U.S. military, which Reagan had strengthened in a determined attempt to win the Cold War, to flex its muscles.[84]

Reagan's combination of masculinity and nationalism shaped and was reinforced by a popular culture that "remasculinized" the country's image of itself.[85] Narratives about the Vietnam War—novels, memoirs, and films —played a leading role in this cultural process. Much like Reagan, who in 1984 tried to close the door on the Vietnam era by presiding over the entombment of an unknown soldier killed in the conflict, Americans were still trying to come to terms with the lost war and the soldiers who fought it.[86] The enormous popularity of Sylvester Stallone's Rambo films demonstrated both the public's fascination with the Vietnam veteran and the symbiotic relationship that existed between the Reagan presidency and much of 1980s popular culture. Centered on the life of fictitious Special

Forces soldier John Rambo, Stallone's films construct the Vietnam veteran as the victim of a disgraced bureaucratic government. The films, however, allow the character (and the nation) to redeem his masculinity and restore a fervent patriotism by providing the opportunity to win the war and defeat the threat of communism.[87]

Susan Jeffords argues that each Rambo film confronted and symbolically resolved various crises in masculinity that presented themselves in the Reagan era.[88] *First Blood* (1982), the initial installment in the trilogy, presents Rambo as a beleaguered veteran whose well-hewn body and masculine defiance contrast sharply with the corpulent, feminized law enforcement officials who harass him. Shortly after traveling to Hope, Oregon, where he learns that the last member of his combat unit has died of cancer, Rambo is arrested by the small-town sheriff, who claims not to like the appearance of the unkempt veteran. To force his prisoner to conform to his expectations, the sheriff instructs his deputies to wash and shave him. After resisting this attempt and escaping from prison, Rambo takes refuge in the forest, where he is forced to defend himself from the inept law enforcement officials and National Guardsmen who trail him. In the face of overwhelming odds, a determined Rambo handily subdues the members of a bumbling local police force and reduces the federally trained part-time soldiers to unskilled cowards. The hero ultimately surrenders, but not before he presents what Jeffords calls "a short history of [the] national deterioration" to which Reagan repeatedly referred. The "soft bodies" of the police and National Guard, bodies that cry with pain or tremble with cowardice, are contrasted with Rambo's imposing physique, which proves its toughness and worth through performance.[89] America had become flaccid during the Carter presidency, the film suggests, and if the country intended to reassert itself, it would have to strengthen both individual and national bodies.

According to Jeffords, the distinction between "soft bodies" and "hard bodies" was an important one in Reagan's ideology. Whereas the stereotypically "soft," languid bodies of "lazy" welfare mothers, drug addicts, the unemployed, and gay men were represented and perceived as being either female or African American, the determined, individualistic, patriotic, and authoritative "hard body" was associated with white men such as Reagan and Rambo. In keeping with Reagan's populist conservatism, which sought to save men from the clutches of a liberal government run amok, the "hard body hero" arose from a social order in which, Jeffords argues, "the men who are thrust forward into heroism are not heroic in defiance of their society but in defiance of their governments and institutional bureaucracies."[90] In *Rambo: First Blood, Part II*, Stallone's character becomes this hero. Incarcerated for the crimes he committed in the first film, an even larger, more physically fit Rambo is approached by his military mentor, Colonel Trautman, who suggests that if his former student agrees to participate in a secret military operation to locate prisoners of war in Vietnam, President Reagan, whose portrait appears throughout the film, might pardon his conviction. Rambo will not assent, however, until Trautman assures him that he will be given a chance "to win this time." This hard body will fight only if indecisive, feminized bureaucrats will untie the hand behind his back and allow him to accomplish his mission.[91]

Just as the Reagan presidency permeated *Rambo*, the film surfaced in the president's rhetoric. Soon after Lebanon freed thirty-nine American hostages in 1985, the president told reporters he had seen "*Rambo* last night" and now knew "what to do the next time this happens."[92] But if Reagan, whose hawkish personality earned him the satiric sobriquet "Ronbo," had in fact watched the film, he would have been impressed by more than just the protagonist's military skills. As Jeffords argues, Rambo embodied an entire constellation of ideologies that mirrored Reagan's, including his ability "to revive the promise of masculinity itself."[93] With its emphasis on male bodies and male bonding, on men saving other men, *Rambo* posited a homosocial world that "produc[ed] an arena of masculine self-sufficiency."[94] Much like Reagan, this well-defined hard body "restored the boundaries not only of the individual masculine figure but of the nation as a whole."[95] Women were an insignificant part of Rambo's world, and when people of color appeared, they were infantilized, notably in *Rambo III*, as Third World residents in desperate need of white Western assistance. As such, Stallone's muscle-bound body clearly demarcated the lines between hard and soft, men and women, white and black, heterosexual and homosexual.[96]

When Springsteen embarked on his stadium tour of the United States in 1985, he found himself enmeshed in the ideologies and symbols that the Rambo films and Reagan represented. In August, the *Chicago Tribune*, coining a slogan that would soon appear on novelty T-shirts and bumper stickers throughout the country, declared Springsteen "the Rambo of rock and roll," a national hero who, like Stallone's character, "only wants America to love him as much as he loves it."[97] According to this editorial, Springsteen reprised "the defiant, good ol' boy, blue-collar skepticism of Merle Haggard," a country musician who expressed opinions that Reagan would have certainly found appealing. Like hard-bodied heroes such as Rambo, Haggard reconfirmed the values of rugged individualism and patriotism. In "Workin' Man Blues" (1969), he describes the difficulty of making ends meet on a tight budget but proudly declares that because he will be "workin' as long as [his] two hands are fit to use," his name will never appear on a welfare check.[98] His populist conservatism also pervades "Okie from Muskogee" (1969) and "The Fightin' Side of Me" (1970), songs that convey a disdain for the counterculture and its politics. Troubled by the protests of largely middle-class students against a war fought predominantly by working-class men, Haggard mocks those who were "harping on the wars we fight" and advises them that if they don't love America, they should leave it.[99]

Even though Springsteen questioned the moral and political motives and ramifications of the war, his masculinity, patriotism, and identification with the working class were enough to attach him to the Reagan-Rambo bandwagon. It was no surprise that "Born in the U.S.A." was the theme song of a Houston nightclub called "Rambose," a popular hangout where "everybody's proud of what . . . Reagan's been doing," waitresses wore fatigues, and the war-zone decor included sandbags, machine guns, and camouflage netting.[100] Many people believed Rambo and Springsteen, and perhaps Ronbo, shared the same politics. Stallone and Springsteen addressed questions of national identity, confronted the legacy of Vietnam, and, in some ways, physically resembled each other: they both had dark shoulder-length hair, wore bandannas as part of their costumes, and flaunted their muscular physiques. To be sure, the heroic and sexualized image that Springsteen cultivated was an important component of his popularity and in large part accounted for his appropriation by the Right.

After forming the E Street Band in the early 1970s, Springsteen had become renowned for performances that, as Will noted, were remarkably physical in terms of endurance and intensity. Throughout these three- to four-hour spectacles, audiences would watch Springsteen sprint from one end of the stage to the other, play his guitar as he stood on Roy Bittan's piano, leap from the top of amplifiers, throw himself into the crowd with unfettered exuberance, and sing with unmitigated passion. Such displays of athletic prowess were clearly sexually charged, particularly in the live concert video of "Rosalita" (1978), in which a group of women pull a very willing Springsteen into the audience and smother him with kisses.[101]

This eroticism became even more pronounced during the Born in the

U.S.A. Tour, largely because Springsteen placed more emphasis on developing and revealing his body. In the fitness craze of the 1980s, the musician changed his diet and began a serious exercise regimen in 1983 that transformed the slender, sinewy frame of the "Rosalita" video into a brawny, well-defined body.[102] In footage from 1978 and 1980, Springsteen covers his thin arms with a sports jacket, but in 1984, he accentuates his burly figure by wearing tattered, tight-fitting jeans and sleeveless, low-cut T-shirts. This new image was particularly well suited for an audience that selected its heroes from the music video network MTV. The video for the album's first single, "Dancing in the Dark," exposed the bulked-up musician to a new generation of fans. Directed by Brian De Palma, the video depicts Springsteen and the E Street Band lip-synching this pop hit in front of a concert audience. Clean-shaven and almost campy, Springsteen wears short hair, a white shirt, jeans, and black boots. His shirt is loosely unbuttoned to reveal his chest, and his sleeves are hiked up to divulge his biceps. As the musician dances around the stage, the camera prominently features his body, cutting from his crotch to his face, from his biceps to his buttocks. These sexualized images are interspersed with shots of the band and an enamored fan, played by actress Courtney Cox, who helplessly coos over the performer. Near the end of the song, Springsteen makes the concert memorable for this excited but embarrassed fan by pulling her onstage for a dance.[103] Provocative enough to titillate yet shrouded in a veil of pop innocence and wholesomeness, the sexuality represented in the video, as Will perceptively noted, evokes the American values of cars and girls, of heterosexual coupling and, perhaps most important, masculine authority. In a decade in which the gender-bending of Boy George, Michael Jackson, Prince, and Annie Lennox had become the norm, Springsteen's representation of manhood was reassuring.

Besides asserting Springsteen's masculinity, "Dancing in the Dark" underscores his whiteness. Since the early 1970s, Springsteen had played with interracial bands, and he was clearly influenced by African American folk music and the sounds of Motown.[104] But as Fred Pfeil argues, rock music is a genre produced and consumed largely by white men, a genre "that defines itself—musically, socially, and perhaps most of all, physically—in diacritical distinction to Blackness."[105] To be sure, Springsteen moves in a stereotypically white manner. Although sexual, his performance style is stilted and deliberate. "Springsteen looks like a member of Up with People," wrote Greil Marcus of the video. "He looks made up. Moving across the stage in seemingly choreographed, marks-on-the-

Bruce Springsteen onstage during the Born in the U.S.A. Tour, 1984. Copyright © Bettmann/Corbis.

boards jerks, he grins like a supperclub singer" trying to win over the all-white crowd in the video.[106] Springsteen's performance, his audience, his status as a rock musician, and, most important, his working-class identity—an identity long constructed as white and male—all point to a rather obvious fact: he belongs to a particular race of singers.[107]

The categories of manhood and whiteness coalesce in Springsteen's confident stage persona, which is more clearly represented in the video of the live electric performance of "Born to Run" (1987). Will is right; there is nothing androgynous about Springsteen. He commands his band and his audience with a sexual authority modeled on Elvis Presley, who, much like Springsteen, drew on African American cultural forms but transformed them into "a sufficiently tamed and whitened product so as to be fit for mass consumption."[108] "He is, indeed," writes Simon Frith of Springsteen, "one of the sexiest performers rock and roll has ever had—there's a good part of his concert audience who simply fancy him, can't take their eyes off his body, and he's mesmerizing on stage because of the confi-

dence with which he displays himself."[109] Band members watch and respond to their leader's every move, and as he struts his muscle-bound
body around the stage, he directs the massive crowds in sing-alongs,
elicits their enthusiasm with well-struck poses, inspires them to bounce
joyfully to his music, and compels them to cheer in unrestrained adulation, which, his exuberance illustrates, he enjoys immensely.

On one level, Springsteen's performance liberates his fans by presenting the possibility of sexual freedom. On another, it reaffirms the power
of masculinity. Springsteen is the Boss, a nickname that points to the
intensely conflicted conditions under which he articulated his politics.
Coined by mid-nineteenth-century artisans, the term "boss," as I have
noted, both distinguished free laborers from black slaves and secured
their manhood. This meaning persisted into the 1980s, for even then
bosses were typically neither female nor black. Springsteen renounced
his sobriquet, but whether he liked it or not, it reinforced his masculinity
and whiteness by connoting mastery and authority. This hard-bodied hero
sang about the rapaciousness of Reagan's America, but in the meantime,
he accumulated more than his fair share of wealth. On the surface, he
seemed to renounce the power and influence of corporate America, but
beneath his rhetoric, he was the product of an intense marketing campaign designed by Landau and CBS Records' top executive Al Teller, who
was determined to sell 10 million copies of Born in the U.S.A.[110] Springsteen
could sing about "the boss man giving you hell," but he was also the chief
executive of a multimillion-dollar enterprise that employed a band and a
sizable support staff, members of which, on one occasion, sued him for
violating labor laws.[111] For all of his talk about powerlessness, Springsteen had become one of the most powerful men in the entertainment
industry, an achievement that could severely limit his political efficacy.

A survey of fans indicates that they readily perceived the connection
between masculine sexuality and authority. A pair of fifteen-year-old girls
who attended one of his 1985 performances recalled seeing "pictures of
[Springsteen] when he was not very cute," but they now thought that with
his pumped-up body he was so "gorgeous," such a "fox," that they would
"marry him" in a heartbeat. Perhaps more instructive were the comments
of a twenty-year-old woman who admired Springsteen's "cute ass" but
also praised his commitment to the United States. "He's the most patriotic guy around," she observed. "I feel patriotic—it's a real turn around
from the hippie days."[112] The sexualized rock and roll of the 1960s had
threatened the social order, but Springsteen's sexuality, like Rambo's,

was perceived as being inextricably bound with national interests. It was a sexuality that prompted Curt Fluhr, a member of Springsteen's first band, to call him "the most heterosexual person [he had] ever met" and a woman in *McCall's* magazine to speculate that he made Americans "feel good" because he was "a real man."[113]

There was, however, one element of Springsteen's sexuality that conservatives, in fact nearly everyone, tended to overlook.[114] Until Springsteen's future wife Patti Scialfa joined his band in 1984, E Street was the site of a tight-knit fraternity of five men whose emphasis on male bonding rang with homoerotic overtones. Whether these men were posing for publicity photographs or performing onstage, they were not reluctant to demonstrate their affection for one another in physical terms. In photo sessions for *The River*, Springsteen poses with his arms around band members; in videos such as "Thunder Road" and "Glory Days," he and the demonstrative Steve Van Zandt sing so close to each other that their mouths nearly touch.[115] Although the band temporarily broke up in 1990, *Blood Brothers* (1996), a documentary directed by Ernie Fritz that chronicles their brief reunion for the recording of Springsteen's *Greatest Hits* (1995), reveals the musicians' affection for one another. In one notable scene, Springsteen approaches Dan Federici, puts his hands on the keyboardist's shoulders, and kisses him on top of the head.

Springsteen's most physical and intense displays of affection typically involve the towering African American saxophonist, Clarence Clemons. Just prior to the scene with Federici, band members tenderly embrace as they celebrate the "Big Man's" birthday, and Clemons announces that "being among these people" is "the best present that a person could have," that these "friends" were "what it's all about."[116] Springsteen, who in the film responds with a firm hug, declared his deep love for Clemons during his 1999 induction into the Rock and Roll Hall of Fame. After thanking each of the band members, including his wife, for the contributions they made to his career, Springsteen followed his customary concert practice of introducing Clemons as the "last but not least" of the E Streeters. His praise for the "Big Man" was tendered in romantic terms. "Something happened when we stood side by side. Some . . . energy, some unspoken story," Springsteen said of their first meeting. "For fifteen years, Clarence has been a source of myth and light and enormous strength for me onstage. He has filled my heart so many nights, so many nights. And I love it when he wraps me in those arms at the end of the night. I want to thank you, Big Man. I love you so much."[117]

Bruce Springsteen kisses saxophonist Clarence Clemons onstage during the Born in the U.S.A. Tour. Copyright © Neal Preston/Corbis.

During the Born in the U.S.A. Tour, the most obvious manifestation of this homoeroticism came when, at the close of the first set of each performance, Springsteen and Clemons embraced each other in a "soul kiss." [118] At the conclusion of "Thunder Road," an unmistakably heterosexual song that culminates with these two musicians triumphantly trading notes on the guitar and saxophone, Springsteen would run the length of the stage, slide on his knees, and be met by Clemons, who embraced and kissed him firmly on the lips. This carefully staged performance has been documented on Springsteen's video anthology but, despite its clear violation of social taboos, has not been widely discussed. Why, in a country that has little tolerance for same-sex relations, has such behavior not prompted someone to question Springsteen's sexual orientation? Certainly George Will would not expect such a "wholesome cultural portent" to frolic about the stage and kiss other men, especially black men, squarely on the lips. How could a conservative pundit such as Will see the soul kiss and still insist that Springsteen's "manner" affirms the "right" American values?

The homosocial and homoerotic love that has been an integral part of the working-class hero's politics cuts two ways. On one hand, it functions conservatively to reinforce the political and economic interests of white men by excluding women and people of color from the privileges that these men enjoy. On the other hand, the hero uses notions of manly love to question sexual conventions and create the possibility of forging social bonds based on love and mutual respect. Embracing the latter of these possibilities, Martha Nell Smith suggests that Springsteen's soul kiss abdicates the power of white masculinity. As this manly musician slides across the stage and finds himself kneeling between Clemons's legs, Springsteen places himself in a subordinate position that Smith describes as "feminine," one in which the saxophonist asserts his imposing physical presence and manhood over Springsteen's, thereby subverting racial and gender hierarchies as well as sexual conventions.[119]

In the mid-1980s, however, Springsteen provided no context for such an interpretation. Despite his homoerotic flirtations and interracial bonding, he ignored the politics of homosexuality and did not address racial issues in any significant way. In fact, his politics largely expressed the original sentiments of Whitman's working-class hero: he lamented the loss of the white male worker's social status and sought to restore his dignity. When read in this context, the soul kiss reaffirms the power and presumed universality of white manhood in a manner that was quite consistent with Reagan's construction of it.[120] Springsteen was so secure in his heterosexuality, whiteness, and enormous popularity that he could engage in homoerotic displays without having to face the political realities of gay male identity and without suffering any consequences. As I argue in my discussion of Guthrie, gay men have been so feminized and the working class so masculinized that even in the 1980s it was virtually impossible to imagine a place or a person in which these two categories could overlap, particularly when conventional definitions of manhood were inseparable from the concept of "family values." Like Reagan and Rambo, the apparently working-class Springsteen was for many Americans a white hard-bodied hero whose masculinity confirmed the values of patriarchy and patriotism, the work ethic and rugged individualism, and who clearly demarcated the boundaries between men and women, black and white, heterosexual and homosexual. His body, argues Pfeil, projected "a certain kind of white working-class masculinity associated with Fordist regimes of mass production and capital accumulation," a sort of nostalgia for the glory days of the white male worker and the economic prosperity he represented.[121] No one commented on Springsteen's homoerotic forays because his masculinity, whiteness, and invocation of the post–World War II past were such an integral part of Reagan's America that they could not possibly be seen as subversive.

That is not to say that the soul kiss could not, if properly contextualized, protest prevailing hierarchies. Much like the homoerotic first chapter of Guthrie's *Bound for Glory*, in which the author embraces an African American hobo and metaphorically erases the distinctions between black and white bodies, Springsteen's kiss could challenge racism, defy constructs of sexuality and manhood, and imagine a community in which men and women, black and white, could embrace one another in the spirit of love and equality. In order to transform his performances from mere appropriation and playful signification to politically significant statements, however, Springsteen would have to do more than, as he told an interviewer, "disassociate [himself] from the president's kind words." [122] He would have to question seriously the privileges and politics of white manhood that were so deeply embedded in the tradition of working-class heroism. These questions would not come until the *Born in the U.S.A.* hype subsided.

8   A Good Clear Eye on the Dirty Ways of the World

Springsteen's Democratic Vistas

" really enjoyed the success of *Born in the U.S.A.*, but by the end of the whole thing, I just kind of felt 'Bruced' out," Springsteen explained in 1992. "You end up creating this sort of icon, and eventually it oppresses you."[1] Springsteen plied his trade so successfully that journalists compared him to a king named Elvis and constructed his story as the triumph of American individualism, the culmination of hard work. Unsettled by such interpretations, Springsteen began to revise his legend and tried to clarify his politics. Throughout the mid-1980s and 1990s, he reaffirmed his commitment to the cultural politics of Woody Guthrie and, particularly in *The Ghost of Tom Joad* (1995), critically examined the constructs of heroism and white masculinity. Grounding his work firmly in an artistic tradition Walt Whitman had engendered nearly a century and a half earlier, Springsteen expanded the rhetoric of republicanism to imagine that the natural rights of freedom and equality might be granted to all Americans, regardless of race, gender, or sexual orientation. His democratic vision was blurred, however, by his blind faith in the republican tradition itself. Rather than adapting Guthrie's materialism to criticize the American political economy, Springsteen recovered Whitman's spiritualism to define economic oppression in moral rather than political terms, a familiar strategy that limited his radicalism and continued to thwart the egalitarian hopes of the working-class hero.

Post-Reagan

Springsteen attempted to clarify his politics almost immediately after Ronald Reagan endorsed him in 1984, but perhaps because the musician wanted to continue to ride the wave of prosperity, perhaps because he lacked a sophisticated political perspective, his response was marked by contradictions. Two days after Reagan claimed him as an ally, Springsteen suggested at a Pittsburgh concert that the president had not listened carefully to his material and dedicated "Johnny 99" to the chief executive. He then began what he called a campaign of "human politics."[2] In Pittsburgh, he presented a check for $10,000 to a food bank administered by United Steelworkers of America Local 1397, the first in a series of donations that put more than $1 million in the coffers of similar programs in the cities he toured. Although Landau's associate, Barbara Carr, and her husband, Dave Marsh, chose the charities, Springsteen's support of labor unions had the potential to distinguish him from Reagan. But because this cultural worker insisted that "people on their own could do a lot" and did not connect his philanthropy to any larger social or political movement, it was easily perceived as a prime example of Reagan's call for volunteerism.[3] And since the tour grossed $117 million in ticket sales and another $30 million in souvenirs, it is fair to say that Springsteen's redistribution of wealth was generous but hardly radical.[4]

Although Springsteen lacked clear ideological commitment, he began to recognize the importance of collective political action. He used "My Hometown," a song about a thirty-five-year-old man who considers relocating his wife and family because he cannot find work, as a sounding board for his ideas. Prior to his performances of this song at his concerts, Springsteen typically encouraged fans to involve themselves in local politics and to design and support programs that would advance the cause of social justice in their hometowns. At a Los Angeles concert, he tried to connect the ideals expressed in his work with the concrete efforts of community activists. The men and women who operated area food banks, he suggested, were the people who took "some of these ideas that I'm singin' about up here tonight and [tried] to make 'em a reality in people's lives. They're trying to make . . . a better and fairer place to live for all . . . citizens. Without them, what I'm doin' up here tonight don't amount to much."[5] He often reiterated such themes when he reprised "This Land Is Your Land," which he introduced by suggesting that Guthrie's song was "about a promise that's eroding everyday for a lot of people" and concluded by making the collectivist, egalitarian pronouncement, "Remember, in the end, nobody wins unless everybody wins."[6]

Following the Born in the U.S.A. Tour, Springsteen tried to sharpen his politics by releasing Live/1975–85 (1986), a compendium of concert recordings that elucidate his position on Vietnam. In an onstage narrative that introduces "The River," Springsteen describes how the war affected individual families by telling of his estranged father's obvious relief when he learned of his son's draft deferment. His cover of Edwin Starr's "War" on the album makes his position even clearer. Explaining that "if you grew up in the sixties, you grew up with war on TV every night," Springsteen addresses the song to the "young people" in his audience. He suggests that the government will be expecting them to fight the "next" war, and unlike Springsteen and his friends, who "didn't have much of a chance to think about how we felt about a lot of things," this generation should consider their options carefully and critically "because in 1985," he insists, "blind faith in your leaders, or in anything, will get you killed." In the angry performance that follows, Springsteen screams that war is "good for absolutely nothin'," an opinion that distinguished him from such hawkish leaders as Reagan.

Springsteen's work still lacked the support of a leftist culture or political movement, however, a problem he sought to rectify by bolstering his connections to Guthrie and the lineage of the working-class hero. In the context of *Live*, "War" punctuates a politically engaged segment that Springsteen initiates with "This Land." Although the performance does not include the "lost" verses of the song, it introduces some of Springsteen's most class-conscious material. "Nebraska," "Johnny 99," "Born in the U.S.A.," and "The River" all reveal Guthrie's political and cultural influence and Springsteen's intentions to follow in his footsteps. He reaffirmed his commitment to this tradition by recording two Guthrie songs for the *Vision Shared* project in 1988 and by occasionally performing them during the Amnesty International Human Rights Now! Tour that same year. Throughout this worldwide musical celebration of the Declaration of Human Rights, Springsteen honed his political viewpoints by issuing a number of heavy-handed commentaries about social and economic justice. In footage from a concert in Harare, Zimbabwe, aired on the Home Box Office Network, he read a prepared statement in which he asked the 15,000 white South Africans in attendance to work toward securing "the dignity and freedom of all the African people." Discerning parallels between South African and U.S. racism, he continued, "Whether it's the systematic apartheid of South Africa, or the economic apartheid of my own country—where we segregate our underclass in ghettoes of all the major cities—there can be no peace without justice. And where there is apartheid, systematic or economic, there is no justice."[7] The words might not have been written by Springsteen, but it was clear that he was acquiring a political education that ultimately manifested itself in his work.

Although part of Live focused on Springsteen's social politics, his next studio album, Tunnel of Love (1987), was an introspective record that, he explained, was "about really letting another person in your life and trying to be a part of someone else's life."[8] Inspired by his relationship with his first wife, Julianne Phillips, from whom he separated in 1988, Springsteen's work carefully examined how constructs of gender shaped social and romantic relationships. Perhaps because he identifies strongly with his mother, he has been sensitive to the conditions in which working-class women live and has expressed a rather egalitarian attitude when it comes to gender. He has acknowledged, however, that "we were all brought up with sexist attitudes," and as the National Organization for Women (NOW) observed in 1982, his persistent use of such terms as "little girl" and "baby" in his songs indicates that some of these attitudes crept into his music.[9] His propensity for constructing work and the crisis of unemployment in largely masculine terms supports NOW's argument, but his treatment of Scialfa and a number of his songs suggest that he has "tried to show a basic respect for people's humanness" in an industry that often exhibits a "denigrating attitude towards women."[10] Well before he began his romance with Scialfa, he remarked that having a woman in the band gave "it more of a feeling of community," and soon after she joined, she became an integral member by stepping out of the traditional woman's role of backup singer, picking up a guitar, and becoming Springsteen's "main foil," a part once reserved for Clemons and Steve Van Zandt.[11]

Springsteen's treatment of Scialfa may have had as much to do with their personal relationship and her musical abilities as it did with his gender politics, but in much of his music, he has made an effort to represent the lives of working-class women with dignity. As early as 1978, "Racing in the Street" empathized with the struggles of a woman whose husband pays little attention to her emotional or material needs. He and his male partner spend most of their time repairing and racing his 1969 Chevrolet, and although this homosocial hobby prevents these men from "dying little by little, piece by piece," it offers her little more than loneliness and depression.[12] Just three years after she and her husband marry—and just three years after Springsteen articulated that "romantic idea" about a man and a woman who would one day drive their car to the promised land—

this young woman "sits on the porch of her Daddy's house . . . / With the eyes of one who hates for just being born." [13] The highway and the young man's romantic promise have not taken her anywhere.

"Racing in the Street" was not the only song in which Springsteen critically explored the myth of heterosexual romance. "Candy's Room," "Point Blank," "The River," "I Wanna Marry You," and "Atlantic City" all depicted less than ideal relationships and empathized with female characters,[14] but whereas these songs tended to present women as victims of unfortunate circumstances, "Spare Parts" (1987) is the story of a woman who has the strength to try to overcome the social relations and myths that shape her life. "This is a song about a woman struggling to understand the value of her own independent existence," Springsteen commented during the Tunnel of Love Express Tour. "The value of the life of her child. Put down her old dreams and parts of her past that are keepin' her down. Trying to find something new and beautiful and meaningful in her life today." [15] The decidedly unromantic scenario in which she conducts this search demonstrates how the relationships of sexuality, gender, and class intersect in the protagonist's life. Springsteen introduces her in a blunt, almost uncouth manner that defies the conventions of popular song: "Bobby said he'd pull out Bobby stayed in / Janey had a baby wasn't any sin." In these lines, Springsteen rewrites more than thirty years of male rock and roll fantasies that celebrate the liberating effects of sexual expression but do not examine the power relations in which they are embedded. Bobby's power play begins when he fails to "pull out." His promise to do so indicates that he and Janey had negotiated the terms of their encounter, but he betrays her confidence, asserting his strength and sexuality in a stereotypically masculine manner that establishes control over both his and Janey's bodies. Social constructs permit him to remain narrowly focused on his own immediate pleasure rather than on the possible long-term effects of his actions. As a mother, Janey will be expected to care for their child, whereas Bobby, who would rather pursue his own individual freedom at the expense of his responsibility, has the ignominious but nonetheless real option of fleeing from the situation. Although the two are engaged to be married, he exercises this option by bolting to the Texas oil fields, leaving Janey in a predictable lurch. Lacking any means of financial support, this young woman moves in with her mother, an arrangement that alludes to the fact that the gendered relations of work provide Janey with few opportunities to support herself and her child. Moreover, it compels the listener to wonder about the absence of Janey's father and suggests that perhaps he too had evaded his commitments and abandoned his family.

After the birth of her son, Janey, deprived of her adolescence and early adulthood, longs for excitement and imagines escaping her past and the arduous burden of motherhood. She recalls the story of a woman from a neighboring town who, perhaps confronted with a similar situation, threw her baby in a river and left it to drown. Although Janey goes so far as to stand in the rushing waters with her son, she reweighs her alternatives before executing her plan. Rather than destroying her baby's life as well as her own, she closes the door on her relationship with Bobby and reclaims the value of her life by pawning her engagement ring, a symbol of broken promise, for some "good cold cash." Janey does not pine for her lover's return, nor does she, like the woman in "Racing in the Street," sit defeated and helpless on the front porch of her father's house. Instead, she asserts what control she can over her "own independent existence" and reaffirms the meaning of her life by discovering something in the love that exists between her and her son. Unlike the grim narratives of *Nebraska*, in which nearly all human relationships, both familial and social, are strained or severed, "Spare Parts" begins to reestablish the bonds that exist between people and suggests the possibility of a social order based on love and understanding rather than on the power relations defined by gender, class, and sexuality.[16]

As Springsteen considers the politics of gender, he also explores the homoeroticism of the soul kiss in a more serious manner. In particular, this eroticism manifests itself in the "Tougher Than the Rest" video, which constructs a continuum between the homoerotic and heteroerotic in a manner that recalls Whitman. The lyrics to "Tougher Than the Rest" do not specify the gender of either the narrator or the person he or she desires, and although Springsteen's voice implies that the narrator is male and his potential lover female, the song provides for a certain Whitman-esque fluidity. Whatever their sex, the two characters are stripped of their romantic illusions about love. Both have learned that rather than waiting for an ideal relationship, you must sometimes "get what you can get."[17] As Martha Nell Smith notes in her provocative reading of the video, the narrator and the object of desire seductively exchange stares until, in the final verse, an offer is tendered in a manner that discloses the sex of neither party: "If you're rough and ready for love / Honey I'm tougher than the rest."[18]

The "Tougher Than the Rest" video explores the sexual continuum through three separate but interrelated narratives: Springsteen and the E Street Band's live concert performance of the song, black-and-white footage of Springsteen and the band performing other songs during the Tunnel of Love Express Tour, and shots of couples posing in a photography booth like those found in amusement parks. The performance of the song both anchors the production and establishes the heteroerotic end of the sexual continuum. A long, plodding instrumental introduction cues the action, and after band members take the stage and purchase tickets to ride through the tunnel of love from a man dressed as a carnival vendor, Springsteen's dark ride begins. The camera slowly and seductively introduces the star's body to the viewer: it focuses on his silver-tipped cowboy boots and gradually exposes his dark jeans, long-sleeved shirt, vest, and bolo tie before giving way to his face. But unlike the Springsteen of the Born in the U.S.A. Tour, who dressed as though he was ready to work his shift at a gas station, this one looks as though he is out for a date. In a sense, he is. As he completes the first verse, Scialfa steps up to a microphone located some thirty feet away from him, and once her eyes meet Springsteen's, the two performers remain transfixed as they harmonize on the song. As their intense, provocative stares re-create the sexual tension and desire that permeate the lyrics, they document the feelings that the couple had been exploring off the stage as well. During the tour, tabloids published intimate photographs of the two musicians, and soon after Springsteen and Phillips divorced, he and Scialfa married.[19]

Whereas the performance narrative suggests that Springsteen's homosocial desire had been displaced by his desire for Scialfa, the only female member of the band, the footage from the tour indicates otherwise. The first narrative may have hidden Springsteen's body from public view, but the second enthusiastically reveals and celebrates it, showing him dressed in tight black jeans and black sleeveless shirts, which, observes Smith, render "the husky-voiced hunk . . . fit for a leather bar."[20] Springsteen kisses female audience members in these segments and welcomes them onstage for a dance, but both his attire and his cavorting recover the familiar homoeroticism of male bonding. As he climbs onto amplifiers and turns somersaults, he also drapes his body, dripping with sweat, around band members. Springsteen was committed to heterosexual relationships, but his conception of manly love was still a central part of his concerts and his politics.

It is possible to conclude that Springsteen is so secure in his heterosexuality that his homoerotic flirtations are, like the soul kiss, mere acts of play that signify nothing. But unlike his performance during the Born in the U.S.A. Tour, the "Tougher Than the Rest" video engages the possibility, if not the politics, of homosexual identity. In the third narrative, which is peppered throughout the first two, couples in love—heterosexual, lesbian, gay, and interracial—pose for the camera, openly hugging, kissing, and touching each other. The song itself does not provide a clear social or political context for images of same-sex love, but as Martha Nell Smith has noted, Springsteen's decision to include these images in a video produced during an era in which family values were touted as the standard to which American civilization must cling challenges rather than confirms the conventions of popular culture.[21]

By representing what is normally and quite acceptably excluded from popular representation and interspersing these representations throughout his own erotic performance, Springsteen practices the politics of inclusion and, like Whitman, intimates that the boundary that separates homoerotic and heteroerotic love is a "thin line."[22] If he and his fans intended to connect their individual freedom to a community of equals in which, as he often told his audiences, "nobody wins unless everybody wins," they had to respect, foster, and disseminate love in all of its guises.[23] "You can use all your powers to isolate yourself, to surround yourself with luxury, to intoxicate yourself in any particular fashion you desire," he explained. "But it just starts eating you away inside because there is something you get from engagement with people, from a connection with a *person* that you just cannot get anyplace else."[24] Like Whitman and Guthrie before him, Springsteen suggests that the bonds of collectivity are formed when individuals engage in meaningful and selfless relations with one another, when they embrace rather than fear other human bodies, regardless of race or gender. To create a society in which an idealized but all-inclusive love for other human beings was actually "tougher than" the values of self-interest, greed, or hate, Springsteen asserts that his audience would have not only to question the economic and racial relationships on which the current social order rested but also to rethink constructions of sexuality.[25]

Springsteen began to explore the politics of sexuality more directly when he contributed to the soundtrack of *Philadelphia* (1993), the Jonathan Demme film about a gay man dying of AIDS. When Demme approached Springsteen, he told him "he was making [the film] for 'the malls,' " that "he wanted to take a subject that people didn't feel safe with and were frightened by and put it together with people they *did* feel safe with."[26] Springsteen's unmistakable heterosexuality and white masculinity made him the ideal man for the job. The Academy Award–winning "Streets of Philadelphia" was decidedly unthreatening, an organ-driven dirge that mourned the loss of a diseased man rather than a topical ballad that agitated for gay rights. The song's ties to the film implied its narrator's sexual orientation, but Springsteen does not disclose his subject's sexuality. As he does in his early songs about economic exploitation, he chooses not to assault oppressive social conventions but instead urges his audience to identify with the afflicted man on a human level, to empathize with his suffering. Relying on the language of brotherhood, Springsteen tries to break down "walls between people," to establish a "particular kind of communion."[27] "So receive me brother with your faithless kiss," sings the narrator as he describes his deteriorating health, "or will we leave each other alone like this."[28] Although the sexual politics of the song remained vague, Springsteen used an interview in the *Advocate*, a gay rights magazine, as an "opportunity" to clarify "where I stand on different issues." Homophobia, he contended, was "an ugly part of the American character," and he "very much" wanted gay men and lesbians to be equal members of his imagined "community."[29] In the early 1900s, Horace Traubel transformed the working-class hero and the language of brotherhood and adhesiveness to suppress Whitman's homoeroticism, but in the 1990s, Springsteen used the same language to try to convince audiences to end discrimination based on sexual orientation.

PAIN, MEMORY, AND HOPE

Following the Amnesty International Human Rights Now! Tour, Springsteen entered a period of psychological depression and intense self-doubt that forced him to turn inward. As a result, his next two albums, *Human Touch* and *Lucky Town* (1992), were mainly celebrations of his recovery, his marriage to Patti Scialfa, and the birth of their first two children. "Better Days" and "Local Hero" commented on the ambivalence he felt about success, "Souls of the Departed" superficially addressed gang violence and the Gulf War, and a remix of "57 Channels (And Nothin' On)" included sounds recorded during the Rodney King riots, but despite the persistent chant of "No justice, no peace," the song made no clear statement about racial politics.[30] When in 1996 Springsteen performed at the Severance Hall tribute to Woody Guthrie, however, he unequivocally announced that he had returned to take up the cultural work of his predecessors.

As he opened his set with "Tom Joad" (1940), his guitar resonated along the open road and reawakened the ghosts of history. Guthrie's lengthy ballad about the protagonist of *The Grapes of Wrath* took Springsteen back to John Steinbeck and John Ford, whose novel and film influenced *Darkness on the Edge of Town*, the pivotal album on which he first "figured out what [he] wanted to write about."[31] Set to the tune of the familiar folk ballad "John Hardy," "Tom Joad" sent Springsteen via *Nebraska*, via the Folkways *Anthology*, via the Carter Family, to McDowell County, West Virginia, where African Americans challenged a racist society. "Tom Joad" directed him to Minneapolis, where, after reading *Bound for Glory*, Bob Dylan learned all seventeen verses of this ballad and could soon be heard singing them in Dinkytown coffeehouses.[32] Springsteen's performance recalled the 1940 Grapes of Wrath Evening, a benefit for agricultural workers organized in New York City by Guthrie's friend and fellow Whitman aficionado, Will Geer. That evening, Guthrie met Pete Seeger, the cultural guerrilla who would later keep his legend alive and who closed the Severance Hall tribute by singing "Hobo's Lullabye," one of Guthrie's favorite songs. And finally "Tom Joad" sent Springsteen back to his native New Jersey, back to Camden, where Guthrie first recorded the song and the Good Gray Poet spent the final years of his life in a modest home on Mickle Street.

These cultural journeys had already presented themselves in Springsteen's *Ghost of Tom Joad*, a largely acoustic album of working-class narratives that, although it resembles *Nebraska*, expresses a vision for the future by imagining ways in which the "meanness" of the social order might be overcome. On *Nebraska* and *Vision Shared*, Springsteen shunned Guthrie's communal politics, but on *The Ghost of Tom Joad*, he enthusiastically embraces the assertion that "everybody might be just One Big Soul" and recommits himself to using his art to help those who are "fighting for their rights."[33] Throughout the album and the tour that promoted it, Springsteen, as Whitman had done before him, constructed economic and racial oppression as a moral problem and tried to forge a culture that is not based on self-interest but that will teach men and women to balance individual freedom with the public good, to value people over profits, to create an egalitarian society based on love and compassion rather than hate and greed. To present his audience with tough moral questions, Springsteen once again relies on the language of the hurt song and the image of the working-class hero, but although he recovers the political potential and some of the shortcomings of these cultural traditions, he revises them to clarify his own cultural politics and avoid the misinterpretation that occurred when the country absorbed him as fully as he absorbed it.

On *The Ghost of Tom Joad*, the hoboes who have been on "the rails since the Great Depression" meet the homeless of contemporary America, where, much as they were in "Vigilante Man," they are "bunked . . . in a barn just like animals" and harassed and beaten by authorities.[34] In the title track, police helicopters keep a watchful eye on Fordesque shanty-towns built beneath bridges, while families, kin to the workers Guthrie saw standing outside the relief office in the original "This Land," stand in a "shelter line," still waiting to feel the impact of the "new world order" that George Bush promised would follow the Gulf War.[35] Springsteen was outspoken in his criticism of the Bush administration's social policies, but the government was not the only institution that he accused of failing to create a kinder, gentler nation. Springsteen also points the gun at organized religion, suggesting that Christianity in particular has shunned its social responsibilities. In *The Grapes of Wrath*, Preacher Jim Casy, whose words Guthrie reiterates in both "Vigilante Man" and "Tom Joad," rejects the practice of saving individual souls in favor of trying to convince everyone they are part of "One Big Soul," a cause for which he sacrifices his life.[36] The homeless preacher in Springsteen's ballad offers no such solutions, however. Rather than embracing the social gospel, he invokes the language and passivity of a fundamentalism that repeatedly aggravated Guthrie and, in Springsteen's era, resurfaced in various components of the religious Right. This man of the cloth recalls the conservatism of the Carter Family and the lyrics of Dylan's "Times They Are A-Changin' " when, sitting helplessly in a cardboard box, he awaits an eternal reward in which "the last shall be first and the first shall be last." [37]

Although Springsteen implies that such conservative ideas have created a culture that largely fails to address the issue of social equality, he acknowledges that the myths he helped perpetuate, particularly those that promise upward mobility, are equally empty. The highway of "Born to Run" was "jammed with broken heroes," but on *The Ghost of Tom Joad*, it was "alive" with broken dreams and "nobody's kiddin' nobody about where it goes." [38] The myth of upward mobility, the hackneyed promise of rock and roll, the romanticized life of the hobo, and even the eternal optimism of Whitman's open road have failed to lead the hard travelers of *The Ghost of Tom Joad* to social and economic justice. What is needed to validate a "one-way ticket to the promised land," Springsteen implies, is an alternative set of symbols and heroes who, like Tom Joad, will confront the pain and history of inequality rather than fleeing from them:

Now Tom said "Mom, wherever there's a cop beatin' a guy
Wherever a hungry newborn baby cries
Where there's a fight 'gainst the blood and hatred in the air
Look for me Mom I'll be there
Wherever there's somebody fightin' for a place to stand
Or a decent job or a helpin' hand
Wherever somebody's strugglin' to be free
Look in their eyes Mom you'll see me." [39]

The Guthrie that Springsteen resurrects is not the road-weary hobo who wanted to run from the world but, as he sang in his performance of "Blowin' Down That Old Dusty Road" at Severance Hall, the cultural worker who vowed to "change this whole damn world around." [40]

"I have decided, long ago," wrote Guthrie in 1946, "that my songs and ballads would not get the hugs and kisses of the capitalistic 'experts,' simply because I believe that the real folk history of this country finds its center and its hub in the fight of the union members against the hired gun thugs of the big owners." [41] Such Guthrie hurt songs as "Ludlow Massacre," "1913 Massacre," and "Talking Centralia" document the violent nature of this history, and although Springsteen has never represented an incident in which a company unleashes "gun thugs" on its workers, "Youngstown" illustrates the violence that corporations commit when they value profits more than people. [42]

Based on Dale Maharidge's *Journey to Nowhere*, a study of the underclass in 1980s America, "Youngstown" reconstructs the history of industrial capitalism through the eyes of an unemployed steelworker. [43] The narrator explains that in 1803 the Heaton brothers built the first blast furnace in the Youngstown, Ohio, area and initiated an industrial economy that sustained the Mahoning Valley for over 170 years. [44] By 1863, Youngstown was the site of a major ironworks, and as the steel industry expanded after the Civil War, local businesspeople were determined to prevent emerging trusts from dominating their town. [45] To that end, George Wick and James Campbell, former employees of Andrew Carnegie, founded Youngstown Sheet and Tube in 1900, which soon dominated the local economy. [46] By 1969, however, Sheet and Tube was acquired by the Lykes Corporation, a

New Orleans–based shipbuilding concern that made much of its fortune transporting supplies to Vietnam.[47] A variety of factors prompted Lykes to close its Campbell, Ohio, works in 1977, a decision that furloughed 4,100 workers. Less than three years later, Youngstown's working people were devastated when U.S. Steel and Jones and Laughlin closed operations, putting another 4,900 people out of work.[48] As support jobs to the mills folded, the city's unemployment rate approached 30 percent in the early 1980s.[49]

Springsteen structures his study of the Youngstown economy around a narrative of military history that illustrates that the workingmen of this community have done their best to live the right way not only by being loyal to their company but also by participating in the Civil War, World War II, and the Korean and Vietnam Wars, each of which was ostensibly fought to preserve or advance a conception of freedom based on capitalism. When the mills close, the narrator declares, much like the veteran in "Born in the U.S.A.," that the promise of this freedom has been betrayed:

> Well my daddy come on the Ohio works
> When he come home from World War Two
> Now the yard's just scrap and rubble
> He said "Them big boys did what Hitler couldn't do."
> These mills they built the tanks and bombs
> That won this country's wars
> We sent our sons to Korea and Vietnam
> Now we're wondering what they were dyin' for.[50]

Working-class sons followed their fathers to the battlefields and the mill, furnishing the bodies and producing the weapons that fought for freedom, but "big boys" like the Lykes Corporation, not the workers, reaped the benefits of their actions. With the help of a liberal corporate state, Lykes accumulated considerable profits by meeting increased wartime demand for its products, but by the 1970s, it no longer needed the men who had paid the cost for their economic freedom. By 1980, more than 10,000 jobs left the Youngstown area, and the federal government provided little assistance to a community that had helped build the country's infrastructure and had given its children to military service. As Lykes pulled out of the Youngstown area, it provided a "guide for Machiavellian managers" that demonstrated that it clearly valued profits over people: it gave its employees no advance notice of the plant closure and provided no services to help them find new jobs.[51] Hitler, suggests the narrator's father, could not destroy the mills or the men who labored there, but with the complicity of the state, the Lykes Corporation could.

Springsteen's penultimate verse situates the history of this working-class town in a national context, asserting that whether an individual labors in the Monongahela Valley or in the mines of Mesabi or Appalachia, the "story's always the same." As international conglomerates absorbed Youngstown's locally owned furnaces, the relationships between community and company, employee and employer became increasingly detached and depersonalized, and once again, profits were given a much higher value than people or places. Standing among the "scrap and rubble" of the old mills, the proud but defeated narrator of "Youngstown" reveals the deep wounds that this dramatic economic transformation inflicted on him:

Seven hundred tons of metal a day
Now sir you tell me the world's changed
Once I made you rich enough
Rich enough to forget my name.

The protagonist's namelessness corresponds to objectified social relations, but more important, it signals an identity crisis. According to Thomas Fuechtmann, Sheet and Tube became "part of the local myth that held together work and family, craft and aesthetics, fellowship and tradition," and when the company shut down, "it was as if a landmark for community and personal identity had suddenly disappeared."[52] Like Whitman's, Springsteen's song of lost occupations defines the crisis in masculine terms. His memory of his "father trying to find work, what that does to you, and how that affects your image of your manhood, as a provider" was a salient one, and for both Douglas Springsteen and the narrator, the "loss of that role is just devastating."[53] When the mills were razed, the narrator's skills and knowledge became essentially useless, his union was rendered powerless, and, most important, his name and his ability to feed his children, in short, his manhood, were taken away from him.

"Youngstown" laments this loss as much as it criticizes corporations, and by constructing work as an entirely masculine activity, it reminds us that the white male heroes on which Springsteen relies carry liabilities when it comes to addressing the politics of gender. But although Springsteen sees unemployment as a crisis in masculinity, he warns that the concept of manhood can inspire destructive behavior. This narrator is too humiliated to imagine ways to address his situation constructively and implies that to preserve his self-respect, he will lash out against the system that betrayed him. "When I die I don't want no part of heaven / I would not do heaven's work well," he proclaims. "I pray the devil comes and takes me / To stand in the fiery furnaces of hell." Simply put, the only way he, much like the main character in "Johnny 99," can regain the dignity he knew when he labored in the mill is to commit a desperate and perhaps destructive act that demonstrates his refusal to be dominated or humiliated, that defiantly replies to the man who forgot his name with the resounding chorus of "The Promised Land": "Mister, I ain't a boy, no, I'm a man." [54]

Whereas "Youngstown" explores what for Springsteen is familiar territory, several songs on *The Ghost of Tom Joad* examine, albeit awkwardly, the politics of race, something that his music previously addressed only indirectly. After moving to Los Angeles in the early 1990s, Springsteen developed an interest in political controversies that involved Mexican immigrants, many of whom entered the country illegally to work in California fruit orchards. Implicitly alluding to the proponents of such anti-immigration policies as Proposition 187, Springsteen explained to his audience at Severance Hall that "the people coming across the border, working for almost no money, doing jobs nobody else wants to do, and encouraged by American businesses to do so, [are] not the problem. But somebody wants to make you think [they are]." [55] His border ballads point the gun at the employment practices of American businesses, advocates of anti-immigration policies, and an exploitative economic system.

The clear antecedent of these ballads is Guthrie's "Deportee (Plane Wreck at Los Gatos)," which Springsteen introduced at the Severance Hall concert as a "favorite" "that explains why . . . [Guthrie's] music has been lasting forever." [56] Guthrie wrote "Deportee" in 1948 after he read a newspaper account of a plane crash in which a group of migrant workers being deported to Mexico were killed. [57] In his eyes, the report trivialized the event and objectified its victims by suggesting that they were *only* migrant workers, a rationale to which he responded by writing one of his most poignant ballads. "Deportee" sketches a history of migrant labor, explaining that American fruit growers created a dependent labor force by hiring immigrants for brief periods, deporting them to Mexico when their contracts expired, and enticing them to spend significant portions of their paltry wages to return to the United States to seek employment again. He then alludes to the fatal crash and poses the central questions that undergird his song and the Springsteen ballads it inspired: "Is this the best way we can grow our good fruit? / To fall like dry leaves and rot on my topsoil / And be called by no name except deportees?" [58] "A folk song ought to be pretty well satisfied to tell the facts and let it go at that," Guthrie wrote in 1940, to present working-class history and then allow the audience to draw its own conclusions.[59] "Deportee" is a remarkably effective example of this approach. By restoring the crash victims' dignity, reestablishing the emotional ties that bound them together, and giving names to the nameless, Guthrie compels his audience to recognize these men and women as members of the human community and evaluate the economic system that contributed to their deaths.

Based largely on newspaper accounts, Springsteen's ballads present a history of racism while providing the possibility of overcoming it, a possibility that he also creates by rehumanizing his protagonists. In "Sinaloa Cowboys," the Mexican brothers Miguel and Louis illegally cross the U.S. border, entering the fruit orchards to perform the jobs that whites will not, until they realize that they can earn more money manufacturing illicit drugs in a methamphetamine kitchen. Springsteen's telling of their story is uncharacteristically awkward and betrays an unfamiliarity, if not an uneasiness, with his subject. The knowledge provided by newspaper reports does not enable him to portray these men with the same depth or sensitivity with which he represents the lives of white workingmen in such ballads as "Youngstown," where his characters normally speak in the first person and talk about their lives on their own terms. Strange rhymes, clumsy phrasing, and a forced Spanish dialect infuse this long, omniscient narrative with an uneasiness that Springsteen magnifies with generic descriptions of the landscape and labor.[60] Like the working-class heroes who came before him, he addresses racial politics but is far more comfortable with representing his own experience and exploring the hardships faced by white working-class men. But even if "Sinaloa Cowboys" is not one of his most effective songs, it represents its subjects with dignity and demonstrates, like "Deportee," that a racially segmented labor market continues to devalue and destroy human life. After the methamphetamine kitchen explodes and Louis is killed, Miguel takes his brother's body to the desert, kisses him, and puts him in a grave that once held the $10,000 they had managed to salvage from their pay. Drawing on "Deportee," Springsteen transforms these despised illegal immigrants into human beings and asks if this meager sum is all a human life is worth. As their father warned them before they departed for the States, the brothers have learned a hard lesson of capitalist exchange: "For everything the north gives it exacts a price in return."[61] Like Guthrie, Springsteen forces us to ask if this is the best way to operate fruit orchards, if this is the best way to value human life.

"Galveston Bay," another cumbersome tale, focuses on more overt forms of racial violence but introduces the possibility for improved race relations. The song is about Le Bin Son, a Vietnamese immigrant, and Billy Sutter, a Vietnam veteran, both of whom operate shrimp boats off the Texas coast. Springsteen tries to convince these men "to recognize each other through [their] veil of differences" by establishing a common ground: they both fought against communists in the war, they share the same occupation, and they both kiss their sleeping children before they leave for work each morning.[62] Despite such similarities, Sutter and his friends are wary of the influx of Asian immigrants, perhaps because the Vietnamese remind them of the war, perhaps because they fear that their new neighbors will compete with them for jobs. Whatever his motivations, Sutter joins the Ku Klux Klan to reclaim "America for Americans" and purge Galveston Bay of its nonwhite residents.[63] Le thwarts the Klan's attempt to set fire to the Vietnamese boats, however, when he kills two of the would-be arsonists. When Le is acquitted, an outraged Sutter vows to avenge the deaths of his white brothers. Armed with a knife, he waits silently in the shadows for an opportunity to kill Le, but when his target approaches, he allows him to pass unharmed. Springsteen's slow telling of this tale creates a suspense that makes the decision all the more momentous.

Although it engages the politics of whiteness, "Galveston Bay" offers hope for the future in individualistic rather than collective terms and does not provide a social context for Sutter's change of heart. But like Guthrie, who revered the individual acts of such heroes as Pretty Boy Floyd and John Hardy and explained the limits of their actions in his writings and performance, Springsteen has used Sutter's moral epiphany to address the subject of collective politics in his concerts. Introducing the song during a 1996 performance in Atlanta, Springsteen compared Sutter's decision to what he called the act of "kindness" that concludes Steinbeck's *Grapes of Wrath*. In this moving scene, Rose of Sharon, who has just miscarried her child, and Ma Joad seek shelter from a violent storm inside a barn, where they encounter a young boy and his dying father. The boy tells Ma that his malnourished father, who has nearly starved because he has insisted that his son eat his share of their scarce food, is in desperate need of sustenance. Unable to find or buy food for him, Rose of Sharon, in a selfless and tender act of compassion, nurses him at her breast.[64]

Despite Springsteen's suggestion that Rose of Sharon's actions parallel Sutter's, the two events are significantly different: her breast-feeding is an act of human kindness that saves a life and establishes close bonds between people, whereas Sutter simply decides not to take a life and ultimately fails to reach out to his intended victim. In fact, the ambiguous lyrics in and of themselves provide no evidence that Sutter reconsidered his racist attitudes; perhaps he was merely afraid to kill Le. Nevertheless, Springsteen suggested in Atlanta that Sutter's story demonstrated that people have the ability to "change" the "part of the world" they "touch." Before collective movements can be formed, people have to recognize that the world can be changed and then assume a sense of responsibility for transforming it.[65]

The glimmer of hope in "Galveston Bay" echoes the "tough optimism" that Springsteen saw in Guthrie, who similarly had faith that an individual "guard or deputy can always change over on the real people's side" and insisted that hope was an essential tool in the struggle for social justice.[66] "I have seen so many dreams, seen them swept aside by weather, and blown away by men, washed away in my own mistakes, that—I use to wonder if it wouldn't be better just to haul off and quit hoping," Guthrie wrote. He could not, however, totally withdraw from the people around him and maintained that the "note of hope is the only note that can help us from falling to the bottom of the heap of evolution." [67]

In Atlanta, Springsteen developed his own tough optimism when he acknowledged his artistic debt to Ford's *Grapes of Wrath* and performed "Across the Border," a song that imagines a place where "pain and memory have been stilled." [68] In the lengthy remarks that preceded this song, Springsteen meticulously described a scene near the end of the film in which the Joad family, along with other residents of a government labor camp, prevent local antiunion agents from instigating a fight during a camp-sponsored dance. The successful social event depicts the virtues of collective action, enables the Joads to enjoy themselves for the first time since they were driven from their Oklahoma farm, and provides a glimpse of the productive, albeit arduous, life they once had there.[69]

At the conclusion of the dance, Tom Joad, who earlier in the film murdered a vigilante for killing his friend, Preacher Casy, learns that the authorities have issued a warrant for his arrest and decides to flee from the camp and leave his family. Before he departs, however, he bids a poignant farewell to Ma, during which he reveals his vision for the future. Inspired by Casy's proclamation that everybody is part of one big soul, Joad has been "thinkin' . . . about our people livin' like pigs" and "wonderin'" what might happen "if all our folks got together an' yelled."[70] Maybe, Joad explains to his mother, "a fella ain't got a soul of his own, but on'y a piece of a big soul—the one big soul that belongs to ever'body."[71] As he departs, he vows to commit himself to fighting against oppression and hatred, telling his mother not to weep because she will see him "wherever you look": "Wherever there's a cop beatin' up a guy," "in the way guys yell when they're mad," and "in the way kids laugh when they're hungry an' they know supper's ready."[72] The next morning, Tom's flight leads his father to doubt his own self-worth and to remark that the Joads had been "takin' a beatin'," but Ma, inspired by her son's newfound faith, urges him to continue his own search for a better life. "Can't nobody lick us," she asserts in the film's final frames. "We'll go on forever, Pa. We're the people."[73]

I would argue that Ford's ending romanticizes the Joads' struggle and represents them as the noble poor who have the strength to endure but not change their situation. Springsteen, however, understood Ma's remarks as a refusal to capitulate to the social forces that keep her down and offered an alternative interpretation. Drawing on the collectivist spirit embodied in the film, the novel, and Guthrie's work, Springsteen suggested in Atlanta that "maybe our salvation" is located not in "individual" achievement but in the progress made by a "collective" society. Maybe, he suggested, our "spirits" "rise and fall together."[74] To inculcate this spirit of collectivity in his audience, Springsteen criticizes a culture based largely on selfish values and suggests that it must be replaced with one that fosters a sense of compassion.

WHAT SEPARATES PEOPLE

As Springsteen challenged the prevailing values of a capitalist society, he faced the problems of doing so within a commercial culture that was wedded to those values. One of the world's wealthiest and most recognizable popular musicians, he became a symbol for the narratives of upward mobility that he deconstructed, and although he sang about the dispossessed and donated portions of his earnings to homeless shelters and food banks, he continued to amass a fortune that enabled him, like the affluent family in "Mansion on the Hill," to live a very comfortable life at the expense of those who lived very difficult ones. Indeed, Springsteen was full of contradictions. His Beverly Hills home reportedly cost $14 million, and in some cases, the Ghost of Tom Joad Tour was used to exploit the people Springsteen purported to help.[75] When concert dates were announced, enterprising agents paid homeless people a meager sum to purchase $30 tickets that the agents then resold for as much as $500 apiece.

Springsteen insisted, however, that neither his fame nor his social status insulated him from the issues or the people he represented. Wealth, he argued in 1985, "is not where the essence of you lies. That's not what separates people. What separates people are things in their heart."[76] Such idealism revealed the limits of his cultural politics and undermined the class consciousness of his work, which clearly demonstrated that the unequal distribution of resources did in fact separate people into social classes. Springsteen readily explored issues of social justice, but he did not seriously question the social system that by his own admission allowed him to lead "an extravagant lifestyle."[77] His working-class background, he maintained, enabled him to bridge the tremendous financial gap that separated him from the people he claimed to represent. As long as your heart was in the right place, as long as you could remember your own working-class experience, money was no object. Even a wealthy man such as Springsteen could remain engaged in the struggle for social and economic justice.

This struggle was more complicated than Springsteen recognized, but he nevertheless understood that if he intended to distinguish his politics from the politics of individualism, he would have to dismantle the mythic persona he had projected during the Born in the U.S.A. Tour and reconsider some of the standards set by the working-class hero. He could not reconcile the interminable contradictions of the market, but if he expected his audience to comprehend his politics of community and compassion, he would have to reintroduce himself "in a very non-iconic role" and downplay "the macho thing" in particular.[78] In fact, in "Real Man" (1992), he mocked the masculinity that he came to represent in the 1980s. When the narrator takes his date to the movies, he renounces what appears on the screen, where he sees "Rambo . . . blowin' 'em down."[79]

When Springsteen recorded *The Ghost of Tom Joad*, he challenged "the rules" of the contemporary recording industry and the expectations generated by his legend in order to articulate his politics in a clearer fashion and prevent his work from being misinterpreted.[80] His power within

Bruce Springsteen onstage at the tribute to Woody Guthrie at Severance Hall in Cleveland, 1996. Copyright © Neal Preston/Corbis.

the industry afforded him the opportunity to make the type of music he wanted to make, and it is unlikely that a lesser-known act would have been able to release such an uncommercial album on a major label. In this sense, his wealth and status actually aided rather than impeded his politics. The album's austere instrumentation, distressing themes, and decidedly unconventional lyrical structures assured that its meaning would not be swept away in a wave of feel-good commercialism, and throughout the rather somber tour that promoted it, Springsteen carefully and quite earnestly elaborated on the political themes of his work. Rather than playing the four-hour stadium shows that George Will found so exciting, he performed two-hour acoustic shows in venues that seated fewer than 5,000 people. Rather than presenting himself as a muscle-bound, rock and roll sex symbol, the forty-six-year-old Springsteen dressed in baggy jeans and biker boots and pulled his hair back in a small ponytail that accentuated his receding hairline.

The shows were not, however, versions of the popular format for MTV *Unplugged*, in which musicians often evoke nostalgia for their younger days by playing their most popular material. Such songs as "Born to Run" and "Thunder Road," songs that built Springsteen's reputation as a rock and roll hero, did not make the set list.[81] Instead, the shows were dominated by the songs of *The Ghost of Tom Joad*, as well as "Adam Raised a Cain," "Nebraska," "Streets of Philadelphia," "Spare Parts," and a bitter, bluesy slide-guitar rendition of "Born in the U.S.A." that recovered the song's hard and defiant edge. Unlike the younger Springsteen, who threw himself into the arms of his audience and encouraged his fans to sing each word with him, the musician muted the "mating call" and asked his audience to pay quiet attention to his lyrics.[82] "A lot of the songs were written with a lot of silence and they need silence to work," he told a Los Angeles audience. "So if you like singing and clapping along, please don't."[83] To encourage his fans to focus on the pain and history he articulated in his songs as well as his politics of compassion and collectivity, Springsteen suspended his highly sexualized, heroic persona to become what one critic called "your neighborhood drinking buddy," a common man with whom a person could commiserate rather than an uncommon man whom people were compelled to idolize and celebrate.[84] The wide acclaim for the 1999 reunion tour with the E Street Band indicates that the image of Springsteen from the mid-1980s will endure in America's cultural memory. But in 1995, Springsteen's sense of history enabled him to understand that "the macho thing"—the working-class hero's defiant white masculinity and the concept of heroism itself—had done more to hinder his cultural politics than it had done to help them.[85] There was, however, an integral part of the working-class hero's character that Springsteen could not bring himself to question.

THE DIRTY WAYS OF THE WORLD

As Springsteen presented this new image, he maintained an unwavering faith that art could change the world and continued to embrace Guthrie's creed that hurt songs must "tell the true battle of our people to get better and better conditions everywhere."[86] Such art, explains Guthrie, "brings your mind out onto an impersonal plane. It puts action and the ways to action clearly before you and educates you about things that have happened in other parts of the world and calls your attention to things happening to other people now. It . . . compares your troubles and hopes and daily work to the worries and hopes and work of everybody else."[87] By urging people to compare their own "troubles and hopes" with others', Guthrie suggests the possibility of using these experiences "like a spring of cold water" to call attention to all social injustices and address them in a collective fashion.[88] These words, which Springsteen likely read in *Pastures of Plenty*, a collection of Guthrie's writings edited by his friend, Dave Marsh, provided the standard for his own work. As Springsteen explained at the Severance Hall tribute, Guthrie's ability to take "you out of yourself" and get "you thinking about the next guy" comprised the "spiritual center . . . of all of Woody's songs."[89] Through the hurt song, Springsteen also presented the historic struggle for social justice and encouraged his audience to reconsider the morality of economic relations. "You can't tell people what to think," he explained. "You can show them something by saying, 'Put on these shoes, walk in these shoes.' People then recognize themselves in characters whose lives on the surface seem to have no relation to theirs."[90] Through such efforts, he shadowed Guthrie's attempt to "make one end of the community feel like they know the other end."[91]

Springsteen embraces the collective impulse embedded in Guthrie's cultural politics but shuns his Marxism, offering a spiritualist rather than a materialist interpretation that seeks to regenerate communal relations through republicanism. His most profound affirmation of this political vision came during a 1987 Carnegie Hall tribute to Harry Chapin (1942–81), who was posthumously awarded the Congressional Gold Medal for his efforts to eradicate world hunger. Before performing Chapin's "Remember When the Music," Springsteen shared stories about his old friend and drew attention to his political commitment. "He was always trying to get me to do something," recalled Springsteen. To raise money for charities, Chapin told his fellow musician that he played "one night for [himself] and one night for the other guy," a strategy that perfectly balanced individuality and communal responsibility. When Springsteen tried "to put [his own] music to some pragmatic use," he remembered Chapin's advice and charged his audience and his peers to do the same. Accompanied by a lone acoustic guitar, he sang about an idealized era when music "brought us all together," when it "set our hearts on fire to believe in things," when it inspired "dreams to live and hope to give." As the final verse approached, Springsteen delivered perhaps his most comprehensive homily on cultural politics:

> I guess there was a time when people felt that music provided you with a greater . . . oh, a greater sense of unity, a greater sense of shared

vision and purpose than it does today. And my generation, we were the generation that was gonna change the world. Thought somehow we were gonna make it a little less lonely, a little less hungry, a little more just place. But it seems that when that promise slipped through our hands we didn't replace it with nothin' but . . . lost faith. And now . . . times are pretty shattered. I got my music, you got yours, the guy up the street, he's got his. And you could kinda sit back and say not cynically but truthfully, well maybe, maybe all men are not brothers. And maybe we won't ever know who or what we really are to each other. But I think Harry instinctively knew that it was gonna take a lot more than just love to survive. That it was gonna take a strong sense of purpose, of duty, and a good clear eye on the dirty ways of the world. So . . . in keeping his promise to himself, he reminds us of our promise to ourselves. And that tonight, alongside Harry, it's that promise that his spirit would have us remember and honor and recommit to. So do something. And may his song be sung.[92]

Springsteen encourages members of his audience to recommit to the promise of America, to practice a modified version of artisan republicanism. He urges them to maintain faith that one day all citizens will enjoy the natural rights of freedom and equality but warns that the realization of this dream will require more than an idealized love. To convert democratic promise into reality, Springsteen suggests, individuals must accept social responsibility, practice active citizenship, be vigilant for abuses of power, and subordinate self-interest to the good of the community. Far from being "bent to extremism," this working-class hero was bent to republicanism. He could question the constructs of masculinity and whiteness, but this part of his political heritage was beyond reproach.[93]

"I think politics are implicit. I'm not interested in writing rhetoric or ideology," explained Springsteen in 1998. "I think it was Walt Whitman who said, 'The poet's job is to know the soul.' You strive for that, assist your audience in finding theirs."[94] Republicanism was such an integral part of working-class heroism that Springsteen accepted it as being non-ideological, as natural truth. He had espoused the same philosophy a decade earlier, contending that the "political implications" of his work came from "personal insight . . . from observations, like, okay, this man is being wasted. *Why* is this man being wasted?"[95] Like Whitman, Springsteen offers an artistic vision that is not, in the words of the Good Gray Poet, "the result of studying up in political economy, but the ordinary sense, observing, wandering among men."[96] He too examines the United States under a moral microscope, expressing doubt in "the ability of the system to address fundamental moral issues" and turning to cultural work to address these issues on his own terms.[97] "A country is judged not just by its accomplishments, but by its compassion, the health and welfare of its citizens," he insists. "That's the core of its spirit."[98] Accepting the responsibility with which Whitman charged all poets, he furnishes "the hints, the clue, the start or frame-work" to nurture this spirit but leaves it to the listener to put his moral advice into practice.[99]

Perhaps more than any contemporary popular artist, Springsteen has kept his eyes fixed firmly on "the dirty ways of the world." When he advised concert audiences not to "vote for that fuckin' Bush," told *Sixty Minutes* that the social programs of the Reagan-Bush years were "failed policies," and explained to the *New York Times Magazine* that he "didn't see anybody, not Clinton or Dole, addressing the concerns of working people" in the 1996 presidential election, he scrutinized the performance of elected officials.[100] When he compared the "economic apartheid" of the United States with the racial apartheid of South Africa and appeared at an affirmative action rally alongside Jesse Jackson, he had his eyes on racism and economic exploitation.[101] When he explored the implications of sexism and homophobia in his music, he was on the lookout for bigotry and hatred. When at the 1997 Kennedy Center Honors he described Dylan's "Times They Are A-Changin' " as a "beautiful call to arms" that "live[s] on in the struggle for social justice in America that continues so fiercely today," he reaffirmed his commitment to participate in that struggle.[102] And when he admitted that he had followed the "dead-end street" of the "cult of personality" and suggested that the "macho thing" had undermined his politics, he gazed in the mirror and stared critically at the working-class hero himself.[103]

"The proof of a poet is that his country absorbs him as affectionately as he has absorbed it," wrote Whitman in *Leaves of Grass*.[104] Springsteen was proof positive. A true believer in the promised land, he invoked republicanism not only to protest economic exploitation and promote collectivity but also to imagine that the ghosts of history, particularly the specters of racism, sexism, and homophobia, could be exorcised from the body politic. His democratic vistas did not, however, extend beyond familiar republican horizons. He defined injustice in moral terms, pointed the gun at unprincipled people, not political structures. This hero learned his job well, inserting himself into a tradition that simultaneously opened and contained the possibility for social change, that prevented him from becoming "bent to extremism." In his own republican words, he was "a concerned citizen," not an "activist."[105] This song had long been sung. A wealthy entertainer such as Springsteen could be radical, but until he put a good clear eye on the dirty ways of the political economy that had permitted him to amass his fortune, until he was willing to abdicate and not merely question the privileges of affluence, whiteness, and manhood, he could not be too damned radical.

ENCORE

This Hard Land

n a preview of Springsteen's 1996 concert at Atlanta's Fox Theater, the *Atlanta Journal Constitution* casually described Springsteen and Bob Seger, another rock musician with blue-collar roots, as "working-class heroes," a term that seemed to apply to a particularly successful artist who expressed "social concerns," confronted the problems of unemployed and "dispossessed Americans," and considered "family problems" and "the need for moral reform."[1] The two musicians have similarities, but Springsteen belongs to a particular race of singers, a lineage he explored in detail when he performed "This Hard Land" for his Atlanta encore. The ideas he articulated in this song, he told his audience, were what he had "in mind" when he spoke about creating a culture based on community rather than individualism, and in many ways, the song "kinda sums . . . up" his career and the cultural history in which it is embedded.[2] "This Hard Land" is a hymn to the working-class hero in which we hear not only the voice of a New Jersey street punk but also the "barbaric yawp" that a printer-turned-poet sounded over the rooftops of Brooklyn in 1855 and the rusty-voiced ballads that an Okie folksinger sang from California to New York.[3] In "This Hard Land" we can hear America singing the praises of democracy and simultaneously trying to come to terms with its limitations.

Written in 1984, the song descends self-consciously from "This Land Is Your Land," recapturing the critical edge of the original manuscript yet sustaining faith in America's democratic promise. "Hey there mister" begins another of Springsteen's common men, "can you tell me what happened to the seeds I've sown."

> Can you give me a reason sir as to why they've never grown.
> They've just blown around from town to town
> Till they're back out on these fields
> Where they fall from my hand
> Back into the dirt of this hard land.[4]

Springsteen reprises the organic, sexualized language that Whitman invoked in his cultural politics and recalls the poet's promise to sow the seeds of democracy and to disseminate adhesive love along the open road. Despite Whitman's unyielding faith and the energy that successive generations of cultural workers expended to cultivate his ideas, these seeds had not flourished as the poet had imagined. The words might be delivered in the voice of a hard-luck dirt farmer, but they could have been uttered by a journeyman printer who abhorred "a morbid appetite for money" or by a radical folksinger who supported the labor movement and courageously fought Jim Crow. Much like the seeds these working-class heroes had planted, Springsteen's had not borne the type of fruit he had expected, but when he identified these men as part of his ancestry, he reclaimed a bundle of moral principles and cultural traditions with which he criticized the morality of capitalism and envisioned an alternative social order based on cooperation and compassion rather than individualism and exploitation. The seeds of freedom and equality may not have germinated, but Springsteen declared his intentions to continue tilling the soil of this hard land.

These working-class heroes often espoused a politics that were as concerned with preserving the social standing of the white male worker as they were with challenging the economic status quo, and although they expressed a commitment to gender equality, they did not always live up to their ideals. Perhaps more than Whitman or Guthrie, Springsteen has explored how constructions of gender have shaped women's lives and, as "This Hard Land" indicates, has at times articulated a gender-inclusive politics. As the narrator embarks on what was previously a predominantly male open road, he is accompanied not by the innocent "girls" of Springsteen's earlier material but by his "sister," a term that connotes a feeling of equality and mutual respect. This brother and sister are still longing to find that place "in the sun" that we first saw in the romantic "Born to Run," but their journey is marked by a struggle that they share equally. Their travels and the promise they offer are utterly romantic, however, and although Springsteen makes the working-class hero's obligatory gesture toward gender equality, in the end his representation of this woman has little political efficacy. In fact, by the penultimate verse, this sister has disappeared from the landscape, and the hero's homosocial world has been reconstituted.

Invoking images of Whitman's tramping artisan, Dust Bowl migrants, and the seeds that appear in the first verse, the travelers of this hard land have rambled "around from town to town / Lookin' for a place to stand," hoping to find a place where they can live with dignity and decency. Springsteen asserts, however, that it is difficult to find such a place when the arid soil, the base of farmers' livelihood, constantly shifts beneath their feet. Recalling the marginal working-class geographies of *Nebraska* and "Pastures of Plenty," this desolate town is so forsaken that "even the rain" fails to fall, leaving the drought-stricken land and the people who live on it particularly susceptible to the effects of an omnipresent wind. Harsh, invisible, and destructive, this wind erodes the landscape in much the same way that human spirits are worn away by the powerful but impalpable dreams of upward mobility and freedom based on consumption, dreams that are worse than lies when they go unrealized not only because they force people to live in poverty but also because they teach them, as Whitman feared, to evaluate their lives in terms of the market, to think of themselves and to be treated by others as second-class citizens. Like the wind that sweeps violently across the landscape, the idealized American dream "stirs you up like it wants to blow you down"; it sets people up for disappointment and despair, humiliation and hurt, far more frequently than it allows them to live with decency and dignity.

Despite such dismal circumstances, the narrator provides hope for the future by looking to the past, by recovering the tradition of Whitman's working-class hero to contest contemporary social relationships. Grounded firmly in this nostalgic vision, "This Hard Land" bemoans the effects of commercialization and mechanization largely because, as Whitman predicted in "A Song for Occupations," they threaten both the communal and homosocial bonds that are formed in the workplace. In Springsteen's idealized conception of the frontier past, folksingers such as Guthrie were at the center of their communities and cowboys cooperated with one another to herd their cattle, but on the contemporary ranch of "This Hard Land," workers get their entertainment from stereos and herd livestock with helicopters. As his narrator listens to the pastoral verses of "Home on the Range" that blare from the tape deck, however, Springsteen revives the romantic promise of the West and male homosocial culture by putting the narrator and his friend, Frank, on horseback. Loosely following the plot of *Seeds of Man*, the novel in which Guthrie and his family look for his grandfather's lost silver mine in Mexico, the characters go prospecting "for lost treasure / Way down south of the Rio Grande."

Although this homosocial coupling reveals the working-class hero's persistent predilection for constructing labor as a masculine activity and for offering a white androcentric view of social justice, it also sustains the hope that society might be reordered along collective lines. Indeed, as these cowboys cross the river, they come to the most beautiful, if not the most fertile, landscape yet to present itself. And, as the closing verse indicates, they begin to forge the idealized homoerotic love on which each hero relied to articulate his vision for the future:

> Hey Frank won't ya pack your bags
> And meet me tonight down at Liberty Hall
> Just one kiss from you my brother
> And we'll ride until we fall
> We'll sleep in the fields
> We'll sleep by the rivers and in the morning
> We'll make a plan
> Well if you can't make it
> Stay hard, stay hungry, stay alive
> If you can
> And meet me in a dream of this hard land.

In what he called "one of my favorite last verses," Springsteen reprises the chorus of Whitman's "Song of the Open Road."[5] As these implicitly white characters flee the routine of industrial society to live spontaneously in the open air, they leave the ethos of competitive individualism behind and run toward a morality based on what Whitman refers to as adhesive love, what Guthrie simply calls "union," and what Springsteen identifies as "community" or "engagement with people." "Camerado, I give you my hand!," sings a triumphantly optimistic Whitman at the conclusion of "Song of the Open Road":

> I give you my love more precious than money,
> I give you myself before preaching and law;
> Will you give me yourself? will you come travel with me?
> Shall we stick by each other as long as we live?[6]

Springsteen's narrator tenders a nearly identical offer to Frank, proposing that they consummate their union at Liberty Hall, a gathering place where, as the name suggests, the ideas of individual freedom and collectivity meet, where communities literally assemble under the name of personal liberty. At this symbolic site, the protagonists express their love freely and naturally in the open air with a soul kiss, an organic, evenhanded sexual exchange that binds them together in an unmitigated equality based on what Whitman would call a "love more precious than money." To form a more perfect union of the body politic, they recommit themselves to disseminating this love along the open road. The seeds of democracy have not yet sprouted as fully as they might, but together these comrades maintain an unwavering faith that they will discover verdant fields and rivers that will nourish the seeds they intend to sow. Their commitment to each other, their regard for each other's humanness, is built firmly on a foundation of equality that, if extended to all social relations, might enable them to meet in the dream of America and reap the fruits of freedom and equality that have long been promised and denied to large numbers of its citizens.[7] The history of this country might be hard and dry, but Springsteen's cheerful, triumphant harmonica solo suggests that the land will one day be fecund enough to grow lush leaves of grass. He still believes in the promised land.

"The past is something that seems to bind us all together with memory and experience," suggested Springsteen in 1987. "And it's also something, I guess, that can drag you down and hold you back as you get stuck in old dreams that just break your heart over and over again when they don't come true."[8] By identifying with the working-class heroes of the past, Springsteen met Whitman and Guthrie in the dream of this hard land and connected himself to a tradition that, despite flirtations with communism, was more interested in recovering the dreams of an idealized past than in creating a revolutionary new social order. Radical but not too damned radical, the hero has evaluated the social relations of capitalism in terms of the dominant language of American democracy, examining the United States under a moral and cultural microscope. Because these heroes believed that the original vision on which the Republic was founded was unflawed, they frequently located corruption and injustice in immoral individuals rather than questioning the political system itself.[9] The unwritten laws of fair exchange were replaced by a morbid appetite for money that depersonalized labor relations, severed social bonds, and uncoupled the promise of individual freedom and social equality. To restore this promise, working-class heroes, notably Guthrie, occasionally supported political reform, but for the most part, they have focused on creating a culture based on love and compassion rather than competition, a culture that would purge injustice from the body politic.

As the past bound this race of singers together, it also weighed them down, for their collective dreams had a way of doubling back on themselves. These working-class heroes all began their forays into cultural politics by trying to redeem the status of the white workingman, but as they explored the economic relationships that shaped the lives of working people, they recognized that the language of class was inextricably connected to those of race, gender, and sexuality. Although these heroes have been committed to racial equality, their preoccupation with the life of the "common man," a figure invariably constructed as being white, often prevented them from questioning the privileges that accrued to their race. Meanwhile, the hero's homosocial conception of love, the basis of his egalitarian vision, created a two-edged sword. Same-sex love challenged sexual and social hierarchies but was often used to exclude women from the workplace and marginalize them in the vision of social justice, a strategy that sometimes shored up the economic privileges of white manhood and effectively reinscribed the gender hierarchies the hero had committed himself to overhauling.

This race of singers has written poignant poems and hard-hitting hurt songs, compositions that have left politically engaged cultural workers an important and enduring legacy and have inspired thousands of people to examine their social consciences. The work of these bards represents no small achievement. But as this backward glance over the roads they traveled draws to a close, as the working-class hero enters his third century, the task taken up by the journeyman poet Walt Whitman remains undone. It seems still that the strongest and sweetest songs of social justice are yet to be sung.

Notes

ABBREVIATIONS

AC   Moses and Frances Asch Collection, Center for Folklife Programs
         and Cultural Studies, Smithsonian Institution, Washington, D.C.
AFC   American Folklife Center, Library of Congress, Washington, D.C.
BW   Woody Guthrie, *Born to Win* (New York: Macmillan, 1965).
CPCP   Walt Whitman, *Complete Poetry and Collected Prose*, edited by Justin
         Kaplan (New York: Library of America, 1982).
CSF   Corporate Subject Files, Folklife Archive, Library of Congress,
         Washington, D.C.
DV   Walt Whitman, *Democratic Vistas*, in Whitman, *Complete Poetry and
         Collected Prose*, edited by Justin Kaplan (New York: Library of
         America, 1982).
GF   Walt Whitman, *The Gathering of Forces*, edited by Cleveland Rodgers
         and John Black, 2 vols. (New York: G. P. Putnam's Sons, 1920).
NUPM   Walt Whitman, *Notebooks and Unpublished Prose Manuscripts*, edited by
         Edward F. Grier, 6 vols. (New York: New York University
         Press, 1984).
PP   Woody Guthrie, *Pastures of Plenty—A Self-Portrait: The Unpublished
         Writings of an American Folk Hero*, edited by Harold Leventhal and
         Dave Marsh (New York: Harper Collins, 1990).
RSF   *Bruce Springsteen: The Rolling Stone Files*, with an introduction by Parke
         Puterbaugh (New York: Hyperion, 1996).
TC   Horace and Anne Traubel Collection, Manuscripts Division, Library
         of Congress, Washington, D.C.
UPP   Walt Whitman, *The Uncollected Poetry and Prose of Walt Whitman*, edited
         by Emory Holloway, 2 vols. (New York: Peter Smith, 1932).
WGA   Woody Guthrie Archive, New York, N.Y.
WGP   Woody Guthrie Papers, Moses and Frances Asch Collection, Center
         for Folklife Programs and Cultural Studies, Smithsonian
         Institution, Washington, D.C.
WWC   Horace Traubel, *With Walt Whitman in Camden*, 9 vols. (vol. 1, 1905;
         reprint, New York: Rowman and Littlefield, 1961; vol. 2, 1907; reprint,
         New York: Rowman and Littlefield, 1961; vol. 3, 1912; reprint, New
         York: Rowman and Littlefield, 1961; vol. 4, edited by Sculley
         Bradley, 1953; reprint, Carbondale: Southern Illinois University

Press, 1959; vol. 5, edited by Gertrude Traubel, Carbondale: Southern Illinois University Press, 1964; vol. 6, edited by Gertrude Traubel and William White, Carbondale: Southern Illinois University Press, 1982; vol. 7, edited by Jeanne Chapman and Robert MacIsaac, Carbondale: Southern Illinois University Press, 1992; vol. 8, edited by Jeanne Chapman and Robert MacIsaac, Oregon House, Calif.: W. L. Bentley, 1996; vol. 9, edited by Jeanne Chapman and Robert MacIsaac, Oregon House, Calif.: W. L. Bentley, 1996).

INTRODUCTION

1. James R. Green, *World of the Worker*, 91–99.
2. Robert K. Murray, *Red Scare*, 213, 222.
3. Giantvalley, *Walt Whitman, 1838–1939*, 268–91.
4. Kirkland, "Americanization and Walt Whitman," 537.
5. Ibid.
6. Sherman, "Walt Whitman and These Times," 4.
7. Ibid.
8. "Whitman No Boudoir Bolshevik," *New York Times*, 5 June 1919, 12.
9. DV, 951, 962.
10. Horace Traubel, quoted in Gollomb, "Would Whitman Be a Bolshevist?," 1, 8.
11. WWC, 3:422.
12. Ibid., 1:223.
13. Michael Gold, "Towards Proletarian Art" (1921), in Gold, *Anthology*, 67.
14. Like the history Denning tells in *The Cultural Front*, my account "is less a story of political divisions than of cultural continuities" (26). The cultural workers I discuss would not always have agreed on how to address issues of economic injustice, but they certainly had similarities. I am more interested in what they had in common than in the internecine struggles that have plagued the Left.
15. Walt Whitman, "Independent American Literature," GF, 2:237–42.
16. Walt Whitman, "Heroes and Hero Worship," GF, 2:290–91. Unless otherwise noted, emphasis in quotations is reproduced from the original.
17. WWC, 1:92; Walt Whitman, "Carlyle from American Points of View," CPCP, 890.
18. Thomas Carlyle, *On Heroes, Hero-Worship, and the Heroic in History* (1841), in Carlyle, *Edicion De Lux*, 307.
19. Ibid., 309–11.
20. Ibid., 334.
21. Ibid., 312.
22. Ibid., 311–12.
23. Ibid., 341; Walt Whitman, preface to *Leaves of Grass* (1855), CPCP, 26.
24. Whitman, preface to *Leaves of Grass* (1855), 24–25.

25. Walt Whitman, "A Backward Glance o'er Traveled Roads," CPCP, 659–60.

26. Ibid., 668.

27. Ibid., 670–71.

28. Ibid., 667.

29. Ibid., 658 (emphasis added).

30. WWC, 2:174.

31. Reynolds, Walt Whitman's America, 176.

32. Walt Whitman, "Starting from Paumanok," CPCP, 176.

33. Walt Whitman, The Eighteenth Presidency!, CPCP, 1318.

34. Whitman, "Backward Glance," 668.

35. Ibid., 669.

36. Sedgwick, Between Men, 3.

37. Woody Guthrie, "Notes about Music," box 1, folder 9, WGP.

38. Lennon, "Working Class Hero."

39. Whitman, "Backward Glance," 672.

CHAPTER ONE

1. Walt Whitman, "Remarks of Walt Whitman, before the Brooklyn Art Union, on the Evening of March 31, 1851," UPP, 1:241–47.

2. Ibid.

3. Walt Whitman, "What Is Music Then?," in Whitman, I Sit and Look Out, 173–74.

4. DV, 939.

5. Walt Whitman, "I Hear America Singing," CPCP, 174.

6. Gorn, " 'Good-Bye Boys, I Die a True American,' " 407. For a discussion of pub culture in the latter part of the nineteenth century, see Rosenzweig, Eight Hours for What We Will, 35–64.

7. Susan Hirsch, Roots of the American Working Class, 11–12; Laurie, Working People of Philadelphia and Artisans into Workers; Schultz, Republic of Labor, 3–36; Rorabaugh, Craft Apprentice, 3–15.

8. Wilentz, Chants Democratic, 95.

9. Polanyi, Great Transformation, 163; E. P. Thompson, "The Moral Economy of the English Crowd," in Thompson, Customs in Common, 201–2.

10. Wilentz, Chants Democratic, 107–42.

11. Laurie, Working People of Philadelphia, 76–77, and Artisans into Workers, 66–72; Schultz, Republic of Labor, 211–33. Wilentz's research reveals that artisans described great disparities in wealth as "artificial distinctions." See Wilentz, Chants Democratic, 93, 157–58.

12. Wilentz, Chants Democratic, 242, 254, 284.

13. Sidney H. Morse, "My Summer with Walt Whitman, 1887," in Traubel, Bucke, and Harned, In Re Walt Whitman, 379. Morse unsuccessfully tried to coax Whitman to make an official statement on the labor question in 1887. Summarizing Whitman's position on unions, Morse writes that the poet believed "it was a

question of manhood if anything. Workingmen's strikes were apt to develop little of that." On Whitman's antiunionism, see Arvin, *Whitman*, 241–43, and Zweig, *Whitman*, 30.

14. Walt Whitman, "Sun-Down Papers [No. 7]," *UPP*, 1:38.

15. Walt Whitman, "Cutting Down Those Wages," *GF*, 1:157–58.

16. Walt Whitman, "Morbid Appetite for Money," *UPP*, 1:123.

17. Gorn, "'Good-Bye Boys, I Die a True American,'" 407. Much like the intimate letters of many middle-class women in the first half of the nineteenth century, the correspondence of young working-class men indicates that they formed intense emotional bonds with one another. See Carroll Smith-Rosenberg, "The Female World of Love and Ritual: Relations between Women in Nineteenth-Century America," in Smith-Rosenberg, *Disorderly Conduct*, 53–76. In 1837, for example, a journeyman printer from New York City wrote that he had "never felt towards any human being—man or woman—so strong and absorbing an affection" (Stott, *Workers in the Metropolis*, 254–55) as he had for the male recipient of his letter. See also Reynolds, *Walt Whitman's America*, 391–403.

18. Gorn, *Manly Art*, 116–17. See also Reynolds, *Walt Whitman's America*, 391–403; Rotundo, *American Manhood*, 75–91; and Denning, *Mechanic Accents*, 167–84.

19. D'Emilio and Freeman argue that same-sex acts were mere sins for which people could repent. They further suggest that the industrial revolution presented opportunities for men to engage in homosexual activity: "For [men], the industrializing economy offered opportunities to explore sexuality outside of marriage, whether on city streets or in the separate sphere of all male activity. The ability to purchase goods allowed men to live free of familial controls, while the city provided anonymity for their actions" (D'Emilio and Freeman, *Intimate Matters*, 122–23). Katz concurs, noting that although homosexual relations were not sanctioned, they were discouraged not because they occurred between same-sex partners but because they did not lead to procreation. See Katz, *Invention of Heterosexuality*, 40–55. For a discussion of the ways in which capitalist expansion created possibilities for a gay identity, see D'Emilio, "Capitalism and Gay Identity," 459–64.

20. *WWC*, 6:343. The historiography of same-sex relations in the nineteenth century is conflicted. In his study of "fraternal love" among abolitionists, Yacavone vehemently argues that the citizens of the "nineteenth century understood and rejected what we would call homosexual acts but had no consciousness of a homosexual persona" ("Abolitionists and the 'Language of Fraternal Love,'" 94). He uses this assertion to discount the apparent homoeroticism that permeated abolitionist language (85–95). Quinn contests Yacavone's claim that homosexual relations were not tolerated. Nineteenth-century Americans, argues Quinn, took part in a "pervasively non-erotic homoculture," but because "they did not have categories to define 'sexuality,' [they] responded to homoeroticism in ways that often seemed restrained, even tolerant today" (*Same-Sex Dynamics*, 402). Yacavone's conclusion may hold true for middle-class abolitionists, but it seems less likely that such blanket statements would cover the working class. See also Reynolds, *Walt Whitman's America*, 397, and Chauncey, *Gay New York*, 66.

21. Walt Whitman, "I Sing the Body Electric," *CPCP*, 119. Ellipses have been reproduced as in Whitman's original texts throughout.

22. Bensman, *Practice of Solidarity*, 54; Rorabaugh, *Craft Apprentice*, 36–38, 42–48. On the importance of manliness in nineteenth-century shop-floor culture, see Montgomery, *Workers' Control in America*, 13–15, and *Fall of the House of Labor*, 30; and Halker, *For Democracy, Workers, and God*.

23. *DV*, 967.

24. Baron, "Acquiring a Manly Competence," 153, and "Contested Terrain Revisited." For a discussion of some of the ways in which workingmen asserted their masculinity in the domestic sphere, see Haag, " 'Ill-Use of a Wife.' " Leverenz argues that an "intensified ideology of manhood [was] a compensatory response to fears of humiliation" that confronted many men in Jacksonian America, particularly those who were forced to labor in bastardized workshops (*Manhood and the American Renaissance*, 4).

25. Roediger, *Wages of Whiteness*, 55–60. See also Saxton, *Rise and Fall of the White Republic*, 183–203.

26. For a reading of how concepts of race and class interacted in the nineteenth-century minstrel show, see Lott, *Love and Theft*, 63–88, 136–68.

27. Walt Whitman, "American Workingmen versus Slavery," *GF*, 1:208–10.

28. Walt Whitman, "Prohibition of Colored Persons," in Whitman, *I Sit and Look Out*, 89–90. Loving does an admirable job of restoring this editorial to its historical context and analyzing the politics of its reproduction in anthologies in *Walt Whitman: Song of Himself*, 230–32.

29. *WWC*, 6:323.

30. Walt Whitman, "Poem of the Black Person," *NUPM*, 4:1346.

31. Rubin, *Historic Whitman*, 207–10; Allen, *Solitary Singer*, 100–105.

32. Walt Whitman, *The Eighteenth Presidency!*, *CPCP*, 1310.

33. Ibid., 2123, 1310.

34. Ibid., 1312.

35. Ibid., 1316, 1318.

36. Ibid., 1309–10.

37. Ibid. (emphasis added).

38. Ibid., 1309.

39. Ibid., 1311 (emphasis added).

40. Erkkila, *Whitman the Political Poet*, 21.

41. Whitman, *Eighteenth Presidency!*, 1323.

42. Walt Whitman, preface to *Leaves of Grass* (1855), *CPCP*, 5.

43. Ibid., 20–21.

44. Ibid., 9.

45. *WWC*, 4:121, 1:283.

46. Reynolds, *Beneath the American Renaissance*, 512–14; Larson, *Whitman's Drama of Consensus*. Larson suggests that Whitman's primary "motive involves the evolution of a consensual framework," the "ideal aim" of which is "to gather together without artificially dichotomizing a host of 'opposite equals' in what amounts to a convocation and tallying of their diverse energies" (xiv).

47. Walt Whitman, "A Song for Occupations," CPCP, 89.

48. Ibid.

49. Thomas, *Lunar Light*, 16.

50. Whitman, "Song for Occupations," 89.

51. Walt Whitman, "Preface, 1876," CPCP, 1011.

52. Fowler, *Human Science*, 699–703.

53. For a discussion of Whitman's concept of adhesiveness and its relationship to the emerging concept of homosexuality, see Lynch, " 'Here Is Adhesiveness,' " 67–96.

54. Cohen argues that in the 1830s even "heterosexuality had a homosocial dimension to it: it was comprehended and validated through the eyes of male friends, instead of being an entirely private matter between a heterosexual couple" ("Unregulated Youth," 36). In his study of Mormon missionaries in the nineteenth century, Quinn argues that Mormon men frequently preferred the company of men to that of women. George Q. Cannon, a counselor to the first Mormon presidency, wrote, "Men may never have beheld each other's faces and yet they will love one another, and it is a love that is greater than the love of woman. . . . It exceeds any sexual love that can be conceived of, and it is this love that has bound the [Mormon] people together" (Quinn, *Same-Sex Dynamics*, 113).

55. Walt Whitman, "Lect. (To Women" [sic], NUPM, 1:341.

56. Reynolds, *Walt Whitman's America*, 399; Whitman, "Lect. (To Women" [sic], 1:341.

57. Erkkila and Yingling both discuss Whitman's politics of the body by relating his vision of adhesive love to democracy. Erkkila argues, "What is clear is that the democratic knowledge the poet receives of an entire universe bathed in an erotic force that links men, women, God, and the natural world in a vision of mystic unity is associated with sexual and bodily ecstasy, an ecstasy that includes but is not limited to cocksucking between men" ("Whitman and the Homosexual Republic," 158). Erkkila is careful to point out that in Whitman, homosexuality must be pursued to further the cause of democracy. Underscoring the connection between sexuality and political economy, Yingling suggests that Whitman outlined "a strategy not of replacing heterosexual with homosexual relations but of rethinking altogether the notion of patriarchal institutions and their control over the individual" ("Homosexuality and Utopian Discourse," 144). I agree with Yingling when he argues, "Male bonding in Whitman is not based on a displacement of desire but on its enactment freely and openly between two men whose sexuality requires no mediating other" (ibid.). But although same-sex love between men clearly challenges standard familial relations, I am less certain that it "rethinks" the notion of all patriarchal structures. Whitman was a strong proponent of the family, and his insistence that the role of women was to raise strong children for the Republic hardly subverts patriarchal structures. In fact, it shores them up by permitting the man to be the breadwinner and leader of the family and allowing him to explore his own sexuality not with other women but with men alone. Whitman's homosexuality is designed to liberate men and challenge certain social conventions, but ultimately it preserves male social power and interests. See also

Sedgwick, *Between Men*, 1–20, in which Sedgwick argues that male homosocial desire does much to promote the political and social interests of men.

58. Walt Whitman, "To the East and to the West," *CPCP*, 285.

59. Walt Whitman, "In Paths Untrodden," *CPCP*, 268; Walt Whitman, "Whoever You Are Holding Me Now in Hand," *CPCP*, 270.

60. Whitman, "Whoever You Are," 271.

61. See Aspiz, *Walt Whitman and the Body Beautiful*, 246–47. Aspiz argues that Whitman wrote against "the entrenched power of prudery" (246).

62. See Killingsworth, *Whitman's Poetry of the Body*, 6–13, 26, 107, and Grossman, " 'Evangel-Poem of Comrades and Love.' " The theme of homosexuality has been predominant in the biographical and critical literature on Whitman, and I am indebted to a number of scholars who have helped me come to an understanding of how sex and same-sex love function in Whitman. Killingsworth's intelligent study has been particularly helpful, as have Erkkila's "Whitman and the Homosexual Republic" and Yingling's "Homosexuality and Utopian Discourse." Erkkila's essay is a reworking of her chapter on the same topic in her extensive study of Whitman's politics, *Whitman the Political Poet*, 155–89. For a survey of how biographers have approached the question of homosexuality, see Kaplan, "Biographer's Problem." As Kaplan suggests, homophobia has shaped, and continues to influence, the ways in which many scholars have interpreted the relationship between sexuality and politics in Whitman's art. In *Walt Whitman's America*, Reynolds argues that Whitman's adhesive love has never been adequately contextualized, and after rectifying this problem by making a quite admirable analysis, he suggests that "Calamus love" is not the equivalent of late-twentieth-century conceptions of homosexual identity (70–90, 390–403). Moon's study, *Disseminating Whitman*, focuses on the various revisions of Whitman's *Leaves of Grass* and makes the interesting observation that Whitman relied on a sexual fluidity to preserve male homosocial relations that were disappearing beneath the weight of domesticity (14). See also Martin, *Homosexual Tradition*, 3–89, which provides a good introduction to the theme of homosexuality in the poet's work. In relation to the argument I make above, Martin suggests that Whitman "did not see adhesiveness as a private matter, whose realization was merely a matter of personal satisfaction. He recognized that the goals of American democracy would always be unrealized as long as adhesiveness had no place and that full spiritual development could not take place until women and men were free to develop their potential for love of members of the same sex" (40). Shively and Schmidgall offer gay interpretations of Whitman's work and connect them to their personal experiences as gay men. Their focus on sexuality is important but often leads to a rather narrow if not ahistorical interpretation of Whitman's work. See Shively, *Calamus Lovers*, and Schmidgall, *Walt Whitman*. For another gay reading of Whitman, see Fone, *Masculine Landscapes*.

63. Walt Whitman, "Behold This Swarthy Face," *CPCP*, 279.

64. *WWC*, 6:342.

65. In *Disseminating Whitman*, Moon argues that Whitman sought "to counter the privatizing, standardizing, domesticizing, misogynist and homophobic social arrangements of industrial, commercial, and (in the post–Civil War era) corpo-

rate capitalism that eventually replaced earlier [homosocial] arrangements" (10). Moon persuasively asserts that Whitman's poetry constitutes a "liminal space" designed to protect the male homoerotic experience from a society that, dominated by middle-class values of domesticity, became increasingly homophobic from the 1830s onward. In *Homosexual Tradition*, Martin suggests that Whitman's homosexuality was diametrically opposed to capitalism: "To the 'capitalism' of heterosexual intercourse (with its implications of male domination and ownership) Whitman opposes the 'socialism' of nondirected sex" (21).

66. Whitman, "Song for Occupations," 89.

67. Ibid.

68. Roediger, *Wages of Whiteness*, 53–54.

69. Whitman, "I Sing the Body Electric," 123.

70. Ibid.

71. Ibid.

72. Ibid.

73. For examples, see Whitman, *Eighteenth Presidency!*, 1319; "Slavers — and the Slave Trade," GF, 1:187; and " 'Home' Literature," UPP, 1:121. Klammer argues that "*Leaves of Grass* portrays African Americans as equal partners with whites in a democratic future and as beautiful and dignified people, the paradigms of a fully realized humanity" (*Whitman, Slavery, and the Emergence of "Leaves of Grass,"* 140). Klammer is right, I think, to suggest that Whitman challenges some racist conventions, but I remain unconvinced that he welcomes African Americans as equals in the republic of labor. So does Beach, who argues that although the figure in "I Sing the Body Electric" is attractive, "the slave is still *observed*, seen from the outside as a silent spectacle needing to be filled with an interiority unavailable to Whitman" (*Politics of Distinction*, 72).

74. Whitman, *Prose Works*, 2:762.

75. Whitman, "Song for Occupations," 90.

76. Whitman refers to "woolypates" in "Song of Myself," CPCP, 39–40.

77. Whitman, "I Sing the Body Electric," 1123.

78. Walt Whitman, "Pictures," NUPM, 4:1301–2.

79. As Christopher Newfield writes of Emerson, Whitman "opposed cruelty and suffering for others, but never modified his vision of the natural economy of market relations to justify democratically determined public-sector intervention" (*Emerson Effect*, 179). Such a position provided the foundation for "liberal racism," which eschewed the recognition of social inequalities manifested in class differences by projecting those inequalities on racial difference and a socially constructed inferiority (190). In Emerson's view, the laissez-faire market is free of value: "Market ideals and racism are completely separable, even if the market sometimes fails to oppose racism" (178). According to the ideology of free labor, the market provides equality of opportunity but fails to guarantee equality of outcome, not to mention equal dispensation of political power. See ibid., 174–208.

80. Whitman, "Song for Occupations," 91.

81. DV, 940.

82. This is not to say that Whitman did not have some effect on women's rights

and did indeed seem to "liberate" some women. See, for example, Anne Gilchrist, "A Woman's Estimate of Walt Whitman," in Traubel, Bucke, and Harned, *In Re Walt Whitman*, 41–55, and Charlotte Abbey, "Freedom and Walt Whitman," *The Conservator* 11, no. 7 (September 1896): 106–7. For succinct critical assessments of Whitman's representations of women, see Erkkila, *Whitman the Political Poet*, 134–38, 308–17, and Loving, "Whitman's Idea of Women." Pollak suggests that by essentializing women as mothers, Whitman represents them as "selfless." His representational strategies, she concludes, posed yet another contradiction in his poetry: "On the one hand, he wished to reinscribe the role of the mother as an enduring archetype of personal and national strength; on the other hand, he wished to liberate women from the inevitable confinements of this role" (" 'In Loftiest Spheres,' " 109). See also Ceniza, " 'Being a Woman,' " 110–34, and *Walt Whitman and Nineteenth-Century Women Reformers*.

83. Sedgwick, *Between Men*, 3.

84. Martin suggests that Whitman's focus on homosexuality enables him to avoid the common practice of viewing women as sexual objects. I agree that Whitman demonstrates "a strong sense of compassion for figures of suffering women," but his compassion has clear social and economic limits. See Martin, *Homosexual Tradition*, 9. Martin's contention is interesting, but Dana Nelson's interpretation of nineteenth-century male relationships in *National Manhood* is in accord with my own. For Whitman, the construct of white manhood became what she identifies as a "marker for civic unity [that] worked as an apparently democratizing extension of civic entitlement. It worked symbolically and legally to bring men together in an abstract but increasingly functional community that diverted their attention from differences between them" (6). The identification of manhood with national unity has, she suggests, "worked historically to restrict others from achieving full entitlement in the United States" (27).

85. Dougherty, *Walt Whitman and the Citizen's Eye*, 54, 5.

86. Whitman, "Song for Occupations," 89–90.

87. Ibid., 90.

88. Ibid., 90–91.

89. Trachtenberg, "Politics of Labor," 130.

90. Whitman, "Song for Occupations," 91–91. See also Trachtenberg, "Politics of Labor," 128.

91. Whitman, "Song for Occupations," 93.

92. Ibid.

93. Ibid.; Whitman, "Song of Myself," 30.

94. Trachtenberg, "Politics of Labor," 128.

95. Whitman, "Song for Occupations," 94.

96. Although Whitman's concept of individualism had much in common with Emerson's, it is important to note that their views of the individual differed in significant ways. See Loving, *Emerson, Whitman, and the American Muse*, 183–91, and Wolfe, *Limits of Literary Ideology*, 6. As Larzer Ziff notes in *Literary Democracy*, Whitman's individual is "far more social" than Emerson's (256). Christopher Newfield suggests that the divergent views that the two men had on sexuality ulti-

mately accounted for their philosophical differences. Newfield demonstrates that in the mid- to late nineteenth century, many middle-class intellectuals, Emerson among them, had conflated their fear of homosexuality with the fear of mob rule. Such men, Newfield argues, constructed a "middle-class masculinity" in which they saw "the point of male existence as self-differentiation, accumulation, and boundary defense, and [saw] America as the place where this is natural" (*Emerson Effect*, 101). Unlike Whitman, Emerson advocated male bonding not between equals but between teacher and student, superior and inferior, and worried that same-sex relations, particularly those that might manifest themselves in the group, had the potential to subvert hierarchy. Indeed, the crowd that Whitman loved was in and of itself a threat to the social order. Such sentiments led Newfield to conclude that "American homophobia has proscribed male homoeroticism in part as a taboo on a kind of politics that takes democracy too far. Male homosexual identity emerged as the continuation of controls on sexual identity in the context of nineteenth-century attempts to validate and restrict the self-governance of the masses" (92). See ibid., 91–128.

97. Whitman, "Song for Occupations," 94.

98. Walt Whitman, "Albot Wilson," NUPM, 1:59–60.

99. Whitman, "Song for Occupations," 95–96.

100. Ibid., 95.

101. Ibid. See also Thomas, *Lunar Light*, 18.

102. Wilentz, *Chants Democratic*, 242.

103. Whitman, "Song for Occupations," 98.

104. Ibid.

105. Moon, *Disseminating Whitman*, 14; Whitman, "Song for Occupations," 96. For a brief discussion of how Whitman's poem also functions as an abstraction, see Trachtenberg, "Politics of Labor," 127.

106. Whitman, "Song for Occupations," 98–99.

107. DV, 981–82; WWC, 6:342. It is interesting to note that "states" is not capitalized here. It was not written by Whitman but rather transcribed by Traubel.

108. Trachtenberg, "Politics of Labor," 131.

109. Whitman, *American Primer*, viii–ix.

110. DV, 930.

111. Trachtenberg, "Politics of Labor," 128–31. For an extended argument that suggests that monolithic definitions of capitalism must be rethought, see Merrill, "Cash Is Good to Eat."

112. Walt Whitman, "Slavery—the Slaveholders," NUPM, 6:2180.

113. DV, 962.

114. Ibid., 939.

115. Ibid., 939, 937.

116. Ibid., 937, 977.

117. Ibid., 990.

118. Walt Whitman, "The Tramp and the Strike Question," CPCP, 1063–65.

119. Ibid., 1065 (emphasis added).

120. WWC, 1:14; DV, 932.

121. DV, 962.

122. Ibid., 935.

123. Ibid., 931.

124. Ibid., 929 (emphasis added).

125. Ibid., 981–82.

126. Ibid., 989.

127. Ibid., 992–93.

128. Ibid., 966.

129. Ibid., 951.

130. Bercovitch, "Problem of Ideology," 644.

131. Ibid., 643.

132. Whitman, "Song of Myself," 27.

CHAPTER TWO

1. Walt Whitman, "Starting from Paumanok," CPCP, 177.

2. Willard provides a detailed account of the making of Whitman's literary reputation in *Whitman's American Fame*.

3. Michael Gold, "Proletarian Art" (1921), in Gold, *Anthology*, 137–38. For an earlier attempt to assess Traubel's radicalization of Whitman, see Bozard, "Horace Traubel's Socialistic Interpretation of Whitman."

4. I have relied on three rather uncritical sources for Traubel's biography: Karsner, *Horace Traubel*; Bain, *Horace Traubel*; and Stoddard, "Horace Traubel."

5. Karsner, *Horace Traubel*, 59. For an extended discussion of Traubel's relationship with Whitman within the context of Whitman's homosexuality, see Schmidgall, *Walt Whitman*, 224–50. Schmidgall concludes, "Though sexual intimacy seems quite unlikely, the relationship between Walt and Horace was extraordinarily close, physical, and gratifying" (226).

6. See Karsner, *Horace Traubel*, 40–49, and Bain, *Horace Traubel*, 11–13.

7. See Karsner, *Horace Traubel*, 40–49, and Bain, *Horace Traubel*, 11–13.

8. WWC, 1:223.

9. Kazin, *Populist Persuasion*, 35.

10. Radest, *Toward Common Ground*, 37.

11. For treatments of the ethical culture movement, see Radest, *Toward Common Ground*, and Friess, *Felix Adler*. These studies provide general information on the early history of the society and Adler's life, and it is clear that both authors were members of the movement. Friess, moreover, was Adler's son-in-law. Both books quote liberally from archival sources but offer rather hagiographic accounts of the movement.

12. Felix Adler, quoted in Friess, *Felix Adler*, 139; Paul Buhle, *Marxism in the United States*, 62–71. Much of the history of ethical socialism has been written on British subjects. For an introduction to the principles of this social philosophy, see Dennis and Halsey, *English Ethical Socialism*, 1–12. Pierson situates ethical socialism in a larger historical context in *British Socialists*, 125–249.

13. Paul Buhle, *Marxism in the United States*, 61.

14. DV, 939.

15. Horace Traubel, "Collect," *The Conservator* 4, no. 3 (May 1893): 33.

16. Horace Traubel, "The Function of an Ethical Society," *The Conservator* 2, no. 7 (September 1891): 53.

17. Ibid.

18. Horace Traubel, "The Ethical Reasons for Social Reform," *The Conservator* 3, no. 1 (March 1892): 4.

19. Horace Traubel, "Craftsmen," *The Conservator* 7, no. 11 (January 1897): 167–68.

20. Traubel, "Ethical Reasons for Social Reform," 4.

21. Snyder, "Walt Whitman's Woman," 7.

22. Traubel, "Ethical Reasons for Social Reform," 4. See also Traubel, "Collect," *The Conservator* 23, no. 2 (April 1912): 17–20, and Bain, *Horace Traubel*, 33–37.

23. Bain, *Horace Traubel*, 33.

24. For a summary of Born's life, see Helen Tufts, "Biographical Introduction," in Born, *Whitman's Ideal Democracy*, xi–xxxvi.

25. Helena Born to Horace Traubel, 11 July 1898, container 53, TC.

26. Helena Born, review of *Women and Economics*, by Charlotte Perkins Stetson, *The Conservator* 9, no. 5 (July 1898): 76.

27. Helena Born, "Inequality in Divorce," *The Conservator* 7, no. 7 (July 1896): 72.

28. Ceniza, " 'Being a Woman' " and *Walt Whitman and Nineteenth-Century Women Reformers*.

29. Helena Born, "Whitman's Ideal Democracy," in Born, *Whitman's Ideal Democracy*, 9–10.

30. See, for example, Helena Born, "Whitman's Altruism," *The Conservator* 6, no. 7 (September 1895): 105–7.

31. Melvin H. Bernstein, Charlotte Endymion Porter and Helen Clarke entry, in *Notable American Women, 1607–1950: A Biographical Dictionary*, ed. Edward T. James (Cambridge: Harvard University Press, 1971), 3:83–85.

32. Helen Clarke and Charlotte Endymion Porter, "A Short Reading Course in Whitman," *Poet-Lore* 6, no. 11 (November 1894): 645.

33. Ibid.

34. Helen Abbot Michael, "Woman and Freedom in Whitman," *Poet-Lore* 9, no. 2 (Spring 1897): 235.

35. Horace Traubel, quoted in Charlotte Porter to Horace Traubel, 20 September 1890, container 96, TC.

36. Charlotte Porter to Horace Traubel, 20 September 1890, container 96, TC.

37. Helen Clarke to Horace Traubel, 5 May 1897, container 59, TC.

38. Ibid., August 1897.

39. Traubel, "Ethical Reasons for Social Reform," 4.

40. Lucius Daniel Morse, "The Future of the American Negro," *The Conservator* 10, no. 12 (February 1900): 183–84; James Walter Young, "The Negro and the South," *The Conservator* 5, no. 12 (February 1895): 185–86.

41. Kelly Miller, "What Walt Whitman Means to the Negro," *The Conservator* 6, no. 4 (July 1895): 70. Miller's essay, which is a very sophisticated discussion of literary representation, is considered in careful detail in Hutchinson, "Whitman and the Black Poet."

42. *WWC*, 6:323.

43. Horace Traubel, review of *The Souls of Black Folk*, by W. E. B. Du Bois, *The Conservator* 14, no. 3 (May 1903): 43.

44. Horace Traubel, review of *The Marrow of Tradition*, by Charles Chesnutt, *The Conservator* 13, no. 3 (May 1902): 41–42.

45. Ibid.

46. Traubel, review of *Souls of Black Folk*, 44.

47. Ibid.

48. Horace Traubel, review of *The Aftermath of Slavery*, by William A. Sinclair, *The Conservator* 16, no. 5 (July 1905): 76.

49. Ibid.; Traubel, review of *Souls of Black Folk*, 44.

50. Traubel, review of *Aftermath of Slavery*, 75–76.

51. Leonard Abbott, "The Democracy of Whitman and the Democracy of Socialism," *The Conservator* 13, no. 9 (November 1902): 136–37.

52. M. P. Ball, "Whitman and Socialism," *The Conservator* 9, no. 3 (May 1898): 40–42 (emphasis added).

53. Abbott, "Democracy of Whitman," 136.

54. *WWC*, 3:385.

55. Katz, *Invention of Heterosexuality*, 51–82.

56. Chauncey, *Gay New York*, 116, 120.

57. Ibid., 111–26; White, *First Sexual Revolution*, 64–65. On late-nineteenth-century reactions to homosexuality, see Kimmel, *Manhood in America*, 97–100.

58. Price argues that George Santayana, William James, and other scholars at Harvard were particularly wary of Whitman's homosexuality. "The Harvard poets wanted to 'embrace' Whitman in a way that neither the preceding nor the succeeding generation of poets could do—because both these generations were bound by different gender codes, ones more proscriptive of male bonding," contends Price. "The modernists felt compelled to transform Whitman into a distanced Homeric progenitor because they could no longer imagine 'embracing' him without being accused, in post-Freudian America, of homosexuality" (*Whitman and Tradition*, 124).

59. Folsom, "Whitman's Calamus Photographs," 200, and *Walt Whitman's Native Representations*, 164–72.

60. Horace Traubel to J. W. Wallace, 1893, quoted in Krieg, "Without Walt Whitman in Camden," 91.

61. Charlotte Porter, "The American Ideal in Whitman," *The Conservator* 7, no. 5 (July 1896): 74.

62. Horace Traubel, "Walt Whitman the Comrade," *The Conservator* 4, no. 1 (March 1893): 7.

63. Ibid.

64. Edward Carpenter to Horace Traubel, 5 September 1905, container 58, TC.

65. See John Addington Symonds to Walt Whitman, 3 August 1890, and Whitman to Symonds, 19 August 1890, in Whitman, *Correspondence*, 5:72n, 72–73.

66. Edward Carpenter to Horace Traubel, 7 August 1905, container 58, TC. In a lecture presented in 1924, Carpenter echoed his opinion on the Symonds letter. He no longer had any doubts that "Whitman was before all a lover of the Male" but recognized that when Symonds inquired about the poet's sexuality, Whitman had little choice but to deny his desires: "he knew that the moment he" declared his love for men, "he would have the whole American press at his heels, snarling and slandering, and distorting his words in every possible way." Attitudes about same-sex love, Carpenter acknowledged, were "pretty bad" in England, "but in the States (in such matters) they are ten times worse." See Carpenter, *Some Friends of Walt Whitman*, 10–12.

67. Carpenter to Traubel, 7 August 1905.

68. William Norman Guthrie, "Apostle of Chaotism," 91.

69. Chapman, "Walt Whitman as Literary Tramp," 147.

70. Ibid.

71. Symonds, *Problem in Modern Ethics*, 119.

72. Eduard Bertz, quoted in "The 'Feminine Soul' in Whitman," *Current Literature* 41 (July 1906): 54–55.

73. Ibid. For a discussion of the Bertz-Schlaf controversy, see Grünzweig, *Constructing the German Walt Whitman*, 187–98.

74. Rivers, *Walt Whitman's Anomaly*, 70.

75. Carpenter, *Intermediate Sex*, 76.

76. Horace Traubel, review of *Intermediate Types among the Primitive Folk*, by Edward Carpenter, *The Conservator* 25, no. 11 (January 1915): 173, and review of *The Intermediate Sex: A Study of Some Transitional Types of Men and Women*, by Edward Carpenter, *The Conservator* 23, no. 12 (February 1913): 188.

77. Yacavone, "Abolitionists and the 'Language of Fraternal Love.'"

78. All quotations in this account are from three letters written from Horace Traubel to Gustave Percival Wiksell, ca. 1904, folder 1, Gustave Percival Wiksell Collection, Manuscripts Division, Library of Congress, Washington, D.C.

79. Gustave Percival Wiksell to Horace Traubel, 1 August 1902, 8 July 1904, container 109, TC.

80. Ed Folsom, foreword to *WWC*, vol. 9. I am in debt to Folsom for calling the Wiksell collection to my attention and for comments he offered when I delivered an abbreviated version of this account at "The Many Cultures of Walt Whitman" conference in Camden, New Jersey, 24 October 1998.

81. Horace Traubel to [Eugene Debs], 16 October 1908, in Debs, *Letters*, 1:286–87. The letter has no addressee, but the editor, J. Robert Constantine, surmises that it was written to Debs.

82. Eugene Debs to Horace Traubel, 8 August 1908, container 63, TC.

83. Ibid., 24 November 1908.

84. Ibid., 12 April 1910.

85. Many progressive reformers, including members of the ethical culture

movement and Christian proselytizers of the Social Gospel, shared this language of love. As Danbom argues, "Christian progressives believed that as men and women put the law of love into operation in their daily lives as voters, workers, employers, consumers, and neighbors, the problems of public life would disappear" (World of Hope, 84). Chauncey and White have argued that homosexuality was more widely tolerated among working-class men than it was among middle-class men. See Chauncey, Gay New York, 106–11, and White, First Sexual Revolution, 92–96.

86. Eugene Debs, "About Walt Whitman," The Conservator 18, no. 5 (July 1907): 73.

87. Ginger, Bending Cross, 232.

88. See Salvatore, Eugene V. Debs, 89, 19, 46–47, 228–29.

89. Paul Buhle, Marxism in the United States, 80.

90. Gertrude Traubel, "Eugene Debs, November 5," The Conservator 21, no. 10 (December 1910): 148.

91. Horace Traubel, "Debs," The Conservator 14, no. 3 (June 1903): 173 (emphasis added).

92. Ibid., 228–29.

93. Horace Traubel, "Collect," The Conservator 10, no. 9 (November 1902): 129–32; James R. Green, World of the Worker, 85–86.

94. Horace Traubel, review of Labor Union Socialism and Socialist Labor Unionism, by William English Walling, The Conservator 23, no. 4 (June 1912): 58, and review of Syndicalism, Industrial Unionism, and Socialism, by John Spargo, The Conservator 24, no. 3 (May 1913): 43.

95. Traubel, review of Syndicalism, Industrial Unionism, and Socialism, 43.

96. Horace Traubel, "How Socialist Altoona Looks to a Visitor," The Conservator 23, no. 5 (July 1912): 72.

97. John Spargo, "Chants Communal," The Conservator 16, no. 3 (May 1905): 45.

98. Eugene Debs, "Horace Traubel and War," The Conservator 27, no. 8 (October 1916): 103.

99. Stoddard, "Horace Traubel," 391–92.

100. On Traubel's involvement with Greenwich Village radicals, see Aaron, Writers on the Left, 7, and Stoddard, "Horace Traubel," 336. Stoddard notes that Traubel was particularly popular among the "Ashcan" school of artists who published their work in The Masses.

101. On Eastman's affection for Whitman, see Hutchinson, Harlem Renaissance, 252–53, 255–57.

102. Dell, "Walt Whitman—Anti-Socialist," 85–86.

103. Dos Passos, "Against American Literature," 271. For an insightful discussion of Dos Passos's use of Whitman, see Price, "Whitman, Dos Passos, and 'Our Storybook Democracy.' "

104. Michael Gold, "Proletarian Realism" (1930), in Gold, Anthology, 203–8. The classic work on literary radicalism in the United States is Aaron, Writers on the Left. Other important works include Deborah Silverton Rosenfelt, "From the Thirties: Tillie Olsen and the Radical Tradition," in Olsen, Tell Me a Riddle, 133–76; Coiner, Better Red, 15–71; and Paula Rabinowitz, "Women and U.S. Literary

Radicalism," in Nekola and Rabinowitz, *Writing Red*, 3. Rabinowitz significantly expands on her arguments in *Labor and Desire*, which carefully examines the ways in which the discourses of class and gender intersect in women's proletarian literature. Foley also offers a revisionist history of the literary Left in part 1 of *Radical Representations*. Foley is particularly effective at delineating the relationship between the Communist Party line on aesthetic and political issues and the artists who both accepted and reformulated these ideas. Wald surveys the shortcomings and strengths of both the "old" and the "new" historiography of the literary Left in *Writing from the Left*.

105. Michael Gold, "The Writer in America," in Gold, *Mike Gold Reader*, 183. For biographical information on Gold, see Michael Folsom, "The Pariah of American Letters," in Gold, *Anthology*, 7–20, and Aaron, *Writers on the Left*, 84–90. For another reading of Gold's interpretation of Whitman, see Tuerk, "Michael Gold on Walt Whitman."

106. Michael Gold, "Towards Proletarian Art" (1921), in Gold, *Anthology*, 67–70. For a discussion of Gold's use of phallocentric metaphors in this essay, see Trask, "Merging with the Masses," 104–7.

107. Michael Gold, "Go Left Young Writers" (1929), in Gold, *Anthology*, 188–89.

108. Faue, *Community of Suffering and Struggle*, 71. Kalaidjian offers an alternative interpretation. He suggests that "the very political vulnerability of the proletarian enterprise" dictated that it must invoke metaphors of masculinity. "Viewed against the era's actual content of political divisions and dissensus," he writes, "the typical symbols of proletarian solidarity . . . stand not so much as phallic icons of working-class hegemony but as uncanny symptoms of its absence" (*American Culture between the Wars*, 138). See also Rabinowitz, "Women and U.S. Literary Radicalism," 3.

109. Michael Gold, "America Needs a Critic" (1926), in Gold, *Anthology*, 139.

110. Hicks, *Great Tradition*, 219, 226.

111. Brenman-Gibson, *Clifford Odets*, 315–20; Wendy Smith, *Real Life Drama*, 196–202; Clifford Odets, *Waiting for Lefty*, in Odets, *Six Plays*, 31.

112. Odets, *Waiting for Lefty*, 29.

113. Ibid., 30.

114. Hicks, *Great Tradition*, 323.

115. Odets, "Democratic Vistas in Drama," 1–2.

116. Timmons, *Trouble with Harry Hay*, 96.

117. Chauncey, *Gay New York*, 332–54.

118. Communist Party of the United States leader Earl Browder made the oft-quoted remark, "Communism is twentieth century Americanism" (James R. Green, *World of the Worker*, 162).

119. See Fishbein, *Rebels in Bohemia*, 83, 111–12, and Chauncey, *Gay New York*, 227–44.

120. On male homosexuality and the Left, see Hekma, Oosterhuis, and Steakley, "Leftist Sexual Politics and Homosexuality." On the "don't ask, don't tell" policy, see Timmons, *Trouble with Harry Hay*, 108–9.

121. Chauncey, *Gay New York*, 46, 106–11, 178.

122. Hekma, Oosterhuis, and Steakley, "Leftist Sexual Politics and Homosexuality," 3.

123. Michael Gold, "Wilder: Prophet of a Genteel Christ" (1930), in Gold, *Anthology*, 200–201.

124. Trask, "Merging with the Masses," 114.

125. Michael Gold, "John Reed and the Real Thing" (1927), in Gold, *Anthology*, 152.

126. Michael Gold, "Thoughts of a Great Thinker" (1922), in Gold, *Anthology*, 7. Trask also discusses "John Reed and the Real Thing" and "Thoughts of a Great Thinker" in "Merging with the Masses," 99.

127. Eastman, "Menshivizing Walt Whitman," 12. See also Trask, "Merging with the Masses," 108–9.

128. Mumford, "Here Is Whitman the Man," 5–6.

129. Lewisohn, *Expression in America*, 200; Bernard Smith, "Literary Caravan," 101.

130. Bernard Smith, "Literary Caravan," 101.

131. Arvin, *Whitman*, 275; Van Doren, "Walt Whitman, Stranger," 283.

132. Arvin, *Whitman*, 282.

133. Ibid., 274, 276.

134. Hutchinson, "Whitman Legacy and the Harlem Renaissance," 202.

135. Ibid., 208–13.

136. Rampersad, *Life of Langston Hughes*, 1:28; Langston Hughes, "I Too," in Locke, *New Negro*, 145, "Old Walt," in Perlman, Folsom, and Campion, *Walt Whitman*, 100, and "Let America Be America Again," in Hughes, *New Song*.

137. Langston Hughes, "The Ceaseless Rings of Walt Whitman," in Perlman, Folsom, and Campion, *Walt Whitman*, 96.

138. Rampersad, *Life of Langston Hughes*, 1:30.

139. Ibid., 215–16.

140. Paul Buhle, *Marxism in the United States*, 139. For other discussions of the relationship between race and Communist Party politics, see Hutchinson, *Harlem Renaissance*, 250–88; Foley, *Radical Representations*, 170–212; Fishbein, *Rebels in Bohemia*, 160–67; and Sitkoff, *New Deal for Blacks*, 139–68. For a black nationalist interpretation of Communist Party involvement in racial politics, see Cruse, *Crisis of the Negro Intellectual*. Because it subordinated racial politics to class struggle, Cruse suggests that the Communist Party, particularly its Jewish members, "assumed the mantle of spokesmanship on Negro affairs, thus burying the Negro radical potential deeper and deeper in the slough of white intellectual paternalism" (147). Kelley challenges Cruse's argument, asserting that African Americans reinterpreted Communist Party politics through their own cultural and ideological lenses and used the party as a springboard for the civil rights movement. See Kelley, *Hammer and Hoe* and *Race Rebels*, 103–58.

141. Michael Gold, quoted in Kelley, *Race Rebels*, 117. For a discussion of Gold's literary representations of African Americans, see James D. Bloom, *Left Letters*, 35–70. In this close and provocative reading of Gold's literary and critical work, Bloom argues that Gold positioned himself as a leftist Caliban who sought to

master bourgeois literary discourse so that he could deploy it against the capitalist class.

142. Kelley, *Race Rebels*, 116–17.

143. Kalaidjian argues that Gold and other radicals failed to tap the revolutionary power of black "vernacular tradition." Hughes, however, "never lost sight of race as a fundamental category of class critique" (*American Culture between the Wars*, 104).

144. Michael Gold, quoted in Hutchinson, *Harlem Renaissance*, 272. Van Vechten authored *Nigger Heaven* (1926), a voyeuristic novel that racializes and exoticizes Harlem street and club life. For a discussion of this novel, see Lewis, *When Harlem Was in Vogue*, 180–89, and Huggins, *Harlem Renaissance*, 102–18. Anderson, who frequently corresponded with Frank and Toomer, particularly when the latter was writing *Cane* (1923), suggested that black folk expression embodied spiritual, emotional, and experiential qualities that were absent from white, urban, industrial society. He wrote to H. L. Mencken, "Damn it, man, if I could really get inside the niggers and write about them with some intelligence, I'd be willing to be hanged later and perhaps would be" (quoted in Lewis, *When Harlem Was in Vogue*, 99).

145. See also Ellen Graff, *Stepping Left*, 36–37.

146. Gold, *Hollow Men*, 48.

147. Foreword to Hughes, *New Song*, 5. Established by communist and radical Jews in the 1930s, the IWO was a multinational fraternal society that grew out of the Workmen's Circle, an organization founded by Jewish socialists in New York City in 1892. See Roger Keeran, "International Workers Order," in *The Encyclopedia of the American Left*, ed. Mari Jo Buhle, Paul Buhle, and Dan Georgakas (New York: Garland, 1990), 379–80.

148. Michael Gold, introduction to Hughes, *New Song*, 6–7.

149. Langston Hughes, "Let America Be America Again," in Hughes, *New Song*, 9–10.

150. Denning, *Cultural Front*, 8. Denning's work is an important reassessment of Popular Front historiography that contends that the movement was not "a marriage between Communists and liberals. The heart of the Popular Front as a social movement lay among those who were non-Communist socialists and independent leftists, working with Communists and with liberals, but marking out a culture that was neither a Party nor a liberal New Deal culture" (5). Denning rightly points out that although the Popular Front was marked by internecine ideological struggles, it was primarily characterized by "cultural continuities" (26) that at times "succeed[ed] in constituting . . . an alternative hegemony" (63). Denning's contention that the Popular Front marked "the first, relatively crude attempt by the left to theorize the social and political significance of modern mental labor" (98) seems a bit misguided, however. As I hope to have demonstrated, Whitman was thinking about mental labor by the mid-nineteenth century, and radicals such as Horace Traubel transferred many of Whitman's ideas about cultural work to the leftists Denning discusses. For a treatment of one of the splinter groups that comprised the Popular Front, see Kutulas, *Long War*. Kutulas sees the movement primarily as a power struggle between established radicals and new radicals.

151. Langston Hughes, "Pride," in Hughes, New Song, 16.

152. Langston Hughes, "Sister Johnson Marches" and "Open Letter to the South," in Hughes, New Song, 26–28.

153. Rampersad, Life of Langston Hughes, 1:336.

154. For a discussion of Hughes's homosexual politics, see Borden, "Heroic 'Hussies' and 'Brilliant Queers,'" 333–45.

155. Langston Hughes, "Blessed Assurance," in Hughes, Short Stories, 231–36.

156. Langston Hughes, "Café: 3 A.M.," in Hughes, Collected Poems, 406.

157. See Kelley, Race Rebels, 103–22.

158. Kelley provides an interesting discussion of this racism. By categorizing nearly all African American literature as "folk" art, the Communist Party suggested that it was not quite as important or sophisticated as that produced by white authors. Kelley argues that this categorization exempted black artists from having to follow the strictures purportedly imposed by proletarian literature and enabled them to articulate a racial politics that, despite the Communist Party's intentions, contained a black nationalist agenda (ibid., 116–20). It is interesting to note that Gold refers to Hughes's poetry as "folk literature" in his introduction to New Song (7).

159. Olsen, Yonnondio, vi.

160. Rosenfelt, "From the Thirties," and Linda Ray Pratt, "The Circumstances of Silence: Literary Representation and Tillie Olsen's Omaha Past," in Olsen, Tell Me a Riddle, 113–31. Surprisingly few scholars have examined Olsen's use of Whitman, despite the obvious connections. Orr briefly acknowledges Whitman's influence in Tillie Olsen and a Feminist Spiritual Vision, 42–43.

161. Walt Whitman, "Yonnondio," CPCP, 626.

162. Tillie Olsen, "Rebecca Harding Davis: Her Life and Times," in Olsen, Silences, 137.

163. Olsen, Yonnondio, 20, 5.

164. Ibid., 6.

165. For a more detailed discussion of this assertion, see Coiner, Better Red, 176–77.

166. Olsen, Yonnondio, 9.

167. Ibid., 40.

168. Ibid., 41.

169. Ibid., 62.

170. Ibid., 62–64.

171. Olsen, quoted in Coiner, Better Red, 159.

172. As Rabinowitz argues, "literary radicals could evoke the narrative of sexual difference to engender classes" in part because it enabled them to eschew "recognition of the more problematic differences within either genders or classes" (Labor and Desire, 95).

173. Olsen, Yonnondio, 64 (emphasis added). A number of scholars have argued that although the Communist Party of the United States was, like the larger society of which it was a part, a sexist organization, it still created significant opportunities for women. See Rosenfelt, "From the Thirties," which relies heavily on

Shaffer, "Women and the Communist Party," and Coiner, *Better Red*, 39–71. Other important sources on the historiography of women and 1930s radical literary politics include Rabinowitz, *Labor and Desire*, 1–96, and Foley, *Radical Representations*, 213–46.

174. Olsen, *Yonnondio*, 75.

175. Walt Whitman, "I Hear America Singing," CPCP, 174.

176. Olsen, *Yonnondio*, 75–77.

177. Whitman, "I Hear America Singing," 174.

178. Olsen, *Yonnondio*, 39.

179. Ibid., 95.

180. Ibid., 67, 96. Rabinowitz offers a reading of the novel that concentrates on the ways in which Mazie confronts the politics of the female body (*Labor and Desire*, 124–35).

181. Olsen, *Yonnondio*, 101–2.

182. Tillie Olsen, "Silences," in Olsen, *Silences*, 37.

183. Olsen, *Yonnondio*, 73.

184. Walt Whitman, "A Song for Occupations," CPCP, 91. For a discussion of Whitman's contradictory representations of women, see Pollak, " 'In Loftiest Spheres,' " 109.

185. Olsen, *Yonnondio*, 64.

186. "American Vision," review of *Walt Whitman, an American*, by Henry Seidel Canby, *Time*, 6 December 1943, 100–102.

187. Michael Gold, introduction to Hughes, *New Song*, 8.

188. DV, 951.

CHAPTER THREE

1. Walt Whitman, "Art-Singing and Heart-Singing," UPP, 1:104–6.

2. Nathaniel Parker Willis, quoted in Levine, *Highbrow, Lowbrow*, 97.

3. Walt Whitman, "Old Actors, Singers, Shows, &c., in New York," CPCP, 1290.

4. Whitman, "Art-Singing."

5. Ibid.

6. Woody Guthrie, "War Songs Are Work Songs," n.d., box 3, Woody Guthrie Correspondence, AFC.

7. Woody Guthrie to Moses Asch, 15 July 1946, PP, 202; Woody Guthrie, introduction to Lomax, Seeger, and Guthrie, *Hard Hitting Songs*, 17.

8. Woody Guthrie, "Notes about Music," box 1, folder 9, WGP.

9. Arlo Guthrie, quoted in *Rolling Stone*, 11 February 1988, 72.

10. Walt Whitman, "Song of the Open Road," CPCP, 307, 305.

11. Ibid., 298, 307.

12. Ibid., 299.

13. For biographical information, I have relied on Klein, *Woody Guthrie*. This scrupulously researched biography provides a detailed and critical account of Guthrie's life as well as the cultural and political context in which he lived.

14. Woody Guthrie, "Thing Called Socialism," PP, 164.

15. Woody Guthrie, untitled autobiographical sketch, PP, 9.

16. On the folk song movement, see Denisoff, *Great Day Comin'*, 133–34; Reuss, "American Left-Wing Interest in Folksong"; and Liebermann, *My Song Is My Weapon*.

17. Klein, *Woody Guthrie*, 72.

18. Ibid., 123–29.

19. Robbin, *Woody Guthrie and Me*, 121. Pascal provides another discussion of Guthrie and Whitman in "Walt Whitman and Woody Guthrie." He also cites a letter from Guthrie's second wife, Marjorie, in which she told Pascal that one of the first gifts she received from her husband was a copy of *Leaves of Grass* (43).

20. Woody Guthrie to Mike Gold, 1 June 1953, Woody Guthrie Correspondence, series 1, box 1, folder 21, WGA.

21. Mike Gold, "Woody's Songs Full of Poverty and Genuine Dirt: Democracy Is Like That," *Worker Magazine*, 13 June 1943, 12.

22. On the Lomaxes and Whitman, see Bluestein, *Voice of the Folk*, 105–16. Bluestein also provides an extended discussion of the ways in which the German folk theorist Johann Gottfried von Herder influenced Whitman.

23. For a discussion of Lomax and Sandburg, see Eyerman and Jamison, *Music and Social Movements*, 60–63.

24. Lomax and Lomax, *Cowboy Songs*, xxx.

25. John Alexander Williams, "Radicalism and Professionalism in Folklore Studies"; Reuss, "American Left-Wing Interest in Folksong"; Jerrold Hirsch, "Folklore in the Making." For further discussion of the role the Lomaxes played in constructing the canon of American folk music, see Filene, " 'Our Singing Country,' " 602–24, and Bartis, "History of the Archive of Folk Song." On the role of folklore in America's search for a distinctive national culture in the 1930s, see Susman, *Culture as History*, 150–83.

26. Lomax and Lomax, *Our Singing Country*, x.

27. Lomax, *Folk Songs of North America*, xvi.

28. "Alan Lomax Brings You the Folk Songs of America," Columbia Lecture Bureau, Alan Lomax CSF.

29. See Klein, *Woody Guthrie*, 153–54.

30. Alan Lomax interview, in Brown, *Vision Shared*.

31. Woody Guthrie to Alan Lomax, 19 September 1940, PP, 51.

32. Woody Guthrie, "My People," BW, 215–17.

33. Woody Guthrie to [Moses Asch and Marian Distler], 2 January 1946, box 4, folder 1, WGP.

34. Untitled manuscript, August 1947, PP, 179–80.

35. Badger, *New Deal*, 15, 17.

36. Bernstein, *Lean Years*, 324, 331.

37. Woody Guthrie to Millard Lampell, March 1941, PP, 51.

38. Woody Guthrie, untitled autobiographical sketch, PP, 3–4.

39. The literature on labor songs is vast. For brief introductions, see Irwin Silber, liner notes to Seeger, *American Industrial Ballads*; Foner, *American Labor Songs*;

Halker, *For Democracy, Workers, and God*; and Archie Green, *Songs about Work*. Cantwell provides an overview of music in nineteenth-century social movements in *When We Were Good*, 22–28.

40. The literature on African American culture and music is comprehensive. See Genovese, *Roll, Jordan, Roll*; Levine, *Black Culture and Black Consciousness*; Barlow, *Looking Up at Down*; and Bastin, *Red River Blues*.

41. James R. Green, *World of the Worker*, 59–69, 85–90; Dubofsky, *We Shall Be All*.

42. See Kornbluh, *Rebel Voices*, for an excellent documentary history of the IWW. Joe Hill's quote is taken from Lori Elaine Taylor, liner notes to Taylor, *Don't Mourn —Organize*. Taylor details the development of the Joe Hill legend in "Joe Hill Incorporated." Taylor also treats the subject in "Politicized American Legend of the Singing Hero." Taylor is perhaps the first scholar to consider the ways in which gender shaped the politics these men espoused. Sam Richards provides a nice summary of Joe Hill's biography in "The Joe Hill Legend in Britain," in Archie Green, *Songs about Work*, 316–31. See also Hampton, *Guerrilla Minstrels*, 60–92, and Archie Green, "Singing Joe Hill," in Green, *Wobblies, Pile Butts, and Other Heroes*, 77–94.

43. Taylor, "Joe Hill Incorporated," and liner notes to *Don't Mourn—Organize*; Richards, "Joe Hill Legend in Britain."

44. See Taylor, "Joe Hill Incorporated," 24–28. On the Composers' Collective, see Liebermann, *My Song Is My Weapon*, 25–49.

45. Klein, *Woody Guthrie*, 188; Taylor, "Joe Hill Incorporated," 27.

46. Klein, *Woody Guthrie*, 213.

47. Lee Hays, interview with Cisco Houston, 10 February 1961, Brooklyn, New York, Cisco Houston Papers, Center for Folklife Programs and Cultural Studies, Smithsonian Institution, Washington, D.C.

48. For a comparison of Guthrie and Hill, see Hampton, *Guerrilla Minstrels*, 97, 127–28.

49. Klein, *Woody Guthrie*, 199.

50. Denisoff, *Great Day Comin'*, 1–76; Liebermann, *My Song Is My Weapon*, 25–66. Folklore was also used by the dancer Sophie Maslow to advocate leftist politics in the 1940s, when she choreographed performances to Guthrie's music. See Ellen Graff, *Stepping Left*, 139–51.

51. Whisnant offers a detailed analysis of this widely circulated stereotype in *All That Is Native and Fine*.

52. Charles Seeger, quoted in Denisoff, *Great Day Comin'*, 134–35. For further details on the Left and folk music, see Reuss, "Roots of American Left-Wing Interest in Folksong," and Liebermann, *My Song Is My Weapon*, 25–66.

53. See Klein, *Woody Guthrie*, 162; Reuss, "Woody Guthrie and His Folk Tradition," 293; and Michael Gold, "Towards Proletarian Art" (1921), in Gold, *Anthology*, 67–70.

54. Klein, *Woody Guthrie*, 162.

55. The communist press criticized Rogers for lacking commitment to revolutionary politics. See Yagoda, *Will Rogers*, 296.

56. For details on Asch's biography, see Goldsmith, *Making People's Music*.

57. Woody Guthrie, untitled autobiographical sketch, PP, 12.

58. Moses Asch, "Moe Asch and Pete Seeger on Woody," taped interview, 7RR-3625, AC.

59. "Folkways Records at the Smithsonian," Moses Asch interview, 1987, narrated by Nick Spitzer, Radio Smithsonian 937, AC.

60. James Fullington, "About Books: Woody Guthrie Expresses Himself about America, His Life, His People," *Columbus (Ohio) Citizen*, 11 April 1943; "Man Who Sings America," *New York Post*, 24 March 1943; *Louisville Courier-Journal*, 2 May 1943; Lewis Adamic, "Twentieth-Century Troubadour," *Saturday Review of Literature*, 17 April 1943, 4; Woody Guthrie, "America Singing," *New York Times*, 4 April 1943 (reprinted in PP, 115–17).

61. For a brief reminiscence of Weatherwax's travels with Woody Guthrie, see PP, 260–61.

62. For a discussion of this daguerreotype, see Trachtenberg, *Reading American Photographs*, 60–70, and Folsom, *Walt Whitman's Native Representations*, 144–51.

63. Walt Whitman, quoted in Kaplan, *Walt Whitman*, 40; Folsom, *Walt Whitman's Native Representations*, 151.

64. WWC, 3:254.

65. Walt Whitman, "Song of Myself," CPCP, 43, 28.

66. Although Weatherwax cropped the photograph that I discuss, a photograph in the WGA indicates that Guthrie was in fact talking to Fred Ross, the manager of the Shafter Farm Workers Community.

67. Woody Guthrie, "Me and the Others," BW, 25.

68. Woody Guthrie, "Prophet Singer," BW, 27–28.

69. Woody Guthrie to Almanac Singers, 8 July 1941, PP, 54.

70. Woody Guthrie, "Greasy String," BW, 122. Pascal quotes this passage to illustrate similarities between Whitman and Guthrie in "Walt Whitman and Woody Guthrie," 52.

71. Woody Guthrie, date book, 18 January 1946, PP, 173.

72. Woody Guthrie, "Me and the Others," 25.

73. Ibid., 26.

74. Ibid.

CHAPTER FOUR

1. Woody Guthrie, *Woody Sez*, 62–63.

2. Ibid.

3. Woody Guthrie, "Big Guns (by the Almanac Singers)," PP, 83.

4. Woody Guthrie, *Songs the People Sing*, 13 February 1945, program 22, WNYC radio, New York, New York, recorded by Moses Asch, ACT-175, and Guthrie Acetate Dubs CDR 5 and 6, AC.

5. Klein, *Woody Guthrie*, 139, 143–44.

6. Woody Guthrie, "This Land Is Your Land," original manuscript, PP, xxiv.

7. Woody Guthrie, "Woody, 'The Dustiest of the Dust Bowlers' (The Tale of

His Travels) (Making of His Songs)," liner notes to *Dust Bowl Ballads*, RCA Victor Records, 1940, PP, 42.

8. Woody Guthrie, "War Songs Are Work Songs," n.d., box 3, Woody Guthrie Correspondence, AFC.

9. Woody Guthrie, "Ranger's Command," *Songs the People Sing*.

10. For another rendition of "Ranger's Command," see Woody Guthrie, *Stinson Collectors Series*, vols. 1–2.

11. Woody Guthrie, "Miss Pavlachenko," in Logsdon and Place, *That's Why We're Marching*. For information on the song, see the liner notes.

12. Woody Guthrie and the Almanac Singers, "Union Maid," in Guthrie, *California to the New York Island*, 35–36.

13. Woody Guthrie to Moses Asch, 15 July 1946, PP, 202.

14. Woody Guthrie, "I Say to You Woman and Man," PP, 182.

15. Will Geer, quoted in Robbin, *Woody Guthrie and Me*, 121–22.

16. Woody Guthrie, "My Best Songs," BW, 53 (emphasis added).

17. Ibid., 47–48.

18. Woody Guthrie, untitled, PP, 229.

19. Woody Guthrie to Moses Asch, 15 July 1946, PP, 200. For a discussion of Guthrie's FBI file, see Wolff, "Opening Woody Guthrie's FBI File."

20. Woody Guthrie, "My Best Songs," 48–50.

21. Walt Whitman, "Song of Myself," CPCP, 51; Woody Guthrie, untitled, PP, 226.

22. Whitman, "Song of Myself," 51; Woody Guthrie, "My Best Songs," 49.

23. Alan Lomax, quoted in Klein, *Woody Guthrie*, 162.

24. Lee Hays, interview with Cisco Houston, 10 February 1961, Brooklyn, New York, Cisco Houston Papers, Center for Folklife Programs and Cultural Studies, Smithsonian Institution, Washington, D.C.

25. Woody Guthrie, *Seeds of Man*, 71–77.

26. Walt Whitman, "To a Common Prostitute," CPCP, 512. For another representation of sexual relations, see Woody Guthrie's book *Bound for Glory*, 270–89.

27. Woody Guthrie, "Dear Prostitute," BW, 99.

28. Woody Guthrie, "My Drunkest Moments," BW, 197.

29. Klein, *Woody Guthrie*, 337–38.

30. Lee Hays and Cisco Houston discuss Guthrie's opposition to abortion in Hays, interview with Houston.

31. Klein, *Woody Guthrie*, 365–68.

32. Woody Guthrie, "My Best Songs," 56.

33. Will Geer, quoted in Robbin, *Woody Guthrie and Me*, 122.

34. Woody Guthrie, untitled, PP, 236.

35. Klein, *Woody Guthrie*, 295.

36. Woody Guthrie, "My Best Songs," 52.

37. Walt Whitman, "I Sing the Body Electric," CPCP, 119.

38. Woody Guthrie, *Bound for Glory*, 19.

39. Ibid., 35.

40. Ibid., 29.

41. Ibid., 31.

42. Ibid., 35.

43. See Widmer, "Way Out."

44. Allsop, *Hard Travelin'*, 212–25; Eric H. Honkkonen, introduction to Honkkonen, *Walking to Work*, 1–17. Honkkonen suggests that the term "gay" may have originated in hobo culture (14). See also John C. Schneider, "Tramping Workers, 1890–1920: A Subcultural View," in Honkkonen, *Walking to Work*, 212–34, and Anderson, *Hobo*, 144–49.

45. See Susman, *Culture as History*, 172.

46. "Forecast," 19 August 1940, *Back Where I Come From*, produced by Nicholas Ray and Alan Lomax, program 10, CBS Radio, Tape AFS 4810, Alan Lomax/CBS Radio Series Collection, AFC. See also Eisenschitz, *Nicholas Ray*, 56–60.

47. Woody Guthrie, untitled, PP, 236.

48. Ibid., 238.

49. Ibid., 232.

50. Ibid., 235.

51. Woody Guthrie, "Educate Me," PP, 242.

52. Woody Guthrie to Pete Seeger, Millard Lampell, and Lee Hays, 8 July 1941, PP, 55.

53. Woody Guthrie to Aliza Greenblatt, 9 July 1942, PP, 91. Aliza Greenblatt was the mother of Marjorie Mazia Greenblatt Guthrie, Guthrie's second wife.

54. Woody Guthrie to Mary Jo Guthrie (sister), n.d., PP, 31. The editors of PP suggest that the letter was written circa 1940.

55. Woody Guthrie, introduction to "Ten Songs," heavily corrected typescript, box 2, folder 3, WGP.

56. Woody Guthrie, quoted in Klein, *Woody Guthrie*, 95.

57. Woody Guthrie, "Slipknot," PP, 36–37, and "The Furguson Brothers Killing," PP, 223–25.

58. Woody Guthrie, "Leadbelly Is a Hard Name," n.d., box 3, folder 8, WGP.

59. Ibid.

60. Woody Guthrie, *Woody Sez*, 136–37.

61. Du Bois, *Souls of Black Folk*, 274.

62. Longhi, *Woody, Cisco, and Me*, 230–39.

63. For a discussion of A. Philip Randolph and the march on Washington movement, see Sitkoff, *New Deal for Blacks*, 314–21.

64. Charles Wolfe, liner notes to Carter Family, *Anchored in Love*. Jeff Place, the head archivist at the Smithsonian Institution's Center for Folklife Programs and Cultural Studies, has become something of an expert in identifying the tunes Guthrie borrowed from other performers, particularly the Carters. He has shared this information with me. See also Hampton, *Guerrilla Minstrels*, 118. For information on Guthrie's relationship to the Carters, see Klein, *Woody Guthrie*, 56, 104, 155.

65. I have relied on a number of sources to reconstruct this narrative, although not all would agree with the details I outline above. Particularly helpful was Chap-

pel, "John Hardy." Other references include Levine, *Black Culture and Black Conscious-ness*, 407–10; Cox, "John Hardy"; Ramella, "John Hardy"; Laws, *Native American Balladry*; and Lomax and Lomax, *Folksong U.S.A.*, 363–64.

66. For a brief discussion of "leaping and lingering," see Lornell, *Introducing American Folk Music*, 53, 58.

67. Trotter, *Coal, Class, and Color*, 21.

68. Ibid. Trotter reports that McDowell County's African American population rose from 3 in 1890 to nearly 15,000 by 1910. For a discussion of the hangings and the black community's response, see ibid., 4, 26, 46, 52. McDowell County may have presented opportunities for its black population, but racism was still preva-lent. Coal miners had occasionally formed interracial alliances in the region, but this cooperative ethos fragmented by the mid-1890s: native-born whites opposed the hiring of African Americans, and in the years that followed World War I, the Ku Klux Klan made its presence felt in nearby Bluefield (129). See also Corbin, *Life, Work, and Rebellion in the Coal Fields*, and Stanley, "Poco Field," 115–220. I am indebted to Tal Stanley for sharing his depth of knowledge about this region.

69. Lomax and Lomax, *Folksong U.S.A.*, 363.

70. Woody Guthrie, "Big Guns," 78.

71. Ibid., 79.

72. Ibid., 79–80.

73. Woody Guthrie, "Leadbelly Is a Hard Name."

74. For a brief synopsis of the 1931–32 Harlan County strike, see Bernstein, *Lean Years*, 377–81.

75. Woody Guthrie, "Leadbelly Is a Hard Name."

76. Ibid.

77. James R. Green, *World of the Worker*, 174–85, 194.

78. Woody Guthrie, *Songs the People Sing*. In *Working-Class Americanism*, a study of textile workers in Woonsocket, Rhode Island, Gerstle finds that radical members of the Independent Textile Union (ITU), which was affiliated with the Congress of Industrial Organizations, regularly deployed the language of Americanism to protest social and economic conditions. Indeed, Woonsocket workers claimed Abraham Lincoln as one of their heroes. Opposing historians such as Susman, who has suggested that the patriotism of the Popular Front was inherently con-servative and procapitalist, Gerstle finds that during the 1930s the ITU co-opted the language of Americanism in a way that "focused . . . insistently on democ-ratizing relations between capital and labor" (5). My discussion of the literary radicals in chapter 2, who used Whitman's brand of radical Americanism to ad-vance an anticapitalist agenda, lends support to Gerstle's thesis, although, as I have argued in chapter 1, faith in American democracy did have the potential both to stimulate and to limit political radicalism. Gerstle argues that the working-class use of Americanism changed dramatically during the war years, however. In the fight against Nazism, this language "was transformed into a pluralist creed focused instead on eliminating racial and religious bigotry from American life. This ideological transformation, which echoed throughout the country, displaced conflict between capital and labor from the central place it had long occupied

in the nation's political consciousness and, in the process, severely weakened the labor movement's claim to speak for the down-trodden and oppressed" (5). Guthrie, however, saw race and labor relations as inextricably entangled and, in his radical use of Americanism, managed to keep both at the center of his critique. Denning builds on Gerstle's thesis, insisting that appeals to Americanism were not "sentimental invocations" but "attempts to imagine a new culture, a new way of life, a revolution" (Cultural Front, 134).

79. Robbin, Woody Guthrie and Me, 110.

80. Pascal, "Walt Whitman and Woody Guthrie," 47.

81. Woody Guthrie, "Woody, 'The Dustiest of the Dust Bowlers,'" 45.

82. Woody Guthrie, "People I Owe," BW, 18–19.

83. Woody Guthrie, "The Great Historical Bum," Songs the People Sing.

84. Ibid.

85. Woody Guthrie to Moses Asch, 15 July 1946, PP, 197.

86. Ibid., 202.

87. Marjorie Guthrie, quoted in Robbin, Woody Guthrie and Me, 132.

88. Hays, interview with Houston.

89. Woody Guthrie to Alan Lomax, 19 September 1940, PP, 50.

90. Woody Guthrie, quoted in "Wrath's Grapes Turn to Wine," New York Sun, n.d., clippings folder, 1943, WGA.

91. Klein, Woody Guthrie, 175–79.

92. Hays, interview with Houston.

93. Woody Guthrie, "Me and the Others," BW, 25.

94. Hays, interview with Houston. Hays remembers that when Guthrie performed with Houston in particular he "liked to keep [Houston] as a harmonizer and a man to back him up rather than to . . . step aside and let [him] come forward."

95. Woody Guthrie, "Prophet Singer," BW, 27–28.

96. Nora Guthrie, interview with author at WGA, 19 December 1996, in author's possession.

97. John Steinbeck, foreword to Lomax, Seeger, and Guthrie, Hard Hitting Songs, 9.

98. Guthrie identifies himself as "just plain old Woody" in his introduction to Lomax, Seeger, and Guthrie, Hard Hitting Songs, 20. For a discussion of Guthrie's working-class pose, see Rodnitzky, Minstrels of the Dawn, 45–62.

99. Outside radical circles, however, most working people had never heard of Woody Guthrie, and when they encountered him and the other cultural workers involved in the folk song movement, they at best tolerated and at worst reacted with hostility toward these politically engaged musicians. "We were under the illusion that we were educating [the workers]," explained Leo Christiansen, director of the San Francisco branch of People's Songs. "We weren't . . . because we didn't talk to them in their language. . . . Their main concern was economic" (quoted in Dunaway, How Can I Keep from Singing?, 132). American workers in the 1940s did strike over noneconomic issues such as safety and workers' control, but on the whole, they were more interested in gaining admission to the finan-

cially secure middle class than in participating in the formation of a socialist state. The reaction of the Meatcutters' Union to the Almanac Singers provides an interesting example of the response of working people to the group's affectations. Invited to perform at the union's 1941 ball, a lavish event held at the upscale Hotel New York, the Almanacs greatly offended their well-dressed audience when they appeared in their standard costume, soiled work clothes. Perhaps the butchers were angered because they thought they were being mocked, perhaps because they saw themselves as much more urbane than these minstrels, or perhaps because they expected a different type of entertainment for their night on the town. At any rate, the butchers did not seem to be interested in listening to class-conscious ballads and promptly drove the Almanacs from the stage. See Klein, *Woody Guthrie*, 221.

100. Woody Guthrie, untitled, PP, xix.

101. BW, 223.

102. Woody Guthrie, "Better World A-Comin'," *Hard Travelin'*.

103. Woody Guthrie, "Thing Called Socialism," PP, 164.

CHAPTER FIVE

1. Robert Shelton, "Woody Guthrie: A Man to Remember," program, Newport Folk Festival, 1960, reprinted by Guthrie Children's Trust Fund, Woody Guthrie CSF; Kael, "Affirmation," 148–54; Hentoff, "Rebel Who Started the Folk-Song Craze"; Charles Kuralt, CBS *Sunday Morning*, 3 March 1988 (videocassette), WGA.

2. Jerome Rodnitzky dubbed Guthrie the "Father of the Now Generation" in his *Minstrels of the Dawn* (49).

3. O'Reilly, *Hoover and the Un-Americans*, 75, 90–94; Caute, *Great Fear*, 487–500, 521–38; Lipsitz, *Rainbow at Midnight*, 157–81; James R. Green, *World of the Worker*, 198–99.

4. James R. Green, *World of the Worker*, 200–202.

5. "The Kids Write to Woody," *Sing Out!* 5, no. 4 (Autumn 1955): 33–34; cover photograph, *Sing Out!* 7, no. 2 (Summer 1957); Woody Guthrie, "Folksongs: How Long?," *Sing Out!* 1, no. 10 (March 1951): 4; Woody Guthrie, "A Letter from Woody Guthrie," *Sing Out!* 2, no. 2 (August 1951): 2, 14.

6. Woody Guthrie, "Folk Songs—'Non-Politickled' Pink," *Sing Out!* 2, no. 11 (May 1952): 10; Wolff, "Opening Woody Guthrie's FBI File," 30.

7. Pete Seeger, "Woody Guthrie—Some Reminiscences," *Sing Out!* 14, no. 3 (July 1964): 25–27.

8. Dunaway, *How Can I Keep from Singing?*, 41.

9. Ibid., 26–32.

10. Alan Lomax, quoted in ibid., 64. For a synopsis of Seeger's boyhood years, see ibid., 33–75.

11. Ibid., 7.

12. Klein, *Woody Guthrie*, 215; Dunaway, *How Can I Keep from Singing?*, 65.

13. Dunaway, *How Can I Keep from Singing?*, 97.

14. Cantwell, *When We Were Good*, 259. Cantwell's interpretation of Seeger is perhaps the most perceptive analysis of this important figure in the folk revival. See the chapter entitled "He Shall Overcome," 241–66.

15. Moses Asch, taped interview by Izzy Young, 13 June 1970, FP-1991-CT, AC.

16. Dunaway, *How Can I Keep from Singing?*, 140–59; Klein, *Woody Guthrie*, 369–72; Cantwell, *When We Were Good*, 178–86; Brown, *The Weavers*; Mary Katherine Aldin, liner notes to the Weavers, *Wasn't That a Time*.

17. Arlo Guthrie, quoted in Dunaway, *How Can I Keep from Singing?*, 143. Cantwell argues that "the Weavers dispelled at once the combative tone of class conflict, the partisanship of electoral politics, and the elitism of the folksong movement itself, marrying Popular Front idealism, ideologically declawed, and the power of folksong to reimagine the lost America that lay in the historical hinterlands behind the great wall of World War II" (*When We Were Good*, 186).

18. Pete Seeger, quoted in Cantwell, *When We Were Good*, 272. Cantwell discusses the Folksmiths briefly in ibid., 274–75. For an interpretation of the role summer camps played in the folk revival, see Cantwell's chapter entitled "Happy Campers: The Children's Underground," 269–312.

19. I thank Joe Hickerson for graciously providing most of the information in the preceding two paragraphs. He kindly shared the Folksmiths' song sampler and business ledgers from his personal collection, as well as his own insights on Seeger and his relationship with Guthrie during discussions with me at the Library of Congress on 11 and 12 November 1996. A recording of Seeger's 1956 concert is housed at the Folklife Archive at the Library of Congress. The set list for the concert is written in Sherover's hand on a concert program located in folder 2, Pete Seeger CSF.

20. The text and program for the 1956 tribute are filed in box 2, folder 8, WGP. For a description of the tribute, see Klein, *Woody Guthrie*, 429–30.

21. Cantwell, "When We Were Good," 43. As the title suggests, Cantwell's essay is a nice summation of the arguments made in his book-length study, *When We Were Good*.

22. Gitlin, *The Sixties*, 1–77; Cantwell, "When We Were Good."

23. Cantwell, "When We Were Good."

24. Ibid.

25. Klein, *Woody Guthrie*, 442–46.

26. Lee Hays, interview with Cisco Houston, 10 February 1961, Brooklyn, New York, Cisco Houston Papers, Center for Folklife Programs and Cultural Studies, Smithsonian Institution, Washington, D.C.

27. Shelton, *No Direction Home*, 21–61. See also Heylin, *Bob Dylan*, and Spitz, *Dylan*. Dylan's first album was entitled *Bob Dylan*.

28. Bob Dylan, quoted in Shelton, *No Direction Home*, 110.

29. Cantwell, "When We Were Good," 53.

30. Klein, *Woody Guthrie*, 444.

31. Bob Dylan, in Brown, *Vision Shared*.

32. Bob Dylan, "11 Outlined Epitaphs," in Dylan, *Lyrics*, 107, originally published as the liner notes to *The Times They Are A-Changin'*.

33. Bob Dylan, "Song to Woody," in Dylan, *Lyrics*, 6.

34. For another discussion of the relationship between Dylan's compositions and Guthrie's, see Hampton, *Guerrilla Minstrels*, 156–57.

35. Bob Dylan, "Talkin' New York," in Dylan, *Lyrics*, 4. In his Dust Bowl ballad about an Okie Robin Hood, Guthrie criticizes bankers and businessmen by suggesting that they commit robberies with fountain pens (Woody Guthrie, "Pretty Boy Floyd," *Dust Bowl Ballads*). Dylan recorded this song in 1988. See *Folkways: A Vision Shared*.

36. Woody Guthrie, *Bound for Glory*, 295–97.

37. Bob Dylan, "Hard Times in New York Town," in Dylan, *Lyrics*, 6–7; Dylan, *Bootleg Series*.

38. For another discussion of Dylan's politics, see Denisoff and Fandray, "Political Side of Bob Dylan." See also Rodnitzky, *Minstrels of the Dawn*, 55–56, 119–21.

39. Dylan, "11 Outlined Epitaphs."

40. Bob Dylan, "Last Thoughts on Woody Guthrie," in Dylan, *Lyrics*, 32–36.

41. Walt Whitman, "A Song for Occupations," *CPCP*, 91.

42. Bob Dylan, quoted in Brown, *Vision Shared*.

43. Cantwell, "When We Were Good," 55.

44. For an extended discussion of the SDS, see Gitlin, *The Sixties*.

45. Shelton, *No Direction Home*, 69, 71.

46. Gitlin, *The Sixties*, 197–98.

47. Shelton, *No Direction Home*, 130–49.

48. Gordon Friesen, quoted in ibid., 142.

49. Bob Dylan, "Masters of War," in Dylan, *Lyrics*, 56; Dylan, *Freewheelin' Bob Dylan*.

50. Cantwell, *When We Were Good*, 350–52; Shelton, *No Direction Home*, 180–83.

51. Phil Ochs, "The Guthrie Legacy," in "Woody Guthrie: A Tribute," *Mainstream*, August 1963, 33, 37, reprinted by Guthrie Children's Trust Fund, Woody Guthrie CSF.

52. Phil Ochs, "Bound for Glory," in "Woody Guthrie: A Tribute," 32.

53. *Broadside*, no. 1 (February 1962).

54. "Woody Works on His Book," *Broadside*, nos. 9 and 10 (July 1962). For a summary of Ochs's role in the folk song movement, see Rodnitzky, *Minstrels of the Dawn*.

55. Woody Guthrie, "I've Got to Know," and Gordon Friesen, "The Man Woody Guthrie," *Broadside*, no. 57 (April 1965).

56. Friesen, "The Man Woody Guthrie."

57. Camilla Adams, "Woody Guthrie: Man or Myth," *Broadside*, no. 71 (June 1966).

58. Friesen even considered the remarks of a young woman who speculated that if Guthrie had come of age in the 1960s, he would have likely joined the Weathermen, a group of young, determined, and violent Marxist-Leninist revolutionaries who, taking their name from a line in Dylan's "Subterranean Homesick Blues," tried to inspire violent action against what they thought was a police state.

Friesen's reply was superficial, if not historically irresponsible: "Of course times are different, but Woody stood firmly against the pigs." As *Broadside* blindly alleged Guthrie's posthumous support for nearly all New Left activities, it threatened, like the conservative cultural workers against whom it fought, to dehistoricize him. Friesen's sentiments notwithstanding, the radicalism of the Popular Front and that of the Weathermen were not one and the same. Inciting working-class teenagers to take up arms against the police was a significantly different political activity than singing union songs. See G. F. [Gordon Friesen], "Woody Guthrie," *Broadside*, no. 120 (July/August 1972). On the Weathermen, see Gitlin, *The Sixties*, 384–401. Irwin Silber echoed the editors of *Broadside* in *Sing Out!* See Rodnitzky, *Minstrels of the Dawn*, 52–53.

59. Irwin Silber, " 'Male Supremacy' and Folk Song," *Sing Out!* 3, no. 7 (March 1953): 4–5, 10 (emphasis added).

60. See also Cantwell, *When We Were Good*, 337, and Gitlin, *The Sixties*, 362–76. Although historical narratives about women in the New Left suggest that they played a subordinate role, it is incorrect to imply that they did not derive any benefits from their involvement. In evaluating the gender politics of the New Left, it is useful to recall the remarks of Tillie Olsen, who has reminded literary historians of the 1930s and 1940s that they must consider their subjects in context. Olsen acknowledges that women were not treated as equals in the Communist Party but maintains that the party was "absolutely ahead of anywhere else" they could have turned in the 1930s. She insists that women "benefited enormously" from their involvement with it. As Olsen might say of her historical moment, the New Left was "a mixed place . . . in a far deeper and [more] complex sense than anybody has begun to approach" (Coiner, *Better Red*, 159).

61. On Dylan's relationship with Baez, see Shelton, *No Direction Home*, 83, 90, 183–90; Spitz, *Dylan*, 276, 287–88, 291–92; and Baez, *Voice to Sing With*, 83–98.

62. Heylin, *Bob Dylan*, 85, 114–15.

63. Fariña, "Baez and Dylan," 83.

64. Bob Dylan, quoted in Shelton, *No Direction Home*, 296.

65. Pennebaker, *Don't Look Back*.

66. Spitz, *Dylan*, 276, 291–92.

67. Bob Neuwirth, in Pennebaker, *Don't Look Back*.

68. Piercy, "Grand Coolie Damn," 430.

69. See Evans, *Personal Politics*, 109–17, 156–92.

70. Baez, *Voice to Sing With*, 152–53.

71. See Gitlin, *The Sixties*, 362–76.

72. Paul Potter, quoted in Evans, *Personal Politics*, 109–10.

73. Piercy, "Grand Coolie Damn," 422, 424, 435–36.

74. "Port Huron Statement," quoted in Gitlin, *The Sixties*, 106.

75. Gitlin, *The Sixties*, 108n.

76. Surprisingly little has been written on the connection between politics and sexuality in this decade. For an introduction, see Bailey, "Sexual Revolution(s)." Bailey suggests that the Yippies in particular linked promiscuity and revolutionary politics.

77. Rodnitzky, *Minstrels of the Dawn*, 53.

78. Paxton, *Rambling Boy*.

79. Ibid.

80. Bob Dylan, quoted in Rodnitzky, *Minstrels of the Dawn*, 71.

81. Bob Dylan, quoted in Shelton, *No Direction Home*, 203, 201.

82. Bob Dylan, "Blowin' in the Wind," in Dylan, *Lyrics*, 53.

83. Bob Dylan, quoted in Shelton, *No Direction Home*, 290.

84. Ibid., 202.

85. Shelton, *No Direction Home*, 269–70.

86. Bob Dylan, quoted in Pennebaker, *Bob Dylan*, 124–25. See Pennebaker, *Don't Look Back*.

87. Pennebaker, *Don't Look Back*; Shelton, *No Direction Home*, 284–85.

88. Pennebaker, *Bob Dylan*, 21.

89. Camus, *Myth of Sisyphus*, 40, 45.

90. Bob Dylan, "Mr. Tambourine Man," in Dylan, *Lyrics*, 173. See also Dylan, *Bringing It All Back Home*.

91. Joan Baez, quoted in Shelton, *No Direction Home*, 186.

92. Jim Rooney, "What's Happening," *Sing Out!*, 15 November 1965, 7.

93. Gitlin, *The Sixties*, 202.

94. Dylan would not, however, lose touch with Guthrie altogether. In fact, in 1992 when he performed at an all-star concert that celebrated the thirtieth anniversary of his first album, he opened with "Song to Woody." Indeed, in the years that followed Guthrie's death in 1967, Dylan and cultural workers of various political stripes reincarnated the folksinger in several political guises.

CHAPTER SIX

1. "Lenin and Woody Guthrie," *Broadside*, no. 116 (November/December 1971).

2. Anheuser-Busch Company, "A Pledge and a Promise," television advertisement, 1991 (videocassette), WGA; Klein, *Woody Guthrie*, 451.

3. Marjorie Guthrie, quoted in Dave Johnson, "Just a Mile from the End of the Line," 11.

4. Greenway, *American Folksongs of Protest*, 275–302; Nat Hentoff, "The Odyssey of Woody Guthrie," Woody Guthrie CSF; Reddy, "Woody Guthrie." For an earlier account of Woody Guthrie's reputation, see Rodnitzky, *Minstrels of the Dawn*, 45–62.

5. Stewart Udall, "A Tribute to Woody Guthrie" (1966), reprinted in Woody Guthrie, *Bound for Glory*, xi.

6. Cary Nelson, *Repression and Recovery*, 40, 37.

7. Ibid., 44.

8. Ashby, *Bound for Glory*.

9. Harold Leventhal, quoted in Demby and McNally, "Bound for Glory"; Harmetz, "Gambling on a Film about the Great Depression," 1, 13; Maslin, "Embalming Woody"; McBride, "Song for Woody"; Kael, "Affirmation"; Schickel, "Bound

for Boredom"; Kauffmann, "Stanley Kauffmann on Films"; Harmetz, "Those Oscar Nominations."

10. Klein, *Woody Guthrie*, 252–53, 269–70.

11. Woody Guthrie, letter to the editor, *New York Herald Tribune*, 25 April 1943.

12. Getchell, "American Grain."

13. Ibid.

14. Woody Guthrie, untitled autobiographical sketch, PP, 9; Woody Guthrie, "Thing Called Socialism," PP, 164.

15. Getchell, "American Grain," 143.

16. Hal Ashby, quoted in McBride, "Song for Woody," 28.

17. BW, 223.

18. "Rock Hall Tribute to Woody Guthrie," VH-1, 17 October 1996 (videocassette), WGA.

19. A sampling of the myriad Woody Guthrie tributes can be found in "Film, TV, Plays, and Tributes," Woody Guthrie CSF.

20. Although tributes have been presented in a variety of venues, I have, except perhaps for the 1956 concert at the Pythian, concentrated on those that, either because they were commercially recorded or because they were attended by prominent recording artists, had the potential to reach a large national audience. A copy of the program and set list for the 1956 "Musical Tribute to Woody Guthrie" at the Pythian is filed in box 2, folder 8, WGP, as is the program for "A Musical Tribute to Woody Guthrie" held at Carnegie Hall in New York City on 20 January 1968. Selections of the performances given at this show and at a 1970 tribute at the Hollywood Bowl were issued on *A Tribute to Woody Guthrie: Highlights from Concerts at Carnegie Hall, 1968, and Hollywood Bowl, 1970*, Warner Brothers/CBS 9 26036-2, 1972, 1976. Although the program for the Carnegie Hall concert includes a list of the songs that were performed, I have not been able to locate similar material for the Hollywood Bowl show, so rather than considering these concerts as two separate performances, I have counted the album that combines performances from both events as one production. *Woody Guthrie's American Song*, a play adapted by Peter Glazer, uses a number of Guthrie compositions to tell the story of his life. It has toured over fifty-five American cities since it was first performed in 1988. See "*Woody Guthrie's American Song* Fact Sheet," 2 January 1996, "Miscellaneous" folder 5, and the program for the 1989 performance of the play at Ford's Theatre in Washington, D.C., "Film, TV, Plays, and Tributes," Woody Guthrie CSF. In 1982, the Smithsonian Institution's Festival of American Folklife organized a tribute concert to Guthrie that was performed on the Mall. Sound recordings of this performance are in "Guthrie Tribute," SI-FP-1982-RR-081-083, Center for Folklife Programs and Cultural Studies, Smithsonian Institution, Washington, D.C. Two albums released by Folkways Records provide details of Guthrie's biography through his music and writings and the recollections of Will Geer: Geer, *Woody's Story* and *Bound for Glory: The Songs and Story of Woody Guthrie*. The score for the film *Bound for Glory*, adapted and conducted by Leonard Roseman and performed by David Carradine, was released by United Artists UA-LA695-H, 1976. Vanguard Records has released a pair of tributes to Guthrie: Country Joe McDonald, *Thinking*

of Woody Guthrie, Vanguard VMD 6546, and *The Greatest Songs of Woody Guthrie*, various artists, Vanguard VSD 35/36. In 1988, CBS Records produced the *Vision Shared* project, a tribute to Guthrie and Leadbelly that included an album and a video featuring popular performers singing Guthrie's and Leadbelly's songs. Because much of the content of these two productions overlaps, I have counted it as one tribute. See *Folkways: A Vision Shared* and Brown, *Vision Shared*. The remaining three tributes I have considered are *Pastures of Plenty: An Austin Celebration of Woody Guthrie; Woody Guthrie — Hard Travelin': Soundtrack to the Film*, Arloco Records ARL 284, 1984; and "Hard Travelin': The Life and Legacy of Woody Guthrie," Severance Hall concert, Cleveland, Ohio, 29 September 1996, tapes at WGA.

21. Kazin, *Populist Persuasion*, 2.

22. Woody Guthrie, "Do-Re-Mi," *Dust Bowl Ballads*.

23. Woody Guthrie, "About: Pretty Boy Floyd," box 1, folder 6, WGP.

24. Woody Guthrie, "Pretty Boy Floyd," *Dust Bowl Ballads*.

25. In the thirteen productions under consideration, "Do-Re-Mi" was performed eleven times, "Hard Travelin'" ten, "Pretty Boy Floyd" nine, variations of "Goin' Down That Road Feelin' Bad" eight, "Jesus Christ" six, "Vigilante Man" five, and "I Ain't Got No Home" four.

26. Carter Family, "This World Is Not My Home," quoted in Klein, *Woody Guthrie*, 118–19.

27. Woody Guthrie, notes on "I Ain't Got No Home," in Lomax, Seeger, and Guthrie, *Hard Hitting Songs*, 64.

28. Ibid.

29. Woody Guthrie, "Vigilante Man," *Dust Bowl Ballads* (emphasis added).

30. Woody Guthrie to Alan Lomax, 19 September 1940, PP, 51.

31. Woody Guthrie, "Vigilante Man."

32. Nora Guthrie described Franti's performance in a conversation I recorded at the WGA, 19 December 1996. Havens's performance has been eliminated on more recent compact disc releases of *Tribute to Woody Guthrie*.

33. *Folkways: A Vision Shared; Tribute to Woody Guthrie*.

34. "Union Maid" has been performed in six of the thirteen national productions under discussion.

35. Moses Asch, liner notes to Woody Guthrie, *Struggle*.

36. Woody Guthrie, *Struggle*. Of the songs compiled on this album, only "Pretty Boy Floyd" and "1913 Massacre" have been included in the tributes. The latter song has been recorded and performed sparsely. See Jack Elliot, in *A Tribute to Woody Guthrie* and *The Greatest Songs of Woody Guthrie*, and Michael Fracasso, in *Pastures of Plenty: An Austin Celebration of Woody Guthrie*.

37. "Pastures of Plenty" has been performed in eleven of the productions, and "This Land" appears in all thirteen.

38. For a discussion of Guthrie's stint with the BPA, see Klein, *Woody Guthrie*, 195.

39. Woody Guthrie, "Pastures of Plenty," *Columbia River Collection* (emphasis added). Pascal also notes this ambivalence in "Walt Whitman and Woody Guthrie," 46.

40. *The Columbia* (1941), cited in Guy Logsdon, "Woody Guthrie: A Biblio-Discography," 18 February 1996, Woody Guthrie CSF.

41. Tom Paxton, "Pastures of Plenty," *Tribute to Woody Guthrie* (emphasis added).

42. Colman McCarthy, "We Need a People's Anthem," *Washington Post*, 16 December 1989, sec. A, 31.

43. Woody Guthrie, "This Land Is Your Land," in Guthrie, *Songbook*, 223–25.

44. See the photocopy of Jack Franklin's 1976 flier in "Miscellaneous," Woody Guthrie CSF, which reads: "Now is the time for 'This Land Is Your Land' to become our national anthem—to sing wherever we meet together! It's up to all of us to pass [the song] around to all our friends, to politicians, to people everywhere in our great land."

45. Klein makes the point in *Woody Guthrie*, 143–44. Arlo Guthrie sings the more radical verses of the song on *Hard Travelin'*, and Harold Leventhal and Dave Marsh include it in *PP*, xxiv.

46. Udall, "Tribute to Woody Guthrie."

47. Arlo Guthrie, quoted in Klein, *Woody Guthrie*, preface.

48. Klein, *Woody Guthrie*, 461–62; Arlo Guthrie, *Alice's Restaurant*.

49. *Hollywood Bowl Tribute* (videocassette), WGA.

50. Woody Guthrie, "Thing Called Socialism."

51. Lampell, *Tribute to Woody Guthrie*, 1.

52. Fadiman, "Minstrel Boy—Japs," 68.

53. For a single-song tribute to Guthrie, see Steve Earle, "Christmas in Washington," *El Corazón*. As he bemoans the complacency of Washington politicians, Earle associates Guthrie with a wide variety of leftist causes, including those represented by Joe Hill, Emma Goldman, Malcolm X, and Martin Luther King Jr.

54. I thank Nora Guthrie for allowing me to listen to the tapes of this performance at the WGA.

55. Ronnie Gilbert, "Union Maid," in "Guthrie Tribute," Center for Folklife Programs and Cultural Studies, Smithsonian Institution, Washington, D.C.

56. Woody Guthrie, "I Say to You Woman and Man," *PP*, 182.

57. Information on DiFranco comes from "The Righteous Babe Story," a press release from the Press Network, in author's possession. DiFranco's quote on sexuality originally appeared in an article by Ray Rogers in *Out*, September 1995, also included in the publicity kit from the Press Network. See DiFranco and Phillips, *The Past Didn't Go Anywhere* and *Fellow Workers*.

58. Billy Bragg, Severance Hall, WGA.

59. Ani DiFranco, "Not a Pretty Girl," *Not a Pretty Girl*.

60. Dafydd Rees and Luke Crampton, *The Encyclopedia of Rock Stars* (New York: DK Publishing, 1996), 424–25.

61. For Bragg's performance of "Which Side Are You On?," see Bragg, *Back to Basics*. For information concerning Red Wedge, see "Red Wedge: The Great Debate," *Melody Maker*, 25 January 1986, 23–26, and "Close to the Wedge," *Melody Maker*, 4 January 1986, 10–11, 39.

62. For Guthrie's performance of "Farmer-Labor Train," see Woody Guthrie, *Long Ways to Travel*.

63. Woody Guthrie, "Tom Joad," *Dust Bowl Ballads.*

64. Springsteen, Severance Hall, WGA.

CHAPTER SEVEN

1. Bruce Springsteen, liner notes to *Greatest Hits.*

2. Eliot, *Down Thunder Road*, 78, 118–19.

3. Orth, "Making of a Rock Star"; "The Backstreet Phantom of Rock," *Time*, 27 October 1975, 48–58."

4. Michner, "Bruce Is Loose"; Greil Marcus, "Springsteen's Thousand and One American Nights," 9 October 1975, RSF, 49–50.

5. Ward, "Night of the Punk."

6. Walt Whitman, "Song of the Open Road," CPCP, 297.

7. Bruce Springsteen, "Born to Run," *Born to Run.*

8. Ibid.

9. Bruce Springsteen, "Thunder Road," *Born to Run* (emphasis added). Beginning in 1992, Springsteen substituted the word "we're" for "I'm" when he performed the song in concert.

10. Bruce Springsteen, "Born to Run" (acoustic), *Video Anthology.*

11. Bruce Springsteen, quoted in Paul Nelson, "Springsteen Fever," 13 July 1978, RSF, 69.

12. Commager and Nevins, *Pocket History of the United States of America*, v–vi.

13. Bruce Springsteen, quoted in Marsh, *Glory Days*, 57. I will rely on Marsh's biography, *Glory Days*, throughout this chapter. Despite his onstage pronouncements about his family, Springsteen has remained very tight-lipped about his life. Marsh, however, has had more access to the artist than any other author. His wife, Barbara Carr, works for Jon Landau's management firm. Moreover, Marsh is a close personal friend of Landau's.

14. Bruce Springsteen, quoted in Fred Schruers, "Bruce Springsteen and the Secret of the World," 5 February 1981, RSF, 117.

15. Bruce Springsteen, quoted in Marsh, *Glory Days*, 285.

16. Bruce Springsteen, "Born to Run," *Born to Run*; Bruce Springsteen, quoted in Schruers, "Secret of the World," 117.

17. Bruce Springsteen, quoted in Marsh, *Glory Days*, 86, 79.

18. Bruce Springsteen, quoted in Marsh, *Born to Run*, 24.

19. Bruce Springsteen, quoted in Marsh, *Glory Days*, 49, 84–88; Joseph Dalton, "Bruce Springsteen, Made in the U.S.A.: My Hometown," 10 October 1985, RSF, 178–87.

20. Bruce Springsteen, quoted in Schruers, "Secret of the World," 112, and in Corn, "Bruce Springsteen Tells the Story," 24.

21. Bruce Springsteen, quoted in Marsh, *Glory Days*, 36.

22. Bruce Springsteen, quoted in Marsh, *Born to Run*, 219.

23. John Hammond, quoted in "Backstreet Phantom of Rock," 57; Eliot, *Down Thunder Road*, 63–77.

24. Springsteen, liner notes to *Greatest Hits*.

25. Bruce Springsteen, quoted in Marsh, *Born to Run*, 217; Springsteen, liner notes to *Greatest Hits*.

26. Bruce Springsteen, "Badlands," *Darkness on the Edge of Town*.

27. Ford, *Grapes of Wrath*. On Springsteen's fascination with this scene, see Marsh, *Born to Run*, 216, and *Glory Days*, 100–101. See also Steinbeck, *Grapes of Wrath*, 40–78.

28. Bruce Springsteen, quoted in Marsh, *Glory Days*, 101.

29. Bruce Springsteen, "The Promised Land," *Darkness on the Edge of Town*.

30. Bruce Springsteen, "Adam Raised a Cain," *Darkness on the Edge of Town*.

31. Bruce Springsteen, "Darkness on the Edge of Town," *Darkness on the Edge of Town*.

32. Springsteen, "Promised Land."

33. Bruce Springsteen, "Factory," *Darkness on the Edge of Town*.

34. Bruce Springsteen, quoted in Marsh, *Glory Days*, 74. On Springsteen and Musicians United for Safe Energy, see Marsh, *Born to Run*, 241–49. For a discussion of Springsteen's involvement with the Vietnam Veteran's Association, see Marsh, *Glory Days*, 67–77, and Steve Pond, "Springsteen, Other Rock Stars Rally to Help Vets," 1 October 1983, RSF, 126–27.

35. Bruce Springsteen, quoted in Marsh, *Glory Days*, 30. On Springsteen's interest in folk music, see ibid., 112.

36. Hank Williams, "Long Gone Lonesome Blues" and "My Bucket's Got a Hole in It," *Hank Williams's 40 Greatest Hits*.

37. Bruce Springsteen, "The River," *Greatest Hits*.

38. Ibid.

39. Schruers, "Secret of the World," 117. See also Pratt, *Rhythm and Resistance*, 193.

40. Hank Williams, quoted in Roger M. Williams, *Sing a Sad Song*, 107.

41. Bruce Springsteen, "This Land Is Your Land," *Live/1975–85*.

42. Bruce Springsteen, quoted in Humphries and Hunt, *Bruce Springsteen*, 53.

43. Bruce Springsteen, quoted in Marsh, *Glory Days*, 102.

44. Chuck Berry, "School Days," *Great Twenty-Eight*; Bob Dylan, "The Ballad of Hollis Brown," *The Times They Are A-Changin'*.

45. For an introduction to Springsteen's use of folk music, see Allister, " 'There's a Meanness in This World.' "

46. Julius Daniels, "Ninety Nine Year Blues," and Carter Family, "John Hardy Was a Desperate Little Man," in Harry Smith, *Anthology of American Folk Music*.

47. Klein, *Woody Guthrie*, 254, 260, 56, 104.

48. Bastin, *Red River Blues*, 196.

49. Marcus, *Mystery Train*, 25.

50. Daniels, "Ninety Nine Year Blues."

51. Baker uses the term "blues geographies" in *Modernism and the Harlem Renaissance*, 106.

52. Daniels, "Ninety Nine Year Blues."

53. For a discussion of prison labor in coal-mining songs, see Archie Green,

Only a Miner, chaps. 6 and 7. Green suggests that "Joe Brown's coal mine" in the song is actually a convict-lease mine in Georgia (386). For historical treatments of convict labor, see Walker, *Penology for Profit*, and Wilson, *Forced Labor in the United States*. Wilson notes that in 1930, approximately 75,000 U.S. convicts produced $100 million worth of goods (35).

54. Levine, *Black Culture and Black Consciousness*, 407–20.

55. The journalist Eric Alterman recapitulates much of this material about Daniels and Springsteen's "Johnny 99" in *It Ain't No Sin to Be Glad You're Alive*, a collection of observations and reminiscences that he wrote about Springsteen in 1999. Although Alterman briefly alludes to an article I published in *Popular Music and Society* in 1996 (Garman, "Ghost of History"), he also draws on my article in his discussion on pp. 130–36.

56. Douglas Fraser, quoted in Hinds, "Ford's Closing at Mahwah Adding to Family Strains." For further information on the shutdown, particularly the ways in which it affected the area surrounding the plant, see Lohr, "Rising Uncertainty in Mahwah," and "Majority from Ford's Mahwah Plant Still Jobless," *New York Times*, 25 April 1982, sec. 1, pt. 2, 56.

57. Aronowitz, *Politics of Identity*, 51; Deakin, "Labor Law and Industrial Relations," 180. Deakin reports that 16.4 percent of the American labor force was unionized in 1988.

58. Bruce Springsteen, "Johnny 99," *Nebraska*.

59. Springsteen, "Dead Man Walkin'."

60. Cullen, "Springsteen's Ambiguous Musical Politics," 13.

61. Bruce Springsteen, quoted in Mikal Gilmore, "Bruce Springsteen: What Does It Mean, Springsteen Asked, to Be an American?," 15 November 1990, RSF, 296.

62. Hank Williams, "A Mansion on the Hill," *Hank Williams's 40 Greatest Hits*.

63. Marsh, *Glory Days*, 227.

64. Ibid.

65. Bruce Springsteen, "Used Cars," *Nebraska*.

66. For an alternative reading of Springsteen's *Nebraska*, see Cullen, "Springsteen's Ambiguous Musical Politics." Cullen argues that *Nebraska* "marks the highwater mark of Springsteen's class consciousness" and reveals its "passivity" as well (12). He further notes that "nowhere in Springsteen's music does anyone attend a demonstration, organize a boycott, or even teach his children to act a little differently" (14). Springsteen's songs are not didactic but simply present a situation and allow the listener to draw his or her own conclusions.

67. Bruce Springsteen, "Born in the U.S.A.," *Born in the U.S.A.*

68. Cullen, "Springsteen's Ambiguous Musical Politics," 3; Marsh, *Glory Days*, 360.

69. Pareles, "Bruce Springsteen—Rock's Populist," 7.

70. Lipsitz, *Time Passages*, 13.

71. Will, *Morning After*, 9–11.

72. For an extended discussion of this incident and Springsteen's response to it, see Cullen, "Springsteen's Ambiguous Musical Politics" and *Born in the U.S.A.*,

1–5, and Kavanaugh, "Ideology." See also Bird, " 'Is That Me Baby?' " Bird offers a provocative analysis of Springsteen's popularity during the Reagan years by placing him in the context of a postmodern culture where " 'meaning' doesn't matter" (48). Although I am willing to admit that commercial culture can obscure artists' intentions, I do not think it is true that an artists' intentions have no meaning at all. To make such a statement seems to me to reduce consumers of popular culture to automatons who are unwilling, if not unable, to process cultural information and reflect on it critically. For a refutation of the claim that lyrics are meaningless, see Lipsitz, *Time Passages*, 101–9.

73. Marsh, *Glory Days*, 264.

74. Bruce Springsteen, quoted in Mikal Gilmore, "Bruce Springsteen Q and A," 5 November–10 December 1987, RSF, 246.

75. Bruce Springsteen, quoted in Kurt Loder, "The *Rolling Stone* Interview: Bruce Springsteen," 6 December 1984, RSF, 154.

76. Bruce Springsteen, "Working on the Highway," *Born in the U.S.A.*

77. For a brief treatment of the ways in which the "meanings" of Springsteen's songs "double back" on themselves, see Anthony DeCurtis, "1986 Music Awards: Artist of the Year," 6 February 1987, RSF, 217–19.

78. Will, *Morning After*, 10–11.

79. Ibid.

80. Ronald Reagan, quoted in Gitlin, *The Sixties*, 217, 357–61.

81. Ronald Reagan, quoted in Wills, *Reagan's America*, 422. For further discussion of the Right's characterization of the New Left as "feminine," see ibid., 403.

82. Rozell, *The Press and the Carter Presidency*, 36–38.

83. Orman, *Comparing Presidential Behavior*, 93–106.

84. For discussions of Reagan's social and economic policies and militarism, see Wills, *Reagan's America*, 192–201, 432–39; Jeffords, *Hard Bodies*, 1–12, 24–28; and Orman, *Comparing Presidential Behavior*, 7–20. After the attempt on his life in 1981, Reagan emphasized the masculine character of such tough-minded economic policy and acts of aggression by using his injured but remarkably fit seventy-year-old body as a metaphor for national progress. As he addressed Congress just weeks after he was shot, Reagan fused his own recovery with the nation's. "Thanks to some very fine people, my health is much improved," he remarked. "I'd like to be able to say that with regard to the health of the economy" (quoted in Rogin, *Ronald Reagan, the Movie*, 4). Through such rhetorical strategies, Reagan, argues Rogin, "was identifying the recovery of his own mortal body with the health of the body politic, his own convalescence with his program to restore the health of the nation." Simply put, he was a "healer, laying his hands on a sick social body," a body whose health could in ensuing months be monitored simply by looking at photographs of the recovered president (4). In 1979, the international press published photographs of Carter collapsing of exhaustion as he competed in a ten-kilometer race (see Orman, *Comparing Presidential Behavior*, 16). In the 1980s, it featured images of Reagan chopping wood and riding horses on his California ranch, representations that attributed his and the nation's recovery to such frontier values as rugged individualism and manhood (see Jeffords, *Hard Bodies*, 25).

85. For a discussion of this concept, see Jeffords, *Remasculinization of America*, 168–85.

86. Ibid., 125.

87. Stallone, *First Blood*, *Rambo: First Blood, Part II*, and *Rambo III*.

88. Jeffords's outstanding studies of the relationship between masculinity, the Reagan presidency, and Vietnam War narratives provides the basis, as the ensuing discussion suggests, for my understanding of the films. See Jeffords, *Hard Bodies* and *Remasculinization of America*.

89. Jeffords, *Hard Bodies*, 35. For full discussions of the film, see ibid., 28–34, and Jeffords, *Remasculinization of America*, 126–28.

90. Jeffords, *Hard Bodies*, 19.

91. Ibid., 34–40; Jeffords, *Remasculinization of America*, 126–36.

92. Ronald Reagan, quoted in Rogin, *Ronald Reagan, the Movie*, 7.

93. Jeffords, *Remasculinization of America*, 138.

94. Ibid., 168.

95. Jeffords, *Hard Bodies*, 27.

96. Ibid., 47–48.

97. "The Rambo of Rock and Roll," *Chicago Tribune*, 9 August 1985, final edition, 18. For a response to this editorial, see Tom Boarman, "Springsteen and Rambo: No Comparison," *Chicago Tribune*, 18 August 1985, final edition, 14.

98. Merle Haggard, "Workin' Man Blues," *Greatest Hits*, vol. 1.

99. Merle Haggard, "The Fightin' Side of Me," *Greatest Hits*, vol. 2. For "Okie from Muskogee," see Haggard, *Greatest Hits*, vol. 1.

100. Connie Stewart, "Newsmakers: Nightclub with Rambo Theme Is Going Great Guns," *Los Angeles Times*, 8 December 1985, pt. 1, 2.

101. Bruce Springsteen, "Rosalita" and "Thunder Road," *Video Anthology*.

102. Marsh, *Glory Days*, 227.

103. Bruce Springsteen, "Dancing in the Dark," *Video Anthology*.

104. See Cullen, *Born in the U.S.A.*, 64–65.

105. Pfeil, *White Guys*, 79.

106. Marcus, "In Your Heart You Know He's Right."

107. Springsteen's fans have often discussed and expressed concern that his audience is overwhelmingly white. See Cavicchi, *Tramps Like Us*, 149.

108. Pfeil, *White Guys*, 74; Bruce Springsteen, "Born to Run," *Video Anthology*.

109. Frith, *Music for Pleasure*, 97.

110. Goodman, *Mansion on the Hill*, 343.

111. Bruce Springsteen, "Night," *Born to Run*. In 1987, roadies Mike Batlin and Doug Sutphin sued Springsteen for overtime pay he allegedly owed them for the *Born in the U.S.A.* tour, for making them pay restitution for damage done to a canoe, and for docking their pay for improperly testing the guitar of E Street Band member Nils Lofgren. Springsteen countersued Batlin, who in deposition said he had taken some of Springsteen's unreleased recordings as well as four of his lyric notebooks, which he sold for $28,000. It was rumored that Springsteen paid Batlin and Sutphin some $200,000 to settle the case. Because few details were leaked to the press, it is difficult to evaluate the issues involved in the case, but it clearly

points to the contradictions of being both a working-class hero and the head of a multimillion-dollar corporation. See RSF, 307, and Eliot, *Down Thunder Road*, 250–51. Both accounts seem biased, the former toward Springsteen, the latter toward the plaintiffs. For further observations on Springsteen as a corporation, see Frith, *Music for Pleasure*, 96.

112. Jill Zeitvogel, Lisa Biscardi, and Amy Human, quoted in Merle Ginsberg, "Bruce Springsteen, Made in the U.S.A.—The Fans: Springsteen's Followers Are Convinced He's Just Like Them," 10 October 1985, RSF, 188–91.

113. Curt Fluhr, quoted in Dalton, "Bruce Springsteen, Made in the U.S.A.," 183; unknown woman, quoted in Pratt, *Rhythm and Resistance*, 194.

114. In his 1987 biography of Springsteen, Dave Marsh parenthetically comments on the "homoerotic undercurrents" of the musician's performance (*Glory Days*, 216).

115. For an example of Springsteen's reference to the E Street Band as "boys," see "Glory Days," *Video Anthology*.

116. Clarence Clemons, in Springsteen, *Blood Brothers*.

117. Bruce Springsteen, in "Rock and Roll Hall of Fame Induction," VH-1, 17 March 1999, television broadcast of 15 March 1999 induction ceremony.

118. The term "soul kiss" is taken from Marsh, *Glory Days*, 187. For an outstanding discussion and description of the "soul kiss," see Martha Nell Smith, "Sexual Mobilities," 841–43.

119. Smith, "Sexual Mobilities," 842.

120. For a discussion of the "universal" themes in Springsteen's music, see Cavicchi, *Tramps Like Us*, 145–47.

121. Pfeil, *White Guys*, 88.

122. Bruce Springsteen, quoted in Loder, "Rolling Stone Interview," 154.

CHAPTER EIGHT

1. Bruce Springsteen, quoted in James Henke, "Bruce Springsteen: The *Rolling Stone* Interview," 6 August 1992, RSF, 321.

2. Marsh, *Glory Days*, 269–81.

3. Bruce Springsteen, quoted in Kurt Loder, "The *Rolling Stone* Interview: Bruce Springsteen," 6 December 1984, RSF, 154; Bird, " 'Is That Me Baby?,' " 44. The information on Marsh is taken from Goodman, *Mansion on the Hill*, 347.

4. Goodman, *Mansion on the Hill*, 346.

5. Marsh, *Glory Days*, 397–98.

6. Bruce Springsteen, quoted in Pratt, *Rhythm and Resistance*, 2. Springsteen makes this remark at the beginning of "Born to Run" (electric), *Video Anthology*.

7. Bruce Springsteen, in "World Stage: The Human Rights Now! Tour," Home Box Office Network, 12 December 1988.

8. Bruce Springsteen, quoted in Steve Pond, "Bruce Springsteen's Tunnel Vision," 5 May 1988, RSF, 264.

9. Bruce Springsteen, quoted in Loder, "Rolling Stone Interview," 163. Loder makes the valid suggestion that the lack of sexist imagery in Springsteen's work

might be connected to his relationship with his mother. For information on the NOW incident, see "Random Notes," 21 January 1982, RSF, 129.

10. Bruce Springsteen, quoted in Loder, "*Rolling Stone* Interview," 163.

11. Bruce Springsteen, quoted in Debby Bull, "The Summer's Biggest Tours Get Under Way: Bruce in the Heartland," 16 August 1984, RSF, 147; Steve Pond, "Bruce's 'Express' Hits the Road in High Gear," 7 April 1988, RSF, 257.

12. Bruce Springsteen, "Racing in the Street," *Darkness on the Edge of Town*.

13. Bruce Springsteen, "Born to Run" (acoustic), *Video Anthology*, and "Racing in the Street."

14. "Candy's Room," "Point Blank," "The River," and "I Wanna Marry You," *The River*; "Atlantic City," *Nebraska*.

15. Bruce Springsteen, "Spare Parts," *Video Anthology*.

16. Martha Nell Smith offers an insightful reading of "Spare Parts" that connects Patti Scialfa's strong performance in the video to the gender politics of the song. "Like Janey," writes Smith, "Patti asserts herself to lead Springsteen himself in the chorus, and thus through performance proclaims that she is not (like a spare part) dispensable, but is in fact an integral part of the band" ("Sexual Mobilities," 844).

17. Bruce Springsteen, "Tougher Than the Rest," *Tunnel of Love*.

18. Martha Nell Smith, "Sexual Mobilities," 845. Smith's reading is very insightful and had a profound influence on my own.

19. Bruce Springsteen, "Tougher Than the Rest," *Video Anthology*.

20. Martha Nell Smith, "Sexual Mobilities," 839.

21. Ibid., 846; Springsteen, "Tougher Than the Rest," *Tunnel of Love*.

22. Springsteen, "Tougher Than the Rest," *Tunnel of Love*.

23. Springsteen, "Born to Run" (acoustic), *Video Anthology*.

24. Bruce Springsteen, quoted in Pond, "Bruce Springsteen's Tunnel Vision," 260.

25. See also Martha Nell Smith, "Sexual Mobilities," 845–46.

26. Springsteen, "*Advocate* Interview," 48.

27. Ibid.

28. For a discussion of Springsteen's use of Catholic thought and imagery, see Cullen, *Born in the U.S.A.*, 164–98. His reading of "Streets of Philadelphia" is particularly insightful (191–95).

29. Springsteen, "*Advocate* Interview."

30. Bruce Springsteen, "57 Channels (And Nothin' On)," *Human Touch*.

31. Bruce Springsteen, liner notes to *Greatest Hits*.

32. Harvey Abrams, quoted in Shelton, *No Direction Home*, 75.

33. Woody Guthrie, "Tom Joad," *Dust Bowl Ballads*.

34. Bruce Springsteen, "The New Timer," *Ghost of Tom Joad*.

35. Bruce Springsteen, "The Ghost of Tom Joad," *Ghost of Tom Joad*.

36. Woody Guthrie, "Tom Joad."

37. Springsteen, "Ghost of Tom Joad."

38. Springsteen, "Born to Run," *Born to Run*, "New Timer," and "Ghost of Tom Joad."

39. Springsteen, "Ghost of Tom Joad."

40. Bruce Springsteen, "Blowin' Down That Old Dusty Road," in "Hard Travelin': The Life and Legacy of Woody Guthrie," Severance Hall concert, Cleveland, Ohio, 29 September 1996, tapes at WGA.

41. Woody Guthrie to Moses Asch, 15 July 1946, PP, 197.

42. Bruce Springsteen, "Youngstown," Ghost of Tom Joad.

43. Maharidge, Journey to Nowhere.

44. Springsteen bases "Youngstown" on details taken directly from ibid., 11–49. This book also provides the structure for "New Timer."

45. Fuechtmann, Steeples and Stacks, 11.

46. Ibid., 16; Buss and Redburn, Shutdown at Youngstown, 20–21.

47. Fuechtmann, Steeples and Stacks, 42.

48. Buss and Redburn, Shutdown at Youngstown, 15, 23.

49. Maharidge, Journey to Nowhere, 35.

50. Springsteen, "Youngstown."

51. Buss and Redburn, Shutdown at Youngstown, 21–22.

52. Fuechtmann, Steeples and Stacks, 56–57.

53. Bruce Springsteen, quoted in Corn, "Bruce Springsteen Tells the Story," 24.

54. Bruce Springsteen, "The Promised Land," Darkness on the Edge of Town (emphasis added).

55. Springsteen, Severance Hall, WGA.

56. Springsteen, Severance Hall, WGA.

57. Klein, Woody Guthrie, 362–63.

58. Woody Guthrie, "Deportee (Plane Wreck at Los Gatos)," in Guthrie, Songs, 29.

59. Woody Guthrie to Alan Lomax, 19 September 1940, PP, 47.

60. Cullen offers a quite different view in Born in the U.S.A., arguing that Springsteen's decision not to cast race relations in familiar black/white terms is visionary (67–72).

61. Bruce Springsteen, "Sinaloa Cowboys," Ghost of Tom Joad.

62. Bruce Springsteen, quoted in Steve Murray, "66th Annual Academy Awards," 6.

63. Bruce Springsteen, "Galveston Bay," Ghost of Tom Joad.

64. See Steinbeck, Grapes of Wrath, 578–81.

65. Bruce Springsteen, Fox Theatre concert, Atlanta, 28 January 1996, author's notes.

66. Springsteen, Severance Hall, WGA; Woody Guthrie, prefatory remarks to "Tom Joad," in Lomax, Seeger, and Guthrie, Hard Hitting Songs, 236.

67. Woody Guthrie, "Notes about Music," box 1, folder 9, WGP.

68. Bruce Springsteen, "Across the Border," Ghost of Tom Joad.

69. Springsteen, Fox Theatre, author's notes. Springsteen has made similar remarks at other performances. See Selvin, "Bruce Sits Down and Sings."

70. Nunnally Johnson, Grapes of Wrath, 142–43.

71. Ibid., 147.

72. Ibid.

73. Ibid., 148. See also Ford, *Grapes of Wrath*, and Steinbeck, *Grapes of Wrath*, 533–38.

74. Springsteen, Fox Theatre, author's notes. For a brief review of the show, see Dollar, "Springsteen Plugs in to Nation's Longings," 6.

75. Springsteen, "57 Channels (And Nothin' On)."

76. Bruce Springsteen, quoted in Kurt Loder, "Bruce!," 28 February 1985, RSF, 169.

77. Springsteen, "*Advocate* Interview," 50.

78. Bruce Springsteen, quoted in Henke, "*Rolling Stone* Interview," RSF, 321.

79. Bruce Springsteen, "Real Man," *Human Touch.*

80. Bruce Springsteen, quoted in Gunderson, "In 'Joad,' Springsteen Answers Ghost of His Past."

81. It is interesting to note that when Springsteen performed on *MTV Unplugged*, most of the show was a full-scale rock concert. See Springsteen, *In Concert: MTV Plugged.*

82. Bruce Springsteen, quoted in Graff, "Q and A with Bruce Springsteen."

83. Bruce Springsteen, quoted in Hilburn, "Storyteller Returns."

84. Dollar, "Springsteen Plugs in to Nation's Longings."

85. "Springsteen Helps Out Striking News Workers," *Boston Globe*, 12 January 1996, 37. At the 28 January 1996 show in Atlanta, Springsteen donated proceeds from souvenir sales to the Atlanta Community Food Bank. On the homeless and ticket sales, see "Agency Pays Homeless to Buy Concert Tickets," *Centre Daily Times* (State College, Pennsylvania), 15 January 1996.

86. Woody Guthrie, "Big Guns," PP, 82.

87. Woody Guthrie, "300 Nazis," PP, 95.

88. Woody Guthrie to Almanac Singers, March 1941, PP, 51.

89. Springsteen, Severance Hall, WGA.

90. Bruce Springsteen, quoted in Gunderson, "In 'Joad,' Springsteen Answers Ghost of His Past."

91. Woody Guthrie to Alan Lomax, 19 September 1940, PP, 51.

92. Springsteen, "Remember When the Music."

93. Cullen also comments on Springsteen's relationship to the republican tradition in *Born in the U.S.A.*, in which he makes several important observations. "Because a republican government places high expectations on its people, and because those expectations are often not met, the characteristic stance of republican art is often protest," he writes. Republican artists such as Springsteen avoid "propagandistic sloganeering" and usually represent "public issues in private terms" (39). Cullen notes, quite correctly, that "America's faith in the republican social contract has never been broken—even when, in the eyes of some, it should have" (42).

Cullen's *Born in the U.S.A.* ultimately connects Springsteen to what appears to be a monolithic "American tradition," a term with which Cullen has expressed his uneasiness. The republicanism he discusses, however, has no distinct boundaries, for anyone and everyone who has ever embraced a tenet of republicanism has apparently influenced Springsteen. In Cullen's view, John Adams, Elvis Presley, Martin Luther King Jr., Stephen Foster, Frederick Douglass, James Fenimore Cooper, Martha and the Vandellas, Walt Whitman, and John Steinbeck all have the same politics. Presley and King are so closely related that they are discussed in a single chapter entitled "Visions of Kings."

Cullen is able to be so inclusive largely because he defines "the art of republicanism" so broadly. In his view, "simplicity, mobility, [and] hope" are the essential characteristics of this tradition (48). Moreover, Cullen seems to be more interested in celebrating republicanism and Springsteen than he is in critically examining them. At the end of his narrative, he states that he hopes he has "convinced a few skeptics that [Springsteen] is an unusually talented man" (201) and praises the musician for articulating "the values of a great people" (198). "When I listen to Bruce Springsteen," he writes in his final sentence, "I remember how to be an American" (202).

I have tried to recognize Springsteen's achievement while simultaneously placing him in an artistic tradition replete with contradictions. As I hope to have demonstrated, the peculiar strain of republican culture that Springsteen embraces is burdened with a conflicted history that has done as much to exclude as it has to include. Because it has invoked constructions of whiteness and maleness, the tradition of working-class heroism is neither as simple nor as heroic as it seems.

94. Springsteen, "Rock and Read," 39.

95. Bruce Springsteen, quoted in Mikal Gilmore, "Bruce Springsteen Q and A," 5 November–10 December 1987, RSF, 244.

96. DV, 930.

97. Bruce Springsteen, quoted in Gunderson, "In 'Joad,' Springsteen Answers Ghost of His Past."

98. Bruce Springsteen, in "Springsteen," interview by Ed Bradley, Sixty Minutes, CBS Television, 21 January 1996.

99. DV, 993.

100. Bruce Springsteen, quoted in RSF, 269; Springsteen, in "Springsteen," interview by Bradley; Bruce Springsteen, quoted in Dawidoff, "Pop Populist," 28.

101. Springsteen, in "World Stage." See Dawidoff, "Pop Populist."

102. Bruce Springsteen, "The Kennedy Center Honors," CBS Television, 26 December 1997.

103. Bruce Springsteen, quoted in Gilmore, "Bruce Springsteen Q and A," 246, and in Henke, "Rolling Stone Interview," 321.

104. Walt Whitman, preface to Leaves of Grass (1855), CPCP, 26.

105. Springsteen, "Rock and Read," 43.

ENCORE

1. DeVault, "Springsteen and Seger," 1.

2. Bruce Springsteen, Fox Theatre concert, Atlanta, 28 January 1996, author's notes; Bruce Springsteen, liner notes to Greatest Hits.

3. Walt Whitman, "Song of Myself," CPCP, 87.

4. Bruce Springsteen, "This Hard Land," *Greatest Hits*.

5. Springsteen, liner notes to *Greatest Hits*.

6. Walt Whitman, "Song of the Open Road," CPCP, 307.

7. Bruce Springsteen, quoted in Kurt Loder, "The *Rolling Stone* Interview: Bruce Springsteen," 6 December 1984, RSF, 163.

8. Bruce Springsteen, quoted in Steve Pond, "Bruce Springsteen's Tunnel Vision," 5 May 1988, RSF, 262.

9. Bercovitch, "Problem of Ideology," 643.

Bibliography

ARCHIVAL SOURCES

Center for Folklife Programs and Cultural Studies, Smithsonian Institution,
    Washington, D.C.
    Moses and Frances Asch Collection
        Folkways Records Archives
        Woody Guthrie Papers
        Pete Seeger Correspondence
    Lee Hays Papers
    Cisco Houston Papers
Library of Congress, Washington, D.C.
    American Folklife Center
        Corporate Subject Files for Woody Guthrie, Alan Lomax, and Pete Seeger
        Woody Guthrie Correspondence
        Alan Lomax/CBS Radio Series Collection
        Alan Lomax Correspondence
    Manuscripts Division
        Horace and Anne Traubel Collection
        Gustave Percival Wiksell Collection
Woody Guthrie Archive, New York, N.Y.
    Woody Guthrie Correspondence

JOURNALS AND MAGAZINES

Broadside   The Conservator
Poet-Lore   Sing Out!

BOOKS, ARTICLES, DISSERTATIONS, FILMS,
AND SOUND RECORDINGS

Aaron, Daniel. *Writers on the Left: Episodes in American Literary Communism.* New
    York: Harcourt, Brace, and World, 1961.
Allen, Gay Wilson. *The Solitary Singer: A Critical Biography of Walt Whitman.* New
    York: New York University Press, 1967.

Allister, Mark. " 'There's a Meanness in This World': Bruce Springsteen's *Nebraska* and Folk Music." *John Edwards Memorial Foundation Quarterly* 19, no. 70 (Summer 1983): 130–34.

Allsop, Kenneth. *Hard Travelin': The Hobo and His History.* London: Hodder & Stoughton, 1967.

Alterman, Eric. *It Ain't No Sin to Be Glad You're Alive: The Promise of Bruce Springsteen.* Boston: Little, Brown, 1999.

Anderson, Nells. *The Hobo: The Sociology of the Homeless Man.* Chicago: University of Chicago Press, 1923.

Aronowitz, Stanley. *The Politics of Identity.* New York: Routledge, 1992.

Arvin, Newton. *Whitman.* New York: Macmillan, 1938.

Ashby, Hal, dir. *Bound for Glory.* Produced by Robert Blumfoe and Harold Leventhal. Screenplay by Robert Getchell. United Artists, 1976.

Aspiz, Harold. *Walt Whitman and the Body Beautiful.* Urbana: University of Illinois Press, 1989.

Badger, Anthony J. *The New Deal: The Depression Years, 1933–1940.* New York: Hill and Wang, 1989.

Baez, Joan. *And a Voice to Sing With.* 1987. Reprint, New York: Plume, 1988.

Bailey, Beth. "Sexual Revolution(s)." In *The Sixties: From Memory to History,* edited by David Farber, 235–62. Chapel Hill: University of North Carolina Press, 1994.

Bain, Mildred. *Horace Traubel.* New York: Albert and Charles Boni, 1913.

Baker, Houston. *Modernism and the Harlem Renaissance.* Chicago: University of Chicago Press, 1987.

Barlow, William. *Looking Up at Down: The Emergence of Blues Culture.* Philadelphia: Temple University Press, 1989.

Baron, Ava. "Acquiring a Manly Competence: The Demise of the Apprenticeship and the Remasculinization of Printers Work." In *Meanings for Manhood: Constructions of Masculinity in Victorian America,* edited by Mark C. Carnes and Clyde Griffen, 152–63. Chicago: University of Chicago Press, 1990.

———. "Contested Terrain Revisited: Technology and Gender Differences of Work in the Printing Industry, 1850–1920." In *Women, Work, and Technology: Transformations,* edited by Barbara Drygulski et al., 58–83. Ann Arbor: University of Michigan Press, 1987.

Bartis, Peter T. "A History of the Archive of Folksong at the Library of Congress, the First Fifty Years: A Dissertation in Folklore and Folklife." Ph.D. diss., University of Pennsylvania, 1982.

Bastin, Bruce. *Red River Blues: The Blues Tradition in the Southeast.* Urbana: University of Illinois Press, 1986.

Beach, Christopher. *The Politics of Distinction: Whitman and the Discourses of Nineteenth-Century America.* Athens: University of Georgia Press, 1996.

Bensman, David. *The Practice of Solidarity: American Hat Finishers in the Nineteenth Century.* Urbana: University of Illinois Press, 1985.

Bercovitch, Sacvan. "The Problem of Ideology in American Literary History." *Critical Inquiry* 12, no. 4 (Summer 1986): 631–53.

Bernstein, Irving. *The Lean Years: A History of the American Worker, 1920–1933.* Baltimore: Penguin, 1960.

Berry, Chuck. *The Great Twenty-Eight.* MCA Records CHD-92500, 1984. Compact disc.

Bird, Elizabeth. " 'Is That Me Baby?': Image, Authenticity, and the Career of Bruce Springsteen." *American Studies* 35, no. 2 (1994): 39–57.

Blewett, Mary. *Men, Women, and Work: Class, Gender, and Protest in the New England Shoe Industry, 1780–1910.* Urbana: University of Illinois Press, 1988.

Bloom, Alexander. *Prodigal Sons: The New York Intellectuals and Their World.* New York: Oxford University Press, 1986.

Bloom, James D. *Left Letters: The Culture Wars of Mike Gold and Joseph Freeman.* New York: Columbia University Press, 1992.

Bluestein, Gene. *Voice of the Folk: Folklore and American Literary Theory.* Amherst: University of Massachusetts Press, 1972.

Borden, Anne. "Heroic 'Hussies' and 'Brilliant Queers': Genderracial Resistance in the Works of Langston Hughes." *African American Review* 28, no. 3 (1994): 333–45.

Boris, Eileen. *Art and Labor: Ruskin, Morris, and the Craftsman Ideal in America.* Philadelphia: Temple University Press, 1986.

Born, Helena. *Whitman's Ideal Democracy and Other Writings.* Edited and with an introduction by Helen Tufts. Boston: Everett Press, 1902.

Bozard, John F. "Horace Traubel's Socialistic Interpretation of Whitman." *Bulletin of Furman University* 20 (January 1938): 35–45.

Bragg, Billy. *Back to Basics.* Elektra/Asylum Records 9 60726-2, 1987. Compact disc.

Bragg, Billy, and Wilco. *Mermaid Avenue.* Elektra Records 62204-2, 1998. Compact disc.

Brenman-Gibson, Margaret. *Clifford Odets, American Playwright: The Years from 1906 to 1940.* New York: Athenaeum, 1982.

Broonzy, Big Bill. *Big Bill Broonzy Sings Folk Songs.* Smithsonian Folkways SF CD 40023, 1989. Compact disc.

Brown, Jim, dir. *A Vision Shared: A Tribute to Woody Guthrie and Leadbelly.* Narrated by Robbie Robertson. CBS Music Video Enterprises 49006, 1988. Videocassette.

―――. *The Weavers: Wasn't That a Time.* Documentary film by Jim Brown Productions, George Stoney Associates, and Harold Leventhal Management in association with the New York Foundation for the Arts, 1981.

Bruce Springsteen: The Rolling Stone Files. With an introduction by Parke Puterbaugh. New York: Hyperion, 1996.

Buhle, Mari Jo. *Women and American Socialism, 1870–1920.* Urbana: University of Illinois Press, 1981.

Buhle, Paul. *Marxism in the United States: Remapping the History of the American Left.* London: Verso, 1987.

Buss, Terry F., and F. Stevens Redburn. *Shutdown at Youngstown: Public Policy for Mass Unemployment.* Albany: State University of New York Press, 1983.

Camus, Albert. *The Myth of Sisyphus and Other Essays.* Translated by Justin O'Brien. 1942. Reprint, New York: Vintage, 1955.

Cantwell, Robert. "When We Were Good: Class and Culture in the Folk Revival." In *Transforming Tradition: Folk Music Revivals Examined,* edited by Neil Rosenberg, 35–60. Urbana: University of Illinois Press, 1993.

―――. *When We Were Good: The Folk Revival.* Cambridge: Harvard University Press, 1996.

Carlyle, Thomas. *Edicion De Lux: Thomas Carlyle.* Boston: Dana Estes and Charles E. Lauriat, 1884.

Carpenter, Edward. *The Intermediate Sex: A Study of Some Transitional Types of Men and Women.* 1908. Reprint, New York: AMS Press, n.d.

―――. *Some Friends of Walt Whitman: A Study in Sex Psychology.* The British Society for Sex Psychology, no. 13. London: Athenaeum Press, 1924.

Carter Family. *Anchored in Love: Their Complete Victor Recordings, 1927–1928.* Rounder CD 1064, 1993. Compact disc.

Cash, Johnny. *The Essential Johnny Cash, 1955–1983.* Columbia C3K 47991, 1992. Compact disc.

Caute, David. *The Great Fear: The Anti-Communism Purge under Truman and Eisenhower.* New York: Simon and Schuster, 1978.

Cavicchi, Daniel. *Tramps Like Us: Music and Meaning among Springsteen Fans.* New York: Oxford University Press, 1998.

Ceniza, Sherry. " 'Being a Woman . . . I Wish to Give My Own View': Some Nineteenth-Century Women's Responses to the 1860 *Leaves of Grass.*" In *The Cambridge Companion to Walt Whitman,* edited by Ezra Greenspan, 110–34. New York: Cambridge University Press, 1995.

―――. *Walt Whitman and Nineteenth-Century Women Reformers.* Tuscaloosa: University of Alabama Press, 1987.

Chapman, John Jay. "Walt Whitman as Literary Tramp." *Public Opinion* 23, no. 5 (July 1897): 147.

Chappel, L. W. "John Hardy." *Philological Quarterly* 9 (1919): 260–72.

Chauncey, George. *Gay New York: Gender, Urban Culture, and the Making of the Gay Male World, 1890–1940.* New York: Basic Books, 1994.

Clark, Christopher. "Household Economy, Market Exchange, and the Rise of Capitalism in the Connecticut Valley, 1800–1860." *Journal of Social History* 13 (Winter 1979): 169–89.

Cohen, Patricia. "Unregulated Youth: Masculinity and Murder in the 1830s City." *Radical History Review* 52 (1992): 33–52.

Coiner, Constance. *Better Red: The Writing and Resistance of Tillie Olsen and Meridel LeSeuer.* New York: Oxford University Press, 1995.

Columbia Country Classics. Vol. 1, *The Golden Age.* Columbia CK 46029, 1990. Compact disc.

Commager, Henry Steele, and Allan Nevins, with Jeffrey Morris. *A Pocket History of the United States of America.* 1942. Reprint, New York: Washington Square Press, 1986.

Corbin, David. *Life, Work, and Rebellion in the Coal Fields: The Southern West Virginia Miners, 1880–1992*. Urbana: University of Illinois Press, 1981.

Corn, David. "Bruce Springsteen Tells the Story of the Secret America." *Mother Jones* (March–April 1995): 24.

Cox, John Harrington. "John Hardy." *Journal of American Folklore* 32, no. 126 (October–December 1919): 505–20.

Cross, Charles. *Backstreets: Springsteen, The Man and His Music*. New York: Harmony Books, 1989.

Cruse, Harold. *The Crisis of the Negro Intellectual*. 1967. Reprint, New York: Quill, 1984.

Cullen, Jim. *Born in the U.S.A.: Bruce Springsteen and the American Tradition*. New York: Harper Collins, 1997.

———. "Bruce Springsteen's Ambiguous Musical Politics in the Reagan Era." *Popular Music and Society* 16, no. 2 (Summer 1992): 1–22.

Danbom, David B. *The World of Hope: Progressives and the Struggle for an Ethical Public Life*. Philadelphia: Temple University Press, 1987.

Davis, Mike. *Prisoners of the American Dream: Politics and Economy in the History of the U.S. Working Class*. London: Verso, 1986.

Dawidoff, Nicholas. "The Pop Populist." *New York Times Magazine*, 26 January 1997, 26–33, 64, 69, 72, 77.

Deakin, Simon. "Labor Law and Industrial Relations." In *The Economic Legacy, 1979–1992*, edited by Jonathan Michie, 173–91. San Diego: Academic Press, 1992.

Debs, Eugene. *Letters of Eugene Debs*. Vol. 1, 1874–1912. Edited by J. Robert Constantine. Urbana: University of Illinois Press, 1990.

Dell, Floyd. "Walt Whitman—Anti-Socialist." *New Review* 3 (15 June 1915): 85–86.

Demby, Betty Jeffries, and Judith McNally. "Bound for Glory: Producing Woody's Life." *Filmmakers Newsletter* 10 (January 1977): 18–22.

D'Emilio, John. "Capitalism and Gay Identity." In *Lesbian and Gay Studies Reader*, edited by Henry Abelove, Michelle Barule, and David Halperin, 459–64. New York: Routledge, 1993.

———. *Sexual Politics, Sexual Communities: The Making of a Homosexual Minority in the United States, 1940–1970*. Chicago: University of Chicago Press, 1983.

D'Emilio, John, and Estelle B. Freeman. *Intimate Matters: A History of Sexuality in America*. New York: Harper and Row, 1988.

Denisoff, R. Serge. *Great Day Comin': Folk Music and the American Left*. Urbana: University of Illinois Press, 1971.

Denisoff, R. Serge, and David Fandray. " 'Hey, Hey Woody Guthrie I Wrote You a Song': The Political Side of Bob Dylan." *Popular Music and Society* 5, no. 1 (1977): 31–42.

Denning, Michael. *The Cultural Front: The Laboring of American Culture in the Twentieth Century*. New York: Verso, 1997.

———. *Mechanic Accents: Dime Novels and Working-Class Culture in America*. New York: Verso, 1987.

Dennis, Norman, and A. H. Halsey. *English Ethical Socialism: Thomas More to R. H. Tawney.* Oxford: Clarendon Press, 1988.

DeVault, Russ. "Springsteen and Seger: They're Older, Tamer, and on the Road Again." *Atlanta Journal Constitution,* 26 January 1996, sec. P, 1.

DiFranco, Ani. *Not a Pretty Girl.* Righteous Babe Records, RBR 007-D, 1988. Compact disc.

DiFranco, Ani, and U. Utah Phillips. *Fellow Workers.* Righteous Babe Records, RBR 015-D, 1999. Compact disc.

———. *The Past Didn't Go Anywhere.* Righteous Babe Records, RBR 009-D, 1996. Compact disc.

Dollar, Steve. "Springsteen Plugs in to Nation's Longings." *Atlanta Journal-Constitution,* 29 January 1996, D6.

Dos Passos, John. "Against American Literature." *New Republic,* 14 October 1916, 269–71.

Dougherty, James. *Walt Whitman and the Citizen's Eye.* Baton Rouge: Louisiana State University Press, 1993.

Douglas, Ann. "Bruce Springsteen and Narrative Rock: The Art of Extended Urgency." *Dissent* 32, no. 4 (Fall 1985): 485–89.

Duberman, Martin. " 'Writhing Bedfellows' in South Carolina." In *Hidden from History: Reclaiming the Gay and Lesbian Past,* edited by Martin Duberman, Martha Vicinus, and George Chauncey, 153–68. New York: New American Library, 1989.

Dublin, Thomas. *Women at Work: The Transformation of Work and Community in Lowell, Massachusetts, 1826–1860.* New York: Columbia University Press, 1979.

Dubofsky, Melvyn. *We Shall Be All: A History of the Industrial Workers of the World.* Urbana: University of Illinois Press, 1988.

Du Bois, W. E. B. *The Souls of Black Folk.* 1903. Reprint, New York: Signet Classic, 1982.

Dunaway, David King. *How Can I Keep from Singing?: Pete Seeger.* New York: McGraw-Hill, 1981.

Dylan, Bob. *Biograph.* Columbia C5X 38830, 1985. Compact disc.

———. *Bob Dylan.* Columbia CL 1779, 1962. Compact disc.

———. *The Bootleg Series.* Columbia C3K 47382, 1991. Compact disc.

———. *Bringing It All Back Home.* Columbia CK 9128, 1965. Compact disc.

———. *The Freewheelin' Bob Dylan.* Columbia CL 1986, 1963. Compact disc.

———. *Highway 61 Revisited.* Columbia CL 2389, 1965. Compact disc.

———. *Lyrics, 1962–1985.* New York: Knopf, 1985.

———. *The Times They Are A-Changin'.* Columbia CK 8905, 1964. Compact disc.

Earle, Steve. *El Corazón.* Warner Brothers 9 46789-2, 1997. Compact disc.

Eastman, Max. "Menshivizing Walt Whitman." Review of *Whitman, An Interpretation in Narrative,* by Emory Holloway. *New Masses* 2 (12 December 1926), 12.

Eisenschitz, Bernard. *Nicholas Ray: An American Journey.* Translated by Tom Milne. 1990. Reprint, Boston: Faber and Faber, 1993.

Eliot, Marc, with Mike Appel. *Down Thunder Road: The Making of Bruce Springsteen.* New York: Simon and Schuster, 1992.

Ellis, Havelock, and John Addington Symonds. *Sexual Inversion.* 1897. Reprint, New York: Ayer Publishers, 1994.

Emerson, Ralph Waldo. *Selections from Ralph Waldo Emerson.* Edited by Stephen E. Whicher. Boston: Houghton Mifflin, 1957.

Ennis, Phil. *The Seventh Stream: The Emergence of Rocknroll in American Popular Music.* Middletown, Conn.: Wesleyan University Press, 1992.

Erkkila, Betsy. "Whitman and the Homosexual Republic." In *Walt Whitman: The Centennial Essays,* edited by Ed Folsom, 153–71. Iowa City: University of Iowa Press, 1994.

———. *Whitman the Political Poet.* New York: Oxford University Press, 1989.

Erkkila, Betsy, and Jay Grossman, eds. *Breaking Bounds: Whitman and American Cultural Studies.* New York: Oxford University Press, 1996.

Evans, Sara. *Personal Politics: The Roots of the Women's Liberation Movement in the Civil Rights Movement and the New Left.* New York: Knopf, 1979.

Eyerman, Ron, and Andrew Jamison. *Music and Social Movements: Mobilizing Tradition in the Twentieth Century.* New York: Cambridge University Press, 1998.

Fadiman, Clifton. "Minstrel Boy—Japs." Review of *Bound for Glory,* by Woody Guthrie. *New Yorker,* 20 March 1943, 68.

Fariña, Richard. "Baez and Dylan: A Generation Singing Out." In *The Dylan Companion,* edited by Eliza Thompson and David Gutman, 81–88. New York: Delta, 1990.

Faue, Elizabeth. *Community of Suffering and Struggle: Women, Men, and the Labor Movement in Minneapolis, 1915–1945.* Chapel Hill: University of North Carolina Press, 1991.

Filene, Benjamin. " 'Our Singing Country': John and Alan Lomax, Leadbelly, and the Construction of an American Past." *American Quarterly* 43, no. 4 (December 1991): 602–24.

Fishbein, Leslie. *Rebels in Bohemia: The Radicals of "The Masses," 1911–1917.* Chapel Hill: University of North Carolina Press, 1982.

Foley, Barbara. *Radical Representations: Politics and Form in U.S. Proletarian Fiction, 1929–1941.* Durham: Duke University Press, 1993.

Folkways: A Vision Shared. Columbia CK 44034, 1988. Compact disc.

Folsom, Ed. *Walt Whitman's Native Representations.* New York: Cambridge University Press, 1994.

———. "Whitman's Calamus Photographs." In *Breaking Bounds: Whitman and American Cultural Studies,* edited by Betsy Erkkila and Jay Grossman, 193–219. New York: Oxford University Press, 1996.

———, ed. *Walt Whitman: The Centennial Essays.* Iowa City: University of Iowa Press, 1994.

Fone, Byrne R. S. *Masculine Landscapes: Walt Whitman and the Homoerotic Text.* Carbondale: Southern Illinois University Press, 1992.

Foner, Philip. *American Labor Songs of the Nineteenth Century.* Urbana: University of Illinois Press, 1974.

Ford, John, dir. *The Grapes of Wrath.* Screenplay by Nunnally Johnson. 1940. CBS Fox Video, 1988. Videodisc.

Fowler, O. S. *Human Science—Or Phrenology.* Philadelphia: National Publishing Company, 1873.

Friess, Horace L. *Felix Adler and Ethical Culture: Memories and Studies.* Edited by Fannia Weingartner. New York: Columbia University Press, 1992.

Frith, Simon. *Music for Pleasure: Essays in the Sociology of Pop.* New York: Routledge, 1988.

Fuechtmann, Thomas G. *Steeples and Stacks: Religion and Steel Crisis in Youngstown.* New York: Cambridge University Press, 1989.

Garman, Bryan. "The Ghost of History: Bruce Springsteen, Woody Guthrie, and the Hurt Song." *Popular Music and Society* 20, no. 2 (1996): 69–120.

Geer, Will, narrator. *Bound for Glory: The Songs and Story of Woody Guthrie.* Edited by Millard Lampell. Folkways FA 2481, 1956, 1961. Phonograph record.

———. *Woody's Story.* Sung by Dick Wingfield. Folkways FA 2930, 1973. Phonograph record.

Genovese, Eugene. *Roll, Jordan, Roll: The World the Slaves Made.* 1972. Reprint, New York: Vintage, 1976.

Gerstle, Gary. *Working-Class Americanism: The Politics of Labor in a Textile City, 1914–1960.* New York: Cambridge University Press, 1989.

Getchell, Robert. "American Grain: An Interview with Robert Getchell." Interview by Richard Thompson. *Sight and Sound* 45, no. 3 (1976): 140–44.

Giantvalley, Scott. *Walt Whitman, 1838–1939: A Reference Guide.* Boston: G. K. Hall, 1981.

Ginger, Ray. *The Bending Cross: A Biography of Eugene Victor Debs.* New Brunswick: Rutgers University Press, 1949.

Gitlin, Todd. *The Sixties: Years of Hope, Days of Rage.* New York: Bantam, 1987.

Gold, Michael. *The Hollow Men.* New York: International Publishers, 1941.

———. *Mike Gold: A Literary Anthology.* Edited by Michael Folsom. New York: International Publications, 1972.

———. *The Mike Gold Reader.* New York: International Publishers, 1954.

Goldsmith, Peter. *Making People's Music: Moe Asch and Folkways Records.* Washington, D.C.: Smithsonian Institution Press, 1998.

Gollomb, Joseph. "Would Whitman Be a Bolshevist?" *New York Evening Post Book Review,* 1 31 May 1919, 1, 8.

Goodman, Fred. *Mansion on the Hill: Dylan, Young, Geffen, Springsteen, and the Head-on Collision of Rock and Commerce.* 1997. Reprint, New York: Vintage, 1998.

Gorn, Elliot. " 'Good-Bye Boys, I Die a True American': Homicide, Nativism, and Working-Class Culture in Antebellum New York City." *Journal of American History* 74, no. 2 (1987): 388–410.

———. *The Manly Art: Bare Knuckle Prizefighting in America.* Ithaca: Cornell University Press, 1986.

Gossage, Leslie. "The Artful Propaganda of Ford's *The Grapes of Wrath.*" In *New Essays on "The Grapes of Wrath,"* edited by David Wyatt, 101–25. New York: Cambridge University Press, 1994.

Graff, Ellen. *Stepping Left: Dance and Politics in New York City, 1928–1942*. Durham: Duke University Press, 1997.

Graff, Gary. "Q and A with Bruce Springsteen." *San Francisco Chronicle*, 17 December 1995, Sunday Datebook, 38.

The Greatest Songs of Woody Guthrie. Vanguard VSD 35/36. Compact disc.

Green, Archie. *Only a Miner: Studies in Recorded Coal Mining Songs*. Urbana: University of Illinois Press, 1972.

———. *Wobblies, Pile Butts, and Other Heroes: Laborlore Explorations*. Urbana: University of Illinois Press, 1993.

———, ed. *Songs about Work: Essays in Occupational Culture for Richard A. Reuss*. Bloomington: Folklore Institute, Indiana University, 1993.

Green, James R. *The World of the Worker: Labor in Twentieth Century America*. New York: Hill and Wang, 1980.

Greenway, John. *American Folksongs of Protest*. Philadelphia: University of Pennsylvania Press, 1953.

Gregory, James. *American Exodus: The Dust Bowl Migration and Okie Culture in California*. New York: Oxford University Press, 1989.

Griffiths, David. "Three Tributaries of 'The River.'" *Popular Music* 7, no. 1 (January 1986): 27–34.

Grossman, Jay. "'The Evangel-Poem of Comrades and Love': Revising Whitman's Republicanism." *American Transcendental Quarterly* 4, no. 3 (September 1990): 201–16.

Grünzweig, Walter. *Constructing the German Walt Whitman*. Iowa City: University of Iowa Press, 1995.

Gunderson, Edna. "In 'Joad,' Springsteen Answers Ghost of His Past." *USA Today*, 1 December 1995, sec. D, 16.

Gunning, Sarah Ogan. *Girl of Constant Sorrow*. Folk-Legacy Records FSA-26. Phonograph record.

Guthrie, Arlo. *Alice's Restaurant*. 1967. Reprise Records 6267-2. Compact disc.

———. *Woody Guthrie—Hard Travelin': Soundtrack to the Film*. Arloco Records ARL 284, 1984. Phonograph record.

Guthrie, William Norman. "The Apostle of Chaotism." *University of the South Magazine* 1, no. 2 (May 1890): 79–91.

Guthrie, Woody. *Ballads of Sacco and Vanzetti*. Smithsonian Folkways SF CD 40060, 1996. Compact disc.

———. *Born to Win*. New York: Macmillan, 1965.

———. *Bound for Glory*. 1943. Reprint, New York: E. P. Dutton, 1976.

———. *Bound for Glory*. Folkways 2481. Phonograph record.

———. *California to the New York Island*. Edited by Irwin Silber. 1958. Reprint, New York: Oak Publications, 1960.

———. *Columbia River Collection*. Rounder CD 1036, 1987. Compact disc.

———. *Dust Bowl Ballads*. Rounder CD 1040, 1988. Compact disc.

———. *Hard Travelin': The Asch Recordings*. Vol. 3. Smithsonian Folkways SF CD 40102. Compact disc.

———. *Library of Congress Recordings*. Rounder CD 1041–43, 1988. Compact disc.

———. *Long Ways to Travel: The Unreleased Folkways Masters, 1944–1949.* Smithsonian Folkways S F C D 40046, 1994. Compact disc.

———. *Pastures of Plenty—A Self-Portrait: The Unpublished Writings of an American Folk Hero.* Edited by Harold Leventhal and Dave Marsh. New York: Harper Collins, 1990.

———. *Seeds of Man.* New York: E. P. Dutton, 1976.

———. *Songs by Woody Guthrie.* New York: TRO-Ludlow Music, n.d.

———. *The Stinson Collectors Series.* Vols. 1–2. Collectibles C O L-C D-5605, 1995. Compact disc.

———. *Struggle.* Smithsonian Folkways S F C D 40025, 1990. Compact disc.

———. *This Land Is Your Land: The Asch Recordings.* Vol. 1. Smithsonian Folkways S F C D 40100, 1997. Compact disc.

———. *Woody Guthrie Folk Songs: A Collection of Songs by America's Foremost Balladeer.* Edited by Pete Seeger. New York: Ludlow Music, 1963.

———. *Woody Guthrie Sings Folk Songs.* Smithsonian Folkways S F C D 40007, 1989. Compact disc.

———. *The Woody Guthrie Songbook.* Edited by Harold Leventhal and Marjorie Guthrie. New York: Grosset and Dunlap, 1976.

———. *Woody Sez.* New York: Grosset and Dunlap, 1975.

Guthrie, Woody, and Leadbelly. *Folkways: The Original Vision.* Smithsonian Folkways S F C D 40001, 1988. Compact disc.

Haag, Pamela. "The 'Ill-Use of a Wife': Patterns of Working-Class Violence in Domestic and Public New York City, 1860–1880." *Journal of Social History* 25, no. 3 (1992): 447–77.

Haggard, Merle. *Greatest Hits.* Vol. 1. Curb Records D2-77646, 1994. Vol. 2. Curb Records D2-77647, 1994. Compact disc.

Halker, Clark. *For Democracy, Workers, and God: Labor Song-Poems and Labor Protest, 1865–1895.* Urbana: University of Illinois Press, 1991.

Hampton, Wayne. *Guerrilla Minstrels: John Lennon, Joe Hill, Woody Guthrie, and Bob Dylan.* Knoxville: University of Tennessee Press, 1987.

Harmetz, Aljean. "Gambling on a Film about the Great Depression." *New York Times,* 5 December 1976, sec. 2, 1, 13.

———. "Those Oscar Nominations: Settling for Second Best." *New York Times,* 28 February 1977, 22.

Hekma, Gert, Harry Oosterhuis, and James Steakley. "Leftist Sexual Politics and Homosexuality: A Historical Overview." *Journal of Homosexuality* 29, nos. 2–3 (1995): 1–40.

Hemphill, Michael R., and Larry David Smith. "The Working American's Elegy: The Rhetoric of Bruce Springsteen." In *Politics in Familiar Contexts: Projecting Politics through Popular Media,* edited by Robert L. Savage and Dan Nimmo, 199–213. Norwood, N.J.: Ablex, 1990.

Henretta, James. "Families and Farms: Mentalité in Pre-Industrial America." *William and Mary Quarterly* 35 (1978): 3–32.

Hentoff, Nat. "The Rebel Who Started the Folk-Song Craze." *Pageant,* March 1964, 102–8.

Heylin, Clinton. *Bob Dylan, behind the Shades: A Biography*. New York: Summit, 1991.

Hicks, Granville. *The Great Tradition*. 1933. Reprint, New York: Macmillan, 1935.

Hilburn, Robert. *Springsteen*. New York: Rolling Stone Press, 1985.

———. "A Storyteller Returns; Springsteen Defines Musical Focus with Images of Steinbeck in Solo Concert." *Los Angeles Times*, 28 November 1995, sec. F, 1.

Hinds, Michael de Courcy. "Ford's Closing at Mahwah Adding to Family Strains." *New York Times*, 21 July 1980, sec. B, 2.

Hirsch, Jerrold. "Folklore in the Making: B. A. Botkin." *Journal of American Folklore* 100, no. 395 (January 1987): 3–37.

Hirsch, Susan. *Roots of the American Working Class: The Industrialization of Crafts in Newark, 1800–1860*. Philadelphia: University of Pennsylvania Press, 1978.

Honkkonen, Eric H., ed. *Walking to Work: Tramps in America, 1790–1935*. Lincoln: University of Nebraska Press, 1984.

Houston, Cisco. *The Folkways Years, 1944–1961*. Smithsonian Folkways SF CD 40059, 1994. Compact disc.

Huggins, Nathan. *The Harlem Renaissance*. New York: Oxford University Press, 1971.

Hughes, Langston. *The Collected Poems of Langston Hughes*. Edited by Arnold Rampersad. New York: Knopf, 1994.

———. *A New Song*. With a foreword by Max Bedacht and an introduction by Michael Gold. New York: International Workers Order, 1938.

———. *Short Stories*. Edited by Akiba Sullivan Harper, with an introduction by Arnold Rampersad. New York: Hill and Wang, 1996.

Humphries, Patrick, and Chris Hunt. *Bruce Springsteen: Blinded by the Light*. New York: Henry Holt, 1985.

Hutchinson, George. *The Harlem Renaissance in Black and White*. Cambridge: Belknap Press, 1995.

———. "Langston Hughes and the 'Other' Whitman." In *The Continuing Presence of Walt Whitman*, edited by Robert K. Martin, 16–27. Iowa City: University of Iowa Press, 1992.

———. "Whitman and the Black Poet: Kelly Miller's Speech to the Walt Whitman Fellowship." *American Literature* 61 (March 1989): 46–58.

———. "The Whitman Legacy and the Harlem Renaissance." In *Walt Whitman: The Centennial Essays*, edited by Ed Folsom, 201–16. Iowa City: University of Iowa Press, 1994.

Indigo Girls. "This Train Revisited." In *1200 Curfews*. Epic Records E2K 67229, 1995. Compact disc.

Jeffords, Susan. *Hard Bodies: Hollywood Masculinity in the Reagan Era*. New Brunswick: Rutgers University Press, 1994.

———. *The Remasculinization of America: Gender and the Viet Nam War*. Bloomington: Indiana University Press, 1989.

Johnson, Dave. "Just a Mile from the End of the Line." *Northwest Magazine*, 2 February 1969, 11.

Johnson, Nunnally. *The Grapes of Wrath*. Screenplay. Hollywood: Script City, 1940.

Johnson, Robert. *The Complete Recordings.* Columbia C2K 46222, 1990. Compact disc.

Kael, Pauline. "Affirmation." Review of United Artists film *Bound for Glory. New Yorker,* 13 December 1976, 148–56.

Kalaidjian, Walter. *American Culture between the Wars: Revisionary Modernism and Postmodern Critique.* New York: Columbia University Press, 1993.

Kaplan, Justin. "The Biographer's Problem." In *Walt Whitman of Mickle Street,* edited by Geoffrey M. Sill, 18–27. Knoxville: University of Tennessee Press, 1994.

———. *Walt Whitman: A Life.* New York: Simon and Schuster, 1980.

Karsner, David. *Horace Traubel: His Life and Work.* New York: E. Arens, 1919.

Katz, Jonathan Ned. *The Invention of Heterosexuality.* New York: E. P. Dutton, 1995.

Kauffmann, Stanley. "Stanley Kauffmann on Films." Review of United Artists film *Bound for Glory. New Republic,* 27 November 1976, 18.

Kavanaugh, James H. "Ideology." In *Critical Terms for Literary Study,* edited by Frank Lentricchia and Thomas McLaughlin, 306–20. Chicago: University of Chicago Press, 1990.

Kazin, Michael. *The Populist Persuasion: An American History.* New York: Basic Books, 1995.

Kelley, Robin. *Hammer and Hoe: Alabama Communists during the Great Depression.* Chapel Hill: University of North Carolina Press, 1990.

———. *Race Rebels: Culture, Politics, and the Black Working Class.* New York: Free Press, 1994.

Killingsworth, M. Jimmie. *Whitman's Poetry of the Body: Sexuality, Politics, and the Text.* Chapel Hill: University of North Carolina Press, 1989.

Kimmel, Michael. *Manhood in America: A Cultural History.* New York: Free Press, 1996.

Kirkland, Winifred. "Americanization and Walt Whitman." *Dial* 66 (31 May 1919): 537–39.

Klammer, Martin. *Whitman, Slavery, and the Emergence of "Leaves of Grass."* University Park: Pennsylvania State University Press, 1995.

Klein, Joe. *Woody Guthrie: A Life.* New York: Knopf, 1980.

Kornbluh, Joyce. *Rebel Voices: An IWW Anthology.* Ann Arbor: University of Michigan Press, 1964.

Krieg, Joann. "Without Walt Whitman in Camden." *Walt Whitman Quarterly Review* 14 (Fall 1996/Winter 1997): 85–112.

Kutulas, Judy. *The Long War: The Intellectual People's Front and Anti-Stalinism, 1930–1940.* Durham: Duke University Press, 1995.

Lampell, Millard. *A Tribute to Woody Guthrie.* New York: TRO, Ludlow Music in Association with Woody Guthrie Publications, 1972.

Lang, Amy Schrager. *Prophetic Woman: Anne Hutchinson and the Problem of Dissent in the Literature of New England.* Berkeley: University of California Press, 1987.

Larson, Kerry. *Whitman's Drama of Consensus.* Chicago: University of Chicago Press, 1988.

Laurie, Bruce. *Artisans into Workers: Labor in Nineteenth Century America.* New York: Hill and Wang, 1989.

———. *Working People of Philadelphia, 1800–1850.* Philadelphia: Temple University Press, 1980.

Laws, G. Malcolm. *Native American Balladry: A Descriptive Study and a Bibliographical Syllabus.* Philadelphia: American Folklore Society, 1964.

Lears, T. J. Jackson. *No Place of Grace: Anti-Modernism and the Transformation of American Culture, 1880–1920.* New York: Pantheon, 1981.

Ledbetter, Huddie (Leadbelly). *Leadbelly Sings Folksongs.* Smithsonian Folkways SF CD 40010, 1989. Compact disc.

Lennon, John. "Working Class Hero." In *John Lennon/Plastic Ono Band,* EMI CDP 7 46770 2, 1970. Compact disc.

Levine, Lawrence. *Black Culture and Black Consciousness: Afro-American Folk Thought from Slavery to Freedom.* New York: Oxford University Press, 1977.

———. *Highbrow, Lowbrow: The Emergence of Cultural Hierarchy in America.* Cambridge: Harvard University Press, 1986.

Leverenz, David. *Manhood and the American Renaissance.* Ithaca: Cornell University Press, 1989.

Lewis, David Levering. *When Harlem Was in Vogue.* 1979. Reprint, New York: Oxford University Press, 1989.

Lewisohn, Ludwig. *Expression in America.* New York: Harper and Brothers, 1932.

Liebermann, Robbie. *My Song Is My Weapon: People's Songs, American Communism, and the Politics of Culture, 1930–1950.* Urbana: University of Illinois Press, 1989.

Límon, Jose. "Western Marxism and Folklore: A Critical Introduction." *Journal of American Folklore* 96, no. 379 (January–March 1983): 34–52.

Lipsitz, George. *Rainbow at Midnight: Labor and Culture in the 1940s.* 1981. Reprint, Urbana: University of Illinois Press, 1994.

———. *Time Passages: Collective Memory and American Popular Culture.* Minneapolis: University of Minnesota Press, 1990.

Locke, Alain, ed. *The New Negro: Voices of the Harlem Renaissance.* 1925. Reprint, New York: Macmillan, 1992.

Logsdon, Guy, and Jeff Place, eds. *That's Why We're Marching: World War II and the American Folk Song Movement.* Smithsonian Folkways SF CD 40021, 1996. Compact disc.

Lohr, Steve. "Rising Uncertainty in Mahwah." *New York Times,* 12 September 1980, sec. D, 1.

Lomax, Alan. *The Folk Songs of North America in the English Language.* London: Cassell, 1960.

Lomax, Alan, Pete Seeger, and Woody Guthrie. *Hard Hitting Songs for Hard Hit People.* New York: Oak Publications, 1967.

Lomax, John A., and Alan Lomax. *Cowboy Songs and Other Frontier Ballads.* 1910. Reprint, New York: Macmillan, 1946.

———. *Folksong U.S.A.* New York: Signet, 1947.

———. *Our Singing Country: A Second Volume of American Ballads and Folksongs.* New York: Macmillan, 1941.

Longhi, Jim. *Woody, Cisco, and Me: Seamen Three in the Merchant Marine*. Urbana: University of Illinois Press, 1997.

Lornell, Kip. *Introducing American Folk Music*. Madison, Wis.: Brown and Benchmark, 1993.

Lornell, Kip, and Charles Wolfe. *The Life and Legend of Leadbelly*. New York: Harper Collins, 1992.

Lott, Eric. *Love and Theft: Blackface Minstrelsy and the American Working Class*. New York: Oxford University Press, 1993.

Loving, Jerome. *Emerson, Whitman, and the American Muse*. Chapel Hill: University of North Carolina Press, 1982.

———. *Walt Whitman: Song of Himself*. Berkeley: University of California Press, 1999.

———. "Whitman's Idea of Women." In *Walt Whitman of Mickle Street*, edited by Geoffrey M. Sill, 151–67. Knoxville: University of Tennessee Press, 1994.

Lynch, Michael. " 'Here Is Adhesiveness': From Friendship to Homosexuality." *Victorian Studies* 29, no. 1 (Autumn 1985): 67–96.

McBride, Joseph. "Song for Woody." Review of United Artists film *Bound for Glory*. *Film Comment* 12, no. 6 (November–December 1976): 26–28.

McCarthy, Colman. "We Need a People's Anthem." *Washington Post*, 16 December 1989, sec. A, 31.

McGhee, Brownie. *The Folkways Years, 1945–1959*. Smithsonian Folkways SF CD 40034, 1991. Compact disc.

McKay, Nellie. "Happy [?]-Wife-and-Motherdom: The Portrayal of Ma Joad in John Steinbeck's *The Grapes of Wrath*." In *New Essays on "The Grapes of Wrath,"* edited by David Wyatt, 47–70. New York: Cambridge University Press, 1994.

Maharidge, Dale. *Journey to Nowhere: The Saga of the New Underclass*. Photographs by Michael Williamson. Garden City, N.Y.: Dial Press, 1985.

Marcus, Greil. "Bruce Springsteen: In Your Heart You Know He's Right." *Artforum*, November 1984, 95.

———. *Mystery Train: Images of America in Rock and Roll*. 1975. Reprint, New York: Plume, 1990.

Marsh, Dave. *Born to Run: The Bruce Springsteen Story*. New York: Dell, 1981.

———. *Glory Days: Bruce Springsteen in the 1980s*. New York: Pantheon, 1987.

Martin, Robert K., ed. *The Continuing Presence of Walt Whitman: The Life after the Life*. Iowa City: University of Iowa Press, 1992.

———. *The Homosexual Tradition in American Poetry*. Austin: University of Texas Press, 1979.

Maslin, Janet. "Embalming Woody." Review of United Artists film *Bound for Glory*. *Newsweek*, 13 December 1976, 104.

Melosh, Barbara. *Engendering Culture: Manhood and Womanhood in New Deal Public Art and Theater*. Washington, D.C.: Smithsonian Institution Press, 1991.

Merrill, Michael. "Cash Is Good to Eat." *Radical History Review* 25 (Winter 1977): 42–71.

Michner, Charles, with Eleanor Clift. "Bruce Is Loose." *Newsweek*, 8 September 1975, 43.

Montgomery, David. *The Fall of the House of Labor: The Workplace, the State, and American Labor Activism, 1865–1925.* New York: Cambridge University Press, 1987.

———. *Workers' Control in America: Studies in the History of Work, Technology, and Labor Struggles.* New York: Cambridge University Press, 1979.

Moon, Michael. *Disseminating Whitman: Revision and Corporeality in "Leaves of Grass."* Cambridge: Harvard University Press, 1991.

Mumford, Lewis. "Here Is Whitman the Man." Review of *Whitman: An Interpretation in Narrative,* by Emory Holloway. *New York Tribune,* 7 November 1926, sec. 7, 5–6.

Murphy, James F. *The Proletarian Movement: The Controversy over Leftism in Literature.* Urbana: University of Illinois Press, 1991.

Murray, Robert K. *Red Scare: A Study in National Hysteria, 1919–1920.* Minneapolis: University of Minnesota Press, 1955.

Murray, Steve. "The 66th Annual Academy Awards, Oscar Night '94: The Jokes, Gaffes, and the Memorable Moments." *Atlanta Journal Constitution,* 22 March 1994, sec. D, 6.

Nathanson, Tenney. *Whitman's Presence: Body, Voice, and Writing in "Leaves of Grass."* New York: New York University Press, 1992.

Nekola, Charlotte, and Paula Rabinowitz, eds. *Writing Red: An Anthology of American Women Writers, 1930–1940.* New York: Feminist Press, 1987.

Nelson, Cary. *Repression and Recovery: Modern American Poetry and the Politics of Cultural Memory, 1910–1945.* Madison: University of Wisconsin Press, 1989.

Nelson, Dana D. *National Manhood: Capitalist Citizenship and the Imagined Fraternity of White Men.* Durham: Duke University Press, 1998.

Newfield, Christopher. *The Emerson Effect: Individualism and Submission in America.* Chicago: University of Chicago Press, 1996.

Odets, Clifford. "Democratic Vistas in Drama." *New York Times,* 21 November 1937, sec. 9, 1–2.

———. *Six Plays of Clifford Odets.* New York: Grove Press, 1982.

Olsen, Tillie. *Silences.* New York: Laurel/Seymour Lawrence, 1983.

———. *Tell Me a Riddle.* Edited by Deborah Silverton. New Brunswick: Rutgers University Press, 1995.

———. *Yonnondio: From the Thirties.* 1974. Reprint, New York: Delta, 1989.

O'Reilly, Kenneth. *Hoover and the Un-Americans: The FBI, HUAC, and the Red Menace.* Philadelphia: Temple University Press, 1983.

Orman, John. *Comparing Presidential Behavior: Carter, Reagan, and the Macho Presidential Style.* New York: Greenwood Press, 1987.

Orr, Elaine. *Tillie Olsen and a Feminist Spiritual Vision.* Jackson: University of Mississippi Press, 1987.

Orth, Maureen, with Janet Huck and Peter S. Greenberg. "Making of a Rock Star." *Newsweek,* 27 October 1975, 57–63.

Pareles, Jon. "Bruce Springsteen—Rock's Populist." *New York Times,* 18 August 1985, 7.

Pascal, Richard. "Walt Whitman and Woody Guthrie: American Prophet-Singers and Their People." *Journal of American Studies* 24, no. 1 (April 1990): 41–59.

Pastures of Plenty: An Austin Celebration of Woody Guthrie. Dejadisc DJD 3207, 1993. Compact disc.

Paxton, Tom. *Rambling Boy.* Elektra Records EKS 7277, 1964. Phonograph record.

Pells, Richard. *Radical Visions, American Dreams: Culture and Social Thought in the Depression Years.* New York: Harper and Row, 1973.

Pennebaker, D. A., dir. *Don't Look Back.* 1967. Reprint, Paramount 2382, 1991. Videocassette.

Perlman, Jim, Ed Folsom, and Dan Campion, eds. *Walt Whitman: The Measure of His Song.* Minneapolis: Holy Cow! Press, 1981.

Pfeil, Fred. *White Guys: Studies in Postmodern Domination and Difference.* New York: Verso, 1995.

Phillips, Dana. "Nineteenth-Century Racial Thought and Whitman's Democratic Ethnology of the Future." *Nineteenth-Century Literature* 49 (December 1994): 289–320.

Piercy, Marge. "The Grand Coolie Damn" (1969). In *Sisterhood Is Powerful: An Anthology of Writings from the Women's Liberation Movement,* edited by Robin Morgan, 473–92. New York: Vintage, 1970.

Pierson, Stanley. *British Socialists: The Journey from Fantasy to Politics.* Cambridge: Harvard University Press, 1979.

Polanyi, Karl. *The Great Transformation.* 1944. Reprint, Boston: Beacon Press, 1957.

Pollak, Vivian. " 'In Loftiest Spheres': Whitman's Visionary Feminism." In *Breaking Bounds: Whitman and American Cultural Studies,* edited by Betsy Erkkila and Jay Grossman, 92–111. New York: Oxford University Press, 1996.

Porterfield, Nolan. *The Jimmie Rodgers Story: The Life and Times of America's Blue Yodeler.* Urbana: University of Illinois Press, 1992.

Pratt, Ray. *Rhythm and Resistance: The Political Uses of American Popular Music.* Washington, D.C.: Smithsonian Institution Press, 1990.

Price, Kenneth. "Whitman, Dos Passos, and 'Our Storybook Democracy.' " In *Walt Whitman: The Centennial Essays,* edited by Ed Folsom, 217–25. Iowa City: University of Iowa Press, 1994.

———. *Whitman and Tradition: The Poet in His Century.* New Haven: Yale University Press, 1990.

Quinn, D. Michael. *Same-Sex Dynamics among Nineteenth-Century Americans: A Mormon Example.* Urbana: University of Illinois Press, 1996.

Rabinowitz, Paula. *Labor and Desire: Women's Revolutionary Fiction in Depression America.* Chapel Hill: University of North Carolina Press, 1991.

Radest, Howard. *Toward Common Ground: The Story of the Ethical Societies in the United States.* New York: Frederick Ungar, 1969.

Ramella, Richard. "John Hardy: The Man and the Song." *Goldenseal: West Virginia Traditional Life* 18, no. 1 (Spring 1992): 47–51.

Rampersad, Arnold. *The Life of Langston Hughes.* Vol. 1, 1902–1941. New York: Oxford University Press, 1986. Vol. 2, 1941–1967. New York: Oxford University Press, 1988.

Rauch, Alan. "Bruce Springsteen and the Dramatic Monologue." *American Studies* 29, no. 1 (Spring 1988): 29–49.

Reddy, John. "Woody Guthrie: Father of the Folk Singers." *Readers' Digest* 92, no. 554 (June 1968): 229–36.

Reuss, Richard. "The Roots of American Left-Wing Interest in Folksong." *Labor History* 12, no. 2 (Spring 1971): 259–79.

———. "Woody Guthrie and His Folk Tradition." *Journal of American Folklore* 83, no. 329 (July–September 1970): 273–303.

Reynolds, David S. *Beneath the American Renaissance.* New York: Knopf, 1988.

———. *Walt Whitman's America: A Cultural Biography.* New York: Knopf, 1995.

Rivers, W. C. *Walt Whitman's Anomaly.* 1913. Reprint, Norwood, Pa.: Norwood Edition, 1976.

Robbin, Edward. *Woody Guthrie and Me: An Intimate Reminiscence.* Berkeley: Lancaster-Miller, 1979.

Rodnitzky, Jerome L. *Minstrels of the Dawn: The Folk Protest Singer as a Cultural Hero.* Chicago: Nelson Hall, 1976.

Roediger, David. *The Wages of Whiteness: Race and the Making of the American Working Class.* New York: Verso, 1991.

Rogin, Michael. *Ronald Reagan, the Movie, and Other Episodes in Political Demonology.* Berkeley: University of California Press, 1987.

Rorabaugh, W. J. *The Craft Apprentice: From Franklin to the Machine Age in America.* New York: Oxford University Press, 1986.

Rosenzweig, Roy. *Eight Hours for What We Will: Workers and Leisure in an Industrial City, 1870–1920.* New York: Cambridge University Press, 1983.

Rotundo, E. Anthony. *American Manhood: Transformations in Masculinity from the Revolution to the Modern Era.* New York: Basic Books, 1993.

Rozell, Mark J. *The Press and the Carter Presidency.* Boulder, Colo.: Westview, 1989.

Rubin, Joseph Jay. *The Historic Whitman.* University Park: Pennsylvania State University Press, 1971.

Salvatore, Nick. *Eugene V. Debs: Citizen and Socialist.* Urbana: University of Illinois Press, 1982.

Saxton, Alexander. *The Rise and Fall of the White Republic: Class Politics and Mass Culture in Nineteenth Century America.* New York: Verso, 1990.

Schickel, Richard. "Bound for Boredom." Review of United Artists film *Bound for Glory. Time,* 20 December 1976, 102.

Schmidgall, Gary. *Walt Whitman: A Gay Life.* New York: E. P. Dutton, 1997.

Schultz, Ronald. *The Republic of Labor: Philadelphia Artisans and the Politics of Class, 1720–1830.* New York: Oxford University Press, 1993.

Schwartz, Lawrence. *Marxism and Culture: The CPUSA and Aesthetics in the 1930s.* Port Washington, N.Y.: Kennikat Press, 1980.

Sedgwick, Eve Kosofsky. *Between Men: English Literature and Male Homosocial Desire.* New York: Columbia University Press, 1985.

Seeger, Pete. *American Industrial Ballads.* Smithsonian Folkways SF CD 40058, 1992. Compact disc.

Sellers, Charles. *The Market Revolution: Jacksonian America, 1815–1846.* New York: Oxford University Press, 1991.

Selvin, Joel. "Bruce Sits Down and Sings." *San Francisco Chronicle,* 1 December 1995, sec. C, 1.

Shaffer, Robert. "Women and the Communist Party, U.S.A., 1930–1940." *Socialist Review* 45 (May–June 1979): 73–118.

Shelton, Robert. *No Direction Home: The Life and Music of Bob Dylan.* New York: W. Morrow, 1986.

Sherman, Stuart P. "Walt Whitman and These Times." *New York Evening Post,* 31 May 1919, 4–5.

Shively, Charley, ed. *Calamus Lovers: Walt Whitman's Working-Class Camerados.* San Francisco: Gay Sunshine Press, 1987.

Sitkoff, Harvard. *A New Deal for Blacks: The Emergence of Civil Rights as a National Issue—The Depression Decade.* New York: Oxford University Press, 1978.

Smith, Bernard. "The Literary Caravan." Review of *Expression in America,* by Ludwig Lewisohn. *Modern Quarterly* 6 (Summer 1932): 101.

Smith, Harry, ed. *The Anthology of American Folk Music.* 1952. Reprint, Smithsonian Folkways, 1997. Compact disc.

Smith, Martha Nell. "Sexual Mobilities in Bruce Springsteen: Performance as Commentary." *South Atlantic Quarterly* 90, no. 4 (Fall 1991): 833–54.

Smith, Wendy. *Real Life Drama: The Group Theatre in America, 1931–1940.* New York: Knopf, 1990.

Smith-Rosenberg, Carroll. *Disorderly Conduct: Visions of Gender in Victorian America.* 1985. Reprint, New York: Oxford University Press, 1986.

Snyder, John Edwin. "Walt Whitman's Woman." *Socialist Woman,* 2 February 1907, 7.

Sobchak, Vivian C. "*The Grapes of Wrath* (1940): Thematic Emphasis through Visual Style." *American Quarterly* 31 (Winter 1979): 596–615.

Spitz, Bob. *Dylan: A Biography.* New York: McGraw-Hill, 1989.

Springsteen, Bruce. *Blood Brothers.* Produced, photographed, and directed by Ernie Fritz. Columbia Music Video 19V 50139, 1996. Videocassette.

———. *Born in the U.S.A.* Columbia CK 38653, 1984. Compact disc.

———. *Born to Run.* Columbia CK 33795, 1975. Compact disc.

———. *Chimes of Freedom.* Columbia 44K 44445, 1988. Compact disc.

———. *Darkness on the Edge of Town.* Columbia CK 35318, 1978. Compact disc.

———. "Dead Man Walkin'." *Music from and Inspired by the Motion Picture "Dead Man Walking."* Columbia CK 67522, 1995. Compact disc.

———. *The Ghost of Tom Joad.* Columbia CK 67484, 1995. Compact disc.

———. *Greatest Hits.* Columbia CK 67060, 1995. Compact disc.

———. *Greetings from Asbury Park, N.J.* Columbia CK 31903, 1973. Compact disc.

———. *Human Touch.* Columbia CK 53000, 1992. Compact disc.

———. *In Concert: MTV Plugged.* Columbia 4738602, 1992. Compact disc.

———. *Live/1975–85.* Columbia C3K 40558, 1986. Compact disc.

————. *Lucky Town*. Columbia CK 53001, 1992. Compact disc.

————. *Nebraska*. Columbia CK 38358, 1982. Compact disc.

————. "Remember When the Music." Lyrics by Harry Chapin. In *Harry Chapin Tribute*, Relativity Records, 1990. Cassette.

————. *The River*. Columbia C2K 36854, 1980. Compact disc.

————. "Rock and Read: Will Percy Interviews Bruce Springsteen." *DoubleTake* 4, no. 2 (Spring 1998): 36–43.

————. "Springsteen: The *Advocate* Interview." Interviewed by Judy Wieder. *Advocate*, 2 April 1996, 47–51.

————. *Tunnel of Love*. Columbia CK 40999, 1987. Compact disc.

————. *Video Anthology, 1978–1988*. CBS Music Video Enterprises 49010, 1989. Videocassette.

————. *The Wild, the Innocent, and the E Street Shuffle*. Columbia CK 32432, 1973. Compact disc.

Stallone, Sylvester. *First Blood*. Produced by Buzz Feitshans. Directed by Ted Kotcheff. Screenplay by Michael Kozoll, William Sackheim, and Sylvester Stallone. Carloco Home Video, 1982. Videocassette.

————. *Rambo: First Blood, Part II*. Produced by Buzz Feitshans. Directed by George P. Cosmatos. Screenplay by Sylvester Stallone and James Cameron. International Video Entertainment, 1988. Videocassette.

————. *Rambo III*. Produced by Buzz Feitshans. Directed by Peter MacDonald. Screenplay by Sylvester Stallone and Sheldon Lettich. International Video Entertainment, 1988. Videocassette.

Stanley, Talmage. "The Poco Field: Politics, Culture, and Place in Contemporary Appalachia." Ph.D. diss., Emory University, 1996.

Stansell, Christine. *City of Women: Sex and Class in New York, 1789–1860*. 1986. Reprint, Urbana: University of Illinois Press, 1987.

Steinbeck, John. *The Grapes of Wrath*. 1939. Reprint, New York: Penguin, 1987.

Stoddard, Donald Richard. "Horace Traubel: A Critical Biography." Ph.D. diss., University of Pennsylvania, 1970.

Stott, Richard. *Workers in the Metropolis: Class, Ethnicity, and Youth in Antebellum New York City*. Ithaca: Cornell University Press, 1990.

Susman, Warren. *Culture as History: The Transformation of American Society in the Twentieth Century*. New York: Pantheon, 1984.

Symonds, John Addington. *A Problem in Modern Ethics, Being an Inquiry into the Phenomenon of Sexual Inversion Addressed Especially to Medical Psychologists and Jurists*. 1896. Reprint, New York: Benjamin Blom, 1971.

Taylor, Lori Elaine. "Joe Hill Incorporated: We Own Our Past." In *Songs about Work: Essays in Occupational Culture for Richard A. Reuss*, edited by Archie Green, 23–36. Bloomington: Folklore Institute, Indiana University, 1993.

————. "The Politicized American Legend of the Singing Hero: Joe Hill, Woody Guthrie, Pete Seeger, Bob Dylan, and Bruce Springsteen." Master's thesis, George Washington University, 1990.

————, ed. *Don't Mourn—Organize: Songs of Labor Songwriter Joe Hill*. Smithsonian Folkways CD SF 40026, 1990. Compact disc.

Thinking of Woody Guthrie. Vanguard VM D 6546. Phonograph record.

Thomas, M. Wynn. *The Lunar Light of Whitman's Poetry.* Cambridge: Harvard University Press, 1987.

Thompson, E. P. *Customs in Common.* New York: Free Press, 1993.

———. *The Making of the English Working Class.* New York: Vintage, 1963.

Thomson, Elizabeth, and David Gutman, eds. *The Dylan Companion: A Collection of Essential Writings about Bob Dylan.* New York: Delta, 1990.

Timmons, Stuart. *The Trouble with Harry Hay, Founder of the Modern Gay Movement.* Boston: Alyson Publications, 1990.

Trachtenberg, Alan. "The Politics of Labor and the Poet's Work." In *Walt Whitman: The Centennial Essays,* edited by Ed Folsom, 120–32. Iowa City: University of Iowa Press, 1994.

———. *Reading American Photographs: Images as History, Matthew Brady to Walker Evans.* New York: Noonday Press, 1989.

Trask, Michael. "Merging with the Masses: The Queer Identity Politics of Leftist Modernism." *Differences* 8 (Spring 1996): 94–131.

Traubel, Horace. *Chants Communal.* Boston: Small, Maynard, 1904.

———. *With Walt Whitman in Camden.* 9 vols. Vol. 1. 1905. Reprint, New York: Rowman and Littlefield, 1961. Vol. 2. 1907. Reprint, New York: Rowman and Littlefield, 1961. Vol. 3. 1912. Reprint, New York: Rowman and Littlefield, 1961. Vol. 4. Edited by Sculley Bradley. 1953. Reprint, Carbondale: Southern Illinois University Press, 1959. Vol. 5. Edited by Gertrude Traubel. Carbondale: Southern Illinois University Press, 1964. Vol. 6. Edited by Gertrude Traubel and William White. Carbondale: Southern Illinois University Press, 1982. Vol. 7. Edited by Jeanne Chapman and Robert MacIsaac. Carbondale: Southern Illinois University Press, 1992. Vol. 8. Edited by Jeanne Chapman and Robert MacIsaac. Oregon House, Calif.: W. L. Bentley, 1996. Vol. 9. Edited by Jeanne Chapman and Robert MacIsaac. Oregon House, Calif.: W. L. Bentley, 1996.

Traubel, Horace, Richard Bucke, and Thomas Harned, eds. *In Re Walt Whitman.* Philadelphia: David McKay, 1893.

A Tribute to Woody Guthrie. Warner Brothers 9 26036-2, 1972.

Trotter, Joe. *Coal, Class, and Color: Blacks in Southern West Virginia, 1915–1932.* Urbana: University of Illinois Press, 1990.

Tsuzuki, Chushichi. *Edward Carpenter, 1844–1929: Prophet of Human Fellowship.* New York: Cambridge University Press, 1980.

Tuerk, Richard. "Michael Gold on Walt Whitman." *Walt Whitman Quarterly Review* 3 (Spring 1986): 16–23.

Van Doren, Mark. "Walt Whitman, Stranger." *American Mercury* 35 (July 1935): 277–85.

Wald, Alan. *The New York Intellectuals: The Rise and Decline of the Anti-Stalinist Left from the 1930s to the 1980s.* Chapel Hill: University of North Carolina Press, 1987.

———. *Writing from the Left: New Essays on Radical Culture and Politics.* New York: Verso, 1994.

Walker, Donald R. *Penology for Profit: A History of the Texas Prison System, 1867–1912.* College Station: Texas A&M University Press, 1988.

Walling, William English. *Whitman and Traubel.* 1916. Reprint, New York: Haskell House, 1969.

Ward, Robert. "The Night of the Punk." *New Times,* 5 September 1975, 61–63.

Warren, James Perrin. *Walt Whitman's Language Experiment.* University Park: Pennsylvania State University Press, 1990.

The Weavers. *Wasn't That a Time.* Vanguard VCD4-147/50, 1993. Compact disc.

Webster, Duncan. *Looka Yonder!: The Imaginary America of Populist Culture.* New York: Routledge, 1988.

Whisnant, David. *All That Is Native and Fine: The Politics of Culture in an American Region.* Chapel Hill: University of North Carolina Press, 1983.

White, Kevin. *The First Sexual Revolution: The Emergence of Male Heterosexuality in Modern America.* New York: New York University Press, 1993.

Whitman, Walt. *An American Primer.* Edited by Horace Traubel. Boston: Small, Maynard, 1904.

———. *Complete Poetry and Collected Prose.* Edited by Justin Kaplan. New York: Library of America, 1982.

———. *The Correspondence.* Edited by Edward Haviland Miller. 6 vols. New York: New York University Press, 1963.

———. *Daybooks and Notebooks.* Edited by William White. 3 vols. New York: New York University Press, 1978.

———. *Early Poems and the Fiction.* Edited by Thomas Brashear. 2 vols. New York: New York University Press, 1963.

———. *The Gathering of Forces.* Edited by Cleveland Rodgers and John Black. 2 vols. New York: G. P. Putnam's Sons, 1920.

———. *I Sit and Look Out: Editorials from the "Brooklyn Daily Times."* Edited by Emory Holloway and Vernolian Schwarz. New York: Columbia University Press, 1932.

———. *Notebooks and Unpublished Prose Manuscripts.* Edited by Edward F. Grier. 6 vols. New York: New York University Press, 1984.

———. *Prose Works, 1892.* Edited by Floyd Stovall. 2 vols. New York: New York University Press, 1963–64.

———. *The Uncollected Poetry and Prose of Walt Whitman.* Edited by Emory Holloway. 2 vols. New York: Peter Smith, 1932.

———. *Walt Whitman of the "New York Aurora": Editor at Twenty Two.* Edited by Joseph Jay Rubin and Charles H. Brown. State College, Pa.: Bald Eagle Press, 1950.

Widmer, Kingsley. "The Way Out: Some Life-Style Sources of the Literary Tough Guy and the Proletarian Hero." In *Tough Guy Writers of the Thirties,* edited by David Madden, 3–12. Carbondale: Southern Illinois University Press.

Wilentz, Sean. *Chants Democratic: New York City and the Rise of the American Working Class, 1788–1850.* New York: Oxford University Press, 1984.

Will, George. *The Morning After.* New York: Free Press, 1986.

Willard, Charles B. *Whitman's American Fame: The Growth of His Reputation in America after 1892.* Providence, R.I.: Brown University Press, 1950.

Williams, Hank. *Hank Williams's 40 Greatest Hits.* Polydor 821 233-2, 1978. Compact disc.

Williams, John Alexander. "Radicalism and Professionalism in Folklore Studies: A Comparative Perspective." *Journal of the Folklore Institute* 11, no. 3 (March 1975): 211–34.

Williams, Raymond. *The Country and the City.* New York: Oxford University Press, 1973.

———. *Culture and Society, 1780–1950.* 1957. Reprint, New York: Columbia University Press, 1983.

———. *Drama from Ibsen to Brecht.* New York: Oxford University Press, 1969.

———. *Marxism and Literature.* New York: Oxford University Press, 1977.

———. *Resources of Hope: Culture, Democracy, Socialism.* Edited by Robin Gable and with an introduction by Robin Blackburn. New York: Verso, 1987.

Williams, Roger M. *Sing a Sad Song: The Hank Williams Story.* Urbana: University of Illinois Press, 1981.

Wills, Garry. *Reagan's America.* New York: Penguin, 1988.

Wilson, Walter. *Forced Labor in the United States.* New York: International Publishers, 1933.

Wolfe, Cary. *The Limits of Literary Ideology in Pound and Emerson.* New York: Cambridge University Press, 1993.

Wolff, Daniel. "Opening Woody Guthrie's FBI File." *Musician,* September 1990, 26–30.

Yacavone, Donald. "Abolitionists and the 'Language of Fraternal Love.' " In *Meanings for Manhood: Constructions of Masculinity in Victorian America,* edited by Mark C. Carnes and Clyde Griffen, 85–95. Chicago: University of Chicago Press, 1996.

Yagoda, Ben. *Will Rogers: A Biography.* New York: Knopf, 1993.

Yingling, Tom. "Homosexuality and Utopian Discourse in American Poetry." With an introduction by Robyn Wiegman. In *Breaking Bounds: Whitman and American Cultural Studies,* edited by Betsy Erkkila and Jay Grossman, 137–46. New York: Oxford University Press, 1996.

Yurchenko, Henrietta. *A Mighty Hard Road: The Woody Guthrie Story.* New York: McGraw-Hill, 1970.

Ziff, Larzer. *Literary Democracy: The Declaration of Cultural Independence in America.* New York: Viking Press, 1981.

Zweig, Paul. *Whitman: The Making of a Poet.* New York: Basic Books, 1984.

INDEX

class hero integral to, 224–25, 258.
See also Adhesive love

Homophobia, 10, 45, 53, 63, 190–91, 235

House Un-American Activities Committee, 136, 141–42

Houston, Cisco, 85, 96, 109, 127–29, 174

Hubbard, Ray Wylie, 181, 182

Hughes, Langston, 11, 60, 67–71, 78, 114, 159

Human Touch (Springsteen), 235

Huntington's chorea, 11, 84, 85, 135, 137

"I Ain't Got No Home" (Guthrie), 94, 179–82, 187, 192

"I Don't Want to Talk About It" (song), 190

"I Hear America Singing" (Whitman), 75–76, 91

Indigo Girls, 189, 190

Individualism, 183; of Whitman, 11, 35, 39, 44, 61, 78; of Guthrie, 128–30; of Dylan, 135–36, 149, 160–63

Industrialization, 6, 7, 19–20, 37

Industrial Workers of the World, 1, 59, 64–65, 92–93, 138, 189

Intermediate Sex, The (Carpenter), 55

International Workers Order, 69, 85, 130

"Iron Throat, The" (Olsen), 71

"I Sing the Body Electric" (Whitman), 21–22, 30–31, 50, 112

"I've Got to Know" (Guthrie), 153–54

Ives, Burl, 114, 115, 118

Jackson, Aunt Molly, 95, 107, 118, 124

Jackson, Jesse, 251

Jackson, Michael, 220

Jefferson, Blind Lemon, 146

Jefferson, Thomas, 45

Jeffords, Susan, 217–18

"Jesus Christ" (Guthrie), 142, 179, 181

Jews without Money (Gold), 87

Jim Crow, 119–20, 125, 173

"Job of Work" (Paxton), 159

"John Hardy Was a Desperate Little Man" (Carter Family), 120–24, 178, 205, 236

"John Hardy Was a Desperate Little Man" (Guthrie), 122–23, 205–6, 208

"Johnny 99" (Springsteen), 205, 207–9, 228–29, 241

John Reed Club, 67

Johnson, James Weldon, 67

Johnson, Robert, 205

Journey to Nowhere (Maharidge), 238

Kael, Pauline, 135

Kameron, Pete, 140

Kansas-Nebraska Act (1854), 24

Karsner, David, 44

Kazin, Michael, 45

Kerouac, Jack, 148, 195

KFVD radio, 86, 118, 125, 130, 172

King, Martin Luther, Jr., 3

King, Rodney, 181, 235

Kingston Trio, 142–43

Kirkland, Winifred, 1–2

Kittredge, George, 87

Klein, Joe, 95, 186, 203, 205

Knights of Labor, 45, 91

Korean War, 137, 153, 239

Kossoy Sisters, 145

Kovic, Ron, 202

"Kum Buy Yah" (song), 142

Kuralt, Charles, 135

Labor movement, 57–58, 91–92, 183, 228; artisans and, 19–20, 21, 91; Whitman's antiunionism, 20, 40, 94; Traubel and, 59; folk song movement and, 85, 120, 124; musical heritage, 91–93; Guthrie and, 94, 120, 123–24, 125, 131, 191–92; World War II and, 124–25; postwar climate, 136–37

Lampell, Millard, 93, 187–88

Landau, Jon, 197, 202–3, 222, 228

Lanier, Sidney, 87

"Last Thoughts on Woody Guthrie" (Dylan), 149

Leadbelly (Huddie Ledbetter), 85, 96, 114, 118–20, 124, 140, 182